Our Osage Hills

Our Osage Hills

Toward an Osage Ecology and Tribalography of the Early Twentieth Century

By John Joseph Mathews
and Michael Snyder

Edited by Michael Snyder

Forewords by Russ Tall Chief
and Harvey Payne

LEHIGH UNIVERSITY PRESS
Bethlehem

Published by Lehigh University Press
Copublished by The Rowman & Littlefield Publishing Group, Inc.
4501 Forbes Boulevard, Suite 200, Lanham, Maryland 20706
www.rowman.com

6 Tinworth Street, London SE11 5AL, United Kingdom

British Library Cataloguing in Publication Information Available

Library of Congress Cataloging-in-Publication Data Available

Library of Congress Control Number: 2020940813

ISBN 978-1-61146-301-9 (cloth)
ISBN 978-1-61146-302-6 (electronic)
ISBN 978-1-61146-303-3 (pbk.)

Dedicated to
my loving parents

Christine Hadley Snyder
Dr. E. Eugene (Gene) Snyder

and to
the Wahzhazhe people

Contents

Essay Titles by Snyder are set in italics

PART I: SCENE SETTING

PART II: BIRDS OF THE OSAGE

PART III: CULTURE AND POLITICS

PART IX: CONSERVATION

PART X: CRITIQUE OF SETTLER COLONIALISM

PART XI: MURDER

List of Photographs

Foreword

By Harvey Payne

John Joseph Mathews was very much a student and lover of wildlife and nature for his entire life. Although he was born in 1894 in Pawhuska on the Osage Indian Reservation, a time pretty early in the settlement of the southern Great Plains, much of the indigenous wildlife was already gone. Since the mid-1700s, the settlers' game plan for what became the State of Oklahoma was to conquer the wilderness and harvest nature's bounty. The bison were historically the most numerous large animals on the plains, but the last re- corded bison in the entire tallgrass prairie ecosystem stretching from Canada to Texas was killed in what is now northern Osage County in about 1851. The Merriam's elk were historically the second most numerous large animals in the southern Great Plains, but they were gone by 1830 because of market hunting. By the time Mathews was a boy, the pronghorn antelope, wolves, mountain lions, bears, passenger pigeons, Carolina parakeets, white-tailed deer, and wild turkeys were also gone.

Mathews's deep love of wildlife and nature is evidenced by his frequent horseback riding exploits through the Osage Hills as a young boy, by his trav- els as a high school boy to the Colorado Rockies, by his degree in geology from the University of Oklahoma, and by his degree in natural sciences from Merton College at the University of Oxford. Additionally, Mathews enjoyed the company of and was influenced by prominent early day conservation au- thors such as Paul B. Sears, author of *Deserts on the March*.

In 1932, Mathews built a cabin on a portion of the land that was allotted to him as a member of the Osage Tribe of Indians pursuant to the provisions of the Allotment Bill of June 28, 1906, when the land that once comprised the Osage Indian Reservation was parceled out to the tribal members. Mathews spent the next forty or so years living in his small cabin and doing what he loved most: observing, studying, photographing, filming, and writing about wildlife and nature, hunting quail, working to help his Osage people and to chronicle their culture, and tromping around his beloved Osage Hills.

It was on April 24, 1973, that I first met John Joseph Mathews. I had started a job in Pawhuska the day before and was invited to be a guest at the local Rotary Club meeting. The speaker for the meeting was none other than John Joseph Mathews. He gave a short talk about prairie chickens and showed a film he had made of the prairie chickens performing their spring courtship displays on a booming ground north of Pawhuska. Each spring the male prairie chickens select a lek (or "booming ground") on a hill or high point where the grass is short to attempt to attract female prairie chickens for mating. The males have a large orange air pouch on each side on their neck that they inflate and do an elaborate "dance" and make many vocalizations. They often fight to determine which males are dominate. Only the one or two strongest males are able to mate with the females. The females indicate their willingness to mate by squatting and flaring their wings, and mating quickly ensues. Some Native American tribes have copied some of the dances of the prairie chickens in performing their tribal dances. To say the least, I was most impressed by Mathews's manifest love of prairie chickens, his ability to capture such an event on film, and his eloquent manner of speaking. Having been raised on a ranch west of Shidler, I was familiar with prairie chickens. We had quite a few of them on the family ranch, so I saw them frequently and even hunted them briefly when Oklahoma had a prairie chicken hunting season. In addition, I was developing a strong interest in photographing wildlife and nature. But I had never seen anything like what Mathews showed at the Rotary Club meeting, and his presentation had a profound impact on my life. I wanted to be like Mathews and photograph prairie chickens and other wildlife.

Later, as I learned more about John Joseph Mathews, I discovered many parallels in our lives and felt that we were almost kindred spirits. We were both born in Osage County, Oklahoma. Mathews spent many hours riding his horse, Bally, over the Osage Hills including land owned by various members of the Mathews family along Big Beaver Creek in western Osage County. Being raised on a ranch in Kay County, Oklahoma, just west of the Kay/Osage County line, I spent much of my childhood riding horses and roaming hills and valleys, much the same as Mathews. In fact, Little Beaver Creek flowed through our family ranch and is the next major drainage west of Big Beaver Creek. Undoubtedly, Mathews and I rode our horses through some of the same Osage Hills. Mathews loved to camp along streams in the Osage Hills and would do so for days at a time. As a child, I would often take some bacon and potatoes and cook my supper along Little Beaver Creek before returning home for the night. Like Mathews, at an early age I was mesmerized by *Wild*

Animals I Have Known by Ernest Thompson Seton. In each chapter Seton described a different wild animal. Because most wild animals were gone from my childhood world, I was particularly engrossed in Seton's comments about the lives of wild animals. Mathews, as well, was greatly influenced by Seton's work and was privileged to meet and work with Seton in New Mexico. The story of John Joseph Mathews's encounter with Seton and other notable guests at Seton Village near Santa Fe is told evocatively by Michael Snyder in one of his essays accompanying Mathews's newspaper articles collected in this book. Mathews and I shared a love of the outdoors, nature, wildlife, and hunting, especially quail hunting.

In *Our Osage Hills*, Mathews vividly evidences with his poetic prose his lifelong love and passion for his Osage people, "The Osage," and its wildlife and nature.

Foreword

By Russ Tall Chief

I consider *Our Osage Hills* a companion to Michael Snyder's biography *John Joseph Mathews: Life of an Osage Writer*. I don't think that one needs to read the two books in any particular order, but I highly recommend reading both books in order to appreciate the context of Mathews's life and writing. Whereas Snyder's first book explores Mathews the man, this second book shares much more of Mathews' own writings, most of which were published in the Pawhuska *Journal-Capital* around 1930. Understanding the period in which Mathews published these articles is important in understanding where his head was, although I think it would be difficult to locate where Mathews's heart was during this period.

As Mathews left his real estate business in Los Angeles in 1928, he also left his wife, daughter, and son. The next year, he moved home to Pawhuska—alone. Although the move was meant to be temporary, Mathews soon began to write regularly for the local newspaper. He assumed the position as secretary of Pawhuska's chapter of one of America's earliest conservation groups, the Izaak Walton League, and devoted his life to hunting, fishing, and observing nature. He appears to have fallen back in love with his hometown and surrounding Osage Hills as one sometimes does upon returning home from years of travel and living in other parts of the world. Mathews's romance with "The Osage" inspired beautiful prose and poetry fused with his expertise in geology, zoology, and other natural sciences. He describes The Osage as "a book in which is written its history . . . open at all times for those who care to read."

On either side of its automobile road are the open pages from which anyone may read as he drives; there is no history more intriguing. It is replete with tragedies and romance which, when compared with man's "earth-shaking" revolutions, causes them to appear as battles of army ants. As one drives

along, not the least interesting thought, as he studies the history on each side
of him, is the consciousness of the fact that he owes the car which he is driving
to geological processes that make the landscape he is enjoying. The original
accumulation and concentration of the hydrocarbons were incidents in the
processes that gave rise to the prairies and blackjack-covered sandstone hills
of the Osage. This is real romance.

Mathews's intense focus on the natural world takes his readers from micro-
scopic to grand perspectives on The Osage, observing how "insects in the
grass roots are sleepy-voices"; how "the cicada, the symbol of midsummer
somnolence, waits until four o'clock to start his chorus of shrill complaint
to the gods of summer"; how "the leaves of the blackjacks stir periodically
in whimsical little breezes, dappling the hot shade under them; the ragged
shade which promises relief from the dancing heat devils, but cannot fulfill
the promise of cool comfort." Mathews's drawings and paintings that accompany his writings do not adequately illustrate what he sees in his mind's
eye. Rather, he paints pictures with his words that illustrate not only just how
one might observe the natural world realistically, but how Mathews sees the
natural world—as a work of art.

> Stand on some hill or ridge that slopes gently and is studded with blackjack.
> The grass is an impressible green, almost velvety. Clouds are racing across the
> sky like great balls of cotton. A half-dozen cattle are grazing. In the distance,
> the hills are blue, a soft blue that is almost indescribable. A painter would tear
> his hair in despair at such a scene. He would have to know something of the
> Osage and its peculiar history to get something of meaning into his picture.
> On looking at his finished canvas, one would have to hear the voice of the
> meadowlark in it and feel that spirit which is the Osage, before he could call
> the result a plausible attempt.

How can one hear the voice of the meadowlark and feel the spirit of The
Osage in a painting? Paint it with words. Mathews's poetic prose paints mas-
terfully for the reader in this passage through the use of simile as "Clouds are
racing across the sky like great balls of cotton." Mathews's assonance rein-
forces the notion of the painter who would "tear his hair in despair" trying to
capture the sensuality of the Osage. Mathews returns again later to the notion
of the Osage as art in describing a sunset: "Then, as the sun slides down the
hazy blue bowl of the sky, the pastel colors of summer come forth to paint
pictures never seen on canvas." Mathews's desire to share the beauty of the
Osage remained prevalent in his writings.

Although this Waldenesque lifestyle appears romantic, one cannot help
but wonder what Mathews was experiencing on a personal level. Leaving
his wife and children with little means of support seems inconsistent with his

compassionate outlook on the beauty and complexity of the world. Mathews was known throughout the Osage as an intellectual and a skillful politician; however, he was also known as a sensitive man who seemed to love children. Osage Minerals Councilman Joe Cheshewalla recalls how Mathews mentored him on his writing when he was a high school student. "I would share my poetry with him and he would work with me on the language," Cheshewalla says. "My teachers were always very impressed with my writing. Little did they know that my editor was Jo Mathews."

Retired nurse Debbie Cheshewalla, Joe's wife, also recalls Mathews's love and devotion to what Snyder calls his "baby," the Osage Tribal Museum, which Mathews both conceived of and secured funding for through the Works Progress Administration. The Osage Tribal Museum would be the first tribal museum established in the country, and Mathews would remain actively involved in its leadership throughout his life. Debbie recalls how even after Mathews's passing, she and others felt and heard his presence at the museum.

> One time, I heard the back door of the museum jiggle like someone was opening the door. Then I heard the scuffling of boots, just as I had heard them when he was alive. Then I could smell him. He would sit by the fire at his home in the blackjacks, so he always smelled like firewood. You always knew he was coming even before you saw him because you could smell the firewood. I think his spirit still visits the museum to keep an eye on things—to make sure that we're taking care of it.

Mathews seems to be a man made of irony. Just as his relationship with his wife and children waned, he embraced a young Joe Cheshewalla and devoted much of his later life to the museum. Moreover, Mathews was simultaneously a conservationist while also an ardent hunter. As a member of the Isaak Walton League, a group of men as devoted to hunting as Mathews, the members worked to preserve wildlife in order to kill it. "Man the hunter must protect his game if he wishes to enjoy it in the future," Mathews writes, and humankind realized this "almost too late," only when "in the Osage we saw our streams polluted with oil, and our game destroyed by transients connected with oil development who killed in all seasons with barbaric unconcern." Mathews battled oil pollution on the Osage reservation while maintaining friendships with oilmen Frank Phillips and E.W. Marland. Mathews even wrote a book devoted to Marland titled *Life and Death of an Oilman: The Career of E.W. Marland*, which was published in 1951. As Snyder notes, Mathews did not blame the elite tycoons as much as the greedy lower-class whites who, "having caught a whiff of wealth, plotted to exploit, and in many cases murder, Osages owning headrights." In an April 17, 1936, letter to Elizabeth Hunt, Mathews described shining oil derricks as "beautiful."

Despite his numerous contradictions, Mathews's writings reveal a gentleman. Michael Snyder passes no judgment on Mathews in this book, but offers important historical context to accurately frame the collection of Mathews's writings in Osage history. These writings may be studied as early examples of creative nonfiction, where prose, poetry, scientific research, journalism, political rhetoric, and satire converge and, at times, collide. In each of the works, ever-present in Mathews's writings is passion. Throughout his life and work, Mathews maintained a zest for life and an unquenchable thirst for knowledge—that was where his head was. Perhaps the Osage Tribal Museum and his desire for justice in all forms, including environmental as well as social and political justice, was where his heart was. Regardless, Mathews expressed the ethos and pathos of many Osage people of that period of time who trusted him as a spokesperson and as an ambassador for the Osage people—a trust that Mathews had to earn upon his return home to his beloved blackjacks.

Introduction

By Michael Snyder

"Every continent has its own great spirit of place. Every people is polarized in some particular locality, which is home, the homeland. Different places on the face of the earth have different vital effluence, different vibration, different chemical exhalation, different polarity with different stars: call it what you like. But the spirit of place is a great reality."

—D.H. Lawrence, *Studies in Classic American Literature*

Rekindled is interest in the life and works of the great Osage author, historian, and naturalist, John Joseph Mathews. In the twentieth century, Mathews was a brilliant intermediary between lower Plains Indian culture and mainstream North American readers, and an intrepid advocate for his Osage Nation. Renewed attention was evidenced by the publication in 2012 of the first volume of what Mathews had planned to be a three-volume autobiography, *Twenty Thousand Mornings*, edited by Susan Kalter. Mathews's accounts of his Victorian-era Indian Territory boyhood in Pawhuska, capital of the Osage Nation, his undergraduate years at the University of Oklahoma (OU), and his thrills as a World War I–period aviator are invaluable. Five years later, an audience was ready for the revelations found within my full-length scholarly biography, *John Joseph Mathews: Life of an Osage Writer*. Further interest was spurred that year by David Grann's true-crime sensation, *Killers of the Flower Moon: The Osage Murders and the Birth of the FBI*, published within a month of *John Joseph Mathews*, to be a Hollywood film directed by Martin Scorsese. David Grann is deeply indebted to Mathews, quoting him in his epigraph and opening paragraph, and using him as a source throughout his fascinating yet flawed bestseller.

The present book offers exciting early lost work by a charismatic figure, plus a wealth of contextual stories and Osage history. Mathews, the brave and dashing aviator, and the first Native American to attend the University of Oxford, is etched upon literary history as a groundbreaking Indigenous author. He is best known for his sole novel, *Sundown* (1934), much inspired by aspects of his own life, and one of the first novels by a Native American author to feature a Native protagonist.[1] A sophisticated Osage intellectual and tribal councilman, Mathews is one of a few early twentieth-century Native writers (others include D'Arcy McNickle and John M. Oskison) who were predecessors of the Native American Renaissance that received attention after N. Scott Momaday's novel *House Made of Dawn* appeared in 1968 and won the Pulitzer Prize the next year.

Our Osage Hills is a new and eye-opening portrait of the Wahzhazhe (Osage) people. For the first time within book covers, Mathews is revealed as a compelling essayist. I discovered, compiled, and edited Mathews's captivating lost articles, and crafted researched commentaries with the intention of creating a literary form that would do justice to Mathews and the Osages. The articles and commentaries interweave to form an Osage-centric chronicle of the Great Depression, an environmental and economic Dark Age in the Osage Nation and the nation surrounding it. Employing historical and biographical methods, my essays limn exemplary events in the relatively new state of Oklahoma, Indian Country, and the Southwest. Recovering and analyzing the history of the Osage Nation during this period becomes a means by which the whole of United States history during the Dust Bowl and the Depression is illuminated. Using Mathews's articles as a cue, a prompt to move through a vast memory palace, my pieces tell a broader story of Osage cultural survivance, continuity, and the struggle for sovereignty; the involvement of Native Americans in high culture performance and music; the novel of the West and novelists in the West; Hollywood as a reflection, however distorted, of the Osage Nation; Indian athletics, especially baseball; and crucially, the beginning of ecological understanding and the emergence of environmental protection. More darkly, the essays also tell of continued White exploitation and violence against Osages during the 1930s; violence within the tribe; and strained race relations among the triangular dynamic of White, Black, and Native.

John Joseph Mathews crafted enriching installments of "Our Osage Hills," his own newspaper column, at least once a week, and as often as three times a week. The lion's share is included herein; omitted are columns that are overly repetitive or quotidian.[2] With wit, flair, and erudition not commonly found in a small-town paper, Mathews promotes conservation, sportsmanship, tourism, and historical and cultural knowledge. He alerts readers to the environmental Dark Age that had struck Osage County, the result of unregulated oil exploitation since the end of the nineteenth century. Appearing in the Pawhuska *Daily Journal-Capital* as the effects of the Great Depression sunk in, from March 14, 1930, through August 28, 1931, these writings form a trove of absorbing work by Mathews that had been forgotten. "Our Osage Hills" were almost completely obscured by time's overgrowth, more readily because they were signed only with the initials, "J. J. M."

Although Mathews tends to focus on natural sciences—zoology, botany, and ecology of the Osage prairie—my commentaries tend to delve into social sciences and history, including the government and politics of the Osage Nation, and the tribe's relationship with Indian agents, other figures of the federal government, and oilmen. The binary of these subjects is arguably artificial, however. Trained in the natural sciences and Darwinism at OU and Oxford, Mathews stresses that humankind is a part of the natural world, and our individual and social behaviors parallel those of other species. With the onset of the Great Depression, he wrote, both Osages and the residents of Osage County who depended on their business patronage would have to adapt to their new economic scenario of drastically reduced Osage headright payments and other repercussions in order to survive. My pieces therefore elaborate connections between Mathews's naturalist writing and the relevant political institutions and economic processes that ultimately are encircled within his view of nature, with *Homo sapiens* being considered another species of mammal.

Shortly before Mathews began composing his crystalline debut, *Wah'Kon-Tah: The Osage and the White Man's Road* (1932), he honed his writing chops producing these columns in Pawhuska. He was writing under pressure to meet deadlines, harkening back to his college journalism days.[3] From 1929 to 1933, Mathews composed a series of hunting yarns and short stories for *Sooner Magazine*, an alumni publication, as a contributing editor, and then associate editor. Joseph August Brandt, Mathews's good friend and a champion of his work, founded and edited the *Sooner*. Joe Brandt had been a fellow student at OU and a Rhodes Scholar at Oxford while Mathews studied there from 1921 through 1924. With OU President William Bizzell, in 1929 Brandt established the University of Oklahoma Press and was its first director. In early 1931 Brandt strongly encouraged Mathews to write *Wah'Kon-Tah*, then he edited the manuscript that Mathews rapidly produced that same year, published it in 1932, and promoted it with the help of Mathews and others at OU Press. With Brandt's intervention, *Wah'Kon-Tah* was even offered as a Book of the Month Club alternate selection, unheard of for a university press book.[4]

Back during the Great War, Mathews had interrupted his education at OU to enlist in the Army. He became an instructor of aviation in the Army Signal Corps. Afterward, he completed college at OU in 1920 with a degree in geology, then went to Oxford and in 1923 earned a second bachelor degree in natural sciences. Studying in Geneva, Switzerland, during the summer after graduation, Mathews met a talented, attractive, sporty young American woman from an affluent family, Virginia Winslow Hopper. "Ginger" was attending an international boarding school nearby. They fell in love and were engaged to be married six months later in Switzerland. Sadly, Mathews almost immediately regretted the engagement and marriage. He had returned to Oxford for one term of graduate coursework in history prior to the wedding, but abandoned notions of pursuing another degree to live with Ginger in Geneva after their wedding in April 1924. Virginia soon became pregnant, and the couple decided they wanted their baby to be born in the United States. They took up residence in New Jersey, in the Newark area where Ginger had grown up, and had a daughter, Virginia Winslow, in March 1925. Late that year, they moved to Pasadena, California, and bought a house, and they had a son, John Hopper, in August 1926. During the late 1920s Mathews tried his hand at being a Los Angeles businessman—buying and selling land—and a family man, but did not prosper in either.

In late 1928, Mathews left his home in Pasadena and subsequently quit his real estate partnership in Los Angeles. Around November, Mathews separated from his wife, daughter, and son, and eventually moved into a room at the University Club of Los Angeles. In October 1929, he left the Golden State and returned to his hometown of Pawhuska, capital of both the Osage Nation and Osage County, where he remained. Like many Osages, whose quarterly headright payments plummeted in the early 1930s, Mathews gave up his former lifestyle and returned to the reservation in reduced circumstances. Like most Americans, Mathews was humbled by the Great Depression. The stock market crashed on October 29, 1929; with black humor, Will Rogers wrote of being in New York City on "wailing day" when "Wall Street took that tail spin," and "you had to stand in line to get a window to jump out of, and speculators were selling space for bodies in the East River."[5] That same day, Mathews wrote a letter to his mentor, author and professor Walter Stanley Campbell (who published under the name Stanley Vestal), to inform him that he had left California and had returned to his homeland. Mathews stayed in an apartment above the Mathews family garage, a separate structure behind the splendid, two-story Spanish-tiled home on 611 Grandview Avenue, with a fountain placed between.[6] In earlier, more prosperous years, the apartment had housed a driver or servant. Inside the home lived three devout Catholics: his mother, Paula Eugenia Girard Mathews (Jennie), plus two of his sisters, younger and unmarried—Lillian B. Mathews (Lilly) and Marie I. Mathews. Their father, businessman, tribal councilman, and banker William Shirley Mathews, had died in 1915. Though Mathews had quit his business in Los Angeles and was living back at home, this was meant to be a temporary situation.

Within five months of his return to Pawhuska, Mathews was a columnist for the local newspaper, supplementing his diminished "natural income," as he called his headright payments. Mathews enjoyed ample time outdoors— hunting, fishing, observing, and thinking, jotting down notes. In a March 1930 letter, he tells Campbell of the joy and sorrow of coyote hunting with dogs. He added: "I am now a columnist in the local paper; a column appearing three times a week, and devoted to the wild life of the Osage, sponsored by the Izaak Walton League. It is really great sport."[7] In California, Mathews may have not succeeded in his life pursuits, but once returned to his homelands among the Osage hills, he budded as an author, eventually found his Osage critical position, and gave back to the community as an Osage councilman: in short, he thrived.

While penning his columns, Mathews served as secretary of Pawhuska's chapter of one of America's earliest conservation groups, the Izaak Walton League.[8] Another official was his friend, Ralph S. Tolson of the Tolson Agency, which did business with the Mathews family, and at time of writing (2019) still deals in real estate and insurance. Ralph was the father of Strat, Melvin, and Ralph, who all knew Jo Mathews and would remark that even before seeing him, one would catch a whiff of wood smoke.[9] Izaak Walton was an English gentleman-author and fisherman of the seventeenth century, best known for *The Compleat Angler* (1653), which celebrates fishing in prose and verse. In 1922, during rapid industrialization, fifty-four sportsmen formed the Izaak Walton League in Chicago with the goal of fighting water pollution and protecting forests and wildlife. Before this league was established, "no integrated citizen defense of our soil, our woods, waters, and wildlife" existed, William Voight, Jr., writes in his history of the group, *Born with Fists Doubled*. The "Ikes" burst into activity, publishing *The Izaak Walton League Monthly*, succeeded by *Outdoor America*. Both magazines attracted celebrated authors; one was bestselling Western novelist Zane Grey, to whom Mathews alludes in "Old Man," a choice column telling the ironic story of a local drifter. Zane Grey, an Ohioan, contributed a column on freshwater fishing, and he and a long list of authors popular in the 1920s also published there: Theodore Dreiser, Mary Roberts Rinehart, Henry Van Dyke, and naturalist and photographer Gene Stratton-Porter, whose first novel, *The Cardinal*, Mathews refers to in one column.[10] In the early 1930s, while Mathews wrote his columns and first book, the Ikes were instrumental in establishing a wildlife refuge in Osage County, stocking it with animals and fish. Although the league faced obstacles, by 1930 they had influenced enactment of game and fish administrative legislation in Oklahoma and eight other states. The

Herbert Hoover administration (1929–1933) regarded conservation mostly as a state-level issue, so it was not until the Franklin D. Roosevelt administration that the federal government took serious interest in conservation projects aligned with those advocated and advanced by the Izaak Walton League.[11] Mathews was a New Deal Democrat and a friend and advocate of John Collier, Roosevelt's successful appointee of Commissioner of the Bureau of Indian Affairs, who served from 1933 to 1944.

Mathews used his education and gift for language to influence public opinion toward preventing wildlife from becoming endangered or extinct. Likewise, beginning a few years later, as a tribal councilman, Mathews used his gift to advocate for the Osage Nation to help them through the Great Depression, serving two four-year terms. An unsigned editorial of January 25, 1931, in the *Journal-Capital*, its style betraying Mathews as the author, informed and warned local readers:

> When the culture pond on Dial Hill, now under construction, is completed, the local chapter will be able to supply stock almost constantly. This stocking will afford sport and recreation for the people of the Osage, and bring back something of the charm that was once synonymous with the name, The Osage.
>
> There is no doubt that the sportsmen of the Osage have had a hint of what a barren, neglected, though natural game and fish country can become, from the experience of many of them who went in quest of quail this last season. The fisherman would soon learn that the semi-polluted streams cannot nourish fry naturally fast enough to afford them good sport without the agency of man. Restocking of streams and cover is a necessity, and all the active protection of the game and fish is essential if there is to be hunting and fishing. For proper protection, cooperation of all sportsmen and lovers of the outdoors is also necessary. . . . This condition is arising all over the United States. The Osage is a natural game and fish country. If we do not do something toward the conservation of our game and fish, it is not unlikely that the Osage Hills will not long remain a public recreation ground.

This was a clarion call to all Osage County to become aware and involved in conservation efforts, and a rationale for his columns and the local chapter of the Izaak Walton League.

Mathews's pieces are influenced by his formal education in geology, zoology, and other natural sciences at the OU and at Oxford. They reflect his belief in Darwinian evolutionary theory and natural selection, but also his Osage critical perspective. Mathews deploys a point of view sympathetic to the Osages and Indigenous people more generally. Successful species adapt in order to survive, and humankind's "development is a part of nature" and its balance, so we must consider ourselves "a part of that life" around us. He takes a scientific point of view, yet as an Osage, stresses that to understand ourselves, humankind benefits from understanding our "brothers of the fields and woods."[12] Mathews also shows an Indigenous perspective when he explains the ecology of the Osage prairie; prior to white settlement, there had been a "delicate balance of nature" in nature. Before the "white man came with his gun and plow, the Indian was included in the balance; he with his bow and arrow was a part of the life," but afterward, wildlife could not "adjust to this new condition." A special cause is the endangered prairie chicken, whose dance and booming on the prairie delighted him and his privileged spring visitors. While coyotes had been able to adapt to humankind's encroachments, it was harder for the prairie chicken to do so.[13]

John Joseph's father, William S. Mathews, was a lover of horses and hunting, and he passed his knowledge and love of them to his son. Like Jo's grandfather, blacksmith and trader John Allen Mathews—who settled among Osages and married two Osage sisters in what is now southeastern Kansas—Will owned horses and stables, and he catered to hunters from outside of the Osage Nation, which was known to be an idyllic hunting range. Along with the family home on Grandview Avenue in Pawhuska, which was later removed to build its replacement in 1927, William owned property out on the family allotment on the prairie outside of town. On this land and all over the county, Jo Mathews whiled away his boyhood days with his beloved dog, Spot, and his handsome horse, Bally. He lay on his back in the tall grass and gazed longingly at the red-tailed hawk "makin' lazy circles in the sky," to quote Rodgers and Hammerstein. He ached to fly, a dream he realized as a student of military aviation, and then as an aviation instructor during the World War I years. As a teenager, Mathews was encouraged to become a natural scientist when he impressed Judge Musseller, an amateur ornithologist, with his skill in classifying birds. He also visited the lodges of Osage camps, played, and observed.

At OU, Mathews spent much time hunting and fishing on and near the Canadian River, which flows near Norman. After graduation from OU, he missed his first term at Merton College, Oxford University, because he, oddly enough, chose to extend his already lengthy hunting trip in the Rockies of Colorado and Wyoming. While at Oxford, Mathews went on a deer hunting trip to Scotland to stalk the legendary red deer of the Highland moors, the quarry of kings of England and chieftains of Scotland, he wrote. Mathews evoked this experience in his first article for the *Sooner Magazine* in April 1929, "Hunting the Red Deer of Scotland," which described his experiences in Argyllshire, Scotland, during 1921. "Hunting in the Rockies" followed the next month. More than one hunting story concluded with a stoic narrator finishing a wounded animal in a coup de grâce. If, in some stories, Mathews kills an animal with detachment, in others he reveals compassion, even empathy.

In the story "Admirable Outlaw" from the *Sooner* of April 1930, a cousin to the column titled "Admirable Bandit" found herein, Mathews expressed remorse and regret for killing a wily coyote he had pursued. He deeply admired coyotes and over the decades, noted seeing and hearing them in his diaries. The title of *Talking to the Moon* honored the coyote's nighttime chorus, and he admired his friend J. Frank Dobie's book, *The Voice of the Coyote* (1957), which, as the Texan folklorist and historian acknowledged, owed a large debt to Mathews. Shooting animals meant sport and sometimes food to Mathews, and he went to great distances and trouble to enter remote habitats and hunt large animals such as bear, bighorn sheep, and wapiti. In "Admirable Outlaw," however, after his dogs have maimed and killed an infamous coyote, Jo Mathews reveals considerable regret.

In Franz Kafka's unfinished novel *Amerika*, the Nature Theater of Oklahoma appears at the end of the text, offering salvation: "The Great Nature Theater of Oklahoma is calling you!" its sign invites. "All welcome! Anyone who wants to be an artist, step forward!"[14] There really was such a theater, and Mathews wrote a draft of the script of "the great drama of Nature," as he put it. In April 1931, Mathews predicted that someday, humankind will "discover in this drama of life romance as great as that found in the Crusades, and tragedy as great as that found in Shakespeare."[15] With this book I attempt to flesh out its characters. Dancing across the stage of the Nature Theater of Oklahoma are the prima ballerinas, Maria and Marjorie Tallchief; walking behind them proudly are their prominent father, Alexander Tall Chief, and their uncle, Eves Tall Chief, an overlooked victim of the Osage murders of the 1920s. This series of coldhearted conspiratorial murders of Osages by whites, and the contemporaneous Tulsa massacre of 1921, in which an entire African American neighborhood was burned, were homegrown manifestations of what historian Timothy Snyder calls "the horror of the twentieth century" in *Bloodlands: Europe between Hitler and Stalin*.[16] Within the Osage Nation, tragic and triumphal sagas of prominent Osage families such as the Tall Chiefs, Lookouts, Red Eagles, Redcorns, and the Mathewses play out over decades of persistent time, narrated in the present book. Indian Territory neighbors and rivals of the Osages, the Cherokees produced creatives such as Will Rogers and playwright Lynn Riggs, who also tread the boards of this theater. They are joined by the opera singer Tessie Mobley, also known as Lushanya, the Chickasaw Songbird, and her Osage actor husband, Louis Brave. Famous twentieth-century writers including Thomas Wolfe and Edna Ferber, and celebrated athletes such as boxer Jack Johnson and the major leaguers Mose YellowHorse of the Pawnee, and Pepper Martin, "the Wild Horse of the Osage," each has a moment in the spotlight.

This book aims to contribute to a tribalography of the Osages, to use the term coined by Choctaw author LeAnne Howe. Tribalography entails synthesizing through narrative the collective experiences of individuals, families, clans, and ancestors into a meaningful form to inform readers about who, in this case, the Wahzhazhe people truly are. Tribalography, Howe explains, derives from "the native propensity for bringing things together" and for "symbiotically connecting one thing to another."[17] In my essays and shorter commentaries I make such connections, providing sociohistorical contexts for significant events and topics Mathews covers in his columns, placing his reflections on nature and ecology, Osage culture, and tourism into dialogue with larger debates over Osage sovereignty, politics, and identity. New and revealing biographical material and insights on significant Osage families trace out, for example, the paths to wealth and power that drew fierce envy and plotting, both among state and federal governments and white individuals, to either control or steal that money by hook or by crook. One such example is my discussion of how the remunerative perks of the position of Osage National Treasurer—a role played both by John Joseph's father, William S. Mathews and Alexander Tall Chief—helps explain the prominence of these families, and why the federal government violated tribal sovereignty in shutting down the Osage National Council at the turn of the century, prior to the establishment of the Osage Tribal Council. Another example of the struggle for Osage sovereignty is my analysis of the role that W.S. Mathews played as a tribal councilman as he and his fellow councilmen were unfairly removed by the Secretary of the Interior in 1913. This book also compares the experiences of neighbors of the Osages such as the Cherokee and the Pawnee and other tribal nations. "Often what happened to one group is intelligible only in light of what had happened to another. But that is just the beginning of the connections," Timothy Snyder writes in *Bloodlands*. In examining violations of sovereignty and, especially at the end of the book, the exploitation and murders of Osages that reached an apex in the early 1920s, like *Bloodlands*, this book contends that oppressive governments and institutions "have to be understood in light of how their leaders strove to master" others' homelands, and how they viewed the oppressed groups and "their relationships to one another." Therefore, like *Bloodlands*, "this study describes the victims, and the perpetrators." It attempts to discuss and analyze "the ideologies and the plans, and the systems and the societies" of Osages, other tribal nations, their White neighbors, and the United States government.[18]

Likewise, working together with Mathews's columns, my essays also serve to elucidate constellations of Native and non-Native artists, writers, poets, and playwrights, making surprising connections to popular culture. As LeAnne Howe explains, "tribalography is a story that links Indians and non-Indians."[19] To give an example of such interrelation, another strong supporter of Mathews and his first book was University of Oklahoma Press employee Betty Kirk, a good friend of the Cherokee playwright and poet Lynn Riggs. The poet enrolled at OU shortly after Mathews graduated in 1920 and shared a mentor in Walter Stanley Campbell (who published as Stanley Vestal). Riggs's folk-play that included songs, *Green Grow the Lilacs*, became the source of Rogers and Hammerstein's enduring musical, *Oklahoma!* Lynn Riggs, a closeted gay man and a friend of Golden Age of Hollywood icons and rivals Joan Crawford and Bette Davis, co-wrote the screenplay of *The Garden of Allah* (1936), starring Marlene Dietrich. That movie was adapted from the bestselling "desert romance" novel of the same name, published thirty-two years earlier. A part of the constellation, Mathews alludes to that novel and its setting of Biskra in a column pondering how to publicize the "romance of the Osage" to draw tourist income.

Many knew Mathews to be kind and generous. In 1931, Violet Willis of Pawhuska, who became a family friend of the Mathewses, was struggling to pay her way through studies at Northeastern State Teachers College (later University) in Tahlequah with makeshift gigs: tutoring, feeding dogs, and lighting coal fires. Violet's educational future did not then seem bright, but her mother had a talk with Lillian Mathews at Immaculate Conception Church in Pawhuska one day, relating her daughter's difficulties. According to Michael Vaught, who interviewed Willis, a few days after this exchange, Violet, in the midst of a gym class, was summoned to the coaches' office, where she, still in her sweaty clothes, was surprised to find the college president and "the dignified, precise-spoken man she came to know as Jo." Following a brief interview, Ms. Willis was hired as an assistant to the dean of women, her education thus safeguarded. Willis said, "I always tried to thank him, even to the end, but Jo always brushed it off." After Violet graduated, she was employed by the Osage Tribal Agency, and later became a secretary for the Osage Tribal Council, which then included Mathews. The councilman valued her shorthand skills and hired her to assist him with his cultural preservation efforts speaking with traditional elders with a translator. Violet Willis remembered Mathews as independent and sometimes unconventional.[20]

Likewise, by reading his newspaper columns, we can sense Mathews's generosity to his community among other facets of his character. Much like Mathews, the book you are reading is somewhat unconventional; thus, its arrangement bears comment. In the pages that follow, this book tends to proceed along a loosely chronological structure, presenting Mathews's columns in the order in which they were originally published. However, I often deviate from this general pattern in favor of grouping columns that address a particular subject and show the evolution of Mathews's thought over time. For example, in his discussion of topics such as "the romance of the Osage" and prairie chickens, we have opportunity to see the introduction and, sometimes, elaboration of themes that he will revisit in his life and later work. In some cases I present Mathews's columns as standalone pieces because their sheer eloquence makes any addendum seem superfluous. Other of Mathews's columns lend themselves to my additional reflections because they often make references or allusions to contemporary events, people, books, or movies. To be precise, when I provide commentary on Mathews's articles, my pieces elaborate content in a given Mathews column and/or they discuss other items and articles about contemporary events usually found in that same day's issue of the Pawhuska *Journal-Capital*, sometimes on the same page or even adjacent to the "Our Osage Hills" column. Overall, my essays aim to annotate Mathews's historical and cultural references, provide additional context, or address other topics relevant to Mathews's writing. By interweaving his columns with my commentaries, this book seeks to amplify Mathews' voice and convey the broad spectrum of Osage familial, social, and cultural history.

NOTES

1. Louis Owens, *Other Destinies: Understanding the American Indian Novel* (Norman: University of Oklahoma Press, 1994), 25, 60; Terry P. Wilson, "John Joseph Mathews," *Native American Writers of the United States*, edited by Kenneth M. Roemer, Dictionary of Literary Biography 175 (Detroit: Gale Research, 1997), 154.

2. Mathews's newspaper columns did not originally bear titles, headlines, or bylines other than "Our Osage Hills, by J.J.M." Along with titling them, I have on rare occasion corrected Mathews's grammar or spelling or made minor changes to diction. Given Mathews's Oxford education, I have maintained any British spellings he used. Where I have deleted repetitive or quotidian material, I have marked this with ellipses. A few additions for clarity are in brackets. The footnotes are mine.

3. At OU, Mathews wrote yearbook copy, features for the *University of Oklahoma Magazine*, and unsigned campus news items for the student newspaper, then called the *University Oklahoman*. After graduating from OU, during the early 1920s his writing style evolved through rigorous sessions with his tutors at Merton College, University of Oxford.

4. In the early 1940s, Brandt served as president of OU before continuing his publishing career as director of the University of Chicago Press, which in 1945 published the hardcover edition of *Talking to the Moon*.

5. Will Rogers, *The Autobiography of Will Rogers*, edited by Donald Day (New York: Lancer, 1963), 192, entry dated October 29, 1929.

6. Mathews to Campbell, October 29, 1929, Box 32, Folder 27, Walter Stanley Campbell Collection (WSC), Western History Collection (WHC), University of Oklahoma, Norman, Oklahoma (OU).

7. Mathews to Campbell, March 24, 1930, Box 32, Folder 27, WSC, WHC, OU.

8. "Walton League Names Officers," *Pawhuska Daily Journal-Capital*, February 4, 1931.

9. "Osage Streams Receive Stock," *Pawhuska Daily Journal-Capital*, November 12, 1930.

10. William Voight, Jr. *Born with Fists Doubled: Defending Outdoor America* (Spirit Lake, Iowa: Izaak Walton League of America Endowment, 1992), 6, 21–22.

11. "Isaak Walton League of America: A Brief History," *Isaak Walton League of America*, www.iwla.org/about-us/history-mission, accessed March 13, 2015; "Osage Streams Receive Stock," *Pawhuska Journal-Capital*, November 12, 1930; see Voight, chapter 7, *Born with Fists Doubled.*

12. J.J.M. [John Joseph Mathews], "Our Osage Hills" column, Pawhuska *Journal-Capital* May 29, 1931, 6 [all Pawhuska *Journal-Capital* articles were copied from microfilm at the newspaper archives of the Oklahoma History Research Center].

13. J.J.M. [John Joseph Mathews], "Our Osage Hills" column, *Pawhuska Journal-Capital* March 23, 1930, section 2, 1; J.J.M. [John Joseph Mathews], "Our Osage Hills" column, *Pawhuska Journal-Capital* March 26, 1930: 6; April 2, 1930; May 5, 1930, 5.

14. Franz Kafka, *Amerika*, translated by Edwin Muir (New York: New Directions, 1946).

15. J.J.M. [John Joseph Mathews], "Our Osage Hills" column, *Pawhuska Journal-Capital* April 4, 1931.

16. Timothy Snyder, *Bloodlands: Europe between Hitler and Stalin* (New York: Basic, 2010), xiii. Full transparency: Timothy Snyder is my brother. Generous as usual, Tim thanks my other brother Phil, a physicist, and me in the acknowledgments (on page 420) for helping him to "frame the introduction."

17. LeAnne Howe, *Choctalking on Other Realities* (San Francisco: Aunt Lute, 2013), 42, 46, 47.

18. Snyder, *Bloodlands*, xix.

19. Howe, *Choctalking on Other Realities*, 46.

20. Michael Vaught, "Osage Scribe," *Oklahoma Today* 46, no. 5 (August–September 1996), 36.

Part I

Scene Setting

"Road Home from the Cattleguard" by John Joseph Mathews
Courtesy of the Osage Nation and the Mathews family

GEOLOGY OF THE OSAGE

Friday, March 14, 1930, #1

The Osage has its own history outside of the part that man has played here. The present topography of the Osage is the result of geological processes, and there is a reason for every sandstone ridge and flint hill, the realization of which adds to the interest by opening a door to another field.

The whole of the Osage is a book in which is written its history. The book is open at all times for those who care to read. On either side of its automobile road are the open pages from which anyone may read as he drives; there is no history more intriguing. It is replete with tragedies and romance which, when compared with man's "earth-shaking" revolutions, causes them to appear as battles of army ants. As one drives along, not the least interesting thought, as he studies the history on each side of him, is the consciousness of the fact that he owes the car which he is driving to geological processes that make the landscape he is enjoying. The original accumulation and concentration of the hydrocarbons were incidents in the processes that gave rise to the prairies and blackjack-covered sandstone hills of the Osage.[1] This is real romance. The stark oil derrick standing out against the horizon is a part of the hills and valleys, not merely because it symbolizes the commercial romance and the material well-being of a race, but also because its own reason for being is found far back in history of those hills and valleys.

SCENE SETTING

The term "the Osage" was used to refer to the Osage Reservation, which became Osage County after Oklahoma statehood in 1907. Although much of the surface land was sold to non-Osages, the Wahzhazhe people communally held onto their subsurface mineral rights, leading to tribal wealth in the early twentieth century after oil was discovered underneath the reservation. Mathews also uses "the Osage" to refer to the Osage tribe as a whole.

John Joseph Mathews majored in geology at the University of Oklahoma (OU), graduating in 1920 after his education was interrupted by World War I. At the time he thought he might become involved in the oil industry. During the war, he served as a military aviator in the U.S. Signal Corps and taught aviation in Texas, and then became a military "aerial chauffeur" in Langley, Virginia. Omitted from this collection are two highly detailed columns about the geology of the Osage. It is possible that Mathews was getting some extra mileage out of a couple of geology papers written for OU or Oxford professors, specially revised for the column.

An advertisement juxtaposed with his debut column ironically befits Mathews's themes that he will introduce in later columns: humankind as a part of nature, and Darwinian natural selection entailing competition for mates. Today we might call sexist and heteronormative the ad for Doctor Pierce's Golden Medical Discovery: "Girls, be Attractive to Men. Nature Intended you Should Be!"

UNIQUE HISTORY OF THE OSAGE

Friday, July 25, 1930, #34

Due to its unique history, the Osage stands out among the other counties of the state. It was a Nation until 1907 when Oklahoma became a state. The council was designated as the "National Council" before that date and the Osage was known as the Osage Nation.[2] The allotment of the lands reserving the mineral rights of the tribe was an example of communistic principles applied within a democracy. The development of the Osage has been influenced by this idea, and a nettle cattle economy has been saved from the monotony of section roads and drab farm houses on every 160 acres; farm houses and plowed fields that would have made the Osage one with every other state, except that in the case of the Osage, only the creek and river bottoms would have been considered seriously as agricultural lands. It is much more interesting since the Osage has been allowed to fulfill its own destiny. It is gratifying that it was not through some stupidity, thrown open to land-hungry hordes, and that it does not bear such a barbaric chapter in its history.[3] Its history has not been Utopian, but primitive chivalry where courage and daring are displayed is not distasteful; there are other human activities in a wild, new country less pleasing and less flattering to a nation of people who believe themselves virtuous.

Farmers who acquire land in the Osage are of the better type; they acquire property through their own efforts and in the end are the most desirable citizens. They have expected nothing from anyone, but have taken advantage of their opportunities and have worked hard for what they have. They contribute much to that charm which is characteristic of the Osage.

The Osage is unique in its topography. Its hills can be seen from almost every direction from adjoining counties. They characteristically stand like green walls' outlines against the horizon; behind them is slight mystery and their very wildness produces interest. One knows instinctively when he has crossed the county line: the indescribable atmosphere of the unusual creeps into his senses.

One wonders if we who live here will ever grow to the stature of the Osage Hills. Man's environment plays a great part in moulding him, but he must come to an appreciation of that environment.

LIFE ADAPTS TO ITS ENVIRONMENT

Friday, March 21, 1930, #4

We have seen that streams adapt themselves to the geology of the district in which they flow. Life also adapts itself to the conditions resulting from geological processes. Trees grow to where they can get water and spring from soil containing the chemicals necessary to them as food. More trees grow on the sandstone hills than on the hills capped with limestone, and yet more trees, and in greater variety, grow in the valleys and flats where the soil is thicker and the water more plentiful.

The sandstone hills, that is, the hills capped with sandstone, are more favorable to the growth of trees, because of the very nature of the sandstone, which is porous and holds water. It consists of quartz grains derived from the original granite, which under the erosion process of water and climate, tend to cause the exposed stratum to break up into large boulders, leaving space between for the growth of trees. While on the other hand, the hills capped with limestone are more often treeless, because the limestone stratum remains intact, and instead of a physical breakup, is more apt to be dissolved by the chemicals in the water with which it comes into contact. Anyone who has been on the limestone prairie has seen "solution holes" in loose rocks lying about. This tendency on the part of the limestone to remain intact does not favor the growth of trees; the thin soil formed above the impervious stratum cannot support such growth, and hence we have the high prairie and the blackjack-covered hills of the Osage; also the valleys to which both type of rock have contributed, giving nurture to sycamores, elms, walnuts, hackberry, and oaks.

Thus does animal life likewise adapt itself to its environment. The natural law of the universe is that each individual exists for the purpose of propagating its own kind: the survival of the species is imperative. In order that the species may remain on the face of the earth, they must have (a) food and water, (b) protection from enemies and the elements, and (c) they must reproduce themselves. Hence adaptation to environment is necessary. Through the ages of development, the species have reached their present stage. Certain foods and water are necessary and the species live where these can be obtained. For protection, many of the species have developed distinguishing characteristics. Some have become fleet of foot; some strong-winged; some have developed strong claws; some exude musk (e.g., skunk); some band together (union gives strength). In the case of the species that prey on others, their weapons for defense are the tools of gaining their food. A defense common to all species is protective coloration. The colors of the feathers or fur are so patterned that when the individual is motionless, he cannot be seen against a natural background. This serves for protection and acquisition of food, and is most effective in the cause of a hen bird sitting on her eggs.

In reproduction, through competition among the males, we have the strongest mating with the strongest, and the weakest killed or outlawed. The survival of the fittest produces strong offspring, and thereby enhances the chances of the species in its battle for existence.

In the next column, we will discuss the drama of life which has as its stage, the bottom of streams, the grass roots, the hills, and the sky. We ought to understand these tragedies and comedies of the Osage, so that we may better understand the participants. Their lives are of the greatest importance to us. The laws that govern them govern us, and our whole economic structure is based on the struggles of the species for existence.

DARWIN AND NIETZSCHE

Suggested in part by several of his columns, over the course of his career, Mathews is often Darwinian and Nietzschean in his outlook, extolling strength, health, intelligence, and beauty as their own natural ends. Yet he reframed this philosophy as traditionally Osage. In *Beyond Good and Evil*, Friedrich Nietzsche posited such attributes were good and their absence bad, and he deconstructs the concept of evil as an illusory product of "slave morality" (e.g., Christianity) that self-servingly protects the weak by preaching mercy and pity. Slave morality restrains strong and talented individuals from exercising their will to power and rising above "the herd." Borrowing from novelist Thomas Wolfe, with whom he socialized in Santa Fe (discussed later), New Mexico, Mathews criticized "the man-swarm" and "the great sheep swarm of America" whose attitudes are easily manipulated by radio and newspapers.[4] He believed in Nietzsche's concept of the Will to Power, and told his sister Marie Mathews, "one may do anything one wants to do if he wants it badly enough and will work hard enough to achieve it."[5] Mathews endorsed social Darwinism and natural selection, and in 1951, he corresponded with evolutionary biologist Julian Huxley, who inspired the title of his unpublished novel, "Within Your Dream."[6] Mathews sounds as though he is familiar with both Darwin and Nietzsche when he declares in the introduction to his tribal history *The Osages* that there was "no Right or Wrong concerning the European invasion; it was only a biological incident as far as the Neolithic man was concerned."[7]

LIFE IS EVER-CHANGING: THE IMPERATIVE TO ADAPT

Friday, May 29, 1931, #81

Every species extant owes its survival as a species to the fact that it was able to adapt itself to the changing conditions. The species as we know them were not always as they are at present in their color, form, and habits. Life is ever-changing; it is a dynamic thing moving on and on through the ages, undergoing adaptations to environment, becoming in fact a series of mutations. Every day, the land masses are changing before our eyes, though in the very life of an individual, or generation, these changes are not palpable. An eternal struggle to survive, a cruel struggle wherein the weak are weeded out and the senile left to die, or left for prey to the enemy species.

Man is not above this struggle of life; he is a part of the life about him, and as a part of this life, he is governed by the same laws. Though he has been a great factor in the struggle of the weaker forms of life, through a wanton, most unbiologic destruction of the species, he is still a part of the life that he destroys. In a few days, his food supply could be wiped out by insects if the pressure that holds their number down were suddenly released, and only a very quick adaptation could save him as a species. The passing of man would not mean the end of the world; it would simply mean that another species would step into his place as the dominant form of life. Man gained his dominance through the development of his nervous system, which has reached a highly developed mentality. This mentality started through necessity of survival. With a weak body, he had to adapt himself in order to survive and in his adaptation, thought and ideas were born, and the world, as a result of this necessitous adaptation, is ruled at present by ideas.

Thus it is with man. He is a biological unit, and cannot separate himself from life as a whole. Every law that governs the swarming ants, the bee, the herds of elephants, applies to man. To understand himself, he would do well to understand and sympathize with his brothers of the fields and woods. He may not understand why flowers are red, purple, or blue, yet he knows that vibrant and pleasing advertisements are helpful to his business. He wonders why, if he thinks about it at all, only a small percentage of the eggs laid by fish hatch into fry, and why out of millions of fry, only a few reach maturity, yet he knows of the necessity of volume sales. He does not see the analogy.

Whether he sells shoes, meat, or shoestrings, he is governed by the laws that govern the species. The species grow lazy and tend to develop ornamentations when their enemies are few and the food supply abundant, which encumber them when the necessity arises for them to adapt themselves to changes. Thousands of species that once lived on the earth exist no more because they were unable to adapt themselves to changes. The seller of shoes, meats, and shoestrings in times of prosperity wastes his energy in ornamentation, which he calls overhead, and thus encumbers himself. Ornamentation may be ideas that he has conceived in his long period of prosperity, which encumber him when changes arrive to which he must adapt himself. Life is virile: the species must be ever ready to struggle for their existence.

Life in the Osage has had to adapt itself through the ages to the natural changes that came about; then, when the European came to the Osage, further adaptation was necessary. The quail, the rabbits, squirrels, coyote, et cetera, have been more or less successful in adaptation, but the prairie chicken has not yet learned that death can spurt from an automobile. But man, through economics upon which his life is based, is now facing a change in the Osage to which he will be compelled to adapt himself, and unless he is too much encumbered by the ornamentation of past prosperity, he will survive through adaptation, or face the alternative of lethargic, enervating stagnation, because in the Osage, men are facing the change while still in the midst of the struggle for the fundamentals.

GREAT DEPRESSION

In the conclusion of the article above, Mathews refers to the necessity of adapting to the straitened circumstances of the Great Depression, which included for the Osages greatly reduced headright payments. Eighteen days after the above column ran, on June 16, 1931, the *Daily Journal-Capital* ran a United Press story reporting that the stock market that day "underwent its most drastic decline since the dark days" of November 1929, and "billions of dollars were clipped from the market values." Between 1930 and 1931, Osage headright payments plummeted by over one-half. Yet despite their reduced income, as we have seen, the Osages "continued to be exploited throughout the 1930s," Terry P. Wilson writes. "Though the tribe had less money, there were no fewer ways they were enjoined to spend it." Alcoholism seemed as prevalent in the 1930s as it had been in the roaring 1920s; from a multitude of hidden illegal stills, a pipeline of liquor flowed. Osage youth were preyed upon by bootleggers, and drugs such as morphine, cocaine, and the more benign marijuana were available. Corrupt guardians would allow "incompetent" Osages to spend freely until they were penniless. In 1938, William Zimmerman, Jr., assistant commissioner of Indian affairs under John Collier and an ally of Mathews, joined the Osage council in urging Congressional action to modify the legislation of the 1920s that was hastening the diminishment of tribal wealth. Zimmerman told the U.S. Senate Committee on Indian Affairs that it was absurd for a guardian "to be in a position of spending this ward's funds until they are absolutely exhausted." Loopholes in laws passed in the 1920s had allowed many Osage homesteads to be lost via sales held to satisfy Osage owners' overdue taxes.[8] Wilson added that "outright robbery and theft actually increased as the Indian camps at Pawhuska, Hominy, and Gray Horse became the special targets of criminals. To aid the single federal law officer assigned to the county, the agency hired three law officers, whose salaries were paid with tribal funds, to be stationed at the camps."[9]

HAWK AND QUAIL: THE BALANCE
OF NATURE BEFORE THE WHITE MAN

Tuesday, January 20, 1931, #49

We have seen that the survival of the species depends upon the food supply. If a shortage of food came about by change in climate, or by the influx of other species that required the same food, the original species had to adapt themselves to this condition by learning to eat other food or by migration. We have seen that the survival of the species also depended on protection. If a new enemy appeared, they had to adapt themselves so they were protect the species against this enemy, either by taking advantage of natural cover, or by the development of defense equipment. If they were forced to migrate, they would have had to adapt themselves to the conditions found in their new home. Those species that, through long immunity from natural enemies, and through a plentiful supply of food, easily obtained, became less active and less alert, would thus be weakened, unable to adapt themselves to the changing conditions, and would become extinct. There is an eternal struggle for existence, and the imperative law of Nature is adaptation to changing condition or extinction.

The changes have occurred constantly through the ages, and the forms that exist today are not necessarily the forms that existed thousands of years ago. The species have changed, and are changing through adaptation. But we cannot think of these changes as going on within a certain number of years. The year is the unit used by man for measuring historical time. The life of man on the earth is very short, and the span of an individual could be measured in minutes of geological time. So naturally these changes and the consequent application of the species are not perceptible to man, and as a consequence, it seems to him that the conditions which exist at present, existed always, and that the species as he knows them are as they were when they made their appearance on the earth.

The species that we know today are the resultant forms from ages of climatic and geological changes that affected their food supply, and their defense against other species; the species are the result of the adaptation to these changes. These species of the Osage played their part, and in their struggles for existence had reached a balance, a condition wherein their struggles against each other gave rise to a dependence upon each other for existence. A delicate balance of Nature.

This was before the white man came with his gun and plow; the Indian was included in the balance; he with his bow and arrow was a part of the life.

To explain this balance of Nature, one must take as an example two species. We shall take the hawk and the quail in the Osage before the advent of the white man. The hawk is a flesh-eater and is very fond of quail; we assume that quail is his food supply, and since there were great numbers of quail, he had a plentiful supply of food. He had few enemies, and he was well equipped for protection in his rending beak and his sharp talons, and this with an abundance of food and adequate protection against his very few enemies, he was able to reproduce and thereby propagate his kind. To assure its continuance, a species has a tendency to great numbers, and by numbers make their position sure; and if nothing stopped them, some species would overrun the earth to the detriment of others. But their numbers are limited by the food supply and their natural enemies. Here comes into play the balance of Nature.

Why then was not the Osage overrun with hawks? Certainly, there were enough quail to sustain a much greater number. Certainly the hawk had adequate protection. If the quail were limited in their numbers by the food supply and by natural enemies, certainly the hawks were not thus limited. What we assume is true, but we must now look to the quail for the answer. The quail is protectively colored; he is fleet of foot and flies very fast for a short distance; he bands into coveys at all times except in the breeding season; he takes advantage of fallen tree tops, undergrowth and briar patches for cover. The hawk hunts from the air, watching intently the ground below, and when he flies on a sunshiny day, he casts a shadow; when he hunts on overcast days, the various species of little seed-eating birds fly ahead of him close to the ground, from cover to cover, uttering chirps of alarm.

It is not necessary for the whole covey of quail to see the shadow of a hawk; one member will communicate the danger to the covey and they immediately "freeze" in their tracks. Here the protective coloring plays its part; they are motionless and the hawk cannot see them against the background of the habitat. If the covey has not been warned by the seed-eaters, or by the shadow, the hawk may be upon them before they know of his presence. They will then then run swiftly to the nearest cover, and the hawk, if he has swooped down on them, is unable to maneuver in the branches of a fallen tree, nor is he able to at the huddled covey under the briars. Thus we see that the coloration, the covey habit, the running ability of the quail, and the protection afforded by the briars, really limit the food supply of the hawk; his food supply is not limited by the number of quail, but by his ability to catch them.

Then again, the hawk is not the only enemy of the quail; he must exist in spite of many enemies, and through adaptation he has become prolific. The hen quail lays from thirteen to twenty eggs, twice and sometimes three times a season, but not over fifty percent of the chicks hatched attain maturity. This lavish overproduction is really protection, inasmuch as the enemies usually catch the weaklings among the adults. The strong are left to mate with the strong for the propagation of the species.

To go back to the hawk, we find that the number of the hawks is limited by food supply, which really depends upon the ability of the quail to protect himself. But there is more to the balance of Nature than this.

Obviously, the hawk with his equipment for defense has the requisite of protection well in hand. A vulnerable spot in the hawk's self-protection is his nest. It is high in a treetop and very conspicuous and cumbersome. High winds could destroy it, and the eggs and nestlings of any bird are delicious food for many species, an even though the hawk is a terrific fighter, his nest is not immune. Then also coming into the balance of nature are many insects and bacilli that destroy many species each year, and this is the case of the hawk, whose numbers are limited by these enemies.

Another point is that the hen hawk only lays two eggs a season, and despite her ability to protect her meat, she is not always sure of bringing up the two nestlings to maturity. Perhaps a certain insect that lays eggs in the leftover flesh of birds, et cetera, which has been brought to the fledglings by the mother hawk, and which become a dangerous food for the former when the eggs have been deposited in it, would eventually wipe out the hawks if it were not for the activity of the crested flycatcher in catching these insects, which are his food supply.[10] Hence we find the number of hawks limited by the insects, and the insects limited by the flycatcher, and the quail indirectly depending upon the insect for protection, and the hawk indirectly depending on the flycatcher.

This, then, is the balance of Nature. This was the status quo before the advent of the white man. In the struggle for existence, each animal, bird, fish, and insect played a role in the Osage, a sort of double role, wherein he fought every other species in order to assure the continuance of his own species, yet served indirectly as a protector to many species.

The balance was delicate; it oscillated a little at all times, and occasionally things happened which threw off the balance for a season or more. For instance, assume that an epidemic has broken out among the rabbits, killing thousands of them between the Kansas line and the Canadian line. The rabbit is one of Nature's most important tools in the universal balance, and when he is scarce, many things may happen in the woods and fields. The scarcity of the rabbit then means in this case a short food supply, not only for the snowy owl and the fierce goshawk that winter in the northern states, but for many other species of birds and animals. These species would in their hunger swarm over the Osage where rabbits could be found, and finding the rabbits insufficient in number to satisfy their voracity, would prey on other species and on each other. This would upset the balance in the Osage, and also the balance north of the Kansas line; perhaps for several seasons, until the remarkably prolific rabbit could repopulate these regions.

We shall see what happened to this balance of Nature when the white man came to the Osage; then we shall be better able to understand what the Izaak Walton League is attempting to do for the wildlife of America.

LOS ANGELES

The closing note of this substantial column is foreboding, implying that dark disturbances to the balance of Nature arrived with the white settlers. The piece seems therefore appropriately juxtaposed with a striking advertisement for seemingly satanic "666 Tablets." Another interesting item is a large ad for The Commodore Hotel in Los Angeles, which attempted to persuade Osages who still had money to indulge in travel and leisure—despite the escalating depredations of the Great Depression. The Broadmoor Hotel in Colorado Springs was another popular destination for Osages. If Mathews read his own column in the newspaper, this lush ad would have been an unwelcome reminder of his forsaken domestic life in Pasadena, and unsuccessful business life in Los Angeles, where he had rented an office in the Pacific National Bank Building. As noted, in February of 1929, Jo permanently left his wife and his two small children in Pasadena. He apparently did not see his daughter Virginia and son John again until 1939, when Ginger Mathews and her sister, Phyllis Hopper, staged an unexpected reunion in Washington, DC, when Jo was there on Osage tribal business.

THE EUROPEAN DISRUPTED A DELICATE BALANCE

Thursday, March 26, 1930, # 6

When the Europeans came to the Osage, the balance of Nature, as we have seen, was in play: a delicate balance wherein insects, birds, animals, flowers and trees contributed to the balance by their struggles for existence.

The tall weeds and grasses grew in the valley "as high as a horse's back," and the wind sang through the undulating grasses on the high prairie. The prairie chicken sent its sonorous, booming call across the limestone hills on spring mornings. The quail whistled in the valleys. Bands of white-tailed deer flicked their ears and stamped their feet in the shade of the blackjacks. Silent-footed panthers prowled along the streams, like ghosts in the dappled shade. The bobcats howled their discontentment from the sandstone bluffs of Sand Creek. In the evenings, wild turkeys could be heard flying up to roost in the sycamores and elms along the creek bottoms.[11]

Then appeared the European with his gun and plow.[12] The wildlife was not able to adjust itself to this new condition, especially those species prized as game. This sudden invasion was not the slow changes of the ages, but a revolutionary change that made adjustment almost impossible. Man had developed the gun in another world and then with it, invaded the Osage. There was no time for adjustment. Had the Indian developed the gun, plow, and motor, the development would have been slow enough so that the species could have adjusted themselves as these things were developed, because after all, man's development is a part of nature, and he must consider himself a part of that life that surrounds him.

True enough, the fields of the invader served as a supplementary food supply for the quail and prairie chicken, and his poultry yard was a heaven-sent boon to the coyote. But the owners of the fields and ranches not only killed wantonly, but killed to protect their stock and grain and the gun, supplemented later by the car, soon destroyed the balance of Nature as it had existed.

The prairie chicken had begun to adjust itself to the man with a gun, when a strange animal appeared, and rolled over the prairie on wheels emitting strange coughs when climbing the hills. He could not adjust himself to this new approach of man in time to save his species.

Not all the species were thus affected by the advent of the white man. The coyote, despite all the ingenuities of man to destroy him, is adjusting himself quickly to the new condition, while the quail seems almost adjusted, with a closed season for his protection. Many of the species not accorded the honor of being game, are adjusting themselves and it is certain that many of them are actually thriving and gaining predominance in numbers under the new balance, having by the new conditions seen the elimination of some of their enemies.

But man the hunter must protect his game if he wishes to enjoy it in the future. The new conditions have placed a too heavy burden upon it and it cannot thrive without his protection. He came to this realization almost too late; the realization came in the Osage when we saw our streams polluted with oil, and our game destroyed by transients connected with the oil development, who killed in all seasons with barbaric unconcern.

This realization gave birth to the local chapter of the Izaak Walton League, and one dreams again of the Osage as a haven of recreation and sport, where public opinion for protection, and interest in wildlife, with an appreciation of how we are favored among people, become a factor in the new balance of Nature.

PAN IS SELECTING HIS REED

Friday, March 28, 1930, #7

Each morning, the cardinal whistles his good cheer, and the robin releases his pent-up feeling in his rapid-fire notes of happiness, which seem to end in a question. The martins have come back to the Council House tower, and the little titmouse and chickadee, singing as they search tirelessly in crannies and niches for places to build their nests. The bands of blackbirds settle in the tops of trees to fuss and quarrel and strut in ludicrous courtships.

In ecstatic song, the meadowlark is telling the prairie world that life is worth living, and in the stillness of every morning, the prairie chicken wends his booming call across the limestone hills, as he struts and poses in his nuptial dance. Frogs are singing from the prairie seepages; their chorus is the very voice of early Spring. High up in the night sky, the snow geese and blue geese are winging their way to lonely marshes and lake-lands in the far north, thrilling us with the honking message of their passing; the snow geese, resting for an hour or more in the fields during the day, are taken for the remnant of a snowbank in early Spring. The "V's" of Canada Geese, honking like the trail-song of aerial hounds, led by wary old ganders, are passing over the Osage to their homes in the north. The red-tailed hawk circles high in the blue, and horned larks duel along the roadsides, in aerial maneuvers that would arise the envy of a pursuit pilot.

A species of dogwood is blooming at the head of sandstone ravines, and the redbud flashes its cheerful red from the creek bottoms. The willows and cottonwoods are beginning to cover themselves with pale green buds. The prairies are turning emerald green. The sportive bass are sending concentric ripples across the surfaces of quiet pools. The cock pheasant walks in dignity with the sun glinting on his gorgeous back, stopping at intervals to send his pugnacious challenge to an aroused world.

The life pulse is high: Pan is selecting his reed. Spring is coming to the Osage.

PUBLIC OPINION IS THE ONLY EFFECTIVE LAW

Sunday, March 30, 1930, #8

After years of killing, carelessness, and disregard, not only of the game of the Osage, but also the future of shooting as a sport and recreation, the white man awoke to the necessity of protecting the game, then to the necessity of restocking the fields and streams. His advent had caused an upset in the balance of Nature, and his devices for the destruction of the species had almost ruined the sport of hunting and shooting. Obviously, it was up to him to do something about it.

In the summer of 1923, the State Game and Fish Commission was created and took to themselves the power to appoint the State Game and Fish Warden. The law creating the Commission empowered them to establish game refuges over the State.

It is gratifying to know that on account of the zeal of the newly formed chapter of the Izaak Walton League, the first of these refuges was established in the Osage in the Autumn of 1923. The men who worked for this refuge were prompted by an intense desire to protect the wildlife of the Osage, and save us and our subsequent generations a natural heritage. Their accomplishment is of interest to us because it assures us of the future of our wildlife, not to mention the interest it must hold for us as being unique as an unselfish enterprise among the many enterprises during the white man's dominance of the Osage. If it had no other interest for us, there would be the interest natural in the unique.

This first game refuge awarded to Osage County consists of 23,000 acres lying in Township 24, Range 7, and is known as "State Game Refuge No.1." This is the main refuge, though there are smaller ones, essentially quail refuges. On the refuge, the League has placed about three hundred pheasants, one thousand quail, ten prairie chickens, and six turkeys. It is thought that on the refuge, there is a remnant of the bands of deer that once roamed the hills of the Osage, but no one seems sure of this. In the streams of the Osage, the League has placed thousands of fish, as well as quail in the smaller refuges, of which there are but twelve, ranging from 40 to 320 acres.

The refuges are adequately patrolled by wardens, but the League is depending on the education of the public for its effectiveness, realizing that public opinion is the hope of the wildlife. There are people in the Osage who would shoot a cock pheasant, believing it to be a "chicken hawk," and there are hundreds who shoot game in all seasons, simply because the law prohibits such shooting, paradoxical as this might seem. If these people derive pleasure from shooting, they must have some sort of appreciation of wildlife, though the instinct is latent; this latter instinct must be developed.

"Wild Turkey" by John Joseph Mathews
Courtesy of the Osage Nation and the Mathews family

They have never stopped to think. They must be made to see the future of wildlife if these activities continue, and as they are brought to see this, public opinion will be gaining thereby, and will grow with every convert. When public opinion is developed for conservation and protection, there will be very little slaughter or all-season shooting of game. Public opinion is the only effective law.

NOTES

1. The blackjack tree is a modest variety of oak found on the prairie, whose low branches form a natural barrier. "When they become older and larger, the lower limbs die and slant downward, forming a perfect protection against anything large enough to harm them. These dead limbs are as hard and as tough as steel lances, capable of tearing hide or clothing," Mathews writes in *Talking to the Moon*. After building a small sandstone home atop a prairie ridge eight miles outside of Pawhuska in summer 1932, he eventually dubbed it The Blackjacks.

2. John Joseph Mathews's father, William Shirley Mathews, served multiple terms on both the Osage National Council and the Osage Tribal Council after 1907, to be discussed.

3. Mathews refers to the Indian Territory land runs of the early 1890s. These runs, which were the byproduct of the allotment of communally owned tribal land, opened up land to white settlement that was previously owned by tribes in Indian Territory, arguably swindled from them through the Dawes and Curtis acts. Boomers had pressured politicians to open the land to settlement. Whoever had the fastest horse could stake their claim on a first-arrival basis. Sooners were criminals who jumped the gun and staked out claims prematurely; they were sometimes even smoked out of caves by federal officers. Land runs or rushes were a dubious method leading to many problems, and the federal government declared them inefficient.

4. John Joseph Mathews diary, June 3, 1952, Box 2, Folder 4, John Joseph Mathews Collection (JJM), Western History Collection (WHC), University of Oklahoma (OU); Mathews diary, June 5, 1957, Box 2, Folder 10, JJM, WHC, OU.

5. Mathews to Marie Mathews, April 16, 1923, Box 1, Folder 22, JJM, WHC, OU.

6. Mathews, correspondence with Julian Huxley, February and March 1951, Box 1, Folder 29, JJM, WHC, OU.

7. Mathews, *Osages: Children of the Middle Waters* (Norman: University of Oklahoma Press, 1961), xiii.

8. Terry P. Wilson, *Underground Reservation: Osage* Oil (Lincoln: University of Nebraska Press, 1985), 150, 151, 156.

9. See Terry P. Wilson, "The Depression Years" chapter, *Indians of North America: The Osage* (New York: Chelsea House, 1988).

10. The Great Crested Flycatcher is a "large, assertive flycatcher with rich reddish-brown accents and a lemon-yellow belly," and its "habit of hunting high in the canopy means it is not particularly conspicuous—until you learn its very distinctive call, an emphatic rising whistle." "Great Crested Flycatcher," *All About Birds*, Cornell Lab of Ornithology, www.allaboutbirds.org/guide/Great_Crested_Flycatcher/id, accessed February 17, 2017.

11. E. E. White, agent to the Osages during the 1880s, wrote, "The Osage reservation is a picturesque country. The uplands are high and rolling, and the valleys broad and fertile. Building stone is abundant, and there are innumerable streams fringed with timber." E. E. White, *Experiences of a Special Indian Agent* (Norman: University of Oklahoma Press, 1965 [1893]), 22.

12. Cf. *Guns, Germs, and Steel: The Fates of Human Societies* by Jared Diamond.

Part II

Birds of the Osage

SAVE THE RED-TAIL

Wednesday, April 2, 1930, #9

Often in his relentless destruction of hawks for the protection of game birds, man makes many mistakes. He reasons that the depredations of one species of hawk are sufficient grounds for the elimination of all hawks, and thereby kills hawks that are actually beneficial to him and the game bird he desires to protect, since they maintain the balance of nature in their destruction of harmful insects and rodents. Mice and other rodents are certainly not helpful to man's crops, and like other species, relieved of the presence of its enemies, would swarm over the fields in countless numbers.

It is difficult to believe that a bird constructed as the hawk is constructed—with sharp, curved talons and hooked beak, sustained by strong wings—can possibly be harmless. It is true that they are all predatory, and it is simply a matter of prey that determines their harmfulness as far as man is concerned. The species that catch his chickens, destroy game birds, are criminals, while the others really aid him. A hawk is not a bandit simply because he happens to be a hawk; the species that interfere with man's plan are the bandits, but unfortunately the whole family suffers because of a few species.

The Department of Agriculture has determined through the examination of stomachs, which species should be killed and which spared; they give the percentage of mice, insects, and game found in each stomach, and the stomachs of some species fail to reveal that they are in the least harmful. These species the Department asks us to protect, not only because they aid in the destruction of harmful rodents, but also because they are in many cases a very pleasing and beautiful bird, a part of the wildlife that surrounds us.

One of the most maligned of all the hawks is the red-tail, so common in the Osage. He is very conspicuous, and it seems that all the deeds of the hawks have been attributed to him. The red-tail is the large hawk that circles in the air and often utters a sound like "kee-kee-kee." One's pleasant memories of childhood in the Osage include the circling of this great hawk against the blue; watching the graceful banks and spirals, and the conspicuous red tail used as a rudder. The watcher lying on his back in the high grass, filled with the dream of flying, makes himself miserable by the desire to fly. It is pleasing to know that this hawk is not just a "chicken hawk," and the Department of Agriculture has acquitted him of criminality.

In another column, the hawks of the Osage will be named and described, the innocent and the guilty alike, but it is hoped that the descriptions of the birds and their actions are clear enough so that the bandits can be distinguished from the others; identification of birds is difficult enough, even with pictures.

SUNDOWN *I: CHAL, GRANVILLE, AND THE RED-TAIL*

Mathews knew hawks like the back of his hand, and he deeply loved this bird of prey. He described more than once gazing up at the circling red-tail hawk as a boy and literally crying tears of frustration at his inability to fly. As a college student, he delivered a paper on "Hawks of Oklahoma" at the Oklahoma City Academy of Science in 1916.[1] The red-tailed hawk was Jo's favorite. In the semi-autobiographical novel *Sundown*, an Englishman, geology Professor Granville, "fascinates" the college-student Osage protagonist, Challenge "Chal" Windzer "with his beautiful words" that "flowed softly" and "were almost lyrical." When Granville visits Chal's Osage prairie while he is working for an oil company during the summer between university terms, he encounters Chal, seemingly randomly, and have a leisurely sit-down to take in the view:

> The red-tail hawk circled down closer as if he would make sure about this un-usual animal that strode so arrogantly across the open prairie. He circled even closer and gave a weak scream, as though he had made up his mind to resent that strange animal's presence. Mr. Granville looked up, watched the circling bird for a second, then said, "I say, Wendzah, this is the buteo borealis,—the red-tail, is it not?"
>
> A thrill came over Chal. Certainly it was his beloved buteo borealis, the red-tail, but—but—who would have thought that anyone else could have been interested in the fact besides himself . . . he was filled with pleasure and wanted to go on talking about the red-tail hawk; about his habits, and about the things he had seen him do, but remained silent. . . . He wanted to tell Mr. Granville that the biological survey didn't know what it was talking about when it said that the red-tail ate only field mice. But he felt ashamed of the disturbance on his inside and sat down again. Mr. Granville was the first person he had ever talked with, except the Osages, who hadn't placed all big hawks under the title of "hen hawks," and all smaller ones under the title "chicken hawks." He wanted Mr. Granville to stay there, even if they didn't say a word.
>
> Mr. Granville, still looking at the graceful circles of the red-tail, said, "Grace-ful beggar—dare say we shall be flying without motors some day—taking advantage of the air currents, sort of thing."[2]

This conversation leaves Chal feeling "more fascinated than ever" with Granville, who later reappears in the novel in yet another role, that of Chal's flight instructor at military flight school, where their close bond continues to grow in a new context.

In these columns, Mathews sought to convey an appreciation and understanding of the nuances of hawks and other species, which Chal and Granville shared, to prevent needless killing of hawks tainted with "criminality."

A BOOMING SYMBOL OF THE HIGH PRAIRIE

Tuesday, April 8, 1930, #12

Many strange and interesting things happen in the Osage at this time of year; it is the time of year when the life of the prairie and sandstone hills is most active. At this time, wildlife reaches its metabolic high point; the keen joy of living and the ecstasies of mating season give rise to song, duels, and strange antics.

The strangest of these nuptial antics, and the most interesting, are those of our most interesting game bird, the prairie chicken. As one watches again the "dancing" of a few birds, where once he watched hundreds, an anger mixed with sadness creeps over him, and he is determined, while lying there on the early morning prairie, to bend his efforts toward the preservation of this great bird, the symbol of the high prairie, whose name should be ever associated with the Osage.

Early, during late March and these April mornings, high on a spot where the grass is short, when the sun is just appearing above the rim, one may hear the sonorous booming of the prairie chicken. The long, rolling sound dominates all the voices of the prairie. The cheerful notes of the meadowlark, the repeated call of the killdeer, and the mournful whistle of the sandpiper (upland plover) form the chorus. The sound can be heard for a great distance, and is produced on the same principle that music is produced from bagpipes: simply the forcing out of air drawn into a bag. The sound is difficult to describe, but sounds like "hoo-oo dundoo-oo dundoo-oo-oo-oo."

The chickens gather on the highest point of their habitat, early in the morning. The cocks then lower their wings, not quite letting them drag as in the case of the turkey-cock. The head is lowered, and the saffron sacs on either side of the neck are filled with air; the pinnate feathers on each side of the neck that cover the sacs are raised above the head so as to look like horns. The tail is raised and slightly spread, and the bird begins a ludicrous dance in circles, the saffron sacs filled out like little balloons, as he sends his voice across the prairie. Suddenly he will run madly toward another cock, who squats to await his attack; they come together and face each other menacingly. They peck at each other rather tentatively, and occasionally fly several feet into the air. Then one of them will strut off and begin his dance again.

It seems a rather senseless series of antics, especially since there are no apparent conclusions brought about by decisive duels. Often, one of the birds will fly away in a purposeful straight flight, but after a while, he returns to the dance to strut and give voice to the hot life surging in him. Often there are other sounds besides the booming: a sort of cackling, and conversational

"Prairie Chicken Hill in June" by John Joseph Mathews
Courtesy of the Osage Nation and the Mathews family

clucking. These sounds may be uttered by the demure little hens, for whose delectation all this display and show of vanity is staged.

The dance will last for an hour or more, then suddenly, without obvious reason, the band will rise and fly off, and the dance is over until the early sun sends its rays across the emerald prairie the next morning.

PRAIRIE CHICKEN

Monday, May 5, 1930, #17

The most interesting game bird in the Osage is the prairie chicken, because of his size, his importance as a game bird, and his habits, of which we know so little. . . . The habitat of this grouse is limited, and he is considered to be a species doomed to extinction. Hence the paucity of numbers gives less opportunity for observation. Due to this fact also is the lively interest shown in him, not only as a game bird but as a species. This alone ought to be sufficient reason why we should do everything possible to save our flocks.

The chicken is admirably adapted to the prairie of the Osage. There is no reason why there should not be thousands of them, instead of the few that have tenaciously held on through years of persecution by thoughtless gunners who have no regard for season or law. He is apparently a very hardy bird and is not affected by the encroachments of the plow, but accessibility of the prairie to the car carrying a thoughtless gunner has been the chief factor in the reduction of his numbers.

These gunners seem to feel vindictive; they, in a spirit of defiance of the law and its representative, the game warden, take pride in outwitting the latter and in shooting the remnant of the great flocks wherever and whenever they find them; it is a sort of determined action to exterminate this great bird inspired by this strange perversity. They fail to appreciate the fact that in a few years, there will be no prairie chickens to slaughter. And that above all, they as lovers of the field and gun will have accomplished nothing except the ruination of their future sport. As long as this slaughter continues, they can hold no hope of ever in the future having the privilege of shooting chickens during an open season. The transient population in the Osage during the oil activity did more damage to our game and especially to the prairie chicken than any other group, in their barbaric disregard for consequences, but it is incredible that people who make their home here could have any other thought than for the protection of that which belongs to them.

The spirit of transgression that seems to have taken hold of the American people, from whatever cause, reacts in this case at least to their own discomfort in the end; they are cheating themselves in their puerile defiance of the law. The prairie chickens of the Osage do not belong to the law or to the warden, but to the public; the warden as a representative of the law attempts to protect them from extinction so that the public may enjoy them and so the sons and grandsons of that public with instinctive tendencies for the outdoors and the chase might have something to shoot, and may have the prairie as it was.

If the people of the Osage could realize what opportunities they have as the "public," as compared to the opportunities of the "public" in Europe and some of the states in the United States, they would guard jealously what they have; they would protect their game and especially that great game bird of their unparalleled prairie, which is their type of game bird, and which according to reports, is fast becoming extinct.

All the game wardens of the state concentrating on the Osage, could not save the prairie chicken, but public opinion is the one effective law, and it is the purpose of this column under the auspices of the Izaak Walton League of America to cause the wanton prairie chicken gunner to realize that he is ruining the future sport we must protect and conserve, and help to build up public opinion for protection, so that there will always be prairie chickens in the Osage and that each year we may have an open season, and enjoy our natural heritage.

VISITORS AND "ARROWFLIGHT"

Mathews loved to take spring visitors to see and hear these notable birds. These included two friends, Paul B. Sears, ecologist and author of *Deserts on the March*, and Joseph A. Brandt, University of Oklahoma Press director and future University of Oklahoma president. Along with his multiple columns celebrating and raising awareness of prairie chickens, Mathews also writes of them in a later short story, "Arrowflight, The Story of a Prairie Chicken," composed in 1963 and published posthumously in *Old Three Toes and Other Tales of Survival and Extinction*, a satisfying animal story collection edited by Susan Kalter. The story ends tragically because a boy, who misrecognizes the prairie chicken as a "chicken hawk," shoots it dead: "The relationship that had existed for so long between the man-animal and the prairie chicken cock lost its natural rhythm for only a moment, and Arrowflight had to die so stupidly."[3]

PROTECT OUR NATIVES: SAVE THE QUAILS

Sunday, November 16, 1930, #42

It seems imperative that we protect our natives. Along with the natural instinct to conserve the native quail of the Osage, and the desire for assurance that there will be future shooting—that this greatest of sports will not be denied us through our own stupidity—is the thought that imported birds will not be wholly satisfactory to us. . . .

If we refrained from shooting this season when birds are apparently few in number, there would undoubtedly be shooting next season if there is a normal winter this year.

We do not care to have on our hands a depleted quail population, especially since we have already a prairie chicken problem, and the task of stocking the Osage with pheasants. Each man must be his own judge in this matter of shooting during the current season. The law of the state allows him to shoot ten quail three times a week from the twenty-first of November 1930 to the first of January 1931. If he understands the situation and is a real sportsman, he will not take advantage of this open season in this county. . . .

Sportsmen who understand that the winter took a great toll of quail in the Osage, know too that these birds propagate very fast under favorable conditions, and that if they are not molested this season, there will be a sufficient number next season to furnish sport for all.

"Head of Cedar Canyon—November" by John Joseph Mathews
Courtesy of the Osage Nation and the Mathews family

GIVE QUAIL A CHANCE

After a few columns of gorgeous nature writing replete with evocative prose-poetry, Mathews turned to a persuasive mode to prevent quail from becoming scarce. He rhetorically appeals to the sportsman's sense of decency, showing respect to his personal freedom of choice as an American, but urging him to do the right thing and show restraint, both for the sake of the species and the sport, without a tone of scolding. Three days later, it was surely Mathews who published an unsigned front page op-ed piece headlined "Give the Quail a Chance." Readers were told: "The quail season opens in Oklahoma Friday, but to the hunters of Osage county, it should not, and probably will not, mean the shooting of these birds."[4] All he was saying is give quail a chance.

QUAIL IN A WORLD OF IRON

Monday, November 24, 1930, #43

Man is not close enough to the struggle that goes on in the fields and woods to determine absolutely cause and effect. He knows that the balance may be thrown off by scarcity of food and epidemics that are in turn often attributed to climate, and that somewhere in the cycle of interdependence of the species on each other, some species will suffer more than others.

There is a serious scarcity of quail in the Osage. Just before the extremely cold weather last winter, and after the season had closed, there were still many birds. Then the Osage suddenly turned to iron, and the cold winds whistled and roared over the prairie and through the black-jacks, carrying before them snow and sleet, forming drifts over the food supply and sifting into the tightest cover, under fallen trees and briar bushes. Crusts formed over the surface, and there was nothing left in all this white expanse, of the natural food upon which the quail covies depend for their existence. The weaker ones were frozen, and the strong ones were forced out of the cover into the open and in search for food. They lost the protection of color against the white snow, and stood out conspicuously as they ran here and there in search of food. The prairie falcon would fly at them, causing them to rise, then take his toll. The relentless low-flying marsh hawk found hunting rather easy.[5] The Cooper's hawk took his quail a day from the frightened, half-starved covies,[6] and the marauding coyote, in this world of iron, picked up and devoured anything he could find in his thorough hunting, from field mice to the tough sinews of a steer carcass. The quail and the rabbit were the ultimate survivors from this cruel whim of Nature. Hundreds of meadowlarks and cardinals froze, and whole covies of quail were found frozen to death in their characteristic circle of protection. The survivors were often weakened by the ordeal to the extent that reproduction was affected.

Many covies migrated from the ridges to the bottoms just before or at the beginning of the storm. Many of these have failed to return, and inasmuch as there are few quails in the bottoms, it would seem that they migrated there only to freeze, or be destroyed by enemies and disease.

Mr. Montgomery, state game and fish warden, has reported that outside of the northern tier of counties, especially those counties of the northeast, the quail in the state are plentiful. The Osage appears on his list of those counties wherein quail are scarce. If the migration theory is correct, it is possible that many of the covies from the ridges of the Osage found their way to some of the southern counties, and have failed to return.

In any case, since the season has opened, many of the sportsmen of the Osage are affirming the statements appearing in this column from time to

"Hoar Frost" by John Joseph Mathews
Courtesy of the Osage Nation and the Mathews family

time, that quail are scarce and that we should refrain from shooting them so that there may be sport for the hunters of the Osage next season. It is not likely that the coming winter will be as severe as the last one, and if this winter is normal, next spring will see thousands of young birds hatched, and by next autumn the cover of the Osage will be filled with covies.

AN IRON-BOUND WORLD

Wednesday, April 23, 1930, #14

The snow of last January and especially the hard, icy crust formed by the sleet, brought about one of the conditions of Nature wherein the white world became a stage upon which was played the tragedy of life. Hunger and death stalked over an iron-bound world, whose very atmosphere seemed metallic, and in the grip of which the species battled for existence.

The balance of Nature is often disturbed by such conditions, as well as through epidemics, the same conditions that the human species must face and survive. When such conditions of hunger among the species, man in the protective role he has assumed, must place his services into the balance, by supplying food and protection, especially since his fields and improvements have destroyed much of the natural food and protection.

It was gratifying to note the number of sportsmen perturbed over the condition of the quail during the snows of last January, and the number who made some attempt to feed them, independently of organized attempts. But the activities of the stockmen and farmers in this matter should be an example to the sportsmen of the towns. Many of them faced the cold winds to carry food to quail and prairie chicken, while some of the sportsmen stood round comfortable stoves and talked about the conditions. The farmers and stockmen can appreciate the struggles of wildlife during such weather, and therefore are in facile sympathy with them, whereas many of the sportsmen of the towns, no matter how intense their delight in wildlife, naturally, surrounded as they are with manmade comforts, are not able to appreciate fully the struggles. We owe much to the rancher and farmer for the protection of game and fish, so there is no reason why a sportsman should feel vindictive when the former asks him not to shoot or fish on his ranch or farm. This prohibition springs often from unsportsmanlike action of the usual few, who are forever creating conditions for which all must suffer.

ON WHITENESS

One of the most evocative and moving stories Mathews published in *The Sooner* magazine is "Hunger on the Prairie," appearing in June 1930, and it bears parallels with the previous column. Its characters are birds and animals enduring harsh conditions of the wintertime on the Osage prairie in a struggle to survive. Mathews writes with vivid imagery and poetic technique: "At night, the stars shone profusely with a twinkling brightness that accentuated the impression of a frigid desolation of whiteness. The crackling trees in the ravines sounded like rifle shots. The air was as metallic as struck steel." Mathews references a desolate, annihilating *whiteness*, alliteratively phrased in the column as "the white world," which is suggestive of racial allegory: "The white world became a stage upon which was played the tragedy of life" for many Indigenous peoples, and "the balance of Nature" was "disturbed by such conditions." Similarly, in the next column, Mathews refers to the "cruel whiteness of winter."

In these pieces, the reader is made to feel great sympathy for the quail and other little creatures who hunt tirelessly for food. The human presence is minimized, yet noted, as food is thrown to the hungry birds. "Hunger on the Prairie" concludes:

> Tracks everywhere and stories of tragedies in the cold silence. The only voices were the muffled caw of a crow winging his way across the prairie, or the pitiful screams of a rabbit in the talons of a hawk or owl; these voices only at rare intervals, then, the silence would descend more profoundly and ominously tense than before.

STRANGE BIRDS

Wednesday, March 18, 1931, #63

In the Osage at this time of the year, one may see strange birds stopping here on their way north. Great flocks of snow geese and blue geese are seen rarely, since they are essentially night-flying birds and seem to hide themselves effectively in the daytime. At this time of year and a little later, however, an occasional flock of these north-flying birds will settle in some field in the Osage. As they sit motionless, they appear from the distance as a remnant of a snowbank. Often the blue geese fly with them, and it is usually these birds that give the observer the clue that the snow remnant or the wind-drifted papers he sees are really some species of bird.

Supposedly, a great number of snow geese are about, but because they usually fly at night, they are seldom seen, even in their nesting grounds. This creates much interest in them.

Around the time of spring plowing, great flocks of seagulls will follow the plow, drifting alongside the man and horses, and alighting behind in the newly-made furrow to eat greedily of the tidbits tuned up. The presence of flocks of these noisy, graceful birds this far inland strikes one as very odd. They are probably gulf birds on a sort of spring reconnaissance.

The curlew comes to the Osage a little later in the spring.[7] Whether he is going east, west, north, or south is difficult to say, and certainly, as he stands erect and motionless on the prairie, he seems to care very little whether he goes anywhere or not. But he is seen rarely, and only for a short time, then disappears, probably to northwest Nebraska and the Dakotas, but unfortunately the dark meat of his body is delicious, and he often appeared on the menus of great eastern hotels in the early days of the Osage.

BIRDSONGS OF THE OSAGE

Thursday, April 30, 1931, #74

Nothing expresses the joy of living more than a robin singing in the top of a blossomed fruit tree. His voice is not remarkable, but his attempt to express something inside him that seems to be bubbling, is remarkable, when one considers his limited notes. If this urge to express himself continues to grow, he will someday drown in his own emotions for which he has no safety valve, and that will be the end of all robins, unless he can develop a smoother, more facile means of expression. No bird tries harder than the robin to convince the world that life is good and life is glorious, and yet this great stream of emotion seemed to be dammed up in his throat, as his heart keeps pumping more and more.

A lone bobwhite on a fencepost can in a few notes express complete contentment. There is no song more tranquil and devoid of the bubbling emotion of most songs of the spring. It is like an Angelus sounding over the fields in the evening and a repeated assurance that "all's well with the world" during the day.[8] There is nothing sad about it, nor is there anything resigned and fateful; it is the song of growing grain, and a plenteous earth filled with peace.

The meadowlark of the prairie has a joyous song; he seems to think that all is gaiety and joy. All day long, he tells the prairie world that life is a song; feeling this himself, he urges it on others. It is gay; it is cheerful, this song of the meadowlark and certainly it is part of the prairie, one of the indispensable voices of the spring prairie, but what dark thought this foolish persistence may create in the mind of a farmer plowing in a nearby field, whose crop was burnt in the summer's drought, and whose mortgage is due.

NOTES

1. "Oklahoma Academy of Science," *Science* 45, no. 8 (March 16, 1917): 271–72.

2. John Joseph Mathews, *Sundown* (Norman: University of Oklahoma Press, 1988 [1934]), 173–74.

3. Mathews, "Arrowflight, the Story of a Prairie Chicken," in *Old Three Toes and Other Stories* (Norman: University of Oklahoma Press, 2015).

4. "Give the Quail a Chance," *The Daily Journal-Capital*, November 19, 1930.

5. *Circus cyaneus*, or hen harrier. Marsh hawk is a historical name for the American form of this migratory bird of prey.

6. Cooper's hawk is a medium-sized, North American bird of prey.

7. Curlews are a group of eight species of medium-to-large birds, characterized by long, slender, down-curved bills and mottled brown plumage.

8. An Angelus here refers to the bell rung to announce the time for the Angelus, a set of prayers to commemorate the Annunciation or the Incarnation.

Part III

Culture and Politics

PORTRAITS OF THE OSAGE

Thursday, April 17, 1930, #13

The Osage is full of pictures. But one can never see these pictures in galleries. They are mostly landscapes, except in the towns where there is still some of the uniqueness of Taos and the southwest generally. There are no pictures of Indian women carrying vessels on their heads, or girls at the loom, but certainly there is enough color and subject matter at the June dances of the Osages. Not only are there the dancers themselves in the rich equipment of the Plains Indian, but there are the little episodes on the side: a woman dressing her dancer under the shade of a tree, or the act of "smoking" a horse.[1] These are the pictures of the town.

Great landscapes are everywhere.

Stand on some hill or ridge that slopes gently and is studded with blackjack. The grass is an impressible green, almost velvety. Clouds are racing across the sky like great balls of cotton. A half-dozen cattle are grazing. In the distance, the hills are blue, a soft blue that is almost indescribable. A painter would tear his hair in despair at such a scene. He would have to know something of the Osage and its peculiar history to get something of meaning into his picture. On looking at his finished canvas, one would have to hear the voice of the meadowlark in it and feel that spirit which is the Osage, before he could call the result a plausible attempt.

There is another picture of the high prairie. A great expanse of sky—the picture is nearly all sky. Reaching the blue on all sides is the emerald-green prairie grass, and here and there, a splash of yellow or white and blue, where the prairie flowers have sprung up.

These pictures and hundreds more are now on exhibition in the Osage. There are no hard benches, tiled floors, or milling crowds to annoy and cause fatigue. One can sit on the grass, and watch and dream unmolested. The best light in which to view these pictures is the light of the late afternoon until sunset, though the setting sun often changes the picture, and makes other pictures of his own which are painted by the master of all painters of pictures, and have never been successfully copied by man.

CHARACTERS OF NEW MEXICO:
THOMAS WOLFE, MABEL DODGE LUHAN, ERNEST
THOMPSON SETON, ARTHUR MANBY,
BUCK DUNTON, AND COMPANY

Just a year and four months before the previous column appeared, John Joseph Mathews had witnessed "the uniqueness of Taos and the southwest," and could thus evoke vivid impressions of women of the Pueblos transporting pots atop their heads and girls working at the loom. Mathews painted scenes with words skillfully, but it is less known that he sometimes literally painted landscapes, showing talent as a visual artist. His canvases evoke the open vistas found near The Blackjacks, his home out on a prairie ridge that he had built from nearby sandstone in summer 1932. Mathews was friends with several artists, which in part drew him to Taos, New Mexico, which had by the 1920s attracted a group of artists, writers, and bohemians.

In November 1928, Jo visited Taos while traveling along the Santa Fe Trail from west to east. At that time, Mathews had just left his wife and two children in Pasadena, and he was traveling alone to Pawhuska for a lengthy visit with his mother and sisters over the holidays, which lasted through January 1929. Mathews spent a day at the home of his friend, Western artist W. Herbert "Buck" Dunton. Buck was collecting material for a portrait of Jo's paternal great-grandfather, William Sherley "Old Bill" Williams, the famous mountain man of Old West lore. A hunter, trader, and expedition leader, Bill Williams as a young man lived among the Osages in what is now Missouri. Around 1813, Bill married Mathews's great-grandmother, a fullblood Osage woman called A-Ci'n-Ga, which is a traditional name used within families to refer to a third or subsequent daughter. While in Taos, Mathews sensed the atmosphere of his legendary ancestor, who later in life maintained headquarters there. Mathews admired Buck Dunton's vivid drawings and paintings of cowboys and Indians, and predicted Dunton would someday become as famous as Frederic Remington.[2] The year before, the Southwestern artist Alexandre Hogue praised Dunton's rare ability "to paint beneath the skin, to analyze the innermost thoughts and character of his models, to make one want to meet the people he paints, even to make one feel that in seeing the pictures he *has* met them."[3] Born in Maine in 1878, Dunton early on became a popular magazine and book illustrator (e.g., Zane Grey's *Riders on the Purple Sage*). A hunter, fisherman, and traveler, Dunton fell in love with the Southwest and cowboy life, and was known to sport a white ten-gallon hat and full cowboy duds.[4] Dunton moved to Taos in 1912, and his path and chosen rugged lifestyle bear many similarities with those of his writer friend, Jo Mathews. Like Mathews, Dunton and his wife eventually divorced after a move west, and she and their two children went back east. Dunton, moreover like Mathews at The Blackjacks, "lived a rather Spartan life, largely refusing modern appliances, sleeping on an open-air porch whatever the weather, and camping in the surrounding area at all seasons both to hunt and to paint wildlife," writes Julie Schimmel in *The Art and Life of W. Herbert Dunton*. The Western artist's creed paralleled that of Mathews: "To live with my own mind, to have few material wants, to enjoy myself in the open and with books, I believe I have found the secret of content-ment," which is "the work you love and the enjoyment of simple things."[5] In 1915, Dunton formed the Taos Society of Artists with painters Joseph Henry Sharp and his close friend and mentor, Ernest L. Blumenshein, both of whom had studied in Paris and painted Indigenous subjects, plus Bert Geer Phillips, Oscar Berninghaus, and Irving Couse. These original members were labeled the Taos Six, but the group soon added Walter Ufer and Victor Higgins, be-coming Los Ochos Pintores; their work was exhibited in major metropolises throughout the east and overseas.[6] Buck Dunton quit the Taos Society of Artists in 1922, however, because of acrimony among its members. For one thing, Ufer had called Ernest Blumenshein a "baldheaded S.O.B." in the lat-ter's absence.[7] It is unknown whether Buck Dunton completed the portrait of Old Bill Williams, though one of his paintings was titled *Mountain Man* and another was alternately titled *The Mountain Man*, their dates unknown. His health began to decline in 1928, the year of Mathews's visit, and he died in 1936 at the age of fifty-seven in his beloved Taos.[8]

Five years and four months after the previous column appeared, Mathews returned to New Mexico, a place that fascinated him. He visited Santa Fe and Taos, traveling solo in the summer of 1935. Around Santa Fe, he socialized with creative people who were fellow guests of his boyhood hero, the author and wildlife artist, Ernest Thompson Seton. In his youth, Jo Mathews adored Seton's illustrated story collection, *Wild Animals I Have Known* (1898), and he references the book a few times in *Twenty Thousand Mornings*. In spring 1915, as a freshman at the University of Oklahoma, Mathews was tasked with writing a humorous piece for his English class, so the hunter penned a parody, "Wild Animals I Have Et."[9]

Born in England in 1860 and raised in Toronto, Canada, Ernest Thompson Seton moved to New York City to pursue his writing career before wending his way to the Southwest. A lover of nature and Indigenous philosophies of nature, Seton eventually became a founder of the Boy Scouts of America and the Woodcraft Indians, later renamed Woodcraft League. Mathews's home-town of Pawhuska boasts the first Boy Scout troop in the United States, which was formed in 1909, a year ahead of the establishment of the Boy Scouts of America. Mathews told Walter Campbell that by July 1935, he had received three letters from Seton and his partner asking when he intended to visit Seton Village.[10] At the College of Indian Wisdom there, established in 1930,

Woodcraft League leaders, campers, and students learned about American Indian arts, skills, and philosophy. Lying south of Santa Fe, Seton Village included adobe buildings and a thirty-two-room castle completed in 1933. Yes, a castle. Despite Susan Kalter's hypothesis that Mathews invented the moniker facetiously, The College of Indian Wisdom was actually a respected institution then, its courses fully accredited by the American Association of Colleges.[11] Mathews believed that Seton's "idea of nurturing Indian culture" was good, but ultimately useless and futile, he wrote to his partner, Elizabeth Hunt, without elaborating.[12] Mathews probably concluded this because Seton's followers for the most part studied Indigenous theory and praxis detached from tribally specific land-based contexts, in a rapidly technologizing, increasingly earth-detached Western world. The Chickasaw storyteller Te Ata Fisher and her partner, Clyde Fisher, a curator who hailed from Ohio, had been to Seton Village the year before and spent two days conversing with Seton and Tony Lujan, the builder from Taos Pueblo who became the fourth husband of patroness and memoirist, Mabel Dodge Luhan. Clyde Fisher found Seton to be "a rare genius, a combination of naturalist, artist and storyteller. His grasp of world history, especially the history of the American Indians, is amazing." Te Ata's response is not recorded.[13] The Dakota historian and author Philip J. Deloria articulates well if rather broadly the function of such appropriations, even if well-intentioned, during the early twentieth century. American Indians, he notes, with their affinity to nature, spirituality, and communal life, were used as a symbol to critique an increasingly urbanized and fragmented modernity. "On silver screen and musical stage, in the summer camps of Camp Fire Girls and Woodcraft Indians," and in retreats such as Taos and Santa Fe,

> Indians evoked a nostalgic past more authentic and often more desirable than the anxious present. By imaging such a past, projecting it onto the bodies of Indian people, and then devising means to appropriate that (now-Indian) past for themselves, white Americans sought reassurance: they might enjoy modernity while somehow escaping its destructive consequences.[14]

For decades, Mathews vividly recalled "that day" in the summer of 1935—"ye gods, the summer Will Rogers was killed"—when he mixed with a group of notable guests at Seton's camp.[15] Although the company was stimulating, they were "all in a funk" because of severe storms and flooding. Jo's compañeros included the watercolorist and naturalist Ellsworth Jaeger and his wife, Zetta, who hailed from Buffalo, New York. A follower and associate of Seton since boyhood, Ellsworth Jaeger had lived among Haudenosaunee, Blackfoot, Apache, Pueblo, and Navajo peoples. Jaeger published *Wildwood Wisdom* a decade later in 1945, the same year in which Mathews's third book

Talking to the Moon appeared, and his how-to book enjoyed a lengthy popularity. Sharing knowledge gathered from indigenes and settlers about living off the land, Jaeger went on to publish six more non-fiction books, and he became a natural history museum curator and a syndicated columnist.[16]

Also in the group was the Southwestern photographer, artist, and author Laura Adams Armer, with whom Mathews became friends. Armer published *Waterless Mountain* in 1931, a contemplative, Newbery Medal–winning novel peopled by Navajos that attempted to convey a Navajo perspective. From a Sacramento family, Armer had earlier worked in the San Francisco Bay area, but left urban bohemian life in favor of becoming neighbors to Hopis and Navajos. At Seton Village, Armer was accompanied by an unidentified artist who was the model for a character in her novel. Anthropologist Oliver LaFarge, who published the Pulitzer Prize–winning novel *Laughing Boy* in 1929, which also centered on Navajo characters, wrote a laudatory foreword to the original edition of *Waterless Mountain*. Although writing of Pueblos, Kiowa author N. Scott Momaday titled his first novel *House Made of Dawn* (1968) after a Navajo ceremonial song, one that Armer transcribes in her novel.[17] A 1969 Pulitzer Prize winner, *House Made of Dawn* followed the modernist paradigm that Mathews established in *Sundown* (1934), telling of an alienated Native American veteran returned to his home community, thereby inaugurating the Native American Renaissance. Amid controversy, in 1928 Laura Adams Armer had filmed a Navajo ceremony, resulting in a historic short documentary, *The Mountain Chant*. Armer was granted access to Navajo sand painting ceremonies and made watercolor copies of their patterns; she was invited to several esoteric Navajo ceremonies conducted by men, to which outsiders and even Navajo women were traditionally not allowed access.[18] Armer published five more books on the Navajos and the Southwest.

The group was joined by Mathews's friend and mentor Walter Stanley Campbell, an English professor at the University of Oklahoma who had urged Mathews to apply to Oxford University. Among others, Mathews, Campbell, Armer, LaFarge, Texan folklorist and author J. Frank Dobie, the Cherokee editor and novelist John M. Oskison, and another of Campbell's mentees, playwright Lynn Riggs, also Cherokee, were to varying degrees part of a burgeoning Southwestern literary regionalist movement. In her introduction to Mathews's *Twenty Thousand Mornings*, Susan Kalter writes that among non-Native authors, "Mathews might be best compared to his friends and models, such as J. Frank Dobie, Jack London, Ernest Thompson Seton, and W.S. Campbell."[19] Using the pen name Stanley Vestal, in 1928 Campbell published a biography of Kit Carson, the legendary mountain man, expedition leader, and unfortunately, serial killer of Indians, who traveled alongside Jo's great-grandfather, Old Bill Williams. Like Old Bill, Carson had lived in Taos and is buried there. Campbell/Vestal became known for incorporating Indigenous perspectives in his books. After extensive field research, in 1932 Campbell published *Sitting Bull, Champion of the Sioux*, which Mathews praised and reviewed for the *American Oxonian*.[20] In January 1933 Mathews wrote:

> Our two books, *Wah'Kon-Tah* and *Sitting Bull*, seem in quite a different way to say the same thing, and certainly the relationship between the Sioux and the Osage is brought out. Our individual Indians have the same reactions and philosophy—It seems to me the parallel is obvious. I am very proud and happy that you have written *Sitting Bull*.[21]

At Seton Village camp, Campbell and Armer delivered multiple speeches apiece, and Mathews wondered if he would ever be asked to speak. Eventually he was invited, and his talk impressed Ellsworth Jaeger very much in particular. Laura Adams Armer afterward called Mathews a sensitive soul. Afterward Mathews quipped in a letter to his partner, Elizabeth Hunt: "If only she could see this 'sensitive soul' hammering people over the head to get what he wants."[22]

In Taos, Mathews mixed with a great American novelist, Thomas Wolfe (or just Tom, as Jo familiarly called him in a letter to Elizabeth Hunt), out on the patio of the Hotel La Fonda. From Asheville, North Carolina, Wolfe had earned widespread critical recognition in 1929 with his debut novel *Look Homeward, Angel*, and he quit his teaching position to write full-time. In the summer of 1935, Mathews recalled, Wolfe was "emotionalized" both by the success of his second novel, *Of Time and the River*, which had been published in March, and "many Martinis." Lois Palken Rudnick claims that with the publication of *Of Time and the River*, "Wolfe entered the ranks of major American writers, while his legend expanded to meet the scope of his intended project: to write the great American novel and get the entire continent into his works." Thomas Wolfe expresses his desire to visit many Western locales known for their Indigenous peoples: "*I will go up and down the country, and back and forth across the great trains that thunder over America. I will go out West where States are square; Oh, I will go to Boise, and Helena and Albuquerque. I will go to Montana and the two Dakotas and the unknown places.*" Such passages also suggest Wolfe's great influence upon Beat Generation author Jack Kerouac, who penned *On the Road*.[23]

With "foam flecks at the corners of his mouth," Wolfe leaned over to Jo: "Mathews, you love this land, don't you?"

The Osage affirmed he did.

"How can you?" he boomed. "It is savage, savage; its fangs gleam. It snarls. My God, what a storm in the Rio Grande Canyon, when I was coming back from visiting Mabel Dodge Luhan—God!" He paused, shivering at his recollection of the tempest. Then Wolfe growled: "drinks—garçon, ober—mozo, drinks!"[24]

Wolfe was lured to Taos by a series of letters and postcards from Mabel Dodge Luhan, the wealthy heiress, patroness of modernist art and literature, memoirist, and devotee of American Indian arts. But "Thomas Wolfe was undoubtedly Mabel's most magnificent failure," Rudnick states. He was one of many artists and writers whom Luhan contacted in her quest for creative people who could share and artistically express her vision of Taos and the people of the Pueblos. "Wolfe's faith in his potential to fulfill a remarkable destiny, his epic vision, and lyrical power made him an ideal candidate to appreciate and celebrate Mabel's garden of the New World," Rudnick concludes.[25] Flannery Burke writes that between 1917 and 1929, a series of visitors to Mabel Doge Luhan's Taos home "transformed northern New Mexico into a cultural hinterland for those on the avant-garde of cultural expression in New York"; beginning in 1924, Wolfe had lived in New York in various hotels and apartments. Things did not go so well. Wolfe arrived at Mabel's place very late, hours after dinner when he was expected, drunk, and accompanied by two young society women he had met in Santa Fe at a luncheon held in his honor, who drove him to Luhan's house. Earlier, he had telephoned Mabel and teasingly asked if it would be all right if he brought over "two whores" he had met; she hung up on him. Upon entering Luhan's home, still inebriated, he promptly put his feet up on an upholstered chair and was told by Mabel's female companion that she had gone to bed, though it was only 9:30 p.m. Wolfe retorted he was used to women waiting up for *him* all night. Instead of allowing himself to be shown to his bedroom, Wolfe left the house with his two new friends, cursing Luhan's name on the way out to the car. Wolfe apparently continued to spurn Luhan's hospitality, staying at the Hotel La Fonda in Taos instead, where he drank and disparaged his would-be host. For her part, Mabel took the high road, sending a polite note saying she regretted any misunderstanding and wished him a pleasant stay in Taos.[26] Sadly, Thomas Wolfe died less than three years later, not quite reaching his thirty-eighth birthday. Even so, he composed a major body of novels and stories that inspired countless authors.

Mabel Dodge had arrived in Taos for the first time in December 1917, and she and her new and third husband, sculptor and painter Maurice Sterne, soon rented the large home of Arthur Manby, a dour English magnate who moved into a back room of the house. Then in his fifties, Manby in his youth had studied art and architecture, so could hold his own in conversation with these aesthetes. Nevertheless, there was something disconcerting about the shadowy Englishman. Mabel was already famous for her "gatherings in Paris, at her villa in Florence, Italy, and in her salon at 23 Fifth Avenue, New York," according to author Frank Waters, who later became her and Tony's friend, joining them in advocating for the people of the Pueblos. Robert Edmond Jones, a noted Broadway stage designer, and Andrew Dasburg, an American modernist painter born in France, soon moved in with the Sterns and Manby.[27] When Jones and Dasburg first visited, they all "spent their days careening around the countryside, attending Pueblo ceremonial dances, buying Pueblo jewelry, and collecting Nuevomexicano santos, painted and carved wooden saint figures common in Nuevomexicano Catholic ceremonies," Flannery Burke writes. Their spirited activities seemed highly suspicious to Arthur Manby, who "insisted that local officials investigate the group for espionage," thinking they might be working for the Germans. Mabel Dodge seemed delighted by the investigation. She wrote her old friend Neith Boyce in 1918 of her naïve impressions:

> We are in the maddest, most amusing country in the world—in the freakiest, most insane village you ever dreamed of and *I* would like to stay forever. . . . We were *so* queer they thought we were German agents importing dynamite! . . . Life is like one long comic opera—with the most exaggerated costumes and colors, and impossible scenery and sunsets. . . . I am in love with all the Indians and they think I am one and talk to me in indian.[28]

Across the street lived painter Bert Geer Phillips, a founding member of the Taos Society of Artists along with Buck Dunton. Mabel was quickly wooed by Tony Lujan (sic), a Taos Pueblo craftsman who later supervised the construction crew that built her new house. Mabel met Tony on her first night in Taos and in hindsight declared it was love at first sight. Heartbroken, Maurice Sterne left New Mexico in August 1918. Ironically, Sterne had visited New Mexico first and had urged Mabel to move there and make the Pueblos and the preservation of their art and culture her life's work. Tony and Mabel were finally married in 1923, and remained so for forty years, until Mabel's death in 1963.[29]

Beginning in 1922, English novelist D. H. Lawrence and his wife, Frieda Lawrence, were drawn into Mabel and Tony's Southwestern circle through correspondence and visits. Spellbound by the land and the people of the Pueblos, the Lawrences resided at nearby Kiowa Ranch during eleven months in 1924 and 1925. Mabel had traded the ranch to Frieda for the manuscript of Lawrence's classic novel, *Sons and Lovers*. In an unconventional arrangement, the painter Dorothy Brett, follower and lover of D. H., lived in a small cabin on the ranch while the Lawrences lived in a large cabin nearby. It was said that D. H. and Frieda Lawrence had tried to recruit followers to form a commune, but Lady Brett was the only taker. The philosophies of Dodge and

D. H. Lawrence on Taos and the Pueblos and many other subjects clashed noisily like a set of cracked cymbals. Lawrence would never write the book that she wanted him to. In fact, according to Burke, Lawrence resisted and rebelled against the women's sphere of power that had been established by Dodge, the Southwestern novelist Mary Austin, and other white women with cultural and financial capital in northern New Mexico. Much like other men in "the Anglo art communities of Taos and Santa Fe," Lawrence "repeatedly tried, both literally and figuratively, to undermine Anglo women's power." Another example is the gay poet and playwright Witter Bynner, Lynn Riggs's friend and mentor who became Mabel's rival. Thomas Wolfe likewise had vehemently rejected such power as he perceived it exercised through Dodge's proxy, apparently without ever actually meeting Dodge face to face. Lawrence moreover objected to Dodge's vision of Indigenous people, rejecting "the kind of primitivism that governed her relationship with Lujan and with other Pueblo Indians." Instead, he "actively mocked Dodge, Austin, and other women for romanticizing" indigenes. Lawrence himself had a complex vision of the Pueblos and like Mabel, engaged a primitivist project, but "it was a dark and disturbing primitivism" that expressed great ambivalence toward Natives, Burke writes. Lawrence famously satirized Dodge with his 1925 story, "The Woman Who Rode Away," in which a naïve Dodge-like protagonist is sacrificed by Natives at the climax. This story was part of an established literary tradition of male writers using Mabel as material. The gay writer Carl Van Vechten had first parodied her New York salon circa 1913 in his comic novel, *Peter Whiffle: His Life and Works* (1922). Witter Bynner satirized Luhan's life in a play called *Cake: An Indulgence* (1926). Sadly, D. H. Lawrence died in March 1930 at the age of forty-four, only six weeks before Mathews's previously cited column appeared.[30]

Mabel's landlord Arthur Rochford Manby, the black sheep of his family, had emigrated from England to New Mexico in 1883 at age twenty-four. Manby's subsequent nefarious deeds are recounted in *To Possess the Land* (1973), a biography by Southwestern author Frank Waters, best known for *The Man Who Killed the Deer* (1942), a novel featuring Pueblo characters. *To Possess the Land* was in turn positively reviewed by Dee Brown, author of the influential *Bury My Heart at Wounded Knee* (1970), a history of American Indians in the West focusing on the late nineteenth century that took a critical tone toward the government and the effects of westward expansion on Indigenous peoples.[31] Over the course of two decades, Arthur Manby lied and schemed his way into possession of vast acreages of land in that area of northern New Mexico called the Antonio Martinez Grant—only to lose most of it without developing it. Manby's rapacious land-grabs serve as evidence of how relatively easy it was, after the 1848 Treaty of Guadalupe Hidalgo, for ambitious white men with capital, or the illusion thereof, to claim tracts that were already justly claimed and often occupied by the descendants of Spanish families and Indigenous peoples of the area, such as Taos Pueblo Indians. Through that treaty, half of New Mexico was acquired by the United States after the Mexican-American War. Differing from most of the artists surrounding him in Taos, Manby disrespected local Indigenous peoples and was paranoid that they were conspiring to kill him. He asked Mabel to be more discriminating when allowing Tony Lujan's Pueblo friends in the house. "Those damn heathen Indians! Their blasted sacred mountain is full of gold and they won't let me get it. They don't want me to have any water for my land. They think all is theirs—land, water, gold, and everything else," he ranted to Mabel. She, of course, sided with the Pueblos, and in 1935 she even filed suit against the "purported village of Taos," claiming that "neither the incorporation of the village nor the election of its officers was legal. Even a member of the national Congress agreed that there was not a single town or business lot in Taos where the legal title was vested in the white man."[32]

Manby's nefarious exploitation was a part of a larger national pattern, and it foreshadowed and overlapped the lying, scheming, and conspiratorial murder that occurred in Osage County during the dissolute 1920s. Philip Deloria writes:

> The story of early twentieth-century land loss is without doubt one of the vilest episodes in the long history of American colonialism. . . . We should not hesitate to mark it, not simply as classically tragic (though it was all that), but as a tragedy marked by cold viciousness—and by the pain, damage, and distrust left in its wake. Indeed, the linked terms *tragedy* and *squandering* provided cover for those who contemplated the transactions.[33]

Osages of the Big Hill Band who owned headrights, mostly living in Fairfax, near the Greyhorse Indian Village, were exploited by dishonest whites, some of whom became family through marriage. The most egregious cases were the scores, perhaps even hundreds, of murders of the Osage reign of terror, perpetrated by ringleader Bill Hale, two of his compliant Burkhart nephews and accomplices, John Ramsey, the Pawhuska banker Herbert G. Burt, and many known and yet unidentified confederates, mostly during the early to mid-1920s. Author David Grann proved what many Osages had known the whole time: many other white men, including prominent citizens, were involved in the crimes or their cover-up, which is further explored later in this volume, especially in Part XI. Many suspicious deaths of fullblood Osages were never investigated. In the Taos area, Manby and his ilk accrued and concealed vast sums in land speculation, ranching, mining, and controlling water rights. Like his fellow entrepreneur E. W. Marland, an oilman and friend of

Mathews—who in 1951 would publish Marland's biography—Manby built a large, lavish home and filled it with art treasures. Similar to Marland's second marriage, Manby's marriage was scandalous. In July 1928, two years after the mysterious death of E. W. Marland's first wife, Virginia Collins Marland, whose friends claimed he mistreated, Marland married the much-younger Lydie Roberts Marland, the daughter of Virginia's sister. Lydie had first been Ernest's niece, and then his daughter through adoption, before he had the adoption annulled earlier that year. As for Arthur Manby, he married Pinky, a sixteen-year-old daughter of a creditor, after she became pregnant, and then cruelly neglected her. Their offspring died stillborn or in infancy, and Manby treated Pinky terribly, driving her away to seek a divorce.[34] In 1922, Chief Bacon Rind said to the Osage tribal council: "There are men amongst the whites, honest men, but they are mighty scarce—mighty few."[35]

In July 1929, Arthur Manby was brutally murdered and decapitated. The mystery surrounding his macabre demise was featured on the front page of *The Daily Journal-Capital* of Pawhuska two days preceding Mathews's column of April 17, 1930. The syndicated account offered readers a sensational, illustrated story set in Taos. Readers no doubt including Mathews were told that "for nine months, the secluded art colony in this little New Mexican city" had been consumed with "one of the strangest murder mysteries ever recorded—a mystery bizarre enough to come straight from the pages of Edgar Allen Poe."[36] Manby's headless corpse had been found in his bedroom, but his head was in the adjoining room. At first, the sheriff arrived at the absurd conclusion that Manby died of natural causes and his head had been bitten off by his dog; perhaps the sheriff was paid to reach that conclusion. Others believed Manby was clearly murdered in grisly fashion. Bizarrely, witnesses claimed to have seen Arthur after his supposed death; therefore, many concluded that Manby had killed another man who resembled him, or had stolen a body, and mangled the corpse to fake his own death, thus eluding creditors who had been demanding money from him and others who wished him dead. As a result of such sensational reportage and pressure from the British consulate, the corpse was disinterred and identified by four men as Manby's.[37] The case was not closed even then, however, because according to Waters, two of the men had never even met Manby and would not have been able to identify him by inspecting a mutilated body; his neighbor Doc Martin "didn't give a damn, and destroyed his autopsy report the minute he found out he was not to be paid for it"; and the fourth man, a dentist, later admitted he lied about Manby's dentures and the man they identified as Manby was actually someone else (probably a neighbor named Brooks who had died around the same time).[38] The painter Victor Higgins, also of the Taos Society of Artists, was convinced Manby had faked his death. Another member, Joseph Sharp, a noted painter of Native Americans, had been traveling in Europe with his wife when the alleged murder occurred; the Sharps were later startled to learn of reports of Manby's death, because they claimed they had seen him in Florence, Italy, on the street, and approached him, only to be evaded.[39] In early 1930, the *New Mexican* reported that Manby was in Italy and had even mailed a photo of himself "to show how he had improved in health." A local real estate agent had seen Manby slouch by his office a couple of days after his putative death; yet another witness spotted Manby in Mexico two years later.[40]

Just as in the Osage reign of terror, a conspiracy lay behind multiple murders, many never investigated. It transpired that Manby was a paranoid despot mysteriously involved with a thuggish secret society that fraudulently claimed to be an arm of U.S. government intelligence and squeezed large sums of money from its members. Manby, after much research, invented this "bunco society," dubbing it United States Secret and Civil Service Society, Self-Supporting Branch, and ran it with Teracita, his partner and lover. Manby lost control of the society and Teracita threw him over for a younger man, the society's messenger, Carmen Duran.[41] Manby was seemingly victimized by Teracita, Duran, and their accomplices. Seven skeletons belonging to decapitated victims were subsequently found in the area by a private detective, Bill Martin. All seven men were associated with Arthur Manby; they may have been victims of the leviathan secret society, which used threats of beheading to keep its members paying up.[42] The more researchers looked into it, the stranger the story grew, stranger than any dime-store novelist could ever imagine. The Manby case remains unsolved.

ONE OF MANY BEAUTIFUL PLACES IN THE WORLD

Thursday, April 24, 1930, #15

Beautifully laid-out farms, with rows of cotton or a great expanse of wheat, waving rows of corn, and cool fields of alfalfa are inspiring, but straight highways running monotonously between miles of fence become tiresome. Drab farmhouses and barns and heaps of rusted implements give the eye no rest after several hours of driving.

Of course, this is the "country," and all countrysides are beautiful. A handful of Holsteins in a meadow or lying in bovine tranquility under the first shade of the trees is picturesque, and a farmer plowing with clouds of dust in his wake may hold one's attention for a time, but how can this compare with the illimitable pastels and vivid greens of the Osage with cattle dotting the landscape? Enter the Osage from any direction and note the change, not only in the landscape, but the very atmosphere that so harmonizes with the prairie and blackjacks.

There are many beautiful places in the world, many of them manmade. There is the grandeur of the Alps, the Rockies, and the Sierras. There are the European villages lying in quiet valleys far from the stream of strident commercialism. Swiss chalets cling to the sides of mountains, and peasants gather grain on steep declivities; there are lone inns on the moors of Scotland and desolate Highland stretches where only the voice of the curlew or the bleat of a black-faced lamb is heard; there is the moonlight on the silent ruins of an ancient civilization; there are the vineyards of France and Italy, and the dreamy countryside of England with their picturesque people drowsy under their traditions. Then there are the vivid splashes of color and the staccato voice of the East with odors that are in themselves romance to the westerner.

From the savagery of an Alpine glacier through myriad pictures of meadows, bubbling streams, sail-reflecting waters, forbidding forests, castles rising above the treetops, or high on the cliffs of the Rhine, and Medieval cathedrals rising like prayers in stone above the squalor of medieval streets, to the jabbering marketplaces of the East; to the camel caravans crossing the Sahara, and lastly to the silence imposing ghostlight of the moonlit ruins of Greece and Rome, there are pictures that would take one's whole lifetime to visit.

It is impossible to compare one of these pictures with another, inasmuch as each picture is complete in itself. Often it depends upon its history and traditions, and always on the fact that man through generations has become a part of it; he lives under its influence and it forms him and molds him, and makes him according to its characteristics, severe and cold or happy and full of song and whimsical dreams; he adapts himself as a part of the animal world, spiritually as well as physically; spiritual development is a part of the processes under which all life develops.

The Osage is one of these pictures: it is complete in itself, and its prairie filled with the song of the meadowlark, its incomparable green expanse dotted with cattle and fading into the blue distance, as well as its brown melancholy of autumn and its cruel whiteness of winter, will affect us who live here; we cannot escape this, but we must gradually learn to appreciate it and love it in order that we might the sooner become a part of it, and come to the full realization that we are fortunate in being a part of it.

A LOSS FOR WORDS

Thursday, May 8, 1930, #18

Now, since the recent rains, the prairie and the blackjack-covered hills have this in common with many wonders of the world: an attempt to describe them with insipid words is impossible. Like flying on a moon at night six-thousand feet above the world and looking down upon one of man's anthills, with its maze of geometrically straight rows of lights leading to a central cluster; like gazing at the Grand Canyon in the early twilight, with the faint voice of a desert mockingbird wafting up from below; like the midnight voice of the nightingale; like the moonlight flooded on an ancient civilization; the starlight on an alpine glacier; or a date-palm etched in the face of an orange moon on the Sahara. Under influence of these, man is dumb. His tendency to name and pigeonhole is frustrated, and that which floods him, that suffusion he calls emotion, overpowers him and he becomes inarticulate; his thoughts are trite and run through his brain in circles, and words are insufficient.[43]

Get out on any highway in any direction from home. It would be better if one could turn off the road, but in any case, go out just before sundown, or just before sunup, stop the car and sit, lose yourself in the world of sound and color. The little bird you hear everywhere and occasionally see swaying on a tall weed, or sitting on a fencepost, attempting to express to the world his joy of life, but whose voice unfortunately bars him from our list of songsters, is the dickcissel, named from the song he should be honored for his dauntless happiness. In the heat of midday in July and August, his voice is the only one heard, and it is welcome. You cannot mistake him; he is everywhere and his "dick—dick—dickcissel" distinguishes him.

We must not confuse an appreciation of the prairie and the hills, and the wildlife about us, with cheap sentiment; the paunchy gods of Hollywood often supply the latter. Men whom we call great are poets, and they express themselves in the building of great business organizations, in architecture, in statesmanship, in philosophy, in literature, and in science.

Theodore Roosevelt left a cabinet meeting to see the first warbler that arrived at the White House gardens one spring. General Allenby studied the botany of Palestine during the campaign, and one understands wrote a book on the subject. Lord Curzon devoted many chapters of his book of travel to the singing sands, and the great waterfalls of the world. We cannot call these men cheap sentimentalists, because they had a full appreciation of the life of which they were a part.

SUNDOWN II: CHAL, GRANVILLE, AND EDMUND ALLENBY

In the previously cited column, Mathews takes pains to justify his appreciation of nature. He is keen to offer evidence that conserving wildlife and paying close attention to natural beauty is not "cheap sentiment," which is implicitly unmanly. Rather, Mathews argues that appreciation of the natural life of which we are all a part is a quality shared by great and hearty men of action, such as his heroes Edmund Allenby, Lord Curzon, and Theodore Roosevelt. "Sentiment" is a quality that was conventionally associated with sensibility and women, primary readers of the sentimental novel, which thrived in the eighteenth century and remained popular throughout the nineteenth century, when it branched into the subgenre of the domestic novel. Valorizing "fine feeling," sentimental novels dramatized scenes of high tenderness and distress, eliciting emotional responses from readers. Exalting feeling over reason, such works raised emotional analysis to a fine art.[44] In 1799, author and philanthropist Hannah More scorned "cheap sentiment" in the novel in her *Strictures on the Modern System of Female Education*: "Such is the frightful facility of this species of composition, that every raw girl, while she reads, is tempted to fancy that she can also write" and her "glutted imagination soon overflows with the redundance of cheap sentiment and plentiful incident, and by a sort of arithmetical proportion, is enabled by the perusal of any three novels, to produce a fourth; till every fresh production, like the progeny of Banquo, is followed by *Another, and another and another!*" By the end of the nineteenth century, it was common for the genre to be criticized as overladen with "cheap sentiment."[45]

Mathews noted in his memoirs a few times that Theodore Roosevelt interested him because of his rugged life hunting and ranching in South Dakota, and Roosevelt only "missed by a slight margin" entering his canon of "tin gods" including Thomas Jefferson, Sir Ernest Shackleton, Marcus Aurelius, and Charles Darwin. To Mathews, raised with horses in Indian Territory, Teddy Roosevelt still had too many vestiges of "dudeism" stuck to him to be sufficiently authentic.[46] Formerly the leader of the Rough Riders, the First U.S. Volunteer Cavalry in the Spanish-American war, Roosevelt embodied an image of robust masculinity. Yet, appealing to Mathews, he was highly attuned to notable birds. One morning President Roosevelt burst into a cabinet meeting: "Gentlemen, do you know what has happened this morning?" The entire cabinet feared a crisis—so it was to their relief that he revealed, "I just saw a chestnut-sided warbler—and this is only February."[47] Like Mathews, Roosevelt had studied natural sciences and sustained a lifelong interest in zoology. Roosevelt's legacy as a president included his conservation efforts, among them the establishment of the National Forest

Service and many national parks, forests, and monuments, bird reserves, and game preserves. Roosevelt's spirit of conservation is being threatened by the current Trump administration that decided to radically slash the size of two national monuments in Utah, Bears Ears by 85 percent, and Grand Staircase-Escalante by 50 percent.[48]

Lord Curzon may not be familiar to readers today but was once a famous aristocratic character. A British Conservative statesman, George Nathaniel Curzon, 1st Marquess Curzon of Kedleston, was known as Lord Curzon of Kedleston between 1898 and 1911, and The Earl Curzon of Kedleston between 1911 and 1921. As Viceroy of India from 1899 to 1905, he created Eastern Bengal and Assam. As Secretary of State for Foreign Affairs, he drew the famed Curzon Line, the proposed border between two emerging states, the Second Polish Republic and the Soviet Union. In 1894 Lord Curzon published his most successful work, *Problems of the Far East*; in 1923 *Tales of Travel* appeared, to which Mathews alludes here. Lord Curzon served as president of the Royal Geographical Society from 1911 to 1914. His best travel writing, marked by an admirable prose style, was collected in 1985 in *Travels with a Superior Person*. Lord Curzon would have been horrified to know that the "superior person" tag, which was taken from a schoolmate's mocking doggerel that rhymed *Curzon* and *person*, became the title of a book bearing his name.

General Edmund Allenby was Mathews's confirmed hero. During Mathews's years as a military aviator stateside, he, an Anglophile, dreamt of flying in Palestine for General Allenby (1861–1936), also known as 1st Viscount Allenby. No less than three times Mathews discusses Allenby, who fought in the Second Boer War and World War I, and is recalled as one of the most successful British generals. Field Marshal Allenby initially fought on the Western Front in France against German forces. Later he famously led British Empire forces against Turkish fighters of the Ottoman Empire and conquered Jerusalem, Damascus, and Aleppo. He commanded T. E. Lawrence, who recounted his experiences in *Seven Pillars of Wisdom* (1926), a book Mathews enjoyed revisiting, which was later adapted into the movie *Lawrence of Arabia*. Historians noted that Allenby, the first Christian conqueror of the Holy City since the Crusades, ordered his men to dismount upon entering the city as a gesture of respect. His greatest victory was the climactic Battle of Megiddo in September 1918, when British forces took Palestine. From 1919 until 1925, Allenby continued to serve in the region as High Commissioner for Egypt and Sudan. Noted for his critical intellect, Allenby was an avid reader of books on diverse subjects ranging from botany to poetry. The fact that in the middle of the Great War,

Allenby was yet "imperturbably studying the botany of the region" held special appeal for John Joseph Mathews.[49]

So it is easy to see why Mathews idolized and identified with Allenby. The two men had many shared interests including horses, birds, and planes. As boys, both Allenby and Mathews spent a great deal of time out in nature: Allenby in West Bilney, Norfolk, England, and Mathews all over the Osage Nation. An account of Allenby's boyhood stated that at West Bilney, he, a brother, and their father "tramped the fields with guns, or sometimes went for long walks through the woods with an axe to cut off dead branches or to blaze trees for cutting." Edmund's parents were both "keen observers of bird-life, and from them Allenby drew the great interest in and love of birds that was to remain with him all his life. From his mother, a keen botanist with a well-stocked garden, Allenby learned the names and care of flowers and plants." A brother of the vicar of Ashbocking, Professor Edward Cowell contributed to Edmund's botanical and taxonomical knowledge.[50] Similarly, Mathews's mother Eugenia (Jennie) also had a beautiful, well-stocked garden, and taught her children and those in the neighborhood about plants and birds. Like Allenby, Mathews was privileged with mentors such as Judge Musseller and his father, who taught him about birds and horses.

In *Sundown*, after becoming an Army pilot in training, Chal again admires with fascination Professor Granville, who has now transformed into Major Granville. The Major appears on the scene to inspect Chal's piloting skills. After Chal lands a plane, Granville approaches him like a suitor, holding a flower in his hand; identifying it as *Yucca elata*, Granville shares with his young mentee that he received a letter from General Allenby, who was sure the flower could be found in their area.

"Yes, Allenby is writing a book on the flora of Palestine, and he had some very queer theories about the Yucca," Granville tells Chal. Major Granville was gathering botanical notes near the base, and he and Allenby were "exchanging data."

That night, Chal lies on his bunk thinking of Granville, recalling the way the Englishman brought him the flower and told him of Allenby's research. Perhaps he also recalled Granville's keen interest in his beloved red-tail hawk. Chal reckons that the reason he is drawn to Granville, and to the notion of Allenby writing down "queer theories" in a book on flora in "the middle of the greatest war in history," was simply because "he was queer himself." This is something that repeatedly concerns Chal.[51] In like manner, in his column, Mathews seems keen to distance any association the reader might have between vocally appreciating natural beauty, and an effeminate sentimentality that might be unfairly dismissed as cheap or queer.

LIFE CYCLES

Sunday, May 11, 1930, #19

The earth processes, like the gradual evolution of life, go on while man's tragedies play, and accomplishments absorb his attention during the short space of this lifetime. Viewed from the ephemeral consciousness that is allotted him, this slow process of tearing down and building up is beyond his comprehension, and though it affects him as a part of the earth's life, he is apt to disregard natural laws in favor of his own customs and superstitions built up through the generations. False reasoning and pride are inspired by privileges that have become tradition. And his insatiable instinct for acquisition reaching far beyond the point of material comforts has been the cause of the crumbling of his great civilizations one after the other, as they complete the cycle from virility, through adolescence, and maturity, senility and decay. The energy used in the fight for survival, and no longer needed for food or defense, is turned into ornamentation, which includes useless luxury and sated appetites. The individual goes through this same cycle; he recapitulates the evolution of the race and the nation; the nation being a glorified tribe of individuals.

All organisms pass through this cycle. Also, rivers may be identified as being young, mature, or old, according to the stage they have reached in their life's history. Their function seems to be the leveling of the hills whence they flow, to deposit the material thus denuded in the flats near their mouths, and when they have completed this task, their usefulness in the scheme of things is at the end, and they ceased to exist as rivers: they will have eroded their own gradient, and there can be no flowing of water from higher to lower levels where there is no incline.

At all times, frost, heat, wind, and water are agents in the gradual tearing down of the Osage hills. The contour is gradually changing due to the minerals removed by these agents, and carried away by the streams.

As we stand on the Bird Creek bridge and watch with fascination or fear the swirling, turgid waters passing beneath, there is an added interest when we realize that suspended in the water are tons of sediments torn away from the sandstone hills, and the materials are being carried away in the form of sediments and in solution, much of this material not stopping until it is deposited in the Mississippi Delta on the Gulf. As we stand there, we actually witness the process of nature in action, and though the hills will look as high and unchanged to us in our lifetime, in time they will be leveled by this process, if some earth movement does not happen to raise the strata again, through the tension that is ever exerted upon the earth's crust. We will remember also that the natural vegetation acting as a deterrent to the erosion process, has in many cases been pulled up for purposes of agriculture, and that the soil thus bared is less resistant to the erosive agents, and as insignificant as it appears, these fields of corn are actually aiding in the tearing-down process of the Osage, and one may see in his lifetime evidence of this wearing-away process, even though it be on a very small scale. . . .

Thus, like the individuals, the race, and organisms as a whole, the river passes though the cycle. At its beginning, the stage of virility, it fights for existence with other nascent streams; it fights its way to the sea through difficulties demanding activity and virility. Then youth, where it is still fighting it way to survival. In maturity, it has defined its drainage system and has reached the apex of its powers; its main stream and tributaries have eroded back to the highest divide and in its struggle, it has annexed all the other streams in the neighborhood and succeeded in shaping its course to the sea over which "conquered" streams must flow. Then senility, the time when it has carried away as sediment the hills and divides: it has worn down to near level its own incline or gradient by its youthful activity and in senility become sluggish, and devotes what energy that remains to it in ornamentation. That is, in whimsically hanging its own channel from one side to the other, and meandering over its broad floodplain. Like it can only survive and realize its power through the constant struggle to perpetuate itself, and when there is no need for such activity, and the obstacles in the way of survival have been eliminated, and if the need arises again for action to safeguard existence, the ornamentation becomes cumbersome, since it was not developed out of necessity.

This is true of civilizations, individuals, elephants, and mayflowers.

ORNAMENTATION AND THE FORCE:
TALKING TO THE MOON

The preceding column represents Mathews's first articulation of his particular understanding of *ornamentation*, which he uses in a later column and elaborates in detail in *Talking to the Moon*. Ornamentation, perhaps first theorized by Charles Darwin with regard to sexual selection in *The Descent of Man, and Selection in Relation to Sex* (1871), is simply an organism's expression not necessary for survival. Very early in *Talking to the Moon*, Mathews writes that he had thought that he

> might find some connection between man's artificial ornamentation and the useless ornamentation among the creatures of my little corner of the earth. I realized that man's artistic creations and his dreams, often resulting in beauty, as well as his fumbling toward God, must be primal, possibly the results of the biological urge which inspires the wood thrush to sing and the coyote to talk to the moon.

Mathews posits a mysterious life force that drives nature he calls, long before *Star Wars*, "the Force." Late in the book, he writes, "Ornamental expression is inspired by the Force among the inhabitants of the ridges just as it is inspired in more privileged man. They have their nuptial dances and their songs, and they all play under the influence of the primal laws, but they also sing and dance and do odd things under the influence of the Force."[52]

Readers familiar with *Talking to the Moon* may note some similarities between that book and Mathews's columns. Both that book and "Our Osage Hills" use a chronological structure and evince close attention to the seasons and Osage land. Using more references to Osage cosmology, *Talking to the Moon* deftly weaves ecological, philosophical, and, occasionally, political concerns into a personal study focusing on the natural environment of his Osage hills and prairies. Evoking traditional Osage culture and the elders who sustained older religious practices that most Osages had retired, *Talking to the Moon* is a meditative, yet paradoxically impersonal memoir. A critical success and the favorite of many aficionados, *Talking to the Moon* was dubbed the Osage *Walden* by more than one critic, including his second wife, Elizabeth Hunt Mathews. "This is John Joseph Mathews' *Walden*," she wrote a year after her partner's death in June 1979, opening her foreword to the University of Oklahoma Press reissue. "It is a book that a Thoreau or a Muir might write, but it is a *Walden* of the plains and prairies, of the 1930s and 1940s, by a Native American." A spiritual descendant of transcendentalist Henry David Thoreau, John Muir was a Scottish American naturalist, author, and conservationist, also known as "John of the Mountains." Arguably, at its best, Mathews's journalistic writing here is on par with *Talking to the Moon*. At times it may even be superior, because his best writing of the early 1930s—exemplified by *Wah'Kon-Tah*—evinces vigor and concision, whereas later works, such as his unfinished autobiography, could meander. This is suggested by a review of *Talking to the Moon* penned by poet Paul Engle, a director of Iowa Writers' Workshop—where Mathews's stepson, John Clinton Hunt, went on to study in the early 1950s. Engle praises Mathews's rendering of conversations with local Osage Indians, ranchers, and cowboys, which are rich in local color, vernacular, and humor. The poet notes, however, a "curious contrast" between Mathews's representation of the speech of local visitors, and the register in which he "quotes himself as talking, for he sounds in this book quite stilted and formal." Engle commends Mathews's plentiful "passages of clean writing" and his "minute observation of animal life," concluding this "wholly compensates" for any small instances of "awkward writing" found therein.[53]

THE MOON

Tuesday, May 13, 1930, #20

How natural it was for primitive people to worship the moon. The soft light flooding the open spaces and creating ghost-lights and shadows in the woods, and spreading over all benign tranquility, with the voices of hundreds of small petitioners floating up from the grassroots and from the shelter of the trees; voices soft with a touch of sadness, paying homage to the mellow light with its own weight, seem to smother harshness.

On the prairie, where no yellow lights flash, nor do the puffs of a motor break the peace, the silence is almost audible and the calm almost oppressive. The scattered limestone rocks seem to float in the eerie light. The distance beckons to unearthly adventure. It is a primeval world, whose valleys are filled with velvety silence; ragged inky shadows reaching down their sides and patches of water in the center, silvered an unrippled. A world far removed from clanking steel and startling disharmony.

On the sandstone hills, the blackjacks stand in dark masses, their leaves like polished metal, unstirring in the ghostly quiet. Their shadows, dense and irregular, lie like fringed garments of sable black. From the grass come the stridulations of the insects in many keys, but in perfect harmony with the dreaming world. The whip-poor-will mournfully repeats his plea like a petulant child convinced of his own virtue. Then, as though to make the silence more perfect, the romance of the night more sad and appealing, from far back in the blackness of the trees, a screech owl complains in quavering tones to the moon.

Man has counted and named the stars; he knows much of the nature of the sun and the origin of the planets, yet his attitude is akin to worship when the moon floods the Osage with silver.

THE PASSING OF RED EAGLES

Mathews's poetic evocation of the moonlit prairie is breathtaking. Moonlight, especially a full moon, is also said to drive irrational behavior, however, forming the root of the word *lunacy*. Three days after the preceding column ran, readers of the Pawhuska *Journal-Capital* learned that the case of Ida Martin, a "Pawnee farm woman" charged with selling wine to a party of fullblood Osages, had been submitted to a jury in the federal court. The alleged sale was blamed by some for the March 1929 death of a young man, Joseph Red Eagle.[54] Born in 1906 from a line of Osage chiefs, Joe Red Eagle was the son of Paul and Cecilia Red Eagle. Paul Red Eagle (1880–1941) served three times as assistant principal chief of the Osages—and during 1923 to 1924 became principal chief after Ne-kah-wah-she-tun-kah passed away in August 1923, amid the horror of the Osage murders.[55] Cecilia Red Eagle's father was Chief Joseph Paw-ne-no-pashe (Not Afraid of Pawnees), or Governor Joe, who headed the Osage council that negotiated the "blanket lease" of the Osage oilfields. The Red Eagle family's land allotments were concentrated in the area of Bigheart, a town in eastern Osage County named for Chief James Bigheart. In a symbolic change, in 1922 the town was renamed Barnsdall after oilman Theodore N. Barnsdall, who had died in 1917, and his Barnsdall Oil Company.[56]

Paul Red Eagle was the son of Henry Red Eagle, or Che-sho-shin-kah, also spelled Tzi-Sho Shinkah (1849–1929), who was a tribal storyteller and successful rancher. Henry Red Eagle served as tribal councilman and assistant principal chief under Chief Bacon Rind, or Wah-she-hah—Star That Travels[57]—and alongside John Joseph Mathews's father, councilman William Shirley Mathews. Will Mathews was proud to serve as tribal councilman, and his only son John Joseph followed in his footsteps. Henry Red Eagle, who signed his name with a thumbprint, married Rosa Pryor, or Sah-me-tsa. Referring to Henry Red Eagle by his surname only, Mathews wrote of his funeral and its broader connotation of the end of a traditional way of life in "The Passing of Red Eagle," a piece for *The Sooner* magazine. Mathews listed Henry as an oral source for his historical masterpiece, *The Osages: Children of the Middle Waters* (1961). The Red Eagle family practiced the peyote ritual of the Native American Church, which many Osages turned to in the early twentieth century after collectively deciding to put away their old traditional religion. Peyote was brought to the Big Hill band of Osages by Mi-ompah-we-li or Moonhead, also known as John Wilson, a Franco-Caddo-Delaware spiritual leader who cultivated a following among the Wahzhazhe. By 1910, the ceremony was firmly established among the majority of fullbloods. Although most Indian agents thought the religion harmless, for decades it continued to be the subject of controversy among county, state, and federal officials. Terry P. Wilson explains that the Osages were often supported by agency superintendents; in 1936, one of them attested that "the Indians who are members of the Peyote Church are our best Indians and do not use alcohol and narcotics." In the 1980s, Wilson reported, "the mixture of peyote, Christian, and old Osage beliefs continued to be intermingled with no apparent uneasiness."[58] The use of peyote in ceremony was sometimes regarded as a means by which an Osage could break from addiction to alcohol and narcotics. "Alcoholism continued to be a problem among the Osages during the 1930s, and many became dependent upon drugs, especially morphine and marijuana," Wilson writes.[59] Prohibition was not lifted until 1933, and alcohol had already been illegal in the Osage Nation.

To return to the Joe Red Eagle case, Mrs. Ida Martin was indicted for selling wine to Pearl McKinley, a wealthy Osage woman, and her uncle, Henry McKinley. They were both of Fairfax, Osage County, and both fullbloods, probably of the Big Hill band, given the proximity of Fairfax to Grayhorse village, the center of Big Hill traditional culture. Members of the Big Hill band in the Gray Horse/Fairfax area were the specific victims of what David Grann and others too broadly call the "Osage murders." Four years later, Pearl McKinley's fortune was the subject of an article in the *Oklahoman* reporting that even an affluent Osage woman could not find living quarters in Fairfax while her home was being remodeled. All houses and apartments were "filled to overflowing," so she found a place in Ponca City and sent her private limousine back and forth to carry her clothes and possessions.[60] Pearl McKinley testified that she and Joe Red Eagle bought a half-gallon jug of wine from Ida Martin, then went to the house of her Uncle Henry and Aunt Mabel McKinley to drink it. Later, the group returned to Martin's farmhouse to buy more wine. Henry and Mabel testified to three visits that night altogether, and the party was all fairly inebriated upon leaving the Martin farmhouse the third time. Henry and Joe Red Eagle, "riding in the backseat of the car while the women drove," started fighting on the way home, Pearl and Mabel testified. They stopped the car, and the men's fight spilled outside. Joe Red Eagle's body was later found in Pawnee County, in a ditch near the Belford Bridge on the Tulsa-Ponca City highway.

Initially, Henry, Mabel, and Pearl McKinley were charged with the murder of Joe Red Eagle. Pearl's case was dropped, however, and Henry and Mabel McKinley were acquitted in October 1929. In retrospect, the acquittal of Henry McKinley seems suspect. In March, it was reported that the body of Red Eagle, who had been stabbed in the head, had been found by three Ralston youths. They saw two women carry Henry McKinley to the car and drive away. Moreover, when Fairfax officers arrested Henry at Pearl's home, he was in a "drunken stupor," his clothes were bloody, and a bloody knife with a broken blade was in his pocket.[61] A district court ruled in favor of the defense, which claimed that despite appearances, it was not Henry McKinley who murdered Joe Red Eagle, but rather the culprit's name was mud—literally. "The state contended that Red Eagle was not killed by knife wounds inflicted during the fight. The defense contention was that he was strangled by mud into which he and McKinley rolled during their fight."[62] It seems unlikely that justice was found for Joe Red Eagle. In May 1930, the *Journal-Capital* reported that Ida Martin, her daughter, and a sharecropper living with them denied that Ida sold any wine to the Osages. They dubiously claimed the Osages were already drunk when they arrived, and Martin was only taking an order for baked goods.[63]

It was symptomatic of the times that at age twenty-three, Joseph Red Eagle, the scion of a line of Osage chiefs, died drunk, stabbed in the head, and drowned in mud, his body abandoned. Precious little is known of Joe, although years earlier in 1920, his perfect attendance record at the Osage Indian School in Pawhuska was reported as widely as Wichita, Kansas.[64] Joe Red Eagle's death speaks volumes of the precarious period in which he lived. The 1920s and early 1930s were a violent and risky time to be a fullblood Osage. They were surrounded by manipulators, crooks, and the constant temptations of drugs and alcohol. It was a violent and corrupt environment in which the Wild West lived on.

Eight years earlier, in 1921, Joe's namesake relative, Joe Redeagle (Hlu-ah-shu-tsa) of Hominy, had died at age sixty under mysterious circumstances, amid the early reign of terror murders. He died of "acute indigestion, after a short illness," it was reported; it is quite possible Redeagle was poisoned, the method used in many cases to conceal murder. This Joe Redeagle left behind a wife, Jennie, and two children, Alice and Louis Redeagle. Handling the funeral arrangements was The Big Hill Undertaking Company of Fairfax,[65] which was owned by Scott S. Mathis, a guardian to seven Osages who died under his watch, at least two of whom were murdered. Mathis and his Big Hill Undertaking Company conspired with kingpin Bill Hale—who owned an interest in the company—and played a major role in covering up multiple Osage murders, further discussed in the final chapter. This knowledge raises suspicion over the elder Joe Redeagle's demise.[66]

Violent tragedy again befell the Red Eagle family in November 1933. The late Joe Red Eagle's older brother, Louis Red Eagle, twenty-eight years old, another son of Paul and Cecilia Red Eagle, was murdered by Jess Dalton, a ranch hand at Red Eagle Ranch, in a "shooting affray over wages" at Red Eagle's home, two miles outside of Hominy in Osage County. Beginning in the late 1920s, Louis Red Eagle had acted as an interpreter to Chief Fred Lookout. His brother Ed Red Eagle, Sr., said that although Louis was a "very

young man," Lookout brought him to Washington, DC several times to interpret. "It was just astonishing to members of the tribe to see a young man"
speaking Osage to Chief Lookout, then telling committees, commissioners,
and the secretary of the interior "things that the Chief had in his mind and
what he wanted for his people." Brutally, Dalton shot Red Eagle below the
heart with a small-gauge shotgun. Then, Caldwell Madison, a youth also employed at Red Eagle Ranch, defended his boss, grabbing a rifle and shooting
Jess Dalton in the legs. (Perhaps Dalton was kin to members of the infamous
Dalton gang that robbed trains and banks in Kansas and Indian Territory during the early 1890s.) Louis Red Eagle was survived by his brother, Eddy Red
Eagle, Sr., who became an assistant chief to the Osages and a friend of John
Joseph Mathews; a widow, May Margaret Rusk Red Eagle; and a twelve-
year-old son, Victor Red Eagle.[67] Louis and May Red Eagle had enjoyed
summering at a cabin outside of Denver, Colorado, and wintering at the warm
seaside climate of Brownsville, Texas.[68]

Fifty years later, another Louis Red Eagle in the family line was horribly
murdered. Though the reign of terror was long over, wealthy Osages were
still being stalked and killed. In the 1980s, Victor Louis Red Eagle, known
by his middle name pronounced as "Lewie," was a great-grandson of two
revered principal chiefs: Paul Red Eagle and Fred Lookout. A fullblood
Osage described as generous and hospitable, and without known enemies,
Louis was the son of Victor G. Red Eagle and Julia Cecilia Lookout Red
Eagle. Louis Red Eagle was reportedly a millionaire, his wealth derived from
owning four Osage headrights. He might be called an openly gay man; he
was a two-spirited person who sometimes dressed in women's garb. Friendly
and hospitable, Louis Red Eagle enjoyed throwing lavish parties in his large
luxurious home outside of Hominy. He hosted guests on the two nights preceding his senseless murder. On October 26, 1987, while "wearing women's
clothing," he shared alcohol and cannabis with fifteen to twenty friends,
his housekeeper testified.[69] Two days before Halloween 1987, Louis was
murdered by seventeen-year-old Maurice Jerome "Trey" Barnes III; many
believed Trey was aided and abetted by his friend and Red Eagle's cousin,
Prentice Antwine Crawford, twenty-one years old. Barnes, possibly with
Crawford's help, struck Red Eagle twice with a bottle, put a plastic bag over
his head, and strangled him for fifteen minutes. After Red Eagle was dead,
Barnes and Crawford stole cash, then attempted to burn his house down by
lighting thirteen fires.

Barnes and his attorney claimed that Crawford and Barnes were practicing
Satanists. Barnes testified that Crawford claimed to be "the son of Satan"
and murdered Red Eagle as a human sacrifice to break a curse that he, Crawford, had placed upon Barnes.[70] Assistant U.S. Attorney Ben Baker said that

Crawford sacrificed a black cat.[71] "Satanic panic" ran amuck in the 1980s; this was the irrational fear of widespread satanic ritual abuse and violence, which was not supported by much evidence when investigated by social scientists. Stories of satanic abuse and murder were promulgated mostly via urban legends and Christian fundamentalist groups, and it is likely that Barnes's attorney deployed such a story as a cover-up. In any event, Crawford flatly denied that he was a Satanist or that he strangled his cousin. Osage County Sheriff's Deputy Larry Sharp testified that investigators who searched Crawford's bedroom found magazines and drawings suggesting he was involved in Satanism. Sharp admitted, however, that he could not tell the difference between a putatively satanic drawing and "works of Indian spiritualism." He may have found the Osage spider symbol on the covers of John Joseph Mathews's books to be satanic. Apparently, whatever was alien to the iconography of mainstream Christian belief was liable to suspicion of demonism.[72] Crawford and Barnes blamed each other for Red Eagle's murder, and the prosecution was not able to prove Crawford murdered his cousin, so he was acquitted of the charge of first-degree murder. Crawford was found guilty of burning his cousin's home, destroying evidence, and failing to report the crime of murder. The U.S. District Judge ordered Crawford to serve eight years for first-degree arson and two years for being an accessory after the fact in Red Eagle's death, but he served less than five years of the prison term.[73] His mother, Sandra Crawford, director of the Cherokee Nation adolescent drug and alcohol treatment center in Tahlequah, helped to destroy bloody clothing worn by her son and Barnes, and was convicted of a charge of accessory after the fact. Trey Barnes pled guilty to second-degree murder and received a twelve-year sentence.[74]

Louis Red Eagle's disloyal cousin, Prentice Crawford, is a tall Native American of Osage, Cherokee, and Dakota ancestry who in the late 1980s and 1990s weighed three hundred pounds.[75] Crawford studied art and drama at Haskell Indian Junior College in Lawrence, Kansas, where many of his ancestors had boarded. After Crawford was released from prison, he returned to Haskell and became student body president. In 1999, Prentice spoke candidly to Deb Taylor, an activist journalist, about being two-spirited. Crawford said he had been around gays and lesbians his whole life, "having known many in his tribe," stressing the presence of two-spirited people among Osages.[76] His late 1999 declaration in the *Liberty Press* that he was gay caused many in the Haskell community to turn against him, Taylor reported. In January 2000, Taylor stated that Crawford was "embroiled in a huge rumor mill at Haskell, with students and faculty alike speculating on his past and present lovers in unbecoming whispers." Haskell representatives failed to understand the traditional acceptance of multiple genders and sexualities found among most Indigenous tribes of North America, and instead voiced homophobic attitudes, it was argued. The same article, however, also reported that Crawford admitted that in his early twenties, he had been convicted of accessory to murder after the fact and served prison time, so this was also likely connected to the censure he received. Under pressure from several parties at Haskell, in early 2000, Crawford resigned his position of president of the Student Senate.[77] Prentice Crawford became an independent movie producer whose film projects include horrific themes.

Returning to the children of Chief Paul Red Eagle and Cecilia Red Eagle, their daughter Mary Red Eagle married Donald Big Elk and had a boy they called Sonny. In 1932 this "rich Osage family" was featured in a story with an accompanying photograph in the *Los Angeles Times*. Inspired by the successes of all-around athlete Jim Thorpe (Sac and Fox) that began in Stockholm in 1912, Donald Big Elk held an ambition to witness an Olympiad, which he and his family did in the summer of 1932. Although Donald was a husband, father, and high school graduate, he was not free to travel on a whim; rather, he "petitioned the government, of which he is a ward, for permission" to travel to Los Angeles for the Olympics. The Bureau of Indian Affairs appointed them a temporary guardian, Paul Trumbley, a friend of the couple. The four of them "motored to Los Angeles in the Big Elk family car." California was already familiar to Donald Big Elk, because he was graduated from Sherman Indian High School, a boarding school in Riverside. After being in Los Angeles for a week, the city Mathews had fled a few years earlier, Donald proclaimed, "this is a swell town."[78] Many Osages took up residence in the Los Angeles area in the 1920s, and there remains a significant Osage contingent in California.

Harry Red Eagle, the oldest son born to Paul and Cecilia, and his brother Eddy Red Eagle, Sr., a World War II Army veteran who served for three years in the South Pacific, survived and fared well. Harry became a tribal councilman, serving on the sixteenth council under Principal Chief Fred Lookout—John Joseph Mathews had been on the preceding two councils under Lookout. Harry Red Eagle ran for principal chief with both the Fullblood party and the Independent party, but not prevailing. Mathews listed Harry Red Eagle, or Xu-tha-zhu-dse, as an oral source for *The Osages: Children of the Middle Waters*, noting that Harry was the grandson of Henry Red Eagle, Tzi-Sho Shinkah.[79] In summer of 1952, Jo and Elizabeth Mathews hosted Eleanor and Rita Lottinville, the daughter and wife of Savoie Lottinville, a friend of the Mathewses and director of the University of Oklahoma Press, plus three of Eleanor's young friends. Jo and Dibbs, as he called her, took their guests to the colorful and entrancing I'n-Lo'n-Schka dances at Hominy Indian Village. With bells chiming and scalplock quivering, Harry Red Eagle and Principal

Chief Paul Pitts memorably walked over to the row of guests to shake hands with each girl and woman.[80] Harry married Mary Pappan and lived until 1965.

Harry and Mary's son, Harry Red Eagle, Jr. (1920–2011), became a much valued servant of the Osages. According to the *Osage News*, he served as committeeman for the June I'n-lo'n-schka dances for the Hominy district and was an Osage language instructor. Beginning in 1978, he served on the twenty-fifth through the twenty-ninth Osage tribal councils under the leadership of Principal Chiefs Sylvester Tinker, George Tall Chief, and Charles Tillman. Harry Red Eagle, Jr., also served as assistant principal chief from 1999 to 2002, to finish his uncle Ed Red Eagle, Sr.'s, term after he died in office. As noted, Ed Red Eagle, Sr., was a friend of John Joseph Mathews, and he served as a pallbearer at his funeral in 1979. For thirty-three years, Harry Red Eagle, Jr., worked at the McDonnell Douglas Corporation in Tulsa and was also a retired cattle rancher.[81] He was thus another example of an Osage who, at the risk of overgeneralizing, lived in two worlds: the White corporate world and the Osage world. The success stories of descendants of Cecilia Red Eagle and Chief Paul Red Eagle balance the sadder fates of other Red Eagles.

THE SQUIRREL IS A NATIVE

"The crows went to honkin' at me when I rode th'ough the Dog Crick timber, and I could see hundreds of squirrels friskin' in the blackjacks."

—spoken by Curly in *Green Grow the Lilacs* by Lynn Riggs[82]

Sunday, May 18, 1930, #21

The squirrel season opened the fifteenth of this month. The shooting of squirrels, though not considered a sport in many states, has always been a sport in the Osage, and ranks with the best, when the squirrel hunter stalks his game with a .22 calibre rifle. A certain skill is necessary when this arm is used, and thereby adds zest to the hunt, and one cannot understand why a shotgun would be used at any time when shooting this game. The game is often torn by the birdshot used, and must undergo a thorough cleaning before all the hair is cleaned from the holes into which the shot has pushed it on entering. Again, during much of the young squirrel season, the woods are full of nesting birds, and the loud booming of a shotgun reverberating along the hills and valleys, is almost like an infringement of the truce between man and the wildlife of the bottoms and blackjack hills. Also, not only is the sport of shooting this nimble animal with a rifle keener, but there is not much chance of slaughter.

From observation, one believes there is good sport in store for the squirrel hunter this season. There are many squirrels on the ridges and in the creek bottoms. Food was plentiful last year, and when this is the case, one looks forward to great numbers, but that is no reason why one should attempt to take his [legal] limit of ten in one day every time he goes out, or for that matter, at any time he goes out. It should not be a case of pride; any one can do it; therefore it is not a distinction, and to boast of "getting the limit" is puerile. The sport is the thing; the opportunity to get out into the leaf-shaded woods, and experience the delights of the chase, and the pleasure of quick and accurate shooting.

The squirrel is a native, and therefore he is ours, and it is up to us to see that he remains in the Osage in great numbers.

WALTER MATHEWS

On the front page of the May 18, 1930, issue containing Mathews's just-cited column, we find news on Osage politics involving John Joseph Mathews's first cousin, Walter Mathews, a son of his father William's brother, Edward Mathews.

In September 1861, Ed and Will Mathews as teenagers fled their home near an Osage settlement in Kansas Territory after Union troops killed their father and burned down his house. John Allen Mathews was a slaveholder who led armed bands of guerillas on raids against Union-sympathizing towns during "Bleeding Kansas." John A. Mathews had married two Osage sisters, the daughters of Old Bill Williams and a fullblood Osage woman called A-c'in-ga: first, Mary Ann, and after she died, Sarah Williams, mother of Ed and Will. Aided for a time by Confederate-sympathizing families, Will and Ed Mathews became itinerant cowboys and ranch hands in Texas. They eventually returned to the Osage Nation after the Osages sold their land in Kansas Territory and moved to their current reservation.

So it was that Ed's son, Walter Mathews, was born on the new Osage reservation. In *Twenty Thousand Mornings*, Mathews writes that Walter Mathews shared an "inherent, imperturbable sense of honor and justice and courage" with his siblings, Annie, Allan, and Owen Mathews. Walter became Jo's hero when he played end on the famous football team at Carlisle Indian Industrial School in Pennsylvania, on which Jim Thorpe famously played a few years later. Walter returned to Pawhuska by 1909. Owen Mathews was also sent to a boarding school, but he ran away and lived at his Uncle William's family home in Pawhuska for a time.[83]

Allegiances and party memberships in Osage politics could shift fairly rapidly. In May 1930, the *Journal-Capital* reported that the Independent party held a meeting called by Paul Red Eagle at the Osage Indian Agency, with Thomas B. Leahy acting as chairman of the meeting. Leahy, a lawyer, would go on to serve on the 14th Osage Tribal Council with Mathews four years later. At the meeting, Walter Mathews was one of five delegates nominated to meet with the Fullblood party and nominate a ticket to represent both parties. At this meeting, the Independent convention recommended Paul Red Eagle for principal chief and Harry Kohpay as assistant principal chief.[84] Walter Mathews, however, ultimately ran as a councilman on the Fullblood party's "National ticket" competing with the Independent party's "Red Eagle Ticket" and the Progressive party,[85] the latter of which won the election in a clean sweep, excepting one Independent councilman.

The Progressive party was embraced by John Joseph Mathews and his late father, William S. Mathews, who was a councilman on both the Osage

National Council and the Osage Tribal Council. The Progressives were headed by Chief Fred Lookout, who continued serving as principal chief after the election on June 2, 1930. Harry Kohpay became the assistant chief, and continued for another term, during which Jo Mathews worked with him while a member of the 14th Osage Tribal Council, his first of two terms. A celebration was held at George Labadie's ranch on June 29. Elected officials were sworn in, speeches were delivered, and barbeque, Osage foods, dances, and hand games were offered to guests. Large photographs of a long line of Osage guests were published above Mathews's column of July 2, 1930. Too bad cousin Walter Mathews never succeeded in his goal of being elected an Osage tribal councilman.[86]

On May 14, 1930, the *Journal-Capital* reported that "Joe Mathews is in Oklahoma City transacting business," and a week later, readers learned that Mathews had "returned from a few days' visit to Muskogee and Tulsa." Because no diaries are available for this period, details of these trips are unknown. At the time he was living in the apartment above the family garage, and he may have used these trips in part to escape from his uprightly Catholic mother and sisters. Mathews continued to spell his nickname as "Joe" until after he became a published author in 1932. After then, it is mostly spelled "Jo."[87]

SUMMER COMES TO THE OSAGE

Friday, May 23, 1930, #22

The trees have reached full leafage, and are casting dense shade over waving green grass. The green expanse of prairie and the spaces between groups of blackjacks are profusely covered with flowers, whose seeds were scattered by hazard, as though by the playful hand of Flora, whimsically entertaining herself. Patches of deep blue and clusters of pale blue and yellow dot the green. Flashing reds and quiet mauves and whites wave in the breeze or nod in the sun.

The mockingbird sings throughout the day and bursts into song during the night out of the sheer joy of living. The oriole sways on the branch of an elm and tells the world in clipped tones that life is good, his notes showing impatience with those who do not appreciate it. The wood thrush sends his evening song from the dense growths of trees, his notes sweetly sad but as liquid as rippling water. The robin takes a few minutes from his domestic cares to give his halting song from the top of a tree. The catbird, with the voice of an immature mockingbird, attempts to imitate his celebrated cousin, but cannot hold his rapid, high-pitched notes. The cardinal flashes through the trees, his scarlet feathers in bold contrast to the quiet shades of green, to perch for the space of a few seconds, and give his clear, whistling song. From convenient fence-posts, the quail whistles his repeated assurance that all is well with the world once more, and the indefatigable dickcissel, swaying on the flower of a weed, contributes to the life-filled world his weak song, a song monotonously repeated throughout the summer when all other songsters have been silenced by the heat.

Mauve cloud shadows move slowly across the green of the prairie. The distant hills become blue, forming a background for grazing cattle. Groups of steers stand and lie under the shade of a lone blackjack, the symbol of summer contentment. On the horizon, a cowboy rides slowly, man and horse in perfect harmony of movement, as the prairie breeze plays with the horse's tail. Far off on the highway, a car moves like some absurd beetle, leaving behind an elongated cloud of dust, which becomes dissipated by the same breeze that whispers in the grass, the same breeze that carries the plover's mournful note, and the plaintive chatter of the killdeer. The crow is more languid as he flies across the hills, and his hoarse caw is less frequent. The little sparrow-hawk hunts grasshoppers with indifference, and the murderous shrike sits for hours in the top of his thorn-bush.[88] The struggle of the species is at a low point, and the world is being filled with thousands of new individuals, that the species may not die.

Thus it is when summer comes to the Osage.

CHIEF BACON RIND, HENRY RED EAGLE, JOHN BIRD, WILLIAM MATHEWS, E-STAH-O-GRE-SHE, AND THE OSAGE TRIBAL COUNCIL VERSUS THE DEPARTMENT OF THE INTERIOR

Four days after the preceding column appeared, a story on the front page of the Pawhuska *Journal-Capital* read: "The ever-thinning ranks of the true old-time fullblood Osages was reduced again today with the death of E-stah-o-gre-she, also known as John Nah-hahscah-she." Born around 1876, E-stah-o-gre-she was described as an honest man, a respectable manager of his business, and "one of the finest old men of the tribe," although he would have been only in his mid-fifties when he died. From 1910 to 1912, he served on the Osage Tribal Council under Principal Chief Bacon Rind and Assistant Principal Chief Henry Red Eagle, and alongside John Joseph Mathews's father, William S. Mathews; in his transactions, he signed his name with a thumbprint. E-stah-o-gre-she was an influential, wise counselor who, during the 1920s prosperity and on, cautioned younger members of the tribe "against drinking liquor and wasting their money." An Osage service was held in his home, and a Catholic service was offered at Immaculate Conception Church in Pawhuska.[89]

While serving as councilmen, E-stah-o-gre-she, William S. Mathews, and several other reputable councilmen and attorneys were swept up in controversy with consequences beyond their control. The federal government, disapproving of an Osage Tribal Council business decision, encroached on Osage tribal sovereignty when Secretary of the Interior Walter L. Fisher, an appointment of President Taft, unjustly removed councilmen from their elected positions. First, in June 1912, soon after the Osage election, Secretary Fisher removed Principal Chief Bacon Rind (Wah-she-hah), Assistant Principal Chief Henry Red Eagle, and Thomas West, a mixed-blood councilman. Bacon Rind and West had been implicated in a 1906 bribery case concerning the leasing of hundreds of thousands of acres to the Uncle Sam Oil Company. In 1913, attorney T. J. Leahy countered that the federal government had set a historical precedent of giving favors and presents to Osage tribal leaders in attempts to influence their decisions, so at the time, Bacon Rind did not understand that his accepting the money was illegal.[90] Leahy also pointed out that Secretary Fisher removed Henry Red Eagle for a reason completely unrelated to the bribery that implicated Wah-she-hah and Thomas West. Red Eagle's election was barred because Fisher had learned that when the council visited Washington, DC, during the previous winter, a bartender sold Red Eagle a half-pint of whiskey, and was subsequently charged with the crime of selling intoxicating liquors to an Indian; Fisher claimed therefore that Red Eagle was drunk and negligent of his duties while in the capital. Showing solidarity, the tribal council refuted this charge, adding that Red Eagle had only missed one meeting, and that one had been hastily assembled.[91]

After Wah-she-hah and Henry Red Eagle were elected, Peter Bigheart plus fourteen more Osages signed a letter sent to the Department of the Interior stating that Wah-she-hah's part in the 1906 scandal should disqualify his election. Peter Bigheart, traditional Osage fullblood and Civil War veteran, had fought against the allotment act with his celebrated relative, former chief James Bigheart. The Secretary of the Interior decreed that Bacon Rind, Red Eagle, and West be removed from office. Despite this order, in early July, Wah-she-hah and his council were formally seated "amid the traditional feasting and dancing" always accompanying the occasion, Terry Wilson writes.[92] Bacon Rind and Red Eagle continued to act as de facto chiefs, and the seven remaining council members continued to regularly meet. Secretary Fisher had told the councilmen to appoint new chiefs, which they chose not to do, and as a result of their exercise of tribal sovereignty, Fisher punished them, removing all seven Osages from their elected positions on the Osage council in January 1913: E-stah-o-gre-she, William S. Mathews, Harry Kohpay, A. F. Brown, Oscar A. Ririe, Peh-tse-moie (Richard Firewalk), and Me-ke-wah-ti-an-kah.[93]

The rationale behind Fisher's arbitrary removal of the remaining councilmen is more complicated than at first appears. In February 1912, the Osage council stunned the Department of the Interior and the powerful Indian Territory Illuminating Oil Company (ITIO), which had long been agitating for a renewal of their "blanket lease," when they announced their tentative approval of the block grant proposals made by the Uncle Sam Corporation, led by H. H. Tucker, plus three more proposals made by local bidders Henry J. O'Connell, Wesley M. Dial, and John Lyman Bird. The ITIO, which was consolidated by Henry Foster prior to his death in 1901, then taken over by his brother, Edward Foster, owned and controlled the Phoenix Oil Company and Osage Oil Company, and supervised the subleasing of the entire Osage reservation.[94] Wesley Dial, former chairman of the State Republican Committee, was a prosperous landowner and businessman who lived on a large homestead north of Pawhuska featuring a panoramic view, which locals called Mount Dial. In 1896, Wesley married Eliza Penn, an Osage widow with a Quaker name, and began advocating for the tribe in dealings with the government. In 1916, Oklahoma historian Joseph Thoburn ventured that Wesley Dial was probably "the most influential white man in the Osage country." Although Dial only had four months of schooling total, "probably no man in Northeastern Oklahoma has handled larger financial sums and more important business transactions" than him.[95] Wesley Dial died in late 1917.

A more vocal advocate for the Wahzhazhe was the Sioux-Osage lawyer and orator John F. Palmer, a mentor to John Joseph Mathews. John Palmer is credited with conceiving the communal plan by which Osages with headrights equally share the oil and mineral wealth of the reservation. Oklahoma Senator Thomas P. Gore, the grandfather, mentor and namesake of author Gore Vidal, called Palmer "the most eloquent Indian alive," and the efforts of Palmer and Dial were celebrated by the *Osage Journal*.[96]

The case of John Lyman Bird is complicated and sometimes troubling. A longtime friend of the Mathews family, Bird was an old-time trader turned banker who had worked for Jo Mathews's father at the Osage Mercantile and then the Citizens National Bank. John was the father of Jack Bird, Jo's longtime friend. John L. Bird reportedly loved and admired the Osages, spoke Osage fluently (and enough Kaw, Ponca, and Omaha for business purposes), and earned the trust of nearly every fullblood. He collected artifacts, photographs, and books about the Wahzhazhe, some of which he later sold to the Osage Nation, becoming the foundation of the collection of the Osage Tribal Museum when it opened in 1938.[97] "The Osages of my day were gentlemen in every sense of the word," John Bird once told John Joseph Mathews, who wrote a lengthy tribute to Bird upon his death for the Pawhuska newspaper, "in a day when there were few white gentlemen in this country." Mathews even went as far as to say that eventually, Bird was so immersed in Osage life that he "became one of them in every respect. He adjusted himself to them so perfectly that his mannerisms and instincts were Indian rather than white. People said he was more Indian than the Osages themselves. The Osages called him *Wah Shinka*, bird." John kept an office in the back of the bank, even after he was no longer employed there, and after the oil boom died, Osage elders sought him out for advice, Mathews wrote. Mathews was apparently not aware of the more questionable side of this family friend. Despite John Bird's more admirable traits, he was nevertheless an usurious Indian loan shark who became filthy rich. Early on, Bird had benefited from a dubious land swindle in which a federal judge ruled against the Osages.

Born in 1864, John Bird was the son of a prominent doctor in northwestern Missouri. At age nineteen, Johnny Bird lit out for "the Osage," Indian Territory, and worked at the Kaw Agency Trading Post co-owned by L. A. Wismeyer of Fairfax and T. M. Finney of Bartlesville, who later became Bird's uncle through marriage. At the time, the same agent served both the Kaws and the Osages, who were descended from the same larger group. This was a good place to be a trader, Mathews explained in his obituary of Bird, because it was near the plains "where the buffalo still moved in small herds. Small though these herds had become, they furnished the Osages and the Kaws with robes for trade to the traders and with hides for their clothing and their lodges as well as meat for the rack and the black kettles." Johnny Bird had been influenced to migrate to the Osage by his younger brother, Dr. R. E. Bird, government physician to the Kaws. Dr. Bird later gave up his medical practice to become a trader in Pawhuska and Gray Horse from 1884 to 1898, when he returned, enriched, to Rock Port, Missouri.[98] Early settler John N. Florer established the Old Red Store at the Osage agency, forming a partnership with Mr. Dunlap. Bird came to Pawhuska to work as a clerk for Florer and Dunlap, licensed Indian traders. In 1888, Bird went to Gray Horse, the village of the Big Hill band of Osages, and established a business with his brother and another partner. In 1891, Bird married Colonel Florer's daughter, Maude, right in the store. They had two children, John Florer Bird (Jack), John Joseph's close friend and University of Oklahoma fraternity brother, and Robert Emmet Bird, named for his uncle. Colonel Florer became very wealthy and wielded great power in the region. The colonel was well known in Washington, DC, and it was said that his sway in the 1890s led to the signing of the original Foster-ITIO oil blanket lease.[99] John L. Bird subsequently engaged in business with his father-in-law for twelve years at Gray Horse under the banner Florer and Bird. Then, in 1906 the men quit that business and went into cattle ranching on their ranch lying east of Gray Horse.

Through his business endeavors, John Bird was able to accumulate a great deal of financial and social capital. In the spring of 1906, he established the Fairfax National Bank with Dyke Carlton Maher and was its first president briefly before serving as its longtime vice president.[100] Prentiss Price and F. Gentner Drummond of Hominy, Osage County, were among the bank's stockholders; Drummond ran his family's business, the Hominy Trading Post, and during the 1920s became involved in several other enterprises. The trading post sold clothes, furniture, even caskets, and had an embalming room on the top floor.[101] D. C. Maher was the cashier, and later secretary and a director of the Big Hill Trading Company in Fairfax; Maher, Homer Huffaker, and John Bird were the incorporators of this mercantile, and Huffaker had been president and general manager.[102] The Big Hill Trading Company later became closely connected with the sinister Osage murders of the 1920s. D. C. Maher was a major link in a banking syndicate fleecing Osages that included Bird, H. H. Brenner, and H. G. Burt—a future conspirator in the Osage reign of terror murders.[103] Back in 1885 when he was eight years old, D. C. Maher had moved with his family from New York to Indian Territory. He worked for an Indian trader at Hominy, becoming fluent in Osage; then he worked for Prentiss Price in a mercantile business. Maher, Price, and a third bought and ran a store in the town of Cleveland, in the Osage, for six years before coming to Fairfax and co-organizing the bank. Maher also owned a cattle ranch and was a breeder of thoroughbred Herefords.[104] He married a younger woman,

Adelia Genevieve Elwell (Veva), in 1904, and they had four children. After D. C. Maher's death, Veva remarried the nefarious H. G. Burt.

John L. Bird accumulated visible authority along with vast capital. When Oklahoma became a state in 1907, and the Osage reservation became known as Osage County, Bird became the first Sherriff of Osage County. After he resigned in 1909, he became associated with the Citizens Nation Bank in Pawhuska, which Jo's father, William S. Mathews, had co-organized and served as president, after it moved from the original frame building that later housed the Constantine Café, to a brick building west of the Council House. John Bird served as vice president of the bank under W. S. Mathews for a period. William Mathews remained a bank director until his death in March 1915, while John Bird "remained associated with the bank through all of its vicissitudes and changes of location, until 1926-27," when he was said to have left due to ill heath, moving into the Triangle Building with his son, Jack. The Triangle Building in Pawhuska, after decades of desuetude and neglect, has been renovated and serves tourists.[105]

In 1909, John Bird was a huge beneficiary of what in retrospect seems not only a violation of Osage tribal sovereignty, but also a legal theft of a valuable and culturally significant piece of Osage land at Gray Horse. The U.S. government forced the Osages to give a tract of land to John Bird's wife, Maude, against the protest of the tribe and a lawsuit taken out by Peter Bigheart. During the allotment period, the land on which the trader John N. Florer lived, traded, built a luxurious home, and raised his family for twenty-five years had been set aside for him, even though he was not Osage, and he was allowed to pay an apprised sum for the land. But the Osage Nation denied the heirs of Florer the right to inherit forty acres of land at Gray Horse after his death, explaining that the land had been a personal grant to John Florer only. The Osages resented the donation of this land to the Florer family, because in their view it was "entirely unnecessary and an injustice to the tribe to take from them this valuable tract." To prevent the land from passing to the Florers, the Osages asked their chief to refuse to sign the deed. Regardless, federal Judge Cotteral ruled against Peter Bigheart and the Osages.[106]

John Joseph Mathews may have been unaware of this incident or the time in early 1915 when John L. Bird was called to testify before the Joint Commission to Investigate Indian Affairs. Bird's own testimony and that of others exposed on public record his usury and the general climate of rank exploitation in the Osage. The Uncle Sam oil lease controversy drew attention to Bird's financial dealings as a banker in Pawhuska and Fairfax, exposing him as a loan shark whose specialty and clientele was Osages. Though Bird may have loved the Osages, he likened them to five-year-old children who turned to their friends for advice with utter trust. "I have the confidence of ninety-nine out of a hundred there. Anything that I say, they absolutely believe is correct. I have never taken a dollar from an Indian in my life that he didn't know I was getting." In March 1913, Bird formed a partnership with H. H. Brenner to issue loans to Osages and to keep the vague book-keeping of such shady dealings separate from those of their respective banks. Locals caustically referred to Brenner and Bird as "the downtown clearing house," including the attorney Preston Shinn, who testified before a joint commission that a similar clearing house operated at the Osage agency, also conducting dubious transactions. A native of Latvia, H. H. Brenner, made his way to the Osage via England and Oxford, Mississippi (William Faulkner's hometown). He became president of First National Bank of Pawhuska and he owned interests in banks at Prue, Foraker, and Bigheart (now Barnsdall), towns in Osage County connected to the oil industry, and served as president of each bank at one time. In 1903, Brenner became president of the Pawhuska Oil & Gas Company.[107] Bird testified that he and Brenner formed the part-nership because bank examiners had wanted the Citizens Bank to part with questionable "Indian notes" that would not stand scrutiny. Brenner charged Osages 40 percent annual interest on loans (10 percent quarterly) when the state law's limit was 10 percent annually. That said, 40 percent, though usu-rious and illegal, was the lowest interest rate that investigators found being charged. According to one Osage, Pawhuskan lawyer J. D. Mitchell had charged an astronomical 10,220 percent interest per annum. The joint com-mission chairman remarked sarcastically that Osage superintendent James A. Carroll had given Bird and Brenner "a very great eulogy for beneficence and philanthropy—and a beautiful eulogy it was—characterizing them as old traders. But it did not occur to me, in the case of a man who was charg-ing 10 per cent a quarter to the Indians, who always paid him, and who never disputed the correctness of his accounts—that there was much philanthropy in that." Superintendent Carroll was well aware of dozens of cases in which Osages had been charged interest much more outrageous than 40 percent, but never reported *any* of them to the district attorney. James Carroll admitted his belief that it was actually good when an Osage squandered his wealth and got in a fix, because then he must learn responsibility: you cannot legislate frugality, he averred. Superintendent Carroll thereby tried to justify how he barely lifted a finger to slow the outrageous chiseling and cheating of Osages transpiring all over Osage County, especially in Fairfax and Pawhuska. Fit-tingly, in July 1914, the Osage council passed a resolution asking for an investigation of the agency, and a petition was circulated asking for James A. Carroll's removal. John Joseph Mathews would later parody the superin-tendent with a rustic, shady character in his novel *Sundown* named Carroll, to be discussed later in this book.[108]

Pawhuskan lawyer Preston A. Shinn, previously attorney for the Osages, testified that other bankers were involved in the Brenner and Bird operation including D. C. Maher of Fairfax, Prentiss Price, George Treadway of Hominy, and one or two more. Invariably, funds paid out to Osages rapidly found their way into the banks controlled by Brenner and Bird.[109] Brenner, Bird, and company would aggressively hunt for old "Indian claims," buy them up, and then take the claims to the agency, seeking payment. After a few weeks, Shinn testified, it became obvious that only certain individuals were given exclusive access to do business with the agency, namely Bird, Brenner, and the parties they represented. These insider parties were given carte blanche, and this became apparent to the general public. Therefore, many individuals who were not in a position to make such collections themselves, "knowing that the managers of this downtown clearing house were getting away with what they wanted, would assign their claims at a discount to these parties." Things degenerated to the point where any Osage, no matter "his capacity" or if he was an alcoholic, could apply for his funds, which would arrive, and were paid out under supervision of Superintendent Carroll. In "scores and scores" of instances, by the time Brenner and Bird finished settling with an Osage's creditors, he or she was nearly penniless: in many cases, their entire payment, at the time $3,820, would already be "wiped out"—in 2018 this sum would be worth a staggering ninety-eight thousand dollars. Around May and June 1913, while the Osage Agency was paying out these funds, frequent poker games were held in the private homes of a group of insiders: A. W. Hurley, who was the president of Pawhuska Citizens Bank (where W. S. Mathews had been president and remained on its board), Bird, Brenner, Carroll, and others. Brenner was implicated in insider trading, having sold shares below value to Carroll, Vernon Whiting, and a third man at the Osage Agency.[110] Shinn testified that in 1914 the "clearing house" was still in place, making illegal loans to Osages. By 1917, H. H. Brenner was the president of Pawhuska Oil & Gas Company, W. T. Leahy was its vice president, and A. N. Ruble, cashier of the First National Bank of Pawhuska, was its secretary-treasurer. A. N. Ruble was the father of Jack Ruble, Jo Mathews's other high school friend and, later, University of Oklahoma fraternity brother who was called Jack.[111]

At least John L. Bird does not seem to have been involved in murder plots. On the contrary, during the mid-1920s, he took action to alert the federal government about the failure of Oklahoma state law enforcement and courts in the investigation and prosecution of the Osage murders. Lonnie Underwood notes in *Osage Indian Reign of Terror* that the Federal Bureau of Investigation learned that in early 1925, John Bird, who had "associated himself with a watchdog agency that advocated for Indian affairs," had alerted Senator Charles Curtis, who had Kaw and Osage ancestry and later became Herbert Hoover's vice president, that the Oklahoma State Court appeared "overwhelmed, helpless and disinterested in prosecuting the Osage murder cases." Bird advised that "the best friend of the Indians was the federal government" and urged a thorough federal prosecution to protect all American Indians in the future.[112]

Although in this instance John Bird advocated on behalf of the Osages, it is concerning that a future murder conspirator, Herbert G. Burt, became a partner of Bird's, taking over half of Brenner's "Indian business." Bird testified that H. G. Burt "takes care of the books and looks after any business that may come up." The attorney Preston Shinn thought Burt was in charge of "the land end of the Citizens National Bank and of the firm of Bird & Brenner" and used sharp practices.[113] Shinn put on the record that H. G. Burt habitually borrowed money at six percent, then would opt not to repay the loan, even though he was able; Burt preferred to continue paying interest, because he could turn around and loan that same money to an Osage at a much higher interest rate, turning a profit. Clearly Burt only cared about enriching himself, heedless of the financial problems this would cause Osages.

According to several pieces of evidence, in 1923 H. G. Burt was a perpetrator in the killing of W. W. Vaughan, the Pawhuskan attorney of Osage murder victim George Bigheart, who had died the day before Vaughan. As will be discussed later in more detail, Vaughan was thrown off a train north of Oklahoma City to prevent him from sharing incriminating information. The guardian of Grace Bigheart, George Bigheart's wife, was none other than John Bird.[114] Preston Shinn first testified to Burt's partnership with Brenner and Bird when he revealed the partnership was involved in graft related to construction. Many houses and barns had been contracted by Osages in 1913, but often, their financing was fishy. In many cases the contracts for these houses were let not to the contractor, but to bankers, and then sublet by these bankers to a contractor, turning a profit. These contracts were drawn up at the Osage Agency under supervision of Superintendent Carroll. Many contractors complained that they were unable to secure any building contracts through the agency, but rather had to acquire them from Bird, Brenner, Burt, or "one or two others" Shinn left unnamed, "who are next to the Indians, and also next to the agency." Some Osages had built as many as three houses that sat unoccupied; the purpose of this frenzy of construction was solely to get Osage money in circulation. Many Osages didn't know how to invest their money, and "his close friends advised him to build," close friends such as John Bird, beloved and trusted by the fullbloods. Needless to say, both Bird and Brenner were also guardians to more so-called incompetent Osages.[115]

Dyke C. Maher of the Fairfax National Bank was the Fairfax point-person in the syndicate or "clearing house" of Bird, Brenner, and Burt. D. C. Maher was another creditor who contrived to have Osage checks from the agency routed directly to him. During the time when Maher was partnered with H. G. Burt, Maher's wife, the former Adelia Genevieve Elwell (Veva), became "good friends" with Burt as their families "were thrown in contact frequently." D. C. Maher died mysteriously on September 22, 1916, at only thirty-eight years of age. Oddly enough, Burt's wife, Mayme McDonnell Burt, died suspiciously exactly a year later to the day. An Independence, Kansas, newspaper reported that early on the day of September 22, 1917, as Mayme Burt and her husband were riding in an automobile, "she became frightened at a bumblebee and jumped out of the machine before her husband could prevent her. She struck on her head and never regained consciousness." Mayme Burt died that night in a hotel room in Caney, Kansas, just over the state line and northeast of the Osage Reservation; the exact location of the accident was unspecified.[116] How long was Mayme Burt, unconscious, left unattended? Why was she not taken to a hospital? It seems unlikely she would have jumped out of a moving car to flee a bumblebee, the gentlest and friendliest of the bees. In retrospect, given what we know of H. G. Burt's character, a more likely scenario is that Burt pulled over to the side of the road in a remote spot and brained Mayme with a blunt object. Or perhaps he reached across her as he drove, flung open her door, and shoved her out—much like he allegedly helped throw W. W. Vaughan, alive or already murdered, out of a moving train. In light of discoveries following her death, it seems quite likely that H. G. Burt murdered his wife in order to marry his mistress, the widow Veva Maher, "a woman of great charm and popularity." Burt may have had a hand in D. C. Maher's death, too. Defying statistical probability, Mayme Burt's parents, the McDonnells, both died within three weeks of their daughter's death. Their suspiciously timed deaths may have been hastened by grief, but it is possible that H. G. Burt hired someone to drive up to remote Cass County, Missouri, to murder one or both of her parents, to accelerate his inheriting her family money (no cause of death can be found for Mr. and Mrs. McDonnell). Veva Maher had moved to Winfield, Kansas, after her husband's death, to educate her children there, she said. In January 1922, amid the Osage murders, H. G. Burt and Veva Maher surprised friends and family members when they traveled from Winfield to Kansas City, where they were married and had their honeymoon. Prosperous H. G. Burt at the time was president of Lumbermen's National Bank of Pawhuska, and owned a large general store.[117]

David Grann deftly tied together strands of evidence to form the case against H. G. Burt as a murder suspect, a major contribution, yet he gives little background or insight into Burt and his past. Burt is not separate from the Bill Hale faction but was part of a network of deep connections going back to Fairfax. One major link Grann failed to make is that Herbert Burt was not just a "Pawhuska banker," but was also, significantly, deeply rooted in Fairfax, close to the village of Gray Horse, the home village of the Big Hill band of the Wahzhazhe people who were the primary targets of the murders (another key distinction that Grann does not make). A serious examination into Burt's background reveals he was deeply connected to several members of the Hale contingent, going way back. These connections were seemingly unnoticed by David Grann, who only noted that Burt and Hale were in ca-hoots and likely divvied up the money resulting from the murder of George Bigheart. A Fairfax newspaper profiling Burt said "H. G. Burt might be properly classed among the pioneer merchants of Fairfax. He located here in the grocery business in 1904" and for years, was "engaged in general merchandising and trading" with the Osages. In 1910, Herbert Burt sold his business to W. E. Copeland, a name that will reappear, and another; then Burt supposedly retired. During those first six years he was in business, "he bought a business house and built a fine home in the Tall Chief addition, which he now occupies with his family. Since selling out, he has invested largely in Osage lands." H. G. Burt invested in, or perhaps more accurately, swindled Osages out of their lands, in sharp practices that were common in those days. Yet on the surface, Burt lived a wholesome family life; his son Harold was in the first Boy Scout troop in Fairfax. H. G. Burt, though already wealthy and claiming to be retired, was in fact not finished with business at all. In a way he was just getting started, about to move into banking in Pawhuska; within a few years, he had joined the shady partnership of Bird and Brenner, issuing loans to Osages at outrageous, illegal interest rates.

By the end of 1919, H. G. Burt was vice president of the Liberty National Bank in Pawhuska, where G. B. Mellott was the president and C. E. Riley was the cashier. Their creepy newspaper ad invited readers to come "actively in touch—in friendly touch—with one of our officers."[118] In September 1922, amid the Osage murders, Burt and Riley traveled to Winfield, Kansas, to tend to business affairs.[119] Oftentimes, White businessmen of Osage County would conduct financial affairs in Arkansas City, Winfield, Independence, and other southern Kansan towns, moving money out of the county and state.

To return to the Osage oil controversy that ultimately removed Bacon Rind, Henry Red Eagle, and W. S. Mathews, many stakeholders including John Bird, Wesley Dial, and O'Connell believed that the ITIO was surreptitiously guided by John D. Rockefeller's Standard Oil Company, which in turn was deeply connected to the Department of the Interior. Standard Oil purchased crude oil from ITIO, which was piped north to be processed at their plant in Neodesha, Kansas.[120] In 1909, the Department of Justice filed a federal antitrust lawsuit against Standard Oil, claiming the company inhibited trade through its preferential deals with railroads, controlling pipelines, and unfair business practices such as price-cutting, deployed to drive smaller competitors out of business. In May 1911, the Supreme Court ordered the dissolution of Standard Oil Company into thirty-four independent companies, ruling it was in violation of the Sherman Antitrust Act.[121] After the Osage tribal council made their announcement, ITIO officers, representatives of the Producers Association, and assorted oilmen all met in Washington, DC, to discuss the four bids with Assistant Secretary of the Interior Samuel Adams and the Osage council. After hearing the discussion, Adams rejected the Osage council's approval of the Uncle Sam block-grants and the independent proposals. In Osage County, reaction was quick and scathing. Secretary Adams was acquiescing to pressure from the ITIO Company, who were in cahoots with Standard Oil, it was claimed.[122] In January 1913, Fisher accused the councilmen of making decisions on oil leases contrary to the best interests of the tribe, and allowing themselves to be unduly influenced by outsiders in business matters. Councilman West apparently made a written confession, but the other council members were not given a forum to defend themselves. Nevertheless, most Osages continued to accept the authority of Bacon Rind and Henry Red Eagle.[123]

This ouster was a violation of Osage sovereignty, the right of the Osage Nation to govern itself. The concept that tribes have an inherent right to self-governance lies at the heart of their constitutional status. Attorney T. J. Leahy and councilman Alpheus H. Brown lobbied aggressively against Fisher's order of a special election to replace the expelled council.[124] Brown instituted legal proceedings, arguing that Fisher lacked the authority to remove the chiefs and councilmen from a position of traditional honor and stature. In late January 1913, members of the Osage council including W. S. Mathews and E-stah-o-gre-she, plus the Uncle Sam Oil Company, retaliated, launching charges with the House Committee on Indian Affairs, seeking a mandamus[125] with the District Supreme Court that would compel Secretary of the Interior Fisher to show why he should not reinstate the removed chiefs and councilmen. They accused Fisher of mistreating the tribal council and the Osages as a whole. By ordering a new council to be elected that would do his bidding, Fisher coerced the Osages to lease with interests of the Standard Oil Company, denying them the right to lease with independent companies. This fired up controversy in Washington, DC, spread by national newspapers.[126]

Unfortunately, the Osage council members were not successful in restoring themselves to office. The federal government subsequently wielded legal power to further punish them. In October 1913, two federal grand jury indictments each were returned in Enid, Oklahoma, against eleven men including officials of the Uncle Sam Oil Company, prominent attorneys, and Osage leaders such as W. S. Mathews—but not E-stah-o-gre-she for whatever reason. Eleven were indicted for conspiring "to balk the department of the interior in the exercise of its governmental functions in the Osage counseling of the Osage lands for oil and gas purposes." They were also indicted with conspiring to "alienate and destroy the confidence of the Osages in their guardian, the secretary of the interior," it was reported. Although the Osages were a nation within a nation, the White man said the Indians needed their guardianship, just as Osage individuals were deemed "incompetent," limited in rights, and assigned guardians, most of whom were on the take. Also indicted was Jo's mentor, the silver-tongued Sioux-Osage attorney, John Palmer.[127]

No evidence was ever found proving corruption or undue influence, however. Secretary Fisher already held the ultimate right of approval of any lease the Osages proposed; therefore, it seems he was punishing the council for proactively planning leases, which was simply an exercise of sovereignty. In 1914 the charges were dropped against Wah-she-hah (Chief Bacon Rind) by Judge Cotterol, who granted a demurrer—an objection that an opponent's point is irrelevant or invalid, while granting the factual basis of the point—to the evidence against him, and in October, all of the indicted were acquitted.[128] A Salina, Kansas, newspaper attacked this case as unjust and abusive to the Osages and the Uncle Sam Oil men. With rhetorical flourish, the *Daily Union* broke down the absurdity of the 1913 charges:

Consider for a moment that these eleven men of character and reputation were indicted for an alleged crime not defined in any statute and forced to defend themselves in court at heavy expense in time and money against the charge of having conspired to thwart the plans of the secretary of the interior. The property involved belonged to the Indians. Eight of the indicted men are Indians and are part owners either in their own right or through their wives and children of the mineral wealth involved. No lease could have any value until it was approved by the secretary of the interior, and that approval was denied. There was no evidence that anyone connected either with the Indians or the oil company used any devious methods of any undue influence in securing the disputed leases. . . . The government had no material interest in the property involved [and thus] could not be defrauded where it had no interests. In the face of all these things, the federal government procured the indictment of these eleven men, thereby branding them as persons of doubtful or criminal character, forced them to come into court and for four weeks defend themselves against charges that if proven, constituted no crime. The United States probably spent a hundred thousand dollars in trying to make a jury believe [they] committed a crime when they undertook to develop the oil and gas resources of the Osage nation through a perfectly open and legitimate contract that provided every safeguard for the interests of the Indians.

It took the jury only twenty-one minutes to reach a verdict of not guilty for all of the defendants. The American people were growing weary of the abuse of federal courts, and many began to believe that "instead of being the seat of justice, the federal bench has become an agency through which the great criminal corporations like the Standard Oil Company punish all those who venture to do business independent of monopoly," the *Daily Union* of Salina, Kansas, declaimed.[129]

Like E-stah-o-gre-she, William S. Mathews, according to both his son and family friend Violet Willis, was known for his profound sense of fairness and honesty.[130] John Joseph Mathews never wrote about his father's unjust removal from the tribal council. The trial was seemingly detrimental to the health of Judge Mathews, as he was known later in life. He died five months later, in March 1915, at age sixty-six. William Mathews's funeral and the exigency of handling of his business affairs interrupted his son's second semester at the University of Oklahoma in Norman, spoiling his chances of playing on the basketball team.

GALLERY: PICTURES OF JUNE

Sunday, June 1, 1930, #23

As June comes to the sandstone hills and the high prairie, there are changes of mood. There is not as much spontaneity and joy of living. Instead there are responsibilities and the care of the young. The erstwhile brilliant males in many cases are beginning to assume the somber colours of the workaday world. During midday, the woods are almost silent; the songs are heard mostly in the early morning and in the late afternoon. The stridulations of the insects seem to accentuate the heat of the day; voices are in harmony with the dreamt languor. The cuckoo raises his voice, a long series of croaks upon which one may put any interpretations, because of the dissatisfaction and remonstrance which he puts in them. He calls on the hottest days, during the summer, and his croaks are a part of the midday voices and the oppressive heat of summer. His croak seems to remonstrate against the heat and the drought, and this fact caused the early settlers in the Osage to call him the "rain crow." They believed he was calling for rain, but certainly his croak is more petulant and insolent than a petition to the rain gods ought to be.

The streams are becoming clear near the sources, but lower downstream, they are still coloured with sediments. Many perch have been taken high up in small branches that feed the heads of the larger streams, and in many cases have become stranded in small pools of water isolated at the heads of these small branches. It is possible they have gone up to spawn.

The cheerful call of the quail is not heard as often this summer as in other years, and one is ready to give credence to the many stories of bevies found frozen during the severe snowstorm last winter. Yet there is still the mystery of the disappearance of these birds from the ridges. Many of them left the ridges just before the storm, or just after it began, and failed to return. It is too early to make a statement about their return to nest in their old haunts. Certainly one does not hear as many calling as in previous summers.

Our gallery of pictures is still open: there is no closing for hot weather. The pictures change throughout the year in form and color. The colors, movement and life of the spring are changing to pastels and the hazy tranquility of summer. The clouds move more slowly across a slightly bluer sky, and the movement of wildlife is more deliberate. The cattle that graze in fields of yellow and white flowers move more contentedly. The hills seem to be sleeping in the heat of the day, burdened with their mature vegetation, and lie dreamily under purple shadows in the late evening. Water glimmers everywhere on the prairie. The grass waves in rhythm with the languorous tempo of June.

INDIAN BASEBALL: THE WILD HORSES OF THE OSAGE

Juxtaposed with Mathews's poetic column in the *Journal-Capital* is a trove of Indian baseball news. Native Americans participated in baseball enthusiastically, and beginning in the late nineteenth century, the game became very popular in Indian Territory and at Indian boarding schools. Lumbee scholar Joseph B. Oxendine reasons: "Baseball is a noble game, a game of tradition, of allegiance and camaraderie. It is played at an unhurried pace, with no clock." The character of the game is therefore consistent with "traditional American Indian traits and attitude toward sport." It is not surprising that young Natives, Osages among them, took to baseball "as soon as it was introduced to them in boarding schools during the last two decades of the nineteenth century."[131]

In the late 1880s and early 1890s, Harry Kohpay (Wah-she-wah-hah), an Osage fullblood known for his muscled physique, became a baseball star at the assimilationist Carlisle Indian Industrial School in Pennsylvania (class of 1891) and at Eastman Business College in Poughkeepsie, New York. Enrolled as a student off and on for fourteen years, Kohpay was a pitcher and infielder who threw hard and tricked batters with an unorthodox delivery. According to his student record, Kohpay was the first Osage to graduate from Carlisle, and he felt that his education empowered him to serve and lead his people.[132] After returning to the Osage, in 1909 Harry Kohpay worked as assistant clerk at the Osage agency and served as secretary and translator for the tribal council. In this capacity, Kohpay joined efforts to remove individuals from the tribal rolls who had been fraudulently enrolled, testifying at length before a Senate commission.[133] He later was elected a tribal councilman himself and in 1913, he was one of the seven who, along with John Joseph Mathews's father, William S. Mathews, were unfairly removed by the Secretary of the Interior. In 1930, literally the day after the preceding column appeared, Harry Kohpay was elected assistant principal chief of the Osages. He was a great advocate of education for the Osages, and made a point of sending his son and daughter to Carlisle Indian School.

Mathews's late Osage father Will Mathews, a sports fan, had financed a semi-professional baseball team in Pawhuska, and he and his wife Jennie were often seen in the stands cheering them on.[134] Indian Territory's embrace of baseball is dramatized by Choctaw author LeAnne Howe in her novel *Miko Kings: An Indian Baseball Story* (2007), partially set in Indian Territory, 1903, prior to Oklahoma statehood. In this novel and in her chapter "Embodied Tribalography" collected in *Choctalking on Other Realities*, Howe has pointed out similarities between baseball and traditional Southeastern Indigenous games that involve sticks, balls, a central mound, and bases but no time limit; moreover, a hitter runs the bases—or four directions—in a counterclockwise fashion, like a stomp dance.[135]

Returning to that day's news, the Pawhuska Indians team defeated the Pawhuska Blues, fourteen to five, in a Memorial Day matchup. The Indians were running strong, with twelve wins and two losses thus far. Later in June, the Pawhuska Indians even beat a "star" touring team, the California Indians, comprised of "graduate athletic celebrities of Sherman Institute of Southern California and other Indian stars assembled from various tribes" around the country. Five days later, the Pawhuska Indians beat the Pawnee Indians.[136]

The Pawnee Nation, neighbors and historical enemies of the Osages, boasted baseball star Mose YellowHorse, who early in his career played for the Pawnee Agency school, Chilocco Indian School, the Ponca City Oilers, and the Arkansas Travelers. In 1917 he achieved a seventeen-zero season record pitching for Chilocco School, and word traveled fast about this prodigy who threw a good fastball and a "sweet curveball." During 1921 and 1922, YellowHorse entered the Major Leagues, pitching for the Pittsburgh Pirates, becoming the first fullblood Native American to play major league baseball, it is claimed. Yet by the early 1920s, many American Indians had played in the Major Leagues. Most famously, Charles Bender (Ojibwe) was a fiery pitcher for manager Connie Mack's Philadelphia Athletics, and the all-around Heracles Jim Thorpe (Sac and Fox) gained renown not only for playing six seasons of baseball with the New York Giants between 1913 and 1919, but also for becoming perhaps the best football player of his generation, and an Olympian who won gold in the decathlon and pentathlon events in 1912, inspiring Sweden's King Gustav to hail him as the greatest athlete in the world. But YellowHorse had a memorable personality and playing style, and although he only pitched thirty-eight games in the Major Leagues, he made a deep impression. He gained notoriety in 1922 for beaning Ty Cobb of the Detroit Tigers in an exhibition game; Cobb, who always crowded the plate and taunted pitchers, had to be carried off the field on a stretcher. According to the story told by YellowHorse's Pawnee friends back home to his biographer Todd Fuller, Cobb was hurling anti-Indian jibes at the pitcher. During the Pawnee's tenure, a chant emerged, "Bring in YellowHorse!" paying homage to his skills as a relief pitcher. "Had the chant endured for a year or two after YellowHorse's departure, it might not be so surprising," Fuller writes, but fans were still yelling the chant more than twenty-five years after the Pawnee last pitched for the Pittsburgh Pirates.[137]

YellowHorse, known for his quick wit and prankish humor along with warm kindness, was quite familiar with the Osages and enjoyed spinning yarns about them. In 1922 he told sportswriter Chilly Doyle humorous stories exemplifying the effects of wealth into the Osage Nation and Osage County generally. Doyle, who found YellowHorse to be "an almost inexhaustible mine of witty and humorous narratives," would seek him out to help fill out his column, "Chilly Sauce," for the Pittsburgh *Gazette Times*.[138] Wealthy Osages had become car aficionados and were trying to outdo one another in the extravagance of their automobiles. "I know one [Osage] fellow who bought a seventeen-passenger touring car with all the latest equipment," YellowHorse said. "The loud car made another chief" so jealous, that he "came up with a white hearse."[139] Stories about Osages buying expensive hearses became common, which can be traced back to a condescending *New York Times* article from 1917 about an Osage oil lessor named Wah-pah-sha-sah, who purchased a hearse for its "ample squatting room," fine curtains, and exorbitant price. Such jokes were a way for non-Natives to cope with the envy and category confusion produced by the sudden advent of "rich, automotive Indians," according to Philip J. Deloria.[140] For non-Osage American Indians, Osage wealth offered an opportunity for intertribal teasing and banter, as exemplified by Will Rogers. In his book *The Pittsburgh Pirates*, sportswriter Frank Lieb noted that YellowHorse's brand of southwestern humor recalled to listeners the late Will Rogers.[141] YellowHorse was also familiar with the lawless oil boom town of Whizbang, or Denoya, in Osage County, officially named for Joseph Frank DeNoya, a local French-Osage personage of some wealth. It was "the toughest town on earth" where everyone "packs a lead pipe for a cane." Whizbang got its name from all of the shooting that happened there, YellowHorse joked. "They whiz all day and bang all night." The notorious town, which sprang up overnight in 1921 after employees of John Joseph Mathews's friend, E. W. Marland, struck oil there, was also said to have been named after *Capt. Billy's Whiz Bang*, a naughty humor magazine with covers featuring color illustrations of flapper cuties. Like John Joseph Mathews, YellowHorse loved to hunt and fish, and he "sometimes preferred a rod and reel to a mitt and ball," Fuller writes.[142]

Four months after Mathews's preceding column ran, the first *Dick Tracy* comic strip appeared in October 1931; its creator Charles Gould, like YellowHorse, hailed from Pawnee, and he and YellowHorse became buddies. Law-and-order-loving Dick Tracy was a response to the lawlessness running rampant in America during the 1920s; the most flagrant example of this near Pawnee was the Osage reign of terror murders. Gould stated he was motivated to create *Dick Tracy* as a reaction to widespread revelations during this period of "fixed juries, crooked judges, bribery of public officials and cops who looked the other way."[143] In 1935, Gould created a character that was loosely based upon Mose YellowHorse called Chief Yellowpony. YellowHorse, like Charles Bender and countless other Native celebrities, had been stereotypically dubbed "Chief" by the media. Unlike

Mose YellowHorse, Yellowpony wore braids and spoke using stereotypical "Indian" interjections, but the character displayed intelligence and insight. YellowHorse seemed amused by the homage, Todd Fuller writes.[144]

During the 1931 World Series—when the very first *Dick Tracy* strip appeared, incidentally—a speedy major league player associated with the Osage was becoming famous to baseball fans. Best known as a St. Louis Cardinals third-baseman and outfielder, John Leonard Roosevelt "Pepper" Martin was born in Temple, Oklahoma, in 1904 and grew up part of a red-dirt-poor Okie family. When he was six, his family moved from a farm to Oklahoma City, and he lived in the state for most of his life. Loved by fans for his gritty working-class style, Martin called Oklahoma City his hometown. Like Mathews and Mose YellowHorse, Martin was an avid outdoorsman and hunter fond of pranks and jokes. When asked how he got so fast, Martin quipped: "Well, I grew up in Oklahoma, and out there, once you start running, there ain't nothin', to stop you!"[145] Pepper told another reporter he "probably learned fast escaping angry farmers and shopkeepers when us kids broke down their fences or snitched their food."[146] Martin was dubbed the "Wild Horse of the Osage" for his fast and forceful base-running and style of play. In one account, the nickname originated with a Rochester, New York, reporter; in another version, Harrison J. "Doc" Weaver, trainer for the Cardinals, had already invented the name, which later caught on while Pepper was personally dominating the 1931 World Series. In only four games, famous baseball writer Red Smith explains, Martin "captured the public as few individuals can do in a team game. It wasn't only his bold larceny on the bases that excited the crowds, or his batting average of .643. It wasn't just his reckless headfirst slides. It was more the sense of joy that characterized his play and somehow communicated itself to spectators." This is the same joie de vivre that Mathews observed in the natural world and sought within his own philosophy of life—in the early 1930s, Martin seemed a natural, born to swing a bat and run the bases.[147]

Still another theory on the origin of the "Wild Horse of the Osage" nickname—memorialized on a plaque at the Oklahoma City minor league baseball stadium owned by the Chickasaw Nation—posits that it arose even earlier, back in the 1920s when Martin played fullback in the Osage Nation for the legendary Hominy Indians football team, which was backed by Osage sponsors enriched by oil headright payments.[148] Specifically, he played in 1922, 1923, and 1929. In 1927, the Hominy Indians famously beat the National Football League champions at the time, the New York Giants. The Hominy Indians disbanded after the 1932 season, probably another victim of the Depression and plummeting headright payments.[149] At any rate, Pepper Martin's tagline, "Wild Horse of the Osage" stuck, apparently leading some, including a writer for Major League Baseball in 2011, to assume Martin was Osage.[150] Martin's parents were Mormon and his father participated in the Land Run, according to biographer Thomas Barthel, yet "it was said that in addition to his Irish background, Martin had some Cherokee blood as well. But there is no evidence of that, simply the appearance of high cheekbones." Regardless, he seems to have been claimed by some Native Americans.

Martin's stellar performance in the 1931 World Series earned him fame, and in that year, he was named the first Associated Press Male Athlete of the Year award. Along with the famed brothers "Dizzy" Dean and Paul Dean, Martin was a part of the Cardinals' celebrated Gas House Gang team, winners of the 1934 World Series. The Gas House Gang was known for their grubby uniforms and appearance, and their rough-and-tumble style of play. A four-time All-Star, Pepper Martin achieved a .298 batting average over his thirteen-year run, and he was the top base-stealer in 1933, 1934, and 1936. In June 1939, "Pepper Martin Day" was held at Sportsman's Park in St. Louis, and Martin was gifted with a ranch in Oklahoma and two strawberry-roan broodmares, which were named Cimarron and Osage by Cardinal fan contest winners.[151] Martin was forever linked with Osage land and people in popular perception.

Pepper loved to play guitar, which he pronounced "gittar," and he formed the Mississippi Mudcats with other Cardinals, playing hillbilly country music at paying gigs. He retired from the Major Leagues in 1944 but continued to coach and manage. Martin hit a low point as a manager of the minor league Miami Sun Sox in 1949 when he choked an umpire and had to be dragged off the field by police, but he also had many successes.

In 1965, Pepper Martin died in McAlester, Oklahoma, and is buried in the small town of Quinton. He was survived by his wife, the former Ruby G. Pope, whom he married in 1927; together they had six children. Martin, like YellowHorse and Mathews, never stopped hunting and fishing, enjoying the outdoors throughout his lifetime.

NOTES

1. *Smoking* refers to the Osage practice of giving gifts such as blankets to honor recipients on Sunday of the June I'n-Lo'n-Schka dances that occur during three weekends at the Osage villages in Gray Horse, Hominy, and Pawhuska.

2. Mathews to Campbell, November 12, 1928, Box 32, Folder 27, Walter Stanley Campbell Collection (WSC), Western History Collection (WHC), University of Oklahoma (OU).

3. Alexandre Hogue, "W. Herbert Dunton: An Appreciation," *Southwest Review* 13, no. 1 (October 1927): 55.

4. Lyn Bleiler and Society of the Muse of the Southwest, *Taos* (Mt. Pleasant, SC: Arcadia, 2011), 94–95.

5. Julie Schimmel, *The Art and Life of W. Herbert Dunton, 1878-1936* (Austin: University of Texas Press, 1984), 14–15.

6. Frank Waters, *To Possess the Land: A Biography of Arthur Rochford Manby* (Chicago: Swallow, 1973), 146.

7. Peter H. Hassrick and Elizabeth J. Cunningham, *In Contemporary Rhythm: The Art of Ernest L. Blumenshein* (Norman: University of Oklahoma Press, 2008), 153–54.

8. Schimmel, *Art and Life of W. Herbert Dunton*, 216, 222.

9. Mathews, *Twenty Thousand Mornings*, edited by Susan Kalter (Norman: University of Oklahoma Press, 2012), 74, 148–49.

10. Mathews to Walter Stanley Campbell, July 6, 1935, Box 32, Folder 27, WSC, WHC, OU.

11. Susan Kalter, Afterword to "The White Sack," *Old Three Toes and Other Tales of Survival and Extinction* (Norman: University of Oklahoma Press, 2015), 160; Historic American Buildings Survey, Indian Village (Seton Village), HABS No. Nm-182, cdn.loc.gov/master/pnp/habshaer/nm/nm0200/nm0207/data/nm0207data .pdf, accessed January 29, 2017.

12. Mathews to Elizabeth Hunt, August 20, 1935, Box 1, Folder 3, John Joseph Mathews Collection (JJM), WHC, OU.

13. Quoted in Richard Green, *Te Ata* (Norman: University of Oklahoma Press), 146.

14. Philip J. Deloria, *Indians In Unexpected Places* (Lawrence: University Press of Kansas, 2004), 166.

15. Mathews, diary, June 3, 1952, Box 2, Folder 3, JJM, WHC, OU.

16. "Ellsworth Jaeger, Naturalist, was 64," *New York Times*, August 6, 1962, 25.

17. Laura Adams Armer, *Waterless Mountain* (New York: Alfred A. Knopf, 1993 [1931]), 91.

18. Catherine Savage Brosman, *Southwestern Women Writers and the Vision of Goodness: Mary Austin, Willa Cather, Laura Adams Armer, Peggy Pond Church and Alice Marriott* (Jefferson, NC: McFarland, 2016), 201–06.

19. Susan Kalter, "Introduction" to *Twenty Thousand Mornings* by John Joseph Mathews, edited by Kalter (Norman: University of Oklahoma Press, 2011), xxi.

20. Walter Stanley Campbell to Mathews, January 2, 1932, Box 32, Folder 27, WSC, WHC, OU.

21. Mathews to Campbell, January [date unknown] 1933, Box 32, Folder 27, WSC, WHC, OU.

22. Mathews to Elizabeth Hunt, August 24, 1935 (JJM 1.3).

23. Lois Palken Rudnick, *Mabel Dodge Luhan: New Woman, New Worlds* (Albuquerque: University of New Mexico Press, 1987), 267; Thomas Wolfe, *Of Time and the River: A Legend of Man's Hunger in His Youth* (New York: Simon & Shuster, 1999 [1935]), 178.

24. Mathews, diary, June 3, 1952, Box 2, Folder 3, JJM, WHC, OU.

25. Rudnick, *Mabel Dodge Luhan*, 267.

26. Flannery Burke, *From Greenwich Village to* Taos (Lawrence: University Press of Kansas, 2008), 2; Andrew Turnbull, *Thomas Wolfe* (New York: Scribner's Sons, 1967), 211, 156–57, 165–67; David Herbert Donald, *Look Homeward: A Life of Thomas Wolfe* (Cambridge, Mass: Harvard University Press, 2002), 238–39.

27. Frank Waters, *To Possess the Land: A Biography of Arthur Rochford Manby* (Chicago: Swallow, 1973), 148–49, 152.

28. Quoted in Burke, *From Greenwich Village to Taos*, 36.

29. Elizabeth Cunningham, *Remarkable Women of Taos* (Taos: Nighthawk, 2013), 42–44.

30. Burke, *From Greenwich Village to Taos*, 2.

31. Dee Brown, "Land Fever: The Strange Jekyll-Hyde Life of Arthur Manby," review of *To Possess the Land: A Biography of Arthur Rochelle Manby* by Frank Waters, *Chicago Tribune*, March 3, 1974.

32. Frank Waters, *To Possess the Land: A Biography of Arthur Rochford Manby* (Chicago: Swallow, 1973), 149, 173.

33. Deloria, *Indians in Unexpected Places*, 151.

34. Waters, *To Possess the Land*, 99–101, 105.

35. Quoted in Terry Wilson, *Underground Reservation*, 147.

36. *The Daily Journal-Capital*, April 17, 1930, 1

37. Waters, *To Possess the Land*, 226.

38. Waters, *To Possess the Land*, 244.

39. Waters, *To Possess the Land*, 244–45.

40. Waters, *To Possess the Land*, 241, 245.

41. Waters, *To Possess the Land*, 192–212.

42. Waters, *To Possess the Land*, 223.

43. In the first paragraph, Mathews speaks from first-hand experience of night flying during the World War I period in Texas; traveling in the Sidi Okba area of the Biskra province in Algeria, there viewing the ruins of the Roman colony at Timgad; and sightseeing the southwestern United States, experiences that are addressed in other columns and commentaries herein.

44. Ann Wierda Rowland, "Sentimental Fiction," *Cambridge Companion to Fiction in the Romantic Period*, edited by Richard Maxwell and Katie Trumpener (Cambridge, 2008), 191–206; "Sentimental Novel," *Britannica Academic*, Encyclopædia

Britannica, November 1, 2017, academic.eb.com.librarynt.occc.edu/levels/collegiate/article/sentimental-novel/66787.

45. Hannah More, *The Works of Hannah More: with a Sketch of Her Life, Volume 1* (Boston: Goodrich, 1827), 359–60; Rowland, "Sentimental Fiction," 191–206.

46. Mathews, *Twenty Thousand Mornings*, 113, 134.

47. Darrin Lunde, *The Naturalist: Theodore Roosevelt, a Lifetime of Exploration, and the Triumph of American Natural History* (New York: Broadway, 2016), 217.

48. Rachel Frazin, "Bears Ears Lawsuit to Proceed, Federal Judge Rules," *The Hill*, October 1, 2019, thehill.com/policy/energy-environment/463775-bears-ears-lawsuit-to-proceed-federal-judge-rules.

49. Quoted in Snyder, *John Joseph Mathews*, 36.

50. "Allenby's Boyhood Days at West Bilney," *Lynn News*, July 8, 1941, reprinted in *East Binch and West Bilney Community Project*, 2010, www.eastwinchandwestbilney.co.uk/personal-vignette/viscount-allenby.

51. Mathews, *Sundown*, 216.

52. Mathews, *Talking to the Moon* (Chicago: University of Chicago Press, 1945), 3, 207.

53. Paul Engle, "Thoreau and Simple Life, Modernized," *Chicago Daily Tribune*, June 17, 1945.

54. "Woman Tried on Charge of Wine Sale to Indians," *Pawhuska Journal-Capital*, May 16, 1930.

55. Lawrence J. Hogan, *The Osage Indian Murders*, second edition (Frederick, MD: Amlex, 1998), 53.

56. "Big Elk and Family Pay City Visit," *Los Angeles Times*, July 1, 1932, 29; Ed Red Eagle [Sr.], interview with Robert Miller [cassette and transcript], Doris Duke Collection, Western History Collection, University of Oklahoma, T-108, vol. 48, p. 2.

57. Also known as Wa-tse-mon-in, Bacon Rind was a grandson of the Osage prophet Wa-tian-kah and was initiated as a priest of the Bear clan prior to converting to the peyote religion. Jon D. May writes: "An Osage political leader of the late nineteenth and early twentieth centuries," Bacon Rind was likely born in Kansas. He was an Osage tribal councilman, served as assistant principal chief in 1904 to 1905, and was elected principal chief in 1912. Bacon Rind, politically "progressive," favored the allotment of the Osage Reservation and development of its oil and natural gas resources. "He remained a traditionalist in customs, however, and always wore native dress and an otter-skin cap. Bacon Rind was a gifted speaker of the Osage language. He spent the last quarter-century of his life representing the Osages on annual visits to Washington, D.C." Bacon Rind, it was claimed, was the most-photographed of all American Indian leaders. He died at Pawhuska, Oklahoma, on March 28, 1932. Jon D. May, "Bacon Rind," *The Encyclopedia of Oklahoma History and Culture*, www.okhistory.org, accessed January 30, 2017.

58. Wilson, *Underground Reservation*, 197–98, 200; Mathews, "Moonhead," chapter 54, *The Osages*, 740–49.

59. Terry P. Wilson, "The Depression Years," in *Indians of North America* (New York: Chelsea House, 2008).

60. "Even Rich Woman Can't Find House in Her Home City," *Oklahoman*, January 5, 1934, 6, Oklahoman Digital Archive, archive.newsok.com.

61. "Three Indians Held for Fatal Shooting," Miami, Oklahoma *News-Record*, March 7, 1929, 10, Newspapers.com.

62. "Indian Couple Freed by Murder Jurors." *Miami Daily News-Record* [Okla.], October 10, 1929, Newspapers.com.

63. "Woman Tried on Charge of Wine Sale to Indians," Pawhuska *Journal-Capital*, May 16, 1930.

64. "Indian Students Show Interest by Attendance Marks," *Wichita Daily Eagle*, March 18, 1920.

65. "Joe Redeagle," *Fairfax Chief*, June 3, 1921, 8, cited by Anna Webb-Storey, "Culture Clash: A Case Study of Three Osage Native American Families," (PhD dissertation, Oklahoma State University, 1998), 100, shareok.org/bitstream/handle/11244/33610/Thesis-1998D-W368c.pdf?sequence=1&isAllowed=y.

66. David Grann, *Killers of the Flower Moon: The Osage Murders and the Birth of the FBI* (New York: Doubleday, 2017), 280–81, 290.

67. "Indian Chief's Son is Killed During Affray," *Miami Daily News-Record*, November 21, 1933; Nancy B. Samuelson, "Dalton Gang," *Encyclopedia of Oklahoma History and Culture*, Oklahoma Historical Society, www.okhistory.org/publications/enc/entry.php?entry=DA006, accessed November 9, 2018; Ed Red Eagle [Sr.], interview with Robert Miller [cassette and transcript], Doris Duke Collection, Western History Collection, University of Oklahoma, T-108, vol. 48, 3–4.

68. Donna Colleen Jones, "The Osages—Louis Red Eagle, Metza Bertha Big Eagle Jones," *Nancy Bellzona's Picture Book*, Electric Scotland, https://www.electricscotland.com/history/america/donna/picturebook/2021.htm, accessed October 29, 2019.

69. "Victim's Lifestyle Described," *Oklahoman*, May 28, 1988, newsok.com/article/2227275, accessed December 3, 2017.

70. Robby Trammell, "Man Gets 12 Years in Slaying," *Oklahoman*, September 2, 1988, newsok.com/article/2237754, accessed December 3, 2017.

71. "Slaying Linked to Satanism," *Oklahoman*, May 27, 1988, newsok.com/article/2227110, accessed December 3, 2017.

72. "Victim's Lifestyle Described," *Oklahoman*, May 28, 1988.

73. Robby Trammell, "Osage Death Case Figure Sentenced," *Oklahoman*, April 21, 1989, newsok.com/article/2263441; Deb Taylor, "Save the Indian: A Story of Two-Spirit, Sacred People, Native Queers," *Liberty Press*, December 1999, reprinted www.debtaylor.com/deb/articles/prentice.html.

74. Robby Trammell, "Satanist Slaying Denied," *Oklahoman*, June 3, 1988, newsok.com/article/2227894; Julie DelCour, "Crawford Convicted in Red Eagle Case," February 24, 1989, *Tulsa World*, www.tulsaworld.com/archives/crawfords-convicted-in-red-eagle-case/article_d8c160ff-1c59-5d6a-abbe-0ef80f5459fa.html.

75. Deb Taylor, "Save the Indian"; Robby Trammell, "Satanist Slaying Denied," *Oklahoman*, June 3, 1988, newsok.com/article/2227894.

76. Deb Taylor, "Save the Indian."

77. "Prentice Crawford is Getting the Shaft at Haskell," *Liberty Press*, January 2000, reprinted in www.debtaylor.com/deb/articles/preditorial.html.

78. "Big Elk and Family Pay City Visit," *Los Angeles Times*, July 1, 1932, 29.

79. Mathews, *The Osages: Children of the Middle Waters* (Norman: University of Oklahoma Press, 1961), 790; Ed Red Eagle [Sr.], interview with Robert Miller [cassette and transcript], Doris Duke Collection, Western History Collection, University of Oklahoma, T-108, vol. 48, p. 8.

80. Mathews diary, July 26, 1952, Box 2, Folder 3, JJM, WHC, OU.

81. "Osage Elder Harry Red Eagle Jr. Passes Away at 90," *Osage News*, August 2, 2011, osagenews.org/en/article/2011/08/02/osage-elder-harry-red-eagle-jr-passes-away-90.

82. The epigram was added to Mathews's column.

83. Mathews, *Twenty Thousand Mornings*, 58–59; "Walter Mathews Student File," Carlisle Indian School Digital Resource Center, carlisleindian.dickinson.edu/sites/all/files/docs-ephemera/NARA_1327_b138_f5448b.pdf.

84. "Independent Osage Hold Convention," *Daily Journal-Capital*, May 18, 1930.

85. "Osages Holding Election of New Officers Today," *Daily Journal-Capital*, June 2, 1930.

86. "Fred Lookout is Reelected Chief of Osage Nation," *Daily Journal-Capital*, June 3, 1930; "Osages to Hold Big Celebration Honoring Leaders," *Daily Journal-Capital,* June 25, 1930.

87. *Daily Journal-Capital*, May 14 and May 21, 1930.

88. The shrike, or butcher-bird, though cute, is carnivorous and impales its victims.

89. "Oldtime Osage Taken by Death," *Journal-Capital*, May 27, 1930, 1.

90. U.S. Congress, House Committee on Indian Affairs, "Leases for Oil and Gas Purposes, Osage Tribal Council," 190.

91. U.S. Congress, House Committee on Indian Affairs, "Leases for Oil and Gas Purposes, Osage Tribal Council," 125.

92. Wilson, *Underground Reservation*, 116.

93. Wilson, *Underground Reservation*, 117.

94. See Donald L. Fixico, Chapter 2, "The Osage Murders and Oil," *Invasion of Indian Territory in the Twentieth Century* (Boulder: University of Colorado, 2011).

95. Joseph Bradfield Thoburn, *A Standard History of Oklahoma*, volume 5 (Chicago: American Historical Society, 1916), 2072–73; "Charged with Conspiring to Defraud the United Natural Gas Co.," *Natural Gas Journal* 8 (1914): 245.

96. Thoburn, *Standard History of Oklahoma* 5: 2048.

97. "Osage Tribal Museum, Library & Archives" [pamphlet], (Pawhuska: Osage Tribal Museum, 2015).

98. John Joseph Mathews, "John Bird, Early Osage Trader, Dies," *Pawhuska Journal-Capital*, January 28, 1935; Robert B. Finney, "John L. Bird," *Osage County Profiles* (Pawhuska, Osage County Historical Society, 1978).

99. Fairfax Area Historical Society, *From a Field of Cane*, 49.

100. Guthrie [Okla.] *Daily Leader*, June 19, 1906, 5.

101. "F. Gentner and Grace F. Drummond," *Osage Country Profiles* (Pawhuska: OCHS, 1978).

102. Fairfax Area Historical Society, *From a Field of Cane*, 72–73.

103. Joint Commission to Investigate Indian Affairs, "Osage Reservation," 1504.

104. Fairfax Area Historical Society, *From a Field of Cane*, "Booze & Banks" sidebar; Thoburn, *Standard History of Oklahoma* 5: 2145.

105. Mathews, "John L. Bird Early Osage Trader Dies," Pawhuska *Daily Journal-Capital*, January 28, 1935, 1; "John L. Bird," *Osage County Profiles* (Pawhuska: OCHS, 1978).

106. Fairfax Area Historical Society, *From a Field of Cane*, 41; "Want Bigheart to Sign Deed to Forty Acres," *Wichita Daily Eagle*, April 15, 1909, 2.

107. Les Warehime, *History of Ranching the Osage* (Tulsa: W.W. Productions, 2000), 134; *Moodys Manual of Railroads and Corporation Securities*, Moodys, 1917, 439.

108. Joint Commission to Investigate Indian Affairs, "Osage Reservation," 1542, 1486.

109. "Exploitation Story Amazes," *Sun* [Coffeyville, Kans.] January 17, 1915, 1, Newspapers.com.

110. Joint Commission to Investigate Indian Affairs, "Osage Reservation," 1476–77.

111. *Moody's Manual of Railroads and Corporation Securities*, 1917, 439.

112. Lonnie Underhill, *Osage Indian Reign of Terror* (Gilbert, AZ: Roan Horse, 2010), 51.

113. Joint Commission to Investigate Indian Affairs, "Osage Reservation," 1504.

114. "Wheeler v. Bigheart," Supreme Court of Oklahoma, 1934, *Justia*, law.justia .com/cases/oklahoma/supreme-court/1934/39251.html.

115. Joint Commission to Investigate Indian Affairs, "Osage Reservation," 1484, 1502, 1503.

116. "Bumble Bee Causes a Death," *Independence Daily-Reporter*, October 2, 1917, 6, Newspapers.com.

117. "Maher-Burt," Winfield [Kans.] *Daily Free Press*, January 25, 1922, 5, Newspapers.com.

118. *Osage County News* [Pawhuska, Okla.], December 12, 1919, Gateway to Oklahoma History, gateway.okhistory.org.

119. Winfield [Kans.] *Daily Free Press*, September 12, 1922, 5.

120. Fixico, *Invasion of Indian Territory*, 31–32.

121. "May 11, 1911: Supreme Court Orders Standard Oil to be Broken Up," *New York Times*, May 15, 2012, learning.blogs.nytimes.com/2012/05/15/may-15-1911 -supreme-court-orders-standard-oil-to-be-broken-up/.

122. Wilson, *Underground Reservation*, 115.

123. U.S. Congress House Committee on Indian Affairs, *Leases for Oil and Gas Purposes, Osage National Council* (Washington, DC: U.S. Government Printing Office, 1913), 130, 156.

124. Wilson, *Underground Reservation*, 117.

125. A writ of mandamus is an order from a court to an inferior government official ordering the government official to properly fulfill their official duties or correct an abuse of discretion.

126. "Fisher Accused of Wronging the Indians to Aid Standard Oil," Salina [Kan.] *Daily Union*, January 28, 1913, 1.

127. "Indictments in Osage Case," *The Liberal* [Kan.] *Democrat*, October 31, 1913, 3.

128. "Tucker and Wilson Freed in Oil Cases," *Independence Daily Reporter* (Kansas), May 28, 1914, 1.

129. "An Infamous Prosecution," *Salina Daily Union*, May 29, 1914, 4.

130. Mathews, *Twenty Thousand Mornings*, 24; Violet Willis, "W.S. Mathews, Early Day Tribe Leader," *Pawhuska Journal-Capital*, September 29, 1972.

131. Joseph B. Oxendine, Foreword to Jeffrey Powers-Beck, *The American Indian Integration of Baseball* (Lincoln: University of Nebraska Press, 2004), ix.

132. Jeffrey Powers-Beck, *The American Indian Integration of Baseball* (Lincoln: University of Nebraska Press, 2004), 187–88; "Harry Kohpay (Wah-she-wah-hah) Student File," *Carlisle Indian School Digital Resource Center*, Dickinson College, http://carlisleindian.dickinson.edu/student_files/harry-kohpay-wah-she-wah-hah-student-file.

133. *Hearings Before the Senate Committee on Indian Affairs on Matters Relating to the Osage Tribe of Indians.* (Washington, DC: Government Printing Office, 1909), 230–44.

134. Osage County Historical Society, *Osage County Profiles*, 27.

135. Howe, *Choctalking on Other Realities*, 174.

136. "Traveling Indian Baseball Team Will Play Here," *The Daily Journal-Capital*, June 18, 1930; "Pawhuska Indians Defeat Pawnee," *Osage Journal*, June 23, 1930, 4.

137. Todd Fuller, *60 Feet, 6 Inches and Other Distances from Home: The (Baseball) Life of Mose YellowHorse* (Duluth: Holy Cow!, 2002), 20, 24, 45, 74, 102–03.

138. Powers-Beck, *American Indian Integration of Baseball*, 155.

139. Quoted in Powers-Beck, *American Indian Integration of Baseball*, 155–56.

140. Deloria, *Indians in Unexpected Places*, 177.

141. Frank Lieb quoted in Fuller, *60 Feet, Six Inches*, 24.

142. Fuller, *60 Feet, Six Inches*, 60.

143. Quoted in Fuller, *60 Feet, Six Inches*,126.

144. Fuller, *60 Feet, Six Inches*, 121–23.

145. Red Smith, "Series: Pepper Martin vs. Philadelphia," *The Ultimate Baseball Book*, edited by Daniel Okrent, Harris Lewine, and David Nemec (New York, Hilltown, 2000), 164.

146. Martin to a Philadelphia *Inquirer* reporter, quoted in Thomas Barthel, *Pepper Martin: A Baseball Biography* (Jefferson, NC: McFarland, 2003), 6.

147. Red Smith, "Series," 164, 251.

148. Plaque beneath a 2007 bust of Martin, stadium of the Oklahoma City Dodgers [formerly RedHawks]; Barthel, *Pepper Martin*, 12, 100–01, 109, 187.

149. Jon D. May, "Hominy," *Encyclopedia of Oklahoma History and Culture*, www.okhistory.org/publications/enc/entry.php?entry=HO024.

150. Charlie Vescallero, "Native Americans Significant to Baseball History," *MLB.com*, Major League Baseball, December 13, 2011, m.mlb.com/news/article/26150368//; see also Osage Tribal Museum, *Osage Timeline*, researched and developed by Lou Brock (Pawhuska, Okla.: Osage Tribal Museum, 2013), 58.

151. "Pepper Martin Given Tribute," *Clarion-Ledger* (Jackson, Miss.), June 19, 1939, 5.

Part IV

Romance of the Osage

TOURISM, HISTORY, AND THE OSAGE INDIAN

Sunday, June 15, 1930, #26

There is no reason why the Osage could not be brought back to its former importance as a sportsman's paradise. There is no reason why lakes cannot be built where good fishing would lure anglers from over the state. It is possible to make the towns of the Osage points of unusual interest to tourists, founded as they are as part of the unique history of the most conspicuous tribe of Indians.

Smoking chimneys and swarming masses are not necessary to make a community important, or for the economic comfort of the citizens. There are such things as beauty and uniqueness wearing the garment of romance, things that have appealed to people over the ages. Thousands of people travel each summer in each of new and strange attractions. Many of them know not what they seek, but are ready to be led; they are receptive to suggestions. The economic well-being of a community depends upon money, and people are the bringers of money, and money with a spirit toward making the communities of the Osage more attractive to tourists, and the development of their natural and historic attractions would in the end mean the prosperity of those communities.

There should be no objection to being called a tourist town. Each town that ever existed had a reason for being. In the case of the towns of the Osage, their reason for being was unusual among the conditions that give rise to towns. The older communities of the Osage were not built as markets for agricultural products, nor did they spring up along routes of travel, nor were they junctions. Neither were they built round fire-belching chimneys of factories. They were trading posts, and their reason for existence was the money sent by the Unites States Government to their wards, the Indians. This money was the communities' reason for being: the presence of this money sent in from the outside, which was given in exchange for the merchandise of the traders.

Then came the large oil royalties from the oil owned by the Indian, and the increase in the money paid to the Indian expanded his buying power and the resultant prosperity of the trader. Only a brief prosperity was experienced. The oil of the Osage was a vast economic resource, and had the communities of the Osage benefitted proportionate to the oil sold, and by the activities of the companies making the explorations, they might have experienced more than temporary prosperity. Unfortunately, the oil of the Osage went to enrich other communities. Perhaps there was much of the goose and the golden egg in it. Many people went to the Osage with their minds filled with the idea of garnering dollars, but few thought of the future of the Osage, even many of those who made it their home. The goddess of fortune smiled and beckoned, and men clutched at her skirts, forgetting that oil is a volatile substance, as volatile and whimsical as Fortune herself; instead of the torch of the goddess, they followed an *ignis fatuus*.[1]

The money paid to the Osage Indian, though, decreasing in amount, is still the economic basis for the existence of these towns, supplemented by small agricultural products and cattle. The erstwhile Osage of fevered activity is left with the towns of the period of its prosperity; it has been hurt little outside a few scars where oil has ruined vegetation, and barbaric field workers have overrun its fields and streams in the wanton destruction of game. The wonder of its rolling green prairie and its blackjack hills remain to us. The older generation of Indian still walks among us with inherent dignity, and his history has just been given another amazing chapter, by the oil that has been pumped out from under his feet and the miniature Klondikes that marred his prairie, picturesque though they were.

The Indian has been the economic basis of the Osage. One wonders if he, his history, and his blackjack hills and prairie, soaked as they are in romance, cannot be used in our economic future.

TOURISM

Mathews's advocacy of promoting tourism in Pawhuska is smart, but it did not seem to catch on at the time. With oil production slumping in the Great Depression of the 1930s after the boom of the 1920s, it behooved the Osages and the townspeople of Pawhuska to find ways to inject money into the local economy. One tactic was to attempt to lure Osages who had wandered elsewhere to bring their spending money back to Osage County.[2] Over the decades, the Osage Tribal Museum (now Osage Nation Museum), the Osage County Historical Museum, Immaculate Conception Church, and the Joseph H. Williams Tallgrass Prairie Preserve have attracted tourists.

Only over eight decades later did Pawhuska seem to begin to realize Mathews's hopes for thriving tourism. Beginning on Halloween 2016, Pawhuska drew large crowds of tourists because of the popularity of The Mercantile, the enterprise of Osage County resident Ree Drummond, the self-styled Pioneer Woman, blogger, author, publisher, television personality, and entrepreneur, who married the wealthy rancher Ladd Drummond. The Mercantile's name alludes to the Osage Mercantile of olden times, once located there. The success of "the Merc" has led to the renovation of the long-vacant Triangle Building across the street, erected during the 1920s heyday. A new hotel there recalls the glory days of the Duncan Hotel. John Joseph Mathews's father William was an early owner of the old Osage Mercantile, and sometimes wrote poetry on Osage Mercantile stationery.[3] It is hoped Ree Drummond and her tourist magnet will find ways to promote Osage arts and culture, and benefit the Osage people.

ROMANCE AND LORE OF THE OSAGE HILLS

Wednesday, February 11, 1931, #54

Wherever the Osage is mentioned, there is ever a display of interest. This interest has a quality that is not found in the natural interests inspired by the mention of other sections of the state. There seems to be something in the name "the Osage" that appeals to the imagination of people, and leads them to expect the unusual. Much of this, of course, has been created by the cheap sensationalism indulged in by newspaper people over the state, when the Osage Indians rose to sudden affluence, and much of it has been due to the same newspaper people's love of catchphrases. There is no phrase more charmingly romantic and more suitable to the uses of those who deal in startling news than the phrase, "the Osage Hills." Here immediately is created in the mind of the average reader a great expanse of inaccessible hills covered with brush and woods, abounding in great grottos and hidden valleys where most anything might happen.

When a story about a murder or train robbery or the looting of a bank comes to light, the Osage hills seem to exist in the mind of the writer solely for the purpose of dragging the escapade from the levels of the prosaic into the dazzling romance found in "penny-terribles." No matter whether society has been insulted in Kansas, or the laws violated in Nebraska or Texas or Missouri, the culprits are invariably "believed to have escaped to the Osage hills," and there endeth in a romantic finis, the incident. The reader is satisfied in his love of the sensational and the adventurous. He can then give his imagination free reign. He can picture the grizzled outlaws sitting in the mouth of a primeval cave in an uncharted valley, playing the guitar in the glow of a campfire, gloriously indifferent to society and its laws.

If all these mal-doers had really escaped to the Osage hills, they would be spying on us from the bole of every blackjack. Hunters would jump them from the long grass on sunny slopes, and watch them bound for the security of sandstone boulders. In election years, candidates would trail them with posters and handbills, and with their supposed numerical strength, they could give complexion to our county administrators. We would then read feature stories of personal interviews, by some entertaining reporter, with "Killer" Dugan, head of the Dugan gang, in lieu of stories of the rich Osages using hearses for pleasure cars.

OUTLAW HIDEOUT

All that said, there was much criminality in "the Osage" in general, and many infamous outlaws truly did hide out in the Osage Hills. These included bank robber Arthur "Pretty Boy" Floyd, called the "Robin Hood of the Cookson Hills" of northeastern Oklahoma, and train robber and bank robber Al Spencer. In *Outlaws*, Robert Barr Smith writes that "the tangled wilderness of the Osage Hills" held a "rich tradition of use for bad men hunted by the law." Trying to locate a fugitive there was "like a game of hide and seek." Mathews himself as a youth ran into a train robber out on the prairie one day while he was out for a ride on his beloved horse, Bally. In *Twenty Thousand Mornings*, he writes of outlaws: "Some of them did come to the Osage Hills. These men were not psychopaths, but quite normal and ignorant, superstitious, unimaginative, humanly cruel, and ferociously vindictive; they were neither psychopathic nor brutish, but just plain 'man'ish."[4]

THE ROMANCE OF BISKRA

Sunday, April 26, 1931, #72

For years, a little Arab town sweltered in the sun on the edge of the Sahara Desert. The merchants sat cross-legged in the shade of their bazaar awnings, looking out upon the world with utter detachment. Children and dogs slept under the shade of buildings during the long summer days, and the women in bright colors moved slowly along the streets, or gossiped during the intervals in their light domestic duties. The men sat in the cafes, sipping vermouth, cassis, or bock, or sat indolently over games. Later, when the brazen sun was descending, the muezzin called from the mosque, and the townsmen took mats from the walls of the cafes, or prostrated themselves in the streets and prayed toward Mecca. Then back to their lethargic occupations. In the hot evenings, the men went to the café Maure, and watched the Ouled Naïls dance to the primitive music of the desert.

For years they lived to the slow tempo, of the heat of summer and the lazy sunshine of winter. The outside world had not heard of Biskra. It was only an oasis in the Sahara surrounded by sterile rocks and sand. Even in winter, when the sunshine flooded the little oasis, and the air was like a tonic, life went on its monotonous rounds.

Then came a man who was filled with the idea of romance, who saw romance in the palms, in the mud walls, in the multicolored merchandise, in the caravans of camels plodding over the desert, in the history of the palm-fringed oasis. Filled with the idea, he wrote a book that became popular, because of the strangeness of the setting and plot. The book was made into a play, and London, Paris, Berlin, and New York were thrilled by the high romance. Soon the sleepy little town was a mecca itself, and people from all over Europe and America came to this romantic spot. Soon, a great casino was built. Soon, many hotels were built with an eye to the atmosphere of the place. Merchants could not keep supplied with merchandise. Camel traders scoured the desert for riding camels, so that tourists could enjoy the doubtful sport of camel-riding, and every other erstwhile loafer became a guide.

Tourists pass the city of Constantine, perched on its basalt rock; they passed up a city that had been sieged by Romans, by Arabs, by the French. It is a city as heavy with historical tradition as many a city in Spain or southern France. They passed up the great ruins of the temple of Timgad and Batna, ruins that were once the cities built on the frontier of the Roman Empire, and guarded by the third capital Legion. They swarmed to Biskra instead because an Englishman had written a popular novel about it, lured on by romance. Not the romance of the past, but the everyday romance of the frustration of two lovers in a strange setting, with palm trees, camels, veiled women, and white burnoused men in the background.

Biskra had not been heard of before this. There were no oil-rich tribesmen or sensational press stories. There are no incomparable rolling hills surrounding Biskra, but only desolate, burning desert. There is one precarious line of steel and rails leading to Biskra, the trains depending upon the whims of the desert. Biskra does not make hosiery, or chewing gum, or mine coal, nor has she extended invitations to hosiery makers, chewing gun manufacturers, or miners of coal. She concentrates on the one thing she has: the selling of romance and atmosphere to a receptive world of romance-seekers.

THE GARDEN OF ALLAH, BISKRA, AND TIMGAD

In this piece, Mathews implies that a romance of the Osages might also be written and published to help draw tourists into Osage County. Tourism would inject money into the local economy, which was sagging from decreased demand for oil during the Depression. His mention of a casino being built to attract tourists seems prophetic. Peering through the fog of a century, it is not readily evident which famous novel Mathews refers to that popularized the small city of Biskra in Algeria, northern Africa. One might at first guess wrongly that Mathews alluded to *The Sheik* (1919), believing that E. M. Hull, the British author of the bestseller, to be a man; after all, the *Times Literary Supplement* misidentified the author, Edith Maud Hull, as male in its review.[5] The controversial Orientalist "desert romance" *The Sheik* was adapted into the famous 1921 silent picture starring sensual Rudolph Valentino. Mathews's description of "the everyday romance of the frustration of two lovers in a strange setting" actually refers to an even earlier, famous desert romance that was a source for *The Sheik*—namely, *The Garden of Allah* (1904), by the prolific English novelist and satirist, Robert Smythe Hichens.

After the novel's success, Hichens and actress Mary Anderson (Mary Navarro) adapted *The Garden of Allah* to the Broadway stage, where it was performed during 1911 and 1912. The fictional setting, Beni-Mora, was understood by reviewers to be the city of Biskra. The plot centers on Domini Enfilden, a young Englishwoman traveler and a devout Catholic virgin, who gradually falls in love with Boris Androvsky, an awkwardly shy and mysterious stranger who is the only other guest at her hotel. Domini and Boris meet and eventually confess their reciprocal love; they marry and head into the vast desert for their honeymoon. Yet Boris has a heavy secret he has hidden from Domini, which puts a damper on the trip: he had been a Trappist monk who, after two decades of service, broke his vows and fled. After much agonizing, Boris decides he must return to the monastery—after impregnating Domini. Although the novel was a big seller in the early twentieth century, and even inspired the name of a Los Angeles hotel that became synonymous with decadence, *The Garden of Allah* is mostly forgotten today.

A film version of *The Garden of Allah* starring Marlene Dietrich, Charles Boyer, and Basil Rathbone was released five years after Mathews's column appeared. None other than Lynn Riggs—the closeted gay Cherokee playwright who entered the University of Oklahoma the semester after Mathews graduated—co-adapted Hichens's novel into a screenplay. Riggs's hit play, *Green Grow the Lilacs*, had ended its successful Broadway run just a month before Mathews penned his column. Lynn Riggs stayed on location in the California desert during filming of *The Garden of Allah*, to be available in the event rewrites were needed. Dietrich biographer Steven Bach writes that Lynn Riggs wandered across sand dunes "in a kind of heat trance." He always found Dietrich "ravishing" and penned such lines for her as "No one but God and I knows what is in my heart," which caused the legend's eyes "to stop upping-and-downing and roll heavenward in disbelief."[6] In her famous accented English, Dietrich declared: "The script—you know it is twash."[7] In a June 1936 letter to his friend, Betty Kirk, a University of Oklahoma Press employee, Riggs remarked: "Dietrich, the bitch, is sometimes ravishing. Boyer (at least in the rushes) is superb."[8] Evidencing the great popularity of this novel in the early twentieth century, that film was its third adaptation—two silent films had already been made in 1916 and 1927. Composer Gustav Holst (*The Planets*), who visited Biskra for health reasons, used Beni-Mora, Hichens's fictional analogue to Biskra, as the title of his three-movement suite that debuted in 1912.

In 1922, Mathews visited Biskra, the capital of the Biskra province in northeastern Algeria. The town of Biskra was known for the belly-dancers Mathews mentions, of the Ouled Naïls people. Younger tribeswomen were, however, "just as notorious for their prostitution as for their dancing," according to critic Roger Benjamin. The Ouled Naïls, Berber tribespeople, were infamous among some Europeans for "sending their younger women to work as socially sanctioned prostitutes in oasis towns," Biskra most prominently. During the modernist period, Biskra had already gained "fame as a wintering place for Europeans: what is these days called sexual tourism," Benjamin states.[9] In Biskra, the guide Ahmed offered Mathews the chance to "visit" with his twelve-year-old niece. Mathews was tempted by her beauty and noted her already full breasts, but became disgusted with himself for considering it. "I must admit there was something rather thrilling about his proposition," he admitted in his diary.

> There had been the desert and intrigue and romance, but when I thought of the twelve years of his niece, I thought also of the harsh poverty of the little cluster of mud houses and tents, protectively colored on the edge of the dun-colored desert, [and] a primitive emotion welled that horrified my cultured senses. I accused myself of abnormality, even though I had had no thought of accepting his offer. I protectively transferred my disgust from myself to Ahmed.

Ahmed made arrangements for Mathews to hunt with two guides. Jo bonded with Mohamed, one of the hunters, much preferring him to his two American companions.

Mathews alludes to Timgad, the Roman ruins he visited, the remnants of a small Roman military colony at Thamugadi near the Aurès Mountains, originally built using a grid plan around AD 100. There, Jo encountered a Latin motto he later painted in "Chinese red" capital letters on his mantel at The Blackjacks: "VENARI LAVARI LUDERE RIDERE OCCAST VI-VERE." Translating the phrase as "TO HUNT, TO BATHE, TO PLAY, TO LAUGH—THAT IS TO LIVE," Mathews adopted it as the "motto of my life at the Blackjacks."[10] Although the letters have faded, they remain clearly legible on the mantle to this day.

TRADITION AND OSAGE ROMANCE

Sunday, May 3, 1931, #75

Oftentimes in the mind of the world, a name is of much more importance than the thing that is indicated by it; the name becomes everything and the object may remain a thing of mediocre interest. Sometimes, a certain geographic feature is made famous by the most obvious of romances built around it and the name of this feature becomes internationally known. It becomes established in the mind of the world and it is a very difficult matter to dislodge it. There may be hundreds of such features like it and some even superior, but the name that has been repeated often, and recurs often in the mind of the world, retains the greatest interest for the world. Often fame, as Marcus Aurelius said, is "a decision of unreason," and often people and things become famous because of their association with other things, and sometimes by mistake. A name, a word, becomes permanently lodged, and it remains to the detriment of that having a better claim.

Humanity clings to tradition; it is one of the strongest forces in life. It is a force in all life. The blackbirds will come to the same elm tree year after year to hold their spring convention, and robins, cardinals, brown thrashers, et cetera, will come to the same tree year after year to build their nests. It would break the British heart to dismantle Oxford, or tear down the Tower. France would go to war if Notre Dame were to be menaced. Englishmen, Frenchmen, blackbirds, and robins are moved by the same force. It must have something to do with survival.

One could imagine the turmoil, the flood of literature, and the frantic broadcasting over the nation if there developed an organized movement to change the name of America. Though our continent was named for an Italian trader who had nothing to do with the discovery of America or the establishment of Europeanism on the continent, Amerigo Vespucci was only a trader who wrote a narrative of his voyage to South America. One would venture that he was quite a salesman as well. Anyway, tradition has made him immortal.

The Osage Hills mean romance to many people over the state, and sporadically, throughout the nation. Even in Paris and London, people have heard of the Osage Indians. The sensational news story of their riding in hearses because of the appeal of their ornateness and luxuriousness has been reprinted at one time or another in many papers. The Osage Hills, according to the newspapers, are the refuge of all bandits who can flee here with convenience. The Osages have been and are still, newspaper and cinema millionaires. Many

Mexicans, Indians of other tribes, "high brown" Negroes, and benighted Nordics and Latins, pose as Osage Indians, for the reflected glory the association of the tribe with oil is supposed to bring.

Here are the beginnings of a tradition in the Osage, while the real Osage of rolling prairie, blackjacks, space and sky is unknown; while the rich romance of the tribe known as Osage is neglected. The very names Pawhuska and Osage have an appeal, but there is no definite association except bandits, oil, murder, graft, and squandering.

"ROMANCE OF THE OSAGES" ON RADIO

In a stinging parting shot, John Joseph Mathews manages to slip in righteous criticism from an Osage perspective. This concludes an article that is otherwise again calling for the production of a "romance of the Osage" that would publicize the area and attract tourism. Mathews made things happen, whether it was Osage romance or a tribal museum. In April 1937, NBC Blue Network broadcast nationwide "Romance of the Osages," a special half-hour radio program that Mathews wrote and hosted, and during which he told two stories. Involving many fullblood and traditional Wahzhazhe singers and storytellers including Chief Fred Lookout, who told a story in Osage, and his son, Freddie Lookout, who translated it, the show was sponsored by the Bureau of Ethnology and recorded at the Tulsa Chamber of Commerce. After the broadcast, Mathews received a package with four aluminum records containing the show (which required a special needle for playback), and decades later he audiotaped them, but what happened to these albums and tapes is unknown. The next year, the Osage Tribal Museum opened; Mathews was largely responsible for conceptualizing and securing federal funding for it. His sister Lillian B. Mathews served as its first curator.[11]

ROMANCE OF THE OSAGE

Tuesday, March 3, 1931, #59

Sometimes, one is thoroughly convinced that the world ought to know about the Osages, and he wonders how this could be brought about without the usual sensational ballyhooing. He would hesitate a long time before subjecting it, and all that it means, wrapped as it is in the unique traditions and teeming with rich interest, to the barbaric yowlings and insincere mouthings of promoters. The thing the world would appreciate in the Osage is that unusual history and that strange fascination of being the one and only—something that is found nowhere else on the globe. There are few tribes of Indians who still carry on their ancient ceremonials just for the pleasure such ceremonials give them. They have learned to show off for money and their ceremonials have in consequence suffered degeneration. It is disgusting to watch a tall, sedate, beautifully dressed and painted Ponca, Cheyenne, or Iroquois add the "Black Bottom" to his repertoire.[12] It is pitiful to watch a trio of Hopis do the "Eagle Dance" listlessly and without meaning, encircled by a group of Kodak-carrying, patronizing tourists.

The Osages dance for the pleasure that such ceremonials give them. The history of their Nation, and the human struggles of the Europeans and mixed-bloods in the relations to this unique Nation of the blackjacks and the prairie, are full of those things that appeal universally—full with very human things, and romance as glittering as that of strange places of the world. It is romance of homespun and buckskin, and charming recklessness.

For these things, the Osages would interest the world.

THE I'N-LO'N-SCHKA DANCES

Wednesday, July 2, 1930, #30

When one watches the Osages dance, he pulls himself up with the realization that he is looking upon a most fascinating vestige of the life that has contributed the most flashing colors to the pages of the colorful history of western America. He is flooded with self-deprecation for his carelessness in ignoring such vivid pictures of old America, neglecting them for the picturesque peoples and customs of other lands. Yet nowhere is such meaning hidden in a ceremonial. Nowhere in the world is there a custom more full of interest in its association with the romantic history of two peoples fighting for a continent, with a life as glamorous, vivid, and sweeping as the expanse of plain sky where it throve.

As the drumbeats start, and the first note of the high-pitched song is lifted, as the gorgeous dancers rise from their seats, one visualizes an emerald prairie, a blue sky with the cottony clouds of June; a circle of tepees, a herd of pinto ponies. Knowing something of the gods of these magnificent people, of the phenomenal approach in their religious beliefs to the accepted theories of a modern scientific world, one is apt to sit dreaming, watching the dance but not seeing, listening to the drums but not hearing. Seeing in his visualization the lithe, brown, half-naked bodies bedaubed in barbaric splendor of another day, instead of sagging bellies and flaccid muscles of prosperity. Carried back into the past but deeply grateful for that spirit that desires to perpetuate the dance in the present, dulled though it may be by the contact with civilization—perhaps modernity is the better word—one resolves to imprint indelibly in his memory every detail of the gorgeous spectacle that has passed before him during his lifetime and preserve as much as possible of its deep significance, preserving the spirit without cheap sentiment and flamboyant heroics, yet remaining true to that spirit that has been so little understood, delving deep below the superficial surface through knowledge of the language and the religion, and through knowledge of the natural environment that shaped both.

Impressions are interpreted by men, and interpretations are influenced by the nature of the man who interprets, and as such, they are valuable insofar as the interpreter is able to catch the spirit through sympathy and inherent knowledge. The Osages and their Hills have suffered through press stories, articles and novels. Inaccurate and bizarre stories have been written by scribblers who have invariably assumed an air of patronage toward a great people; they have sacrificed truth on the barbaric altar of sensationalism. Not in the actual writing lies the harm; the English in which they are written bars such stories from any literary importance, but such fantasies are taken by thousands of people as factual. In a country where such importance is placed upon efficiency and cold facts, it seems that such drivel would be inharmonious, and unacceptable to a people who call themselves civilized.

It behooves us of the Osage to collect our material, to preserve the spirit of our history before it passes, and by so doing obviate future collections of fantastic incidents under flaring cinema titles.

LAKOTA VISITORS AT THE JUNE DANCES

The close of Mathews's column presents an early manifesto articulating some of Mathews's cultural preservation goals. Osages and their neighbors should collect and preserve their own stories, write their own history. In line with this ideology, eight years later in 1938, the Osage Tribal Museum, Mathews's baby, would open. Mathews conceptualized the museum and secured Works Progress Administration funding for it. He was aided by his friends and contacts in Washington, DC, such as Commissioner of the Bureau of Indian Affairs John Collier and Assistant Commissioner William Zimmerman, who were both appointed by President Franklin D. Roosevelt. Mathews was a Democrat New Dealer, a vocal and public supporter of Collier and the Wheeler-Howard Act, the Indian New Deal.

Mathews attended the dances regularly, but like his protagonist Challenge Windzer, he did not dance with his people. An article from June 1931 suggests how the June I'n-Lo'n-Schka dances have changed since the 1930s, or at least their perception. They are referred to as "the annual Osage war dances" and described as "open to the public," which has not been the case for some time. Today only Osages and invited guests of the Osages are welcome at the dances. In 1931 the Osages were visited by a party of twenty Lakotas from the Oglala Lakota Pine Ridge Agency, led by a Sioux and Cheyenne dancer, singer, and drummer called Chief Black Horse, formerly known as Buffalo Chips. Chief Black Horse thrilled listeners as he told of his presence at Custer's last stand, and of his onstage appearances with Buffalo Bill Cody's Wild West Show for six years. "Although past 80 years old, the Chief demonstrated an agility and fervor in his dancing Saturday that far surpassed the performance of the younger bucks," a journalist wrote, using stereotypical language of the day.[13]

NOTES

1. A will-o-the-wisp, a deceptive goal or hope, the term is derived from the name for the light that appears over swampy ground due to combustion of gas from decomposed organic matter.

2. See Terry P. Wilson, "The Depression Years" chapter, *Indians of North America: The Osage* (New York: Chelsea House, 1988).

3. Raymond Redcorn III, personal interview, January 7, 2013, Pawhuska.

4. Robert Barr Smith, *Outlaws: Tales of Bad Guys Who Shaped the Wild West* (New York: Rowman and Littlefield, 2013), 115–16; John Joseph Mathews, *Twenty Thousand Mornings*, edited by Susan Kalter (Norman: University of Oklahoma Press, 2012) 76–77.

5. Laura Frost, "The Romance of Cliché: E. M. Hull, D. H. Lawrence, and Interwar Erotic Fiction," *Bad Modernisms*, edited by Douglas Mao and Rebeca L. Walkowitz (Durham, NC: Duke University Press, 2010), 102.

6. Steven Bach, *Marlene Dietrich: Life and Legend* (Minneapolis: University of Minnesota Press, 2013), 215.

7. Quoted in Jace Weaver, "Foreword," *The Cherokee Night and Other Plays by Lynn Riggs* (Norman: University of Oklahoma Press), ix.

8. Quoted in Phyllis Cole Braunlich, *Haunted by Home: The Life and Letters of Lynn Riggs* (Norman: University of Oklahoma Press, 1988), 141.

9. Roger Benjamin, *Orientalist Aesthetics: Art, Colonialism, and French North Africa, 1880-1930* (Berkeley: University of California Press, 2003), 100, 165.

10. Mathews, *Talking to the Moon*, 194.

11. Snyder, *John Joseph Mathews*, 98, 100.

12. The "Black Bottom" was an energetic dance that became a Jazz Age craze during the mid-1920s, its origins in Southern rural African American dances. Jazz pianist and composer Jelly Roll Morton wrote "Black Bottom Stomp" in 1925, recording it with his Red Hot Peppers the next year.

13. "Old Sioux Warrior, Present at Custer Massacre, Among Gayest Dancers at Osage Pow-Wow Here," *Journal-Capital*, June 21, 1931.

Part V

African Americans

"EE SA RAH N'EAH'S STORY" AND ZORA NEALE HURSTON'S "SPUNK"

Written in Pawhuska in May of 1931 and published in June, "Ee Sa Rah N'eah's Story" is set on the outskirts of the dance arbor or pavilion where the I'-Lo'n-Schka June dances take place. Perhaps the best story that Mathews ever published, it appeared in *The Sooner* magazine and was much later reprinted in a collection of early American Indian short stories, *Singing the Spirit*. The story begins with the narrative frame device of a boy very similar to the young Mathews listening to the title character, who wears moccasins and a scalplock.

> When the women were decorating their men for the June dances, he could always be found on the edge of the camp, sitting cross-legged, in utter detachment, and there I always searched for him. Though I loved the kettle-drum and its circle of singers, and of course was fascinated by the gyrations of the gorgeous dancers, I grew weary of this spectacle through long familiarity.[1]

Jo observed and imitated the movements of the dancers with his fingers, but he never participated.

Like the title character, Mathews was at the figurative "edge of the camp" of traditional Osage culture, in the margins between white and Osage society. The elder Osage's story centers on a Pawnee who kills a panther, concluding with a supernatural twist. "Ee Sa Rah N'eah's Story" has much in common with the Harlem Renaissance author Zora Neale Hurston's 1925 short story "Spunk," set in a small rural African American community in Florida. Hurston's story also involves a wild black cat in which, characters in each story believe, lives a reincarnated human soul. Both stories make use of dialect and draw from Southern and Southwestern folk story tropes, some shared in common between Native Americans and African Americans.[2]

PAWHUSKA FLOOD

On June 16, 1930, the *Journal-Capitol* printed a huge headline: "CITY DAM-AGED BY FLOOD." Several houses were swept away and others were ripped from their foundations. Readers learned that "residents of the negro section were returning to their water-soaked homes today after being driven out in one of the worst floods since 1915, when the entire business district was flooded." This result might be called a small but typical example of institutional racism. African American residents were sequestered in homes on lower land more subject to flooding. Some white or Osage families were "marooned" or had water flow into their homes, but the African American population of Pawhuska got it worst by far.

Such discrimination cannot be blamed on White residents alone. Any Black residents of Pawhuska had only been present in real numbers sometime after Oklahoma statehood and the establishment of Osage County in 1907, a year after the Osage Allotment Act. In 1905, the *Osage Journal* estimated only six Negroes at most were living on the entire Osage reservation.[3] Many Osages fought for the Confederacy in the Civil War; some had been convinced to do so by John Joseph Mathews's paternal grandfather, John Allen Mathews, a Kansas Territory bushwhacker who married two Osage sisters. Other Osages fought for the Union. The Civil War was incredibly destructive to the Osages, and in their confusion over loyalties, they realized the bloody struggle had something to do with the *Nika-sabe*, who therefore may have been stigmatized. Mathews wrote in *The Osages*:

> It had been explained to the Little Ones in some manner that the Heavy Eye-brows were fighting over the *Nika-Sabe*, but there were so few of *Nika-Sabe* there on the prairie to fight over. The abstractions were too much for the Little Ones, and they couldn't see any reason for these wild, unthinking men murdering each other, burning houses and whole communities, and shouting themselves into uncontrollable emotionalism.[4]

During the 1880s and 1890s, Negroes were expressly forbidden by the Osage Constitution. In late 1881, led by James Bigheart, the Osage National Council signed the Constitution of the Osage Nation. In 1884, Article XII was amended, while W. S. Mathews was national treasurer. Section 1 stated bluntly that "from and after the passage of this act, the negroes residing within the Osage Nation shall be ordered to get out." Section 2 declared that any citizen of the Osage Nation would be subject to a fifty dollar fine for "employing any negro upon this reservation." Section 3 requested the U.S. Indian Agent to "take such action as is necessary to have all negroes put out of the Osage Nation."[5] Intermarriage between Osages and African Americans was historically very rare.

JACK JOHNSON AND RALPH ELLISON

Mathews's column on the romance of the Osage of May 3, 1931, in which Mathews refers to African Americans pretending to be Osage, was juxtaposed with an advertisement for an upcoming performance of a touring act in Pawhuska: Jack Johnson's Big Vaudeville Show. This engagement was promoted by Tom Galvin, who later became a rancher and a good friend of John Joseph Mathews after he married Mathews's cousin, Marie Girard, the daughter of his Aunt Amelia "Minnie" Girard and Uncle Nicholas Girard, a brother of Jo's mother, Pauline Eugenia Girard Mathews (Jennie). During the performance, Jack Johnson, the flamboyant former heavyweight champion and folk hero to many African Americans, was slated to perform three two-minute rounds of exhibition boxing. The son of former slaves, Jack Johnson, the "Galveston Giant," was the first African American world heavyweight boxing champion, reigning from 1908 to 1915. According to biographer Geoffrey Ward, during a time "when whites ran everything in America, he took orders from no one and resolved to live as if color did not exist." Jack Johnson was the epitome of American individualism despite his color.[6]

In Ralph Ellison's 1940 short story, "Afternoon," the *Invisible Man* author draws from his Oklahoma City childhood, describing the skylarking and conversation of two boys, Buster and Riley, who both cope with poverty and abuse.[7] Riley vows to "learn to box like Jack Johnson" just so he can "beat the hell outa" his abusive father, prompting Buster to acclaim "Jack Johnson, first colored heavyweight champion of the world!" and wonder "where he is now." Wherever he is, Riley replies, "ain't nobody messing with him."[8] Johnson's ostentatious style and three marriages to White women stoked controversy and criticism from both the Black and White press. In another Ralph Ellison story, "A Storm of Blizzard Proportions," the narrator, an African American soldier stationed in England, faced with the chore of leaving a blue-eyed Welshwoman who loves him, cannot stop thinking of Jack Johnson. "In spite of all those women," he likes Johnson because the boxer "went where he wanted to go and did what he wanted to do. No matter what they said. That's what a man has to do."[9] Johnson, the protagonist thinks, was "a man engaged" and "a man enraged" who "defined the world in his own terms."[10] Jack Johnson's 1910 bout with James J. Jeffries was called "the fight of the century." Many Euro-Americans regarded Jeffries as the "great white hope" who might seize Johnson's title, and Jeffries' defeat prompted both race riots and celebration. In "Afternoon," Riley says his father constantly sings: "If it hadn't a been / for the referee / Jack Johnson woulda killed / Jim Jeffrie [sic]." The story concludes with Buster looking at a wasp, possibly symbolizing the oppressive ethnic WASP, as he further contemplates the wonder that is Jack Johnson.[11]

Johnson had been charged under the Mann act for traveling with a young White woman who soon became his wife, even though the Mann Act was not yet in effect. He was imprisoned and his career put on hold. Johnson was convicted in 1913, but skipped bail and fled the country. Theresa Runstedtler writes: "In his day, Johnson was the most famous black man on the planet. Not only did he publically engage racial segregation within the United States, but he also enjoyed the same brazen and unapologetic lifestyle abroad, one of conspicuous consumption, masculine bravado, and interracial love."[12] Jack Johnson returned to the States in 1920 and served a prison sentence. In his later years, he participated in exhibition boxing matches, and in the late 1920s, began a second career in band leading.

In December 1929, Jack Johnson was filmed at the Checkers Club in Harlem, leading a jazz band with a baton. Before the band breaks into the infectious "Tiger Rag," he announces to the cameras: "Ladies and gentleman, I have been requested by many to tell you just how I knocked out so many of my o-pponents. As far as I am concerned, that day has past. I have a new way of knocking them out, and I will show you." Hot-cha-cha! Also touted on Johnson's vaudeville program for Pawhuska were "Blue Singers," comedians, tap dancers, and "the big Jack Johnson Jazz Orchestra," guaranteeing audiences "two hours of high class entertainment." Forty years later, trumpeter Miles Davis paid tribute to the pugilist with a jazz-fusion LP called *Jack Johnson*, providing soundtrack music for a documentary.

One wishes for a time machine that would allow an experience of this performance. This program of African American entertainment starring the provocative Jack Johnson surely raised eyebrows in a small city on the prairie that, until the early twentieth century, did not allow Black people to reside or even work there.

CHICKASHA LYNCHING

Contemporary news reporting the state of race relations in Oklahoma con-
trasted violently with the placid natural scenes that Mathews limns. To the
right of Mathews's column of June 1, 1930, is the continuation of a shocking,
upsetting news story of White savagery: a lynch mob in Chickasha.[13] Today
Chickasha is known for the University of Sciences and Arts of Oklahoma,
which from 1912 to 1965 was Oklahoma College for Women, the alma mater
of the Chickasaw orator and performer, Te Ata Fisher. This Chickasha incident, preceded just weeks before by a horrific lynching in Sherman, Texas,
was the last recorded lynching in the state of Oklahoma. Henry Argo, an
African American man of nineteen years described as slow-witted, the son of
a local iceman, was accused of raping and assaulting a White woman, Angie
Skinner, wife of a sharecropper, and choking her infant in her small, dugout
home outside of Chickasha. Just a month before, Argo had been charged with
assaulting an African American girl, but the case was thrown out when the
accuser failed to appear, and he had a previous juvenile offense.[14] According
to Oklahoman civil rights hero Ada Lois Sipuel Fisher, who challenged segregation at the University of Oklahoma, there was "suspiciously little evidence
of any crime at all," however, including no marks on the neck of the infant
boy, but "those facts emerged" only later.[15]

Rather than letting justice take its course, a mob of boys and men gathered
around the Grady County Courthouse, growing to a thousand, and a lengthy
and destructive standoff ensued. The guards were totally ineffectual; a military patrol from Fort Sill eventually arrived to attempt to impose order. The
lynch mob, totally out of control, cut all the building's wires and cables, set
the edifice aflame, broke open a hole in a wall, and stormed the county jail. A
man climbed up and shot Henry Argo through the bars of his cell. Mr. Skinner, husband of the woman allegedly assaulted, gained access through the
hole, and stabbed Argo twice near the heart. Skinner later threatened to gather
a posse to "wipe out" the Black residents of Chickasha, recalling the horror
of the Tulsa race riot and massacre of spring 1921 in which over a hundred,
perhaps hundreds, of Black people died, around eight hundred were injured,
and at least a thousand families were left homeless after the Greenwood
neighborhood was burnt to the ground. An African American guard, Private
Melvin Stringfellow, was shot through the head. Henry Argo was reportedly
refused treatment in Chickasha and was driven to Oklahoma City, fifty miles
away, where he finally succumbed. In *The Tragedy of Lynching* (1933), Arthur F. Raper writes: "The Attorney General of Oklahoma announced that his
office would cooperate in the prosecution of the lynchers of Henry Argo. But
here, as elsewhere, the handling of the case was left in the control of the lo-

cal prosecuting officer and nothing has come of it."[16] Ada Lois Sipuel Fisher confirmed there "never was a successful prosecution for Argo's murder." She concluded that "the experience left scars on both the white and black communities. It takes a long time for any town to get over something like a lynching. It took Chickasha a very long time indeed."[17]

In a January 31, 1931, column, Mathews writes: "After him comes the mob. They attack him from above, from below, from the sides . . . he dodges to the side and down, but his attackers are relentless. He cannot cope with them. They become more excited and more daring. The mind of the mob holds them, and they become ecstatic in their lust to destroy." Mathews is not describing the Greenwood massacre or the Chickasha lynching, but rather an attack of crows and other birds upon a hectored owl. But just as he later does in "Singers to the Moon," Mathews makes pointed parallels between these brutal birds and a despicable form of human behavior, the lynch mob. Decades later, Mathews wrote a coyote story called "Singers to the Moon," which was posthumously published in *Oklahoma Today* in 1996, and in 2015 collected by editor Susan Kalter in *Old Three Toes and Other Tales of Survival and Extinction*. In this story, Mathews uses the perspective of a clever coyote he names Lineback to highlight the animal's intelligence and intra-species communication skills. Thus he elicits our sympathy for coyotes, who were being pitilessly hunted down and falling victim to cyanide traps implanted in the ground. Mathews lamented the persecution of the coyote, and in a January 1945 diary entry, he even dubbed an organized coyote hunt in Osage County a barbaric "attempt at mass murder."[18]

I wish to highlight a striking, previously unnoted rhetorical link that Mathews suggests in sympathy for the coyote, and implicitly, for persecuted groups of human beings. The two human characters in "Singers to the Moon" are Sammy, the rancher, and Sheb, the cowhand. When Sammy is away, Sheb enjoys roping young coyotes and "hanging them from fence posts so that people could see them from the County Road." Sheb seems to realize there is some shame in doing this, however, because when Sammy is present, he "turned them loose, seeming to agree with Sammy that it was much more fun running them with greyhounds."[19]

Mathews's references to a mob of men with guns in a country town setting out to commit "murder," or to hanging bodies where they can be seen from the road, gesture at the series of horrific lynchings of African American and Native American men that were all too common in the southern and western United States in the late nineteenth and early twentieth century, including Oklahoma. Of all the lynchings in Indian Territory and Oklahoma carried out between 1885 and 1930, about 10 percent of the victims were Native American. One of the most infamous lynchings was that of Laura Nelson and L. D. Nelson, in May 1911 outside of Okemah, the boyhood hometown of not only folksinger Woody Guthrie but also two of Mathews's friends, newspaperman Walker Stone and Houston oilman Ralph A. Johnston. Guthrie's father took part in the lynching; the Black couple's bodies were hanged from a bridge over the Canadian River. Photographs of the awful scene were sold as postcards. Woody Guthrie later wrote songs about the incident. In 1932 Will Rogers, who became famous with his rope tricks, wrote bitterly in his column: "In the glorious old state of Oklahoma, rope is not just an implement it's a tradition. Our history has been built on citizens dangling in the air by a rope and some escaped the dangling that would have made better history."[20] Mathews embedded a subtle rhetorical link to underscore his belief that organized killing sprees directed at a particular group, regardless of the group's color or even species, are immoral and savage. Although his column argues that humankind is a part of nature, Mathews with subtlety reminds us that we as a species have the intelligence and ability to rise above mob mentality and atavistic violence.

NOTES

1. John Joseph Mathews, "Ee Sa Rah N'eah's Story." *Sooner Magazine* 3 (June 1931): 328–29.

2. Zora Neale Hurston, "Spunk," *The New Negro*, edited by Alain Locke (New York: Simon & Schuster, 1997 [1925]), 105–11.

3. *Osage Journal*, December 10, 1905, quoted in Wilson, *Underground Reservation*, 47.

4. Mathews, *Osages*, 624.

5. "Constitution of the Osage Nation," *Treaties and Laws of the Osage Nation*, as Passed to November 26, 1890, compiled by W. S. Fitzpatrick (Cedar Vale, KS: Cedar Vale Commercial, 1895), reprinted www.loc.gov/law/help/american-indian-consts/PDF/02016475.pdf, accessed December 10, 2017.

6. Geoffrey Ward, *Unforgivable Blackness: The Rise and Fall of Jack Johnson* (New York: Knopf, 2004), 3–4.

7. Ralph Ellison, "Afternoon," *Flying Home and Other Stories* (New York: Vintage, 1996), 42–43.

8. Ellison, "Afternoon," 43.

9. Ellison, "A Storm of Blizzard Proportions," *Flying Home and Other Stories* (New York: Vintage, 1996), 149.

10. Ellison, "A Storm of Blizzard Proportions," 150.

11. Ellison, "Afternoon," 44.

12. Theresa Runstedtler, *Jack Johnson, Rebel Sojourner* (Los Angeles: University of California Press), 1.

13. "Chickasha Mob Burns Courthouse to Get at Negro," *Daily Journal-Capital*, June 1, 1930.

14. Arthur F. Raper, *The Tragedy of Lynching* (Chapel Hill: University of North Carolina, 1933), 373.

15. Ada Lois Sipuel Fisher, *A Matter of Black and White: The Autobiography of Ada Lois Sipuel Fisher* (Norman: University of Oklahoma Press, 1996), 45.

16. Raper, *Tragedy of Lynching*, 17.

17. Fisher, *Matter of Black and White*, 48

18. Mathews diary, January 14, 1945, Box 1, Folder 47, John Joseph Mathews Collection, Western History Collection, University of Oklahoma.

19. John Joseph Mathews, "Singers to the Moon," *Oklahoma Today*, August–September 1996, The OKT Reader section, II–VII.

20. Will Rogers, *Autobiography of Will Rogers*, entry for May 12, 1932, 252.

Part VI

Autumn

SUMMERTIME

Sunday, July 13, 1930, #32

The grass is less green. The seed pods and the white clusters of white and yellow flowers give the whole a less vivid color, as though the grass was fading under the intense rays of the summer sun. Yet there is beauty: not the emerald, vivid beauty of spring, but a sadder, softer beauty that expresses the tranquility and calm of heat. Every voice is softened to harmonize completely with this lethargic calm; no echoes or sounds carry for a long distance, subdued instead by the heaviness of high temperatures.

The insects in the grass roots are sleepy-voices and the birds limit their calls to lazy communication; only the dickcissel sits in the dazzling sun and sends forth his weak call throughout the day. Even the cicada, the symbol of midsummer somnolence, waits until four o'clock to start his chorus of shrill complaint to the gods of summer. On the higher hills, the leaves of the black-jacks stir periodically in whimsical little breezes, dappling the hot shade under them, the ragged shade that promises relief from the dancing heat devils, but cannot fulfill the promise of cool comfort. Along the streams, the cattle stand with fretful stolidity in the thick bushes, silently defending themselves from the flies, their forms reflected vaguely in sun-spotted water. A cicada falls buzzing from a sycamore into the water and spins there until some lazy bass or perch rises to gulp him down in a swirl of water, the concentric little waves making the reflection of trees and cattle crazily animated.

Then, as the sun slides down the hazy blue bowl of the sky, the pastel colors of summer come forth to paint pictures never seen on canvas. The haze of heat softens the colors and outlines of the trees and the hills, until the former appear as indistinct clumps on the distant ridges and the latter seem intangible in mauve and lilac. They become more evanescent and unreal as the sun approaches the horizon and changes to orange, adding to the dream-picture a touch of pink. The foreground is dotted with cattle, grazing with detachment that is peculiarly bovine.

The heat of the day is over. Soon the great red moon appears on the eastern horizon, as material and distinct as a plaque of brass, brick-red as though scorched, climbing out of the prairie to liberate itself from the earthly heat.

It climbs higher and soon becomes a small bright disc, flooding the Osage with its silver, making ragged shadows under the trees, and causing the rocks to float in the eerie light. The heat of the day is forgotten as a breeze springs up and rest is found in the magic beauty of a summer's night.

THE END OF A SPECIES IS THE ONLY DEATH

Sunday, August 3, 1930, #36

There is something poignant about the dying out of a species. The last individual of that species appeals to us in a sad way. We think of its being the last thing on earth with a particular form and coloration. In all the world there is nothing like it, and in all probability there will never be another thing like it. It must be thrilling to look at such a bird and know that we are looking at the last one of the race; that we are witnessing drama in the world organisms, and that we are watching in that last individual the symbol of termination; the only real death that can possibly occur on earth. The end of a species is the only death.

THE LAST DANCE OF THE HEATH-HEN

In the preceding column excerpt, Mathews goes on to quote two long paragraphs from a report by ornithologist and photographer Herbert K. Job, who was a collaborator with the celebrated author and naturalist John Muir, co-founder of the conservationist Sierra Club. On Martha's Vineyard, off the coast of Massachusetts, Herbert Job witnessed the last dance of the heath-hen, which Mathews calls a "close cousin to our prairie chicken," in fact a subspecies of the greater prairie chicken. With that precedent in mind, the reader is asked to imagine the "possible fate of the prairie chicken, if public opinion is not aroused on his behalf." Job concludes by comparing endangered birds to Native Americans, alluding to James Fennimore Cooper: "These dancing, strutting valiants represented, as it were, 'the last of the Mohicans.'" Job's evocation of this event, imbued with pathos, inspired a short story that Mathews wrote in the early 1960s, "The Last Dance."[1]

INTIMATIONS OF AUTUMN

Thursday, August 14, 1930, #38

Each day the grass grows paler. The sere leaves have begun to fall from the trees, giving the hills and valleys an atmosphere of autumn, but without the gaiety of color and change, without the promise of frosty mornings and lazy sunshine, and the vociferous V's of geese overhead. It is not apparent that nature is preparing for a change, but more the appearance of hopelessness and the end of resistance. One senses silent resignation to the blazing persecution of the sun riding supreme in the hot skies, and to the breath that swirls and eddies over the prairie and through the trees, breezes impregnated with the sun's rays as are reflected from the sweltering earth and radiated from the sandstone, breezes that move the curling grasses and rattle through the prematurely yellowed cornstalks and cause the dry whispering among the leaves, breezes that carry only the occasional bawl of a fly-weary steer and the heat song of the cicada.

But Nature is bountiful at this season. The seeds are ripening and the berries are come to maturity. Decaying logs are full of larvae and myriads of young insects hop and fly over the fields and woods. On the mornings following the days of humidity, every herb, leaf and grass blade has its drops

"Cedar Canyon" by John Joseph Mathews
Courtesy of the Osage Nation and the Mathews family

of water for the prairie and blackjacks, and there is much seepage among the clay and shale beds in the limestone of the wooded hills. Many of the birds may be seen with wings raised and mouths open, and their voices are hushed, but they are not suffering except in cases where water is not obtainable. Many of them are uncomfortable from being fat through inactivity. As in the case of man, when there is abundance, they grow lethargic. A mother quail will lie for hours under the shade of a bush in perfect contentment, while her brood scattered around her search half-heartedly for food.

The constant struggle of the species is at ebb; food is plentiful, and there is a truce on the prairie and among the blackjacks; a truce that will give the juveniles time to grow in strength and knowledge, so they may be competent to carry on the struggle when the cold winds howl over an iron world, and Nature bares her fangs.

EPHEMERAL LAND OF ENCHANTMENT

Thursday, October 30, 1930, #39 [2]

The dreamy, lazy gold of August precedes the glowing yellow and gold of September, giving way to the mellow gold and flaming reds of October that make the Osage a land of enchantment for a few days.

First, the sumac appears in a brilliant flash of crimson against the background of black jacks; against fields of brown, and along the roads. The scarlet groups on the hillsides appear like blood oozing wounds.

Later, the cottonwoods change to pale yellow, and the blackjacks seem to go mad in rivalry for frenzied gaiety before the winter death. Tranquil and glinting in the midday sun, expressing the richness of maturity, with a hint of the sadness of mutability and mortality that gives life much of its interest: the symbol of that bitter-sweetness that has much to do with the romance of living. As the setting sun turns the horizon to orange and red, and the mauve of twilight floods the distant hills, the mad colors stand out boldly and crazily like colored bits of material dropped from the sky by the hand of some careless pagan god.

The Autumn is the beginning of death, the last glorious manifestation of life before the silence of winter. The Mardi Gras of Nature, it is a season of activity and excitement.

"Blackjack Catkins" by John Joseph Mathews
Courtesy of the Osage Nation and the Mathews family

The tragedies and emotions of reproduction hold the insect world, but the humming activity of Autumn has a different meaning from the lazy humming of the Spring. The voices of the woodpeckers are heard throughout the day, storing winter's foods; the squirrels make many trips a day along the ground and up and down trees in the creek bottoms and along the ridges where the sun-dappled shadows are athrill with life. The honking geese traveling in V's and etched against the orange glow of the Autumnal sunset, give life to a picture already replete with color. The bluebirds, with soft voices of vague restlessness, are forming in flocks. The robins call to each other in tones of pathos and discontent, and the vulgar Bluejay cries in hoarse impatience, his thoughts divided between this strange restlessness and his alert watchfulness for the unique. The ever-present crow flies high above the painted trees and makes a fuss out of all proportion to the seriousness of his existence. The coyote complains of his lot to the cold, uninterested moon, and the little screech owl quaveringly appeals to the eerie spirits of the night, while the great barred owl sends his booming hunting call echoing along the still creek bottoms, freezing the furry hunters of the lower world in their tracks.

Color, extravagant and exuberant display; fevered activity and restlessness: the assembling of Nature's cast in the drama of Life, before the final curtain of winter.

VIVID COLORS OF AUTUMN IN THE OSAGE

Thursday, November 6, 1930, #40

It is impossible. Words cannot be used to interpret the emotions inspired by Autumn in the Osage. The gold—the old gold, the mellow gold—the fire reds, the soft crimson, the orange, the flaming reds and the dark and light greens, are all in riotous display. It is the sparkling, abandoned, melancholy gypsy dance of the death of a season. Hillsides gleam in the sun, fantastically painted in colors and combinations never seen on a palette, never reproduced by man. Hillsides dressed for the festival of Nature's Mardi Gras, changing as the sun climbs the sky and descends behind the high prairie of the west, changing as the moon climbs and floods them with cold silver and eerie silence. Vivid colors evoke the madness and rapture of abandoned living, summer losing herself in the emotions of extravagant farewell. Yet these colors also give the impression of melancholy and tranquility. . . .

Then, when the moonbeams search out and expose things hidden in the inky shadows, the 'coon walks calm with assurance along the water's edge, stopping to fish out with dexterous hand-like paw anything that glints in the ghostly light. The barred and horned owls vie with each shadow, and the

"November Glory" by John Joseph Mathews
Courtesy of the Osage Nation and the Mathews family

coyote's voice projects from the prairie in petulant controversy with his kind. The insect chorus is silent; there is no voice from the grassroots, except on very rare occasions, the frightened squeak of a mouse. Another voice of the autumnal nights is the bell-like baying of trailing hounds, echoing along the bottoms, facing out in the distance or approaching as the tortuous trail is worked out, the change of voice telling the hunter of the vicissitudes of the chase, working up a crescendo of emotions that reaches its apex in the excited medley that means "treed."

NOTES

1. Collected in Mathews, *Old Three Toes and Other Tales of Survival and Extinction*, edited by Susan Kalter.

2. Issues of the *Daily Pawhuska Journal-Capital* published from August 17 through October 29, 1930, are missing and not available on microfilm at the archives at the Oklahoma Historical Society's Research Center in Oklahoma City or at the Pawhuska Public Library. Sadly, unless preserved copies turn up, Mathews's "Our Osage Hills" columns from this period are lost. Therefore, my numbering system at this point refers only to the available columns.

Part VII

Man in Nature

NATURE IS THE GREAT SOURCE

Friday, June 6, 1930, #24

One is never lonesome when he wanders alone in the Osage; he is not lonesome if he is aware of all that goes on about him. He cannot be lonesome if he attempts to understand what is around him and attribute to it the importance which is its due. Many of us have been steeped in the artificialities of life and so coddled by the comforts of populated communities, that we feel strange and foreign, and perhaps superior to the life of the fields and prairie. It is perhaps because we have not had a full experience with men and cities and that dazzling whirligig we call civilization. By lack of experience, we feel that happiness and complete living are found where people strive by the millions—in the swarming streets where defeat, worry, greed, lust, and anxiety are worn like masks. It is there where lonesomeness is found.

In the heart of every man is the yearning for the woods and open spaces. Oftentimes, he dreams of outdoor life that is essentially unreal and romantic. He visualizes life in the wild as it is depicted by the advertisements of railways and from the ideas he has received from certain types of romantic literature, but the yearning is natural and the men who do not know nature feel the same desire as those who have experienced the many moods and phases, though his conceptions are ridiculous to the latter.

Nature is the great source. Our economic system is based upon the struggle of the species; the flowers were advertising their pollen long before man appeared, and fish and insects went in for mass production and volume before we claimed the natural process as a discovery. The herds and flocks of animals and birds formed for protection were the basis for our society formed for the same purpose. Each bird and animal lives under the laws and traditions of its species, as man lives under the laws of society; as he lived under the laws springing naturally from tradition and opinion, which hold in the progressive stage of his evolution. Man, animal, and birds as units in society, the herd and the flock, owe allegiance for the protection he received, and is therefore governed as an individual for the ultimate protection of all.

Man, it would seem, is better for living in constant touch with nature, and attempting to understand through her the meaning of things that surround him, whether he be devoted to the gods of commerce or a devotee of politicians who appeal in many cases with mere drivel, to his inherent tendency to heroize. In order to understand the present, man must know something of the past of the race, and in order to understand something of nature, the source of all.

The world's greatest music attempts to interpret the languorous rippling of a brook or the majesty of a storm; often the depiction of passion and love. Artists have tried to transfer the beauty of nature's pictures to canvas and the results have become famous as examples of great art. Literature is full of man's attempt to describe heat, cold, storms, and tranquil moonlight. The interpretations of other people, whether in music, oil paints, or words, may have the power to lift us out of ourselves for a time; they give us happiness, and the genius displayed in their creation has made them immortal as invaluable contributions to civilization. We may not be creative; we may feel unable to interpret for others that which we see and feel, but each one of us has in varying degrees the genius to educate ourselves to a better understanding, so that our appreciation may become greater, and thus we attain a happiness that is impossible to many millions. We live in a country unique for its beauty and interest. We have the music of the wind in the prairie grass and trees, and the beauty and majesty of electric storms. There are pictures that would cause an artist to tear his hair in despair, and the wonder of the phases in which nature displays herself, makes words inadequate.

One wishes to bring the attention of those who live in the Osage to its incomparable beauty, and bring about an appreciation of the wildlife within its boundary, both of the conservation of that wildlife for the pleasure which will spring from the proper valuation of nature and from its accessibility.

DOG, DUCK, AND BUFFALO

Monday, December 8, 1930, #44

To the man who loves shooting, there is nothing more thrilling than to watch one or more bird dogs working out the cover. Thrilling are the moments when the dog has disappeared for a short time, then appears suddenly rustling the fallen leaves and panting with tongue hanging out, and the sight of a dog on the stand, then again during the few minutes of rest when he looks up into his master's face with more than vocal admiration. These thrills make of man a god for a few hours. A mute understanding between man and dog contributes to the happiness of both: the egotistical man, sure of the complete adoration of his dog, and the happy dog filled with insane joy of living and the consciousness of having the unqualified approval of the god, his master.

In this season of scarcity, the real sportsman does not carry a gun but is satisfied with the pleasure of "working the dog." All the thrill is there except the actual shooting. There is even an added thrill this season in the genuine hunter's knowledge that that he is assuring himself of shooting for the future.

Thousands of ducks were killed several years ago by some epidemic. Naturalists and scientists were wondering for some time whether they were poisoned by the alkaline eaters of the western lakes, or whether their deaths were due to some other cause. Whatever the cause, thousands of ducks were found dead and dying. We of the Osage have noticed this effect on the flights over the Mississippi Valley. We are on the edge of the great flights down the valley, and naturally when the number of individuals shrinks from one cause or another, we of the fringe are the first to notice it. If one were to chart these great fights and draw lines on the map of the United States from the northern breeding grounds to the Gulf, indicating the area covered by the annual flights, he would find those lines would be drawn closer and closer together during the last decade; the lines east of the Mississippi river would come closer to the river and confine the denser flights to a smaller area.

Once, when the writer of this column was a small boy and spent many hours at the Indian Camp, admiring the stolid dignity, and wondering at the geniality of a number of the older men of the tribe, one of the smiling-eyed old fellows described to him the passing of the buffalo. He drew a figure on the ground with the general outlines of a pear. This represented the area in the Great Basin occupied by the great herds. He pointed to a spot in the upper southeastern part of this figure and smiled. Then he drew in the salt fork of the Arkansas, part of the Arkansas, and two small creeks which this writer understood to be Little Beaver of Kaw County and Big Beaver of the Osage. He indicated that buffalo roamed this region in the millions. Then he drew a smaller figure within the larger, of the same general shape; he hesitated, then indicated that in the margin between the outer and inner lines, the buffalo had disappeared. He drew a smaller figure inside the second one, then smaller and smaller ones each time, indicating that the herds were to be found only within the area represented by the successively smaller figures as the years advanced. Finally, the last figure represented a small area in the great Basin between the Platt and the Arkansas rivers, and then he drew small scattered circles within the last figure to represent the last, bewildered, persecuted bands. Then with a grunt of disgust, he obliterated the whole drawing.

The buffalo herds were migratory just as the ducks are migratory. They roamed north in summer and in the autumn came south in millions, and the effects of slaughter were first evident on the edges of the great herds.

COYOTE: ADMIRABLE BANDIT

Monday, December 22, 1930, #45

Of all the denizens of the Osage, there is none more interesting than the coyote. The invasion of hordes of people connected with the oil activity, and the gradual encroachments of the farmer on the ranges have not discouraged this very clever wolf. Guns, hounds, and poisons are useless against him. He has always ranged the Osage and perhaps will always be here in great numbers.

Pioneers of the reservation tell of the wolves and of a very peculiar little animal called the swift. There are perhaps a few wolves still haunting the sandstone escapements and the wooded streams and hills of the county, but the swift has certainly disappeared. It is not unlikely that the wolf will soon be gone from the haunts where he was found in great numbers, but it is credible that there is not one who can say there is one less coyote roaming the prairie than were at the beginning.

The processes of survival have worked havoc on the wolf packs, and the swift, never numerous wolf has been able to adapt himself to the changes that have come about. The wolf is predatory. He has few enemies outside of man. If the smaller, less ferocious coyote has held his own and has been able to adapt himself to the activities of man, why could not the larger, more ferocious wolf do the same? It is very likely a case of intelligence. The wolf's fear of man is a resentful, unreasoning fear, while that of the coyote, if his attitude can be called fear, has reason in it. It is cupidity. He does not depend entirely upon his strength or his fleetness, but uses his wits. He has that intelligence found in the animal world that gives to certain species quick adaptation to changes, perhaps that same intelligence that gave man his place in life. The wolf desired, and by strength and numbers killed with ferocity. He pitted his strength against man, and would not deign to adapt himself for the future benefit of his species. He warred openly and was defeated. The coyote, on the other hand, has never really feared men; he has simply adapted himself to man and the conditions that he has brought about.

Before the European came to the Osage, the coyote had probably not eaten the flesh of the domestic chicken, nor had he eaten watermelons. He saw a few Indian dogs, perhaps, which were certainly unable to catch him. He was never fired at. Yet in a short time he learned to distinguish between the long legs of the greyhound and the short legs and flopping ears of the slow trail-hound. He learned to eat with relish, watermelons and chickens and other things the European cultivated. He learned that a long, gleaming "stick" in the hands of a man was capable of spouting death and pain. He soon learned that a person in flapping skirts and sunbonnet was harmless, and that he could catch chickens with impunity despite her excited shouting, while her mate was a person to be respected, especially if he were afoot, and carried the gleaming "stick." It has even been said that a female coyote will establish her den and bring up her family almost within sight of one ranch house, but steal chickens as food for her offspring from a ranch or farm several miles distant, leaving the flock of her host intact.

Here is adaptation well exemplified. It is the law of the species: adaptation is necessary to the survival of the species. Many of the smaller birds and animals have gone from the Osage because they were unable to adapt themselves to the changes that the European brought. The coyote is probably the largest wild mammal in the Osage, if one excepts the few wolves, and the possibility of a deer or two. Yet his numbers do not decrease. His voice still thrills the listener on the night prairie, and he affords sport as he leads the hounds over the hills, often sending them back to their master with hanging tongues and heaving flanks. Defeated. But when he is caught, he fights effectively and silently with every ounce of his strength, until he is torn to pieces and the savage light dies out of his eyes.

A Chicken thief, a melon thief, a destroyer of prairie chicken nests. A marauder unexcelled, but an admirable bandit who contributes something indispensable to the life of the Osage.

COLORS OF WINTER AND ANIMISM

December 28, 1930, #46

Color does not go from the Osage. Colors play on the prairie from sunup to sundown, colors that would make an artist despair. Pastels mostly, silver greys on the bare branches, and the soft browns of the blackjack leaves. The tinted brown grasses change as the light changes, and mauves and pinks are suggested by the distance. The white boles of the sycamore in the creek bottoms suggest color, gleaming startlingly in the lazy sun of midday. There are no old reds and yellows of autumn, or the definite emerald greens of summer and spring, but subdued and sleepy seem the colors of midwinter. The green patches that sometimes appear under the trees are soft, and blend with the soft browns. Often, red berries in the creek bottoms almost shout for attention, but the grey stems of reeds and the mouse-colored trunks of the trees make of them only a touch of cheer. One such bush will give life to a whole valley; perhaps Nature's way of attracting attention to one of her masterpieces of winter.

There was much beauty in the conceptions of primitive man. He filled the woods and fields with gods, and attributed to them certain powers. He gave personality to inanimate objects, and gave to trees and animals the virtues and vices of man. In every disturbance was seen the activity of a god. Earth became to him a great mother, bearing the seeds of life. His gods were often vengeful, and not infrequently impish. When the storms bent the trees and the lightning flashed, and the thunder roared like celestial artillery, he prayed to appease awful gods; he wore amulets and charms and placed baubles on crude altars. In the serenity of sunshine, and the lethargic days of plenty he did homage to beauty. He was in close contact with Nature and could appreciate her moods. He read meaning into the most trivial thing, and this appreciation, this concept of Nature is pleasing to us now. He felt the teaming life about him, and his worship, though crude, can never be distasteful to more civilized minds. There is a personality of the woods and fields; the whole meaning of life is there.

SUPPLICATION TO WAH'KON-TAH

During this period, while John Joseph Mathews was in his mid-thirties, he struggled with his purpose and identity. Earlier in the month, on December 3, 1930, he typed a memorable letter to his friend and mentor, Professor Walter Stanley Campbell (author Stanley Vestal). Mathews had been depressed for two weeks, feeling that his life had gone sour. He was trying to write a novel inspired by his experiences at Oxford in the early 1920s, inspired and excited by recent conversations with Campbell, but his drive had sputtered out. "I need you tonight," Jo confessed to Walter, and considering the length of his letter, he might have added, like the late rock star Michael Hutchence of INXS, "'cause I'm not sleeping." Mathews described a weekend of partying with a free-spirited group of "smoldering youths" of his acquaintance in Independence, Kansas. Jo thought the trip would lend diversion, but these Jazz-Age Jayhawks, having taken libertinism to the limit, were jaundiced, even incoherent. A University of Kansas co-ed half Jo's age announced her boredom, then fondled Jo's chest "like some half-hearted kitten" and offered him her lithe body. Mathews was thirty-five when he wrote this "Lost Generation" letter to Campbell, much older than these "flaming youths," and had been raised with Victorian values. Instead of excitement, he found only weary degeneration. Bare thighs, nude swimming parties, naughty stories, promiscuous sex, even drunken orgies, had left these youths "stupefied and listless, like children tired of their toys."

Surrounded by White decadence and his own depression, Mathews told Walter he thought he might have to resort to "charms and amulets," or to praying "fervently to strange gods." He reflected on this. "Perhaps the gods of my red ancestors are jealous of my Europeanization, and think to win back my homage by causing disorder in my life. It may be that I shall turn to them; to Wahkanda, the Great Spirit, since the Greek gods have been of little aid." Turning to a notion of Osage traditional religion, he grasped at something familiar from boyhood that might lend succor.

> Oh Wahkanda, Intatsa, it is I, John, son of the Lame One, who comes to you with distressed heart and bleeding soul like the wounded bird in the grass. It is I, John, who has looked upon the ways of the white man and thought them good. I, John, Oh Wahkanda, the wanderer in many lands far from home; far from the black-jacks and the whispering prairie, am come back to you.

The Lame One was William S. Mathews, who injured his leg when a horse fell upon him; the leg had to be amputated and replaced with a prosthetic leg. This was very rarely mentioned by anyone.

Mathews then shared his devotion in animistic terms, having described animism more detachedly in his column:

> Know, Oh Wahkanda, that he has loved in awe the blinding lightning of your temper, revealing the trees like ghosts when nights are black; that he has loved in fear the thunder of your anger echoing over the prairie, and has known in admiration the howling winds of your disfavor, when trees cried in frenzy and bent in homage to your majesty. Oh, Wahkanda, also has he loved you when your hot breath rattled the leaves of summer, and dried the water in the streams; when you sent the heat devils to dance over the prairie and dazzle the eyes of your children. He has revered you when you have painted the leaves of autumn with whimsical abandon; when the sumac becomes a bleeding wound in the hillside, and your hand guides the honking V's of geese across the sky. His lips, Oh Wahkanda, have moved in the prayer of a strange tongue, when you with generous strokes splash the west with crimson and gold, and tint the twilight hills with purple. He has dreamed of you. Oh Wahkanda, drive into my soul the spirit of the prairie, which gave birth to mine own people, that in my creations I might glorify them, and thereby glorify you Oh Wahkanda, by speaking a language that is a true one. Turn mine eyes into mine own heart that I might see what is written there by your hand, and lift from my shoulder the tinsel mantle of deception and the sackcloth of convention, that my limbs may be free for action. Purge my heart and mind, Oh Wahkanda, of the phantasies of civilization, and fill the void with the things of earth; the truths that lie unheeded, and the true philosophy.

The personal and lyrical tone of this letter differs sharply with the public voice Mathews employs in his column, yet the vivid natural descriptions are familiar. Concluding his letter to Campbell, Mathews summarily dismissed this reverie as "crazy thoughts." In fact, it turned out to be a serious statement of intent that would guide the direction of his literary career.[1]

LEARNING MANY THINGS ABOUT MAN IN NATURE

Wednesday, January 7, 1931, #47

These are delightful days, with the hills and fields flooded with sunshine, the air cold and ringing like the tinkle of ice in a glass. The woods are athrill with life, busy life. The squirrels sun themselves on limbs, running here and there. Sometimes they are purposeful and at other times, just playful and filled with curiosity. Several species of woodpeckers talk as they busy themselves with dead tree trunks. The cardinal flashes through the undergrowth, adding color to the dull-grey stems, uttering his clear, flute-like chirrup. The titmouse, the junco, the chickadee, and many species of sparrow feed and chatter among the reed stems. The blackbirds hold daily meetings in the tops of trees, or cover whole fields in the feeding. The horned larks, when they are not flitting along prairie roads, follow the feed wagons as the fodder is pitched off to the cattle. The vulgar jay is somewhat subdued, yet when the sun warms him he comes out of his lethargy, and continues his search for novelties. Sometimes it is his good fortune to find a basking squirrel spread out in careless posture on a limb, and then he calls to the jay tribe to view the marvel. How they curse and scold, and fill the air with abuse! "What a scandalous thing it is that this robber should lie sunning on a limb, right out in the open; an affront to all decent people of the woods," they say. Of course, it is the case of the pot and the kettle. One can learn many things about man in Nature.

Sometimes the woods ring with the excited voices of a band of crows. Filled with indignation and anger, their raucous voices also carry a note of apprehension and nervousness. They sit in the tops of trees, in a circular group; they take turns flying up into the air and alighting again in another tree top. They dart down toward an object in a tree that is the centre of the group, each one scolding like a disgruntled fishwife all the while. The object of their attack is a great horned owl, sitting like some parasitic growth, solemnly blinking his displeasure. When he is first discovered, he attempts to ignore these black demons, by remaining motionless, but this is not possible after some cursing crow has pecked him sharply in the head. He becomes angry, but is helpless in the semi-blindness. He just sits and takes the abuse stoically, losing his composure occasionally by snapping at one of his persecutors. For hours they will taunt him, and all the while their number will grow by the addition of indignant crows from fields and woods and prairie. Finally, with some owlish curse on the whole species, he spreads his broad, silent wings and flaps away, always through the treetops, because of the small protection they afford him. After him comes the mob. They attack him from above, from below, from the sides. Often after a sharp peck, he dodges to the side and down, but his attackers are relentless. He cannot cope with them. They become more excited and more daring. The mind of the mob holds them, and they become ecstatic in their lust to destroy. His only hope is to lose them in heavy timber and after losing them, sit like some grotesque growth on the limb of tree, using his color and his immobility for protection.

MAN AS AN ANIMAL

Wednesday, July 9, 1930, #31

Man has gone to nature for his knowledge; he has imitated Nature in all that he has done. Not that this is unique inasmuch as he is a part of Nature, but he often forgets that he owes so much to this life which includes him, and attributes so much to his own superiority and originality, failing to see that he is only an imitator. He fails to see that mass production is the principle of the species in perpetuating their kind; that the nuptial plumage of the birds and the varied colors of flowers are advertisements, and that sex as a lure was exploited by nature long before man thought of large billboards depicting pretty girls in bathing suits, or the suggestive postures on cinema posters.[2] His whole economic system is built up on the economics of the species in their struggle for survival, and his social system springs from economic necessity.

Many of us are dreamers. We dream not only of the betterment of mankind, but of a Utopia. We struggle against things as they are, toward something infinitely better, and in so doing, ignore blissfully our origin. Our dreams remain things of vapor and we remain earthbound, tied irrevocably to the sordid business of self-preservation and perpetuation of our species, struggling on through the centuries, romancing and dreaming our dreams, but passing inevitably through Nature's cycle of youth, maturity, senility, and decay, handing on the spark of life and our accumulated knowledge to those who follow. Learning more of ourselves each generation, through knowledge becoming more and more our brother's keeper, and thus evolving according to natural laws against which we struggle in our dreams, we become more and more humane, and with each generation, new light is thrown on our history, and our origin and place in Nature, and with it a better understanding of ourselves.

These dreams may influence our ultimate evolution. The development of the nervous system that made our intellectual life possible is new. There are great possibilities in the further development of man's intellect, and man's dreams may be in the manifestation of the divine spark in him which is at this stage far beyond his comprehension. Yet in his present stage, he has developed far from his ancestors. Man's first dim dream of God, and his clumsy propitiation seem to us nothing more than ruthless savagery and lust, just as our conception will seem crude to those who follow in the future. But as we live our short span, we have only a short time in which to seek some kind of understanding. The beauty we find in dreams will not suffice; we cannot find happiness in struggling against the laws that bind us as a part of Nature. We must strive to understand Nature and her ways, so that we may have a better understanding of man as an animal, and through such an understanding, see the beauty of the life of which we are a part and the reasonableness and the romance in the natural laws under which we live. We will come to appreciate and interpret life for ourselves, each according to his limitations. We shall then find the harmony, the beauty, the romance that is in Nature, and find the joy in living.

ADAPTATION AND ILLUSIONS OF NATURE

Sunday, February 1, 1931, #51

If the temperatures of the summer were to continue on through the autumn and winter, it is true that the sap in the trees would descend and the leaves would turn red, yellow, and brown, and fall to the ground. The trees would attain that insensitiveness that they assume for the metabolic low stage of life, even though there were no cold winds and iron-hard temperatures. The grasses would turn brown, and the earth in general would assume the characteristics of winter. This is the habit of Nature.

In California, thousands of eucalypti trees have been planted. The eucalyptus is a native of Australia, and its habit therefore is to assume seasonal changes just the reverse to those found in California. In the spring, which is really the autumn for the imported tree, it begins to "change" its leaves; the tree is never bare, but the change occurs in about the same way that a bird or domestic hen moults. New leaves take the place of old one immediately. How long will it take this foreign tree to adapt itself to the seasonal changes in California, no one is able to say, but adapt itself it certainly will. Adaptation is one of the necessary laws of Nature; upon adaptation depends the survival of the species.[3]

The trees, plants, grasses and all the denizens of the woods would prepare for winter, even though the temperature remained even. They would follow the habit of Nature. But the fact that unseasonable weather in the months of January and February often brings forth buds and the early appearance of insects and frogs is not easily explicable. It would seem that pursuant to the habit of nature, the temperature would have nothing to do with the swelling of buds and the hatching of the young from insect eggs, et cetera. But obviously this is not the case. Nature is often misled by warm sunshine and seems inspired to awake and bloom, very often to her detriment. To anyone who goes to Nature for the explanation of all things, this would seem puzzling, yet it would inevitably occur to him that this unseasonable swelling into life is the manifestation of that force that is very source of dreams and activity. To put it into our own language, the false spring inspires nature to activity, though the illusion is often blasted by the arrival of lower temperatures, just as illusions are born and blasted in the life of man. Why could not this then be the same force which man calls Hope—the force that has influenced the activity of mankind since the beginning?

One can account for man's acquisitiveness through the law of survival in Nature. The urge to reproduce himself, and the instinct to protect the young, as well as the instinct to band himself in community, have their roots in Nature. Man's system of economics, under which comes his use of feminine beauty, his use of color, as well as the use of the tragic and the morbid in advertising and the daily news, has Nature as the source. His dream of the supernatural, his creative tendency, his resistance and his gratitude, are found in the processes of biological changes. In all activity relating to these natural tendencies, he is being what he is—that which he cannot escape until he has evolved into another state. Why then, one wonders, is this apparent lapse on the part of Nature, this tendency to bloom and spring into renewed life, through the inspiration of unseasonable warmth and balminess, not a quiet, unobtrusive indication of that hope that "springs eternal" in the breast of man?

Of course, hope has other sources in Nature, but as an indication of hope in the manifestation of Nature, this early awakening of life is a striking analogy. The idea is pleasing.

NOTES

1. Mathews to Campbell. December 3, 1930, Box 32, folder 27, Walter Stanley Campbell Collection, Western History Collection, University of Oklahoma.

2. C.f. Richard O. Prum, *The Evolution of Beauty: How Darwin's Forgotten Theory of Mate Selection Shapes the Animal World-and Us* (New York: Doubleday, 2017). Its publisher describes it as a "major reimagining of how evolutionary forces work, revealing how mating preferences—what Darwin termed 'the taste for the beautiful'—create the extraordinary range of ornament in the animal world."

3. Mathews uses the term "adaption," equivalent to "adaptation." Because the latter became the common term, I have inserted it in the place of "adaption."

Part VIII

Osage Women and Others

RED EAGLE REDUX: ROSA AND HENRY

On December 8, 1930, the same day that Mathews's column "Dog, Duck, and Buffalo" ran, the *Journal-Capital* reported that "one of the few remaining old-time Osage fullbloods," Mrs. Rosa Pryor Red Eagle, or Sah-me-tsa, had passed away. She was "one of the oldest and best-loved women of the tribe" and the widow of Henry Red Eagle, Che-sho-shin-ka, "one of the best known Osages," who predeceased her in October 1929. Rosa was also the aunt of Julia Pryor Mongrain, who married Fred Lookout, longtime principal chief of the Osages; Julia Lookout's parents were Stephen Mongrain and Mary Pryor.[1] Rosa's husband, Che-sho-shin-ka, as a boy had fought alongside his father against General Custer when the officer was embattled near the future site of Oklahoma City. For ceremonials, Henry proudly maintained tradition, using war paint and wearing traditional Osage attire.[2] Mathews described Henry Red Eagle's funeral in a "The Passing of Red Eagle," a piece published in February in *The Sooner* magazine:

> It was not so much the long painted figure in the finery of his race that caused emotion of sharpest regret, and brought brave efforts to check visible evidence of the disturbance within, but the end of an epoch. A past of which there is little evidence other than a few faded ribbons, a few pictures, and a disconnected story in the precarious memories of those whose chief interests were trade, and in many cases, actual existence.

"Rosie" Red Eagle and Henry Red Eagle were the parents of Paul Red Eagle, who was an assistant principal chief of the Osages—and during 1923 and 1924, principal chief—and of an adopted daughter, Mary Pitts of Hominy, a notable Osage Quaker and a leader of Women's Club projects. "The Mother of the Hominy Meeting," Mary Pitts was also the mother of a future principal chief, Paul Pitts, who was also active with Hominy Friends Meeting, and among Quakers became widely known as a spiritual leader.[3] Paul Red Eagle led the tribe during the traumatic years of the Osage reign of terror murders, years during which Mathews was abroad studying at Merton College, Oxford University.

CIMARRON *MANIA:*
EDNA FERBER, LOUIS BRAVE,
LUSHANYA, AND CHIEF BACON RIND

As Mathews's "Our Osage Hills" columns appeared, *Cimarron* mania was sweeping Osage County. Pawhuska, the Osages, and the Mathews family all had connections to the film, the bestselling novel, and its author, Edna Ferber. Beginning with the success of Ferber's novel in 1929, which was serialized in newspapers the next year, and intensifying in May 1930, with newspaper reports of the rapid filming of its adaptation, *Cimarron* mania spread like a prairie fire across vast Osage County.

In June 1930, Doran C. Cox, assistant director of *Cimarron*, along with cameramen from RKO studios of Hollywood, arrived in Pawhuska and began shooting prairie and oilfield scenes. No doubt Mathews, living in town at the Mathews home, had heard of their arrival. Cox proclaimed the movie would portray the "transformation of Oklahoma from a desolate prairie to a land of thriving cities." The first scene of the movie depicting the land rush of 1889 required five thousand people and a thousand wagons; twenty cameras would shoot for three days, at great expense, Cox said.[4] Doran Cox was also tasked with spotting authentic-looking Osages, whom he would invite to return to Hollywood with him to appear as extras in the film.

Edna Ferber's story dramatizes Oklahoma land runs and the Osage tribe, before and after the discovery of oil under their reservation, and Ferber visited with Mathews family members during her research for the book. Ferber, a popular Jewish playwright and novelist from the Midwest, was already celebrated for her Pulitzer prize–winning *So Big* (1924) and *Show Boat* (1926), which in 1927 was adapted into a musical. In 1928, while Mathews was living in California, Ferber spent significant time in Osage County. Phillip Fortune, Jo's cousin through adoption, said that Ferber, while visiting Pawhuska, stayed at the Mathews family home at length and interviewed Jo's sister, Lillian Mathews, a local historian, about the history of the Osages and their interactions with settlers.[5]

While visiting Pawhuska, Ferber tried to gain access to former Indian agent Laban Miles's journals, but was denied. These journals instead became a major source for John Joseph Mathews's successful first book, *Wah'Kon-Tah: The Osage and the White Man's Road*, which he composed from July through November 1931, right after wrapping up his *Our Osage Hills* column. In fall 1932, *Wah'Kon-Tah* was published by the University of Oklahoma Press and chosen as an alternate Book of the Month Club selection. This evocative, literary non-fiction work tells the story of the Osages from 1878 to 1931, using the point of view of the Quaker Indian Agent to the Osages, Major Laban J. Miles. The Friend had been a neighbor and friend of the Mathews family; Jo interviewed an elderly Laban Miles after he returned to Pawhuska from California in October 1929. Prior to Laban Miles's death in April 1931, he gave Mathews his journals, saying he hoped the budding writer could do something with them; these and Jo's interview notes became his sources for his first book.

Intrepid Edna Ferber was again stymied when she attempted to interview Alexander Joseph Tall Chief, the affluent father of future prima ballerinas Maria and Marjorie Tallchief. Maria Tallchief writes in her memoir that during Ferber's research trip to Osage County, the novelist visited Fairfax and made efforts to schedule an interview with the prominent Osage, think-ing Alex had information she desired. Edna Ferber was blocked, however, by Ruth Porter, his wife and the girls' mother, a strong Kansan woman of Scots-Irish ancestry. Maria Tallchief recalled: "She was jealous. Daddy was extremely handsome, attractive to women. Although Ferber wasn't known for her good looks, I believe Mother was afraid Daddy would fall in love with the sophisticated novelist and abandon us."[6]

Osages and other Natives became involved with the making of *Cimarron*, illustrating how Hollywood interacted with and represented American Indi-ans. In May 1930, *The Daily Journal-Capital* reported that "two Pawhuska Indians, Louis Brave, fullblood Osage, and his wife Lou-scha-enya, the Chickasaw Hummingbird, have connected with the 'talkies' in Hollywood."[7] The Braves were both actors and Lou-scha-enya, or Lushanya, born Tessie Mobley, was an opera singer renowned both for her voice and beauty. From the Ardmore area, the daughter of a white father and a Chickasaw mother, Lushanya grew up in a bicultural environment. She became interested in opera in high school and sang in college, but was also especially close to her maternal grandmother, "who, it was said, spoke no English but taught her to do beadwork and identify useful herbs and foods," writes Richard Green, biographer of Lushanya's Chickasaw contemporary, Te Ata Fisher, storyteller and performer. Te Ata and her husband, Clyde Fisher, visited John Joseph Mathews at The Blackjacks in 1934, an example of the Indian Territory social network of creative folk that spread during this period. Lushanya had the opportunity to study music in Europe, and it is said that when she made her operatic debut at La Scala in Milan, Italy, the enraptured audience lost control of their senses, covering her hands and feet with copious kisses.[8] Her Osage husband Louis Brave signed a contract with RKO Pictures as "Indian technical advisor" for *Cimarron* and Lushanya assisted. While on the job in Hollywood, Lushanya unintentionally scored the part of Matape in a Ziegfeld movie called *Whoopie!*, a Southwestern and Indian musical comedy starring the Jewish singer and entertainer Eddie Cantor playing a hypochondriac who travels to Arizona for a rest cure. Florenz Ziegfeld, Jr., who also produced the film of Ferber's *Show Boat*, glimpsed lovely Lushanya on the set one day and immediately ordered a screen test. Florenz was the producer of the famous Ziegfeld Follies stage show revues, which featured not only their celebrated chorus girls, but also Eddie Cantor and his lifelong friend, Cherokee entertainer Will Rogers, who enjoyed early success with his lariat tricks and homespun wit prior to becoming a massive movie star, then a syndicated columnist.

The then-famous composer Charles Wakefield Cadman had discovered Lushanya's talent, and in the late 1920s he launched her career as a soloist in the "Indian Ceremonials" event held at the Hollywood Bowl. Cadman's one-act opera *Shanewis: The Robin Woman*, lyrics by Nelle Richmond Eberhardt, among many other pieces, employed "an unadorned Osage song, sung in a traditional style largely untouched by Cadman's alterations and orchestrations," and provided one of Lushanya's signature songs. Philip Deloria identifies *Shanewis* as a milestone in American musical history, a precursor of what he jocosely calls "the sound of Indian" (i.e., the music heard in countless movie and television show soundtracks, pop songs, and even sporting events that rapidly signal that the hills—or plains as the case may be—are alive with "Indians," often on the warpath). The soundtrack of *Cimarron* is in fact an early example of the Indian sound of which Cadman was a co-creator, Deloria notes. The most successful composer of the so-called Indianist movement in American classical music, Charles Wakefield Cadman blended tribal tones and timbres with nineteenth-century Romanticism. The movement was popular during the first two decades of the twentieth century, a time when one could find many examples of operatic treatments of American Indian life and music, some more successful than others. Cadman lived among Omahas and Winnebagos and studied their instruments, and he studied the anthropological work of Alice Fletcher and Francis La Flesche, the latter an Omaha himself, who studied the Omahas and Osages. Cadman even assisted La Flesche in recording Native songs and drew from those same recordings. With a charitable view, Philip Deloria writes that Cadman refused merely "to imagine an Indian sound but looked, instead, to Native originals for his sources." Cadman borrowed Native songs, usually Osage or Omaha, and embellished their melody lines with harmony and rhythm that "faithfully captured the essence of the original." He saw himself as engaged in translation, representing Indigenous meanings "in compelling music forms," Deloria writes. Cadman toured a popular lecture on American Indian music with the Creek-Cherokee singer Tsianina Redfeather singing and educating mainstream America on Indigenous music and culture. To his discredit, however, Cadman appropriated an Osage song, placing it in a different context without asking the permission of the tribe. Moreover, Nelle Eberhardt's libretto was often stereotypical and un-tethered from original musical meanings, working at cross-purposes against Cadman's music and intentions, Deloria concludes.[9]

Often holding a background in both Indigenous music traditions and Indian boarding school bands and choirs, Native Americans in the early twentieth century participated widely in such high-culture realms as opera, art song, and chamber music, defying mainstream expectations and stereotypes, and showing Natives to be co-creators of cultural modernity, not anomalies. *Shanewis: The Robin Woman* opened in 1918 at the New York Metropolitan Opera, and was also performed in 1919—making it the first opera composed by an American to be performed at the Met two years in a row—and it toured other cities such as Denver and Los Angeles. Back then, the Creek and Cherokee singer Tsianina Redfeather, billed as Princess Redfeather, whose semi-autobiographical stories inspired the story of *Shanewis*, was Cad-man's featured vocalist. The story centered on a Native girl gifted in music, sponsored by a rich Californian clubwoman, who leaves her reservation in Oklahoma to study music in New York. Redfeather reprised the role in 1926 at the Hollywood Bowl before Lushanya picked up the mantle.[10] The name Lou-scha-enya, which she took to mean "songbird," became attached to Tes-sie Mobley's name; she was oft called the Songbird of the Chickasaws, the Chickasaw Songbird, or the Chickasaw Hummingbird. During the 1930s, she studied at the State Academy of Music in Berlin and gave solo vocal perfor-mances in Los Angeles and Chicago. In 1937, she performed at the corona-tion of King George VI before meeting him and Queen Elizabeth. That year she gave her most celebrated solo performance in the title role of Verdi's *Aida* with the Chicago Opera Company at the Trieste Opera House in Italy. She later married Ramon Vinay, a distinguished tenor of the Metropolitan Opera, and retired to focus on managing his career.[11]

John Joseph Mathews's first wife, Virginia W. Mathews, or Ginger, was a singer and more so a dancer who performed in joint recitals with Charles Wakefield Cadman, linking her to Lushanya. Ginger, using her training at the Brilliantmont School in Geneva, Switzerland, gave dance concerts in Cali-fornia and New York using her stage name, Anna Pavia. Ginger's recital with Cadman, her role as Minnehaha in a performance of *Hiawatha* at the Rose Bowl, and her marriage to an Osage man, all suggest Ginger Mathews was much intrigued by American Indian culture.[12]

The presence of Osages in the film was used as a selling point to promote the release of *Cimarron* in theaters. During February and March 1931, to pub-licize *Cimarron*, newspapers around the country hyperbolically claimed that "fifty-one millionaires" had "appeared as 'extras' in Radio Pictures' *Cimar-ron*." At the age of eighty, Wah-she-hah (Star That Travels) or Chief Bacon

Rind, joined by fifty more Osages, had "journeyed to Hollywood to appear in the Edna Ferber epic to ensure authentic Indian types. They are among the richest men in the United States, as the result of the oilfields developed on their lands in the Osage Nation. Louis Brave, full-blooded Osage and university graduate, acted as interpreter for the Indians."[13] Mathews remarked with irony in a later column that despite vicissitudes in fortunes, "the Osages have been and are still, newspaper and cinema millionaires." Sadly, Louis Brave and Tessie Mobley were divorced later that year, perhaps in part due to the stress of a dual Hollywood career in the media spotlight. Wah-she-hah, who had become a much-photographed Osage celebrity, died the following year.

Pawhuska celebrated the release of the movie *Cimarron*—directed by Wesley Ruggles and starring Richard Dix and Irene Dunne—with a special *Cimarron* page of tie-in ads for local businesses in the *Journal-Capitol*, on March 25, 1931. The copywriters of the movie ad did not fear risking hyperbole: "Drama Terrific as All Creation, an Avalanche of emotion sweeping into oblivion all that has gone before—WROUGHT FROM THE SOUL OF A MIGHTY PEOPLE WRITTEN IN FIRE ACROSS THE SCREEN!" Get me to the Ki-He-Kah Theatre immediately!

Cimarron was well received upon release. *Variety* hailed it as an "elegant example of super film making," a "spectacular western" offering "action, sentiment, sympathy, thrills and comedy—and 100% clean."[14] *Cimarron* was nominated for seven Academy awards and won three, the first Western to win the Oscar for Best Picture, and the only one to win it for nearly sixty years, until 1990 when *Dances with Wolves* took the prize.[15] While *Cimarron* has merit, despite the accolades, its appeal is perhaps more modest today. In 1960, director Anthony Mann filmed a second adaptation, and this version starring Glenn Ford and Maria Schell is better known, but lacking the authentic backdrop of Osage County.

OUR ENVIRONMENT SHAPES OUR PHILOSOPHY

Sunday, January 11, 1931, #48

> Man-made heights and man-made canyons,
> Paved with cement hard and cold.
> Harsh sounds of maddening hurry,
> Rasping screams of steel 'gainst stone
> God-made heights and God-made canyons,
> Paved with verdure green and cool.
> Bird songs and spacious freedom,
> And above the sky's blue dome.
>
> —Marie Mathews

Certainly the natural environment of the peoples of the earth has affected their characteristics, has affected their literature, their art, their music and their conception of immortality. Just as species vary with environment, and develop in harmony the nature of their surroundings, so has the race of mankind developed. There is a great difference between the song-loving and carefree Italians and the northern Scotsman or the Norwegian. The harsh deserts of North Africa and Arabia have colored the thoughts and attitude of the bands that roam over them. On the deserts, life is harsh, and this harshness has affected architecture, literature, laws and religion. In the North there is harshness, but it is not the same. Here it may be called severity, lacking fervor, but mixed with a gloomy mysticism. Amidst the gloomy forest lands, and frowning hills of the north, during the long winters, man is much indoors with his thoughts. Nature is ice-locked or fog-bound, creating depression of spirits, which gives birth to mystic conceptions and gloomy superstitions. As the pagan religion of Rome was colored by the many peoples of different environment who accepted it, so is Christianity, born as it was on the burning sands and sun-reflecting rocks, colored by the environment of the peoples who follow its teaching. Their interpretations must differ, just as the environments which make them what they are differ.

Where man has existed for hundreds of years in certain regions, the nature of his surroundings are reflected in him, and all that he thinks or does reflects his natural environment. Man attempts to interpret that which he sees, that which he knows and feels through inheritance. Whether his interpretations are by the medium of art, music, architecture, literature, religion, or law, he is interpreting Nature, and especially that manifestation of Nature that has molded his race.[16]

In the ghostly half-light, one finds a dreary though pleasing desolation. No sound is heard except the sad chirrup of the horned lark,[17] and at rare intervals, the exaggerated bawl of a discontented steer, invisible somewhere among the hills. Silence is felt in the long interval, silence like velvet. A hiker's footfalls are in cadence with his almost audible pulse, as he feels cool moisture against his hot face. A lone tree appears suddenly, like a thing of the imagination, unreal and disembodied. The vague outline of the hills is exaggerated and fantastic, like stage setting. Familiar objects become unreal, and loom grotesquely. The world has become small, and its objects grow large and forbidding and strange. There is no sky curving to the brown hills to give the impression of definiteness. All is indefinite except one's pulse and the thud of his footfalls. Here is mystery and adventure and a most pleasing ethereal solitude, when the prairie is shrouded in mist.

MARIE IMOGENE MATHEWS

Although Marie Mathews was known to be a poet, the untitled poem in the previous section is the only one known to be published, though one hopes more of her work might be discovered. Born in 1897, Marie Imogene Mathews was John Joseph's favorite sibling, the middle sister among his three younger sisters, between Lillian and Florence. Josephine was firstborn, and John Joseph was the only surviving male child. Like her sisters Josephine and Lillian, Marie Mathews played piano; Florence played harp, and Jo as a child reluctantly studied violin. Unfortunately, because of rheumatism, Marie became almost totally deaf at the age of twelve. Like her brother and Lillian, Marie was a student of local history. Like her mother and sisters, Marie was devoutly Catholic, and like Lillian and Florence, Marie earned a bachelor's degree from Saint Mary-of-the-Woods College in Terre Haute, Indiana. Taking college classes together, Lillian took lecture notes for Marie, but became a bit vexed when Marie earned higher scores on exams. Jo thought Marie was the smartest of the family, describing her as logical, tranquil, and possessing a strong sense of justice. In a letter written at Merton College in April of 1923, Oxford University, he urged introspective Marie to be more proactive: "The world will not draw you out; you must obtrude yourself upon the world."

According to family lore, Marie Mathews became acquainted with J. C. Penney on a ship while she and Florence were globetrotting in the early 1920s, funded by their Osage headright payments. During a shared voyage, James Cash Penney apparently became enamored of the much younger Marie. Not long after returning to the States, the entrepreneur opened a J. C. Penney store in Pawhuska, largely as a pretext to see her, and arrived in town for the grand opening in fall 1925. Marie, however, was shy or embarrassed by the extravagant attentions of this two-time widower, and she refused to emerge from the Mathews family home to see him, Florence's daughter Fleur Jones said.[18] In June 1930, Marie was the maid of honor at her little sister Florence's wedding to Michael Feighan, looking "lovely in a frock of pink net made princess-style, with hat and shoes of matching color."[19] Lillian and Marie lived in the Mathews family home on 611 Grandview Avenue for many decades, until their deaths, and the home began to fill up with books, ephemera, artifacts, and other items. Marie Mathews, who gradually became something of a recluse, died in December 1988, about a month shy of her ninety-second birthday, leaving Lillian alone in the home.

FLORENCE MATHEWS AND MICHAEL A. FEIGHAN

On June 21, 1930, in Pawhuska, Jo Mathews gave away his baby sister, Florence Julia Mathews, in marriage to Michael Aloysius Feighan of Lakewood, Ohio, near Cleveland. Mathews nicknamed Florence "Dooley" after the character Mr. Dooley, the creation of Irish American humorist Finley Peter Dunne, because she had an answer for everything, her daughter Fleur Jones said.[20] Florence earned a bachelor of arts degree from Saint Mary-of-the-Woods College in Terre Haute, Indiana, and enjoyed traveling. Michael A. Feighan was a Princeton graduate finishing a degree at Harvard Law School. From an affluent Irish Catholic family, Feighan went on to join the family law firm; then he sustained a lengthy political career as a Democrat in the House of Representatives in Washington. Mathews and Feighan were both Democrats and anticommunists; Michael became one of Jo's many political contacts in the capital, which he visited fairly regularly as a tribal councilman (1934–1942) and later, informal advocate for the Osages. During the 1960s, Feighan knew President John F. Kennedy and worked closely with President Lyndon B. Johnson.

Florence and Michael's wedding ceremony occurred at historic Immaculate Conception Church in Pawhuska. The church boasts an array of beautiful stained glass windows, including two commissioned by the Mathews family to honor the patriarch, William S. Mathews, who died in 1915. "Indian Love Call," an enduringly popular tune from the 1924 operetta-style musical *Rose-Marie*, was featured during their ceremony.[21] Florence and Michael's firstborn son, Michael Aloysius, Jr., arrived in April 1931, William Mathews (Bill) followed in 1934, and Florence Marie (Fleur) was born in 1940. Tragically, in August of 1942, at age eleven, Michael A. Feighan, Jr., was killed in an accident involving a drunk driver. (Mathews's loss of his nephew must have been especially difficult, because only three months earlier, Jo and Elizabeth Mathews had been in a one-car accident with Jo at the wheel, which resulted in the death of the talented bird photographer, Lorene Squire, from Harper, Kansas, whom Jo admired.) The Feighan family moved from Lakewood, Ohio to Washington, DC, the next year.

Florence Mathews Feighan, as the wife of a career Congressman, gave tours of Capitol Hill homes to veterans with disabilities and their families, headed the 78th Congress Club, and advocated for American Indian rights. Feighan family members in various combinations made many visits to Pawhuska to see family. In 1976, Fleur Feighan married an industrialist, Hugh Jones, and they resided in Massachusetts. Bill Feighan, a gay man who made forays into business and Ohio state politics, never married. He made many visits to Pawhuska, some said to curry favor with his Aunt Lillian Mathews, who held the purse strings of the Mathews family estate. Florence Mathews died in January of 1980, seven months after her big brother, and Michael A. Feighan lived for twelve more years. The family seems to have prospered, because at Florence's death, the Feighans owned three homes, located in Lakewood, Ohio; Washington, DC; and Scottsdale, Arizona.

OSAGE WOMEN'S TEA:
BEHIND EVERY GREAT MAN

The interwoven biographies of the participants of an Osage women's tea party of January 1931, and those of their influential husbands, tell a rich story of the Osage Nation and its history of relations with the U.S. government in the late nineteenth and early twentieth centuries. These stories serve to introduce or develop several key figures in Osage history and politics. On January 18, 1931, a week after Marie Mathews's poem was published in her brother's column, the Pawhuska paper's front page announced: "In one of the most elaborate social affairs of the season, Mrs. J. George Wright [Irene Basford Wright], Mrs. T. J. Leahy [Bertha Rogers Leahy], and Mrs. Fred Lookout Sr. [Julia Pryor Mongrain Lookout] will be hostesses to the fullblood Osage Indian women of the county at the Wright home." A formal tea party was hosted from 4:00 to 6:00 p.m., with Mary [Lookout] Standing Bear, assisted by Julia Whitehorn, Minnie Fletcher, and Maggie Hickey, pouring and serving. Those four women were each daughters of present or former chiefs.[22]

By 1904, Julia Pryor Mongrain had married Fred Lookout, who became a longtime, honored principal chief of the Osages, and a friend and colleague of John Joseph Mathews. In the early 1880s, Quaker Indian agent Laban J. Miles—or "Thick Hand" as the Osages called him in their language—sent both Julia and Fred Lookout to Pennsylvania, where they studied at the Carlisle Industrial Indian School. Carlisle was supervised by Colonel Richard H. Pratt, who is notorious today for his credo paraphrased "kill the Indian, save the man." Julia Pryor was a great-granddaughter of Chief Pah-huh-skah, or White Hair, namesake of the city of Pawhuska and the White Hair Memorial near Hominy. In 1904, Pratt, who tracked the progress of former students, noted on Julia's record that she was "all right, progressive, but gambles."[23] Around the same time, Pratt noted that Fred Lookout, a landowner, was "doing as well as anyone on the reservation."[24] Spiritually, the Lookouts were practitioners of the peyote ceremony of the Native American Church, and in their fashion Fred grew his hair long and braided it. Politically, young Fred was a protégé of Principal Chief James Bigheart, also a fullblood.[25] By 1908, Lookout was assistant principal chief, and he later became principal chief when he replaced Bacon Rind (Wah-she-hah, Star that Travels), who had been removed by Secretary of the Interior Fisher after the 1912 election, discussed in Part III. A deeply respected and compassionate leader, Fred Lookout served as principal chief from 1913 to 1914, 1916 to 1918, and from 1924 all the way to his death in 1949.[26] Julia Lookout and Chief Fred Lookout are buried atop Lookout Mountain, a tall hill outside of Pawhuska, beside a large granite memorial. Their daughter Mary Nora Lookout, who poured and served at the tea party, had married Eugene George Standing Bear, an Oglala Sioux. Mary and Eugene George's grandson is the current (2020) principal chief of the Osages, Geoffrey Mongrain Standing Bear. Another great-grandson of Fred Lookout is E. Sean Standing Bear, an artist who contributed to the excellent book *Art of the Osage* by Garrick Bailey and Daniel Swan. At the Osage women's tea, Mary Wilson Lookout, who married Fred and Julia's son, Frederick Morris Lookout (Freddie), performed a piano solo. Freddie Lookout was a repeated guest at Jo's sandstone home on the prairie, The Blackjacks, during the late 1940s and 1950s.[27]

The ancestry of Bertha Rogers Leahy blended Cherokee, Osage, French, and Scots-Irish strands. Bertha was the great-granddaughter of John Martin, the Cherokee Nation's first supreme judge. She was the daughter of Judge Thomas L. Rogers, who fought for the Confederacy under the Cherokee General Stand Watie, served for several years on the Osage Council, and became the first chief justice of the Supreme Court of the Osage Nation.[28] Judge Rogers's father, his namesake, married Ellen Lombard, a French-Osage woman. Judge Rogers married Nancy Martin, who hailed from a prominent Cherokee family. Judge Rogers, as a Cherokee-Osage married to a Cherokee, helped the Osages negotiate with the Cherokees, from whom they had purchased their land in Indian Territory after being pressured to sell their remaining reservation in Kansas in 1871 per the Drum Creek Treaty of 1870. His daughter, Bertha Rogers, married attorney T. J. Leahy, a crucial figure in the history of the tribe because of his sustained legal work for them.

Born at the Osage Mission in Neosho County, Kansas, Timothy John Leahy (T. J.) settled in Pawhuska in 1892 to practice law after having done business there since 1884. He hailed from a prominent regional family. Although Terry Wilson refers to T. J. Leahy as a mixed-blood Osage allottee, Thoburn specifies that both of T. J.'s parents were Irish-born.[29] In 1921, Leahy stated "Practically all my life has been spent among the Osages. Outside of my immediate family, I have a good many relatives who are part Osage Indian blood." Back at the Neosho Mission in Kansas Territory, he said, "there were more Osage Indians living around me then than there are now."[30] In 1911, as oil development in the Osage was booming, T. J. Leahy clashed with the Barnsdall Oil Company, who cut the fence enclosing his pasture and farmland, and hauled in lumber to build an oil derrick. Leahy removed the lumber and repaired his fence. The conflict ended up in court, and Leahy's "right to refuse drillers entry into a cultivated enclosure was upheld," Wilson writes.[31] Six months before that, T. J. Leahy became an officer, and his mixed-blood cousin, William T. Leahy, became president of a new organization they co-founded with other mixed-bloods, called the Osage Protective Association (OPA). The OPA petitioned Congress to pass legislation preventing the Department of the Interior from "taking further action affecting the leasing of Osage land for oil exploitation without the tribe's advice and consent."[32] On Independence Day 1924, Leahy gave a speech commending the brave Osages who had served in the U.S. military during World War I, which included John Joseph Mathews. Leahy pointed out that these men had been under no legal obligation to serve, as they were not even U.S. citizens, yet they and other Natives served in a higher ratio than the national average.[33] T. J. Leahy served as a U.S. commissioner and on the Oklahoma Constitutional Convention. He was a special assistant U.S. attorney during the prosecution of the 1920s Osage reign of terror murders,[34] which necessitated three trials over nearly four years, until state and federal prosecutors won a final conviction in 1929. Even so, a minimum of a dozen murders linked to the case were left unsolved, according to Wilson, and many more were unreported or uninvestigated.[35] This was in part because of the vanity of J. Edgar Hoover, director of the new Federal Bureau of Investigation (FBI). Hoover wanted U.S. citizens, who were scandalized by lurid newspaper accounts of the murders, to believe that the FBI had caught their man, ringleader William K. Hale. They could not connect Hale to some of the murders, however.

T. J. Leahy's cousin and president of the Osage Protective Association, William T. Leahy married Bertha Rogers's Cherokee-Osage sister, Martha Rogers.[36] W. T. Leahy is a perplexing case, and records of a scandal that surrounded him yield information that may shed light on John Joseph's father, William S. Mathews, Leahy's predecessor as treasurer on the Osage National Council. According to Thoburn, W. T. Leahy was born at the Old Osage Mission at St. Paul, Kansas, and spoke Osage fluently; his mother was French and Osage and his father was Irish.[37] Wilson, however, calls the mixed-blood W. T. Leahy an intermarried citizen, not recognizing his Osage ancestry. According to Wilson, under Principal Chief James Bigheart's leadership, the Osage council became intensely involved in attempts to oust W. T. Leahy from the tribal roll. They accused him of embezzling tribal funds while employed as treasurer of the Osage Nation for four years, prior to the abrogation of the Osage National Council by the federal government in 1900. W. T. Leahy refused to vacate his Pawhuska office in the council house where he practiced law. In 1903, Secretary of the Interior Ethan Hitchcock ordered Agent Oscar Mitscher to remove W. T. Leahy both from the annuity payment list, which the Osage council had ordered over a year before, and from his office. "For want of adequate documentation of guilt or innocence," however, "the inquiry into Leahy's affairs ended inconclusively as the larger issue of enrollment pushed all other business from the council's agenda," Wilson states.[38]

The positioning and prerogatives of the office of the treasurer itself, established in the early 1880s when the Osage National Council was formed, were most unusual; they explain a portion of the accumulation of wealth in the Mathews family. Wilson writes: "If the Osages were especially zealous in balancing the powers of the executive and legislative branches of their government, the provision rounding out the executive with the office of national

treasurer seems peculiar for the latitude allowed holders of that appointment."
Per the Osage Constitution drafted in late 1881, the treasurer handles the
receipt and disbursement of all public monies, and retains a staggering 10
percent of all sums that pass through his hands.[39] William S. Mathews was
appointed by Governor Joe, or Joseph Paw-ne-no-pashe (Not Afraid of Pawnees), also called Big Hill Joe, to be the Osage National Council's first treasurer, serving from 1882 to 1886, and his brother, Edward M. Mathews, was
appointed the first clerk.[40] Governor Joe, the Osage Nation's first governor,
had negotiated with the U.S. government and the Cherokees to purchase the
Osage Reservation in Indian Territory. William Mathews and William Leahy,
who succeeded him as treasurer, acquired a great deal of wealth during their
respective terms as treasurer and each became involved in banking. At various times, W. S. Mathews organized and was the president or director of four
banks. With the timing of the end of W. T. Leahy's term with increased oil exploitation, he especially stood to rake in large sums. Leahy was the president
of a bank, the vice president of two banks, and the director of a fourth bank.
By 1917, he was the vice president of Pawhuska Oil & Gas Company.[41] Cha-
ching! W. S. Mathews was an organizer and the first president of Pawhuska
National Bank, where Leahy later became a vice president.[42] Despite the
scandal that swirled around W. T. Leahy, agent Oscar Mitscher chose him
the following year to be a part of the delegation that traveled to Washington,
DC, to discuss the proposed allotment act. The group also included W. S.
Mathews, Bacon Rind, Fred Lookout, James Bigheart, Peter C. Bigheart,
Heh-scah-moie, Black Dog, Shun-kah-mo-lah, and Eves Tall Chief.

Alexander Tall Chief (Alex), a brother of Eves Tall Chief, and father of
future prima ballerinas Maria Tallchief and Marjorie Tallchief, was another
treasurer of the pre-1900 Osage National Council, under Principal Chief
James Bigheart.[43] Like W. T. Leahy and W. S. Mathews, Alex Tall Chief got
rich. Maria Tallchief recalled: "As a young girl growing up on the Osage
reservation in Fairfax, Oklahoma, I felt my father owned the whole town. He
had property everywhere. The local movie theater on Main Street, and the
pool hall opposite, belonged to him. Our ten-room, terra-cotta-brick house
stood high on a hill overlooking the reservation."[44] The Tall Chiefs showed
generosity when they hosted a Christmas social in their home in 1913; two
wagonloads of thirty boys and girls "enjoyed games and refreshments in the
gaily decorated home."[45] The Tall Chief family enjoyed summering in Colorado Springs, golfing and swimming at the Broadmoor Hotel. Alex Tall Chief
had capital ample enough to move to Los Angeles to pursue his daughters'
music and dance careers. "Like many in the wealthy Osage tribe, Daddy
never worked a day of his life," Maria wrote, albeit he oversaw his business
affairs and worked for the tribe as treasurer. As was the case with Jo Mathews,
who sometimes labored long hours on research and writing, yet also claimed

to have never worked a day of his life, the phrase is hyperbolic. Yet it suggests the freedom that many Osages enjoyed, thanks to their headright payments in the late teens and 1920s. Another trait was shared by Alex Tall Chief and Jo Mathews, unfortunately. Maria Tallchief lapses into stereotype when writing that her father "was a modern-day Osage in another respect. He drank." Excessive drinking and drugs became a serious problem in Osage County in the 1920s and 1930s, exacerbated by copious bootleggers and crooked doctors.

Prominent Osage women sipped tea at their soiree while enjoying a piano solo played by Helen Tallchief, a cousin of Maria and Marjorie Tallchief who had attended Mount Carmel Academy in Wichita and Colorado College in Colorado Springs.[46] Osage wealth being both blessing and curse, Helen's life was beset by problems. Born in 1906, Helen was a daughter of the late Eves Tall Chief (Tse-to-hah), Alex's brother and a fullblood. Eves Tall Chief, a graduate of Haskell Indian School in Lawrence, Kansas, had been William S. Mathews's friend and fellow councilman from 1900 to 1904, during the pre-allotment period when the federal government refused to recognize the authority of the Osage National Council. Mathews, recollecting the mourning of his father's death in March 1915, believed it was Eves Tall Chief of the Buffalo Face clan who led a mourning party of five or six Big Hill men of the Buffalo Face or Buffalo clans. They rode on horseback up the hill to the Mathews family home on Grandview Avenue and tied their horses near his mother Jennie Mathews's celebrated flower garden. Mathews recalled: "I went to the door and held it open for them, and they came in one after the other, seeming, as they actually did on the trail, to step into the exact footprints of the one in front." The fullbloods gathered around a portrait of Will, and "there with faces uplifted to the portrait, they chanted the Song of Death, wherein the Great Mysteries were asked why they had taken away" his father's remaining days.[47] Eves Tall Chief was a talented steer roper and musician, and a practitioner of the Native American Church. In 1919, he was part of an Osage delegation headed by John Abbott that traveled to Washington, DC, to combat a bill that would prohibit the use of peyote, violating their constitutional freedom of religion. The bill passed in the House but failed in the Senate. Eves even won awards at the Oklahoma State Fair for his "fine chickens."[48]

Helen Tallchief was the oldest of Eves's many children, a daughter of Beatrice, his first wife. After Beatrice died, Eves married Rose, a pretty redhead from Ralston, a nearby town in Pawnee County, just over the Osage County line, and they settled in the Gray Horse area.[49] Russ Tall Chief said that according to the family story that he grew up hearing, his great-grandparents Eves and Rose met in an unusual way. One night, the mischievous mixed-blood was out riding his horse after knocking back a few drinks, and he decided he would shoot out the lights of Ralston. His horse took a fright from the gunshots and threw him, knocking him unconscious right in front of a hotel owned by Rose's family. The family took Eves into the hotel, and Rose helped tend to him. Although Rose was only eleven and a lot younger than Eves, the two later fell in love and were married.[50] Rose and Eves had five sons: Eves, Jr. (George), John, Andrew, Harry (Apache), and Timothy Tall Chief.

In October 1926, four years before Helen Tall Chief played piano at the women's tea, her father Eves Tall Chief died at age forty-nine, by all indications murdered—a little-noted victim of the Osage reign of terror. According to Eves's son, George Tall Chief, Eves had agreed to serve as a witness for the prosecution against William King Hale, the Osage murder kingpin with whom Eves had done business, in the murder trial of Henry Roan. On the Sunday that Eves Tall Chief died, he pulled his automobile into a filling station in Fairfax, Osage County. It is believed he was planning a trip to Oklahoma City, where he intended to testify against Hale that week. The *Oklahoman* reported that Eves Tall Chief, "prominent in tribal affairs, dropped dead in a filling station while trying to use the telephone." He may have been trying to reach his contact in the capital, to be updated on the murder trial. At noon on the previous day, in Oklahoma City, the government's prosecution team had unexpectedly rested their case against Hale and John Ramsey, after hearing the testimony of Fairfax bank cashier, Charles E. Ashbrook, whose wife was the nominal guardian of murder victim Henry Roan (Ashbrook's forgotten villainy is exposed in Part XI of this book). Court spectators were "startled" by this abrupt terminus because the prosecution had made their case in only three-and-a-half days, so much shorter than the previous trial of Hale and Ramsey in Guthrie, Oklahoma, which had stretched out for weeks. Most therefore believed the prosecution would continue to call witnesses for a good while longer.[51] The Fairfax gas station attendant saw Eves Tall Chief slump over, and, mistaking him for drunk, called the police instead of a doctor. The Fairfax policeman who arrived clearly "discerned that intoxication was not the cause of the Indian's collapse" and phoned the Tall Chief family physician, Dr. J. M. Reid, but Tall Chief was dead by the time the doctor arrived.

Scores of Osages and some white men, such as lawyers Barney McBride and William W. Vaughan, who sought justice for slain Osages, had already suffered similar fates at the hands of white predators. It is no surprise, therefore, that Tall Chief family members were "greatly alarmed" and "frightened" for their safety, as the *Oklahoman* reported. They requested an immediate investigation into the cause of death including a "chemist's analysis of the stomach," which the jury promptly ordered. Dr. J. M. Reid testified he had prescribed two medications to Tall Chief, and that one of them, if taken in a large enough dose, could be lethal; however, an examination of two pillboxes found in his car "did not bear out" any conjecture that Eves might have taken excess medicine. In fact, Tall Chief had been healthy and "hearty," and the prescriptions he had obtained, the physician and a druggist's clerk testified, could have had "no bearing on his general health."[52] Some believed Mr. Tall Chief was killed by ingesting a poisoned glass of whiskey, a common method of murder during this period in Osage County; however, according to witnesses and descendants, he did not drink, and the policeman had already ruled that out, presumably by noting the absence of a liquor bottle or its telltale scent on Tall Chief's person.[53] The cause of death remains mysterious; in retrospect, considering family accounts and the cases of others who were killed because they planned to share evidence or testify against Hale, it seems clear that Eves Tall Chief was murdered by someone in the Hale contingent based in Fairfax to prevent his testimony.

Following Eves Tall Chief's death, his sons were sent to boarding schools and military schools. John Tall Chief lived in Fairfax, ranched in that area with his wife, Pat, and served on the Osage Tribal Council from the 1970s through the mid-1990s.[54] Born in 1916, George Tall Chief, a talented football player, earned a master's degree and became an educator and coach, and served as principal chief of the Osages from 1982 to 1990. George, who died at age ninety-six in 2013, was the father of Timothy Tall Chief, a popular powwow Master of Ceremonies and the father of Amy Tall Chief, actor, filmmaker, and Osage Casino entertainment director, and Russ Tall Chief, educator, playwright, and university diversity office director.

During the modernist period, throughout the 1920s, 1930s, and beyond, Osages and other Native peoples were used as fodder for colorful but condescending newspaper stories. Five years after the women's tea, Helen Tallchief became the subject of gossipy syndicated items that sensationalized her headright wealth. In June 1934, Helen married Wesley Lee Robertson, a Choctaw baritone opera singer who used the name Chief Ishtiopi or Ish-ti-opi professionally. By 1920, Philip J. Deloria explains, just as there was already a tradition of singing Indian "Princesses," so was there a "parallel tradition of what might be called 'singing chiefs.' Perhaps best known were the Iroquois baritone Oskenonton and the Yakama singer Daniel Simmons" (aka actor Chief Yowlachi).[55] Wesley Robertson was well educated, having earned degrees from the University of Oklahoma and Columbia University; he also had vocal training in the east. Born in Caddo, Oklahoma, Robertson was the descendent of Choctaw war chiefs and the great-grandson of Joel Henry Nail, the first elected chief of the Choctaws after the tribe's removal from their Mississippi homelands to Indian Territory. Beginning in the mid-1920s, Ishtiopi sang in concert in Europe, New York, and California.[56] He lived in Oklahoma City before taking up residence in the posher Beverly Hills, where his wife Helen joined him. In November 1934, Helen Tallchief

Robertson assisted Ish-ti-opi in a typical recital he gave in Los Angeles County, to the Covina Woman's Club, as she read a story of "the feast of the corn" dressed in "the picturesque costume of the Navajo." Ish-ti-opi, donning white buckskin and headband, beads, and moccasins, and later a long war bonnet, told stories, acted, and sang Indigenous and Indian-themed songs, including several compositions by ethnomusicologist Homer Grunn.[57] Robertson believed Grunn's Indian music lost "none of the beauty of the tribal songs."[58]

Helen and Wesley's marriage unfortunately ran into trouble. According to a patronizing story of July 1936, Robertson's Indian sense of masculine pride was injured when Helen, accustomed to a pampered lifestyle because of her Osage headright wealth, slept late mornings and made the singer prepare his own meals and perform other household chores. Once, Helen even locked Wesley out of their home; he subsequently sought a divorce.[59] Five months later, Helen's personal life was again news as an Associated Press story shed light on her domestic trouble: "A wealthy Osage Indian, Mrs. Helen Tallchief Robertson, sued Miss Batisha Matuzoff, Hollywood milliner, today for $75,000 damages," claiming that Matuzoff had stolen the affections of her husband.[60] Helen later returned to Fairfax, Osage County. Prima ballerina Maria Tallchief writes that when renowned choreographer George Balanchine, her mentor and husband from 1946 to 1952, was on his deathbed in 1983, he wore on his wrist "the turquoise-and-silver American Indian bracelet my cousin Helen Tall Chief Robertson had given him when he and I visited my family in Fairfax, Oklahoma a few years after our wedding forty years earlier."[61] Russ Tall Chief said family members including his Aunt Cecilia Tall Chief recalled Helen as an eccentric, artistic, and extravagant woman who did theater, played piano, and wore amazing dresses. Helen Tall Chief died in 1976 and is buried in Fairfax Cemetery.[62]

Born in South Dakota, Irene Winnifred Basford was married in 1925 to a much-appreciated agent to the Osages, J. George Wright, their advisor and ally. At the time of the women's tea, Wright had just retired, much to the sadness of the Osages. Irene had worked in Washington, DC, in the offices of the Secretary of the Interior and the Bureau of Indian Affairs.[63] George Wright had served as an agent to Lakotas at the Rosebud Sioux reservation, Commissioner to the Five Civilized Tribes in Muskogee, then Superintendent to the Osage Agency from 1915 through 1930. He had been compelled to step down by the Commissioner of Indian Affairs in Washington, because he, favored by the Osages, had already received a one-year extension allowing him to serve past the legal retirement age of seventy. Wright's forced retirement overrode the recommendations of both the Osage tribal council and members of Congress, the *Journal-Capital* reported in December 1930. Terry Wilson calls

Wright an indefatigable Bureau of Indian Affairs lifer who tried to be ethical, repeatedly alerting the council when "several oil companies were making an extra, unearned profit on the tribe's royalty oil."[64] Chief Fred Lookout was quoted: "Mr. Wright has been fair and honest with us. He has taught us to preserve our money, that we shall not want. We do not know what will become of us when he goes. We do not want him to leave. He is our friend." Fred Lookout presented Wright with a shiny new LaSalle automobile, the gift of the tribe. LaSalle was a General Motors luxury brand, built by their Cadillac division. Wah-she-hah (Chief Bacon Rind) felt that a more traditional present, a spotted pony, was more appropriate. "Mr. Wright has been good to us," he said. "I will remember and love Mr. Wright as long as I live."[65] This tribute was reported nationwide in a syndicated story. Joseph B. Thoburn, professor of history at the University of Oklahoma, wrote in *A History of Oklahoma*: "When the complete history is written of the American Indian's adjustment" to the white man's system, running through it "like a shining vindication of one's too frequently abused faith in human nature" will be the story of "how wisely, sanely, honestly, and humanely" J. George Wright "administered Indian affairs for nearly half a century." His replacement, D. E. Murphy, met with the approval of the tribe, and Principal Chief Fred Lookout said it was gratifying to the Osages that the department had actually followed their endorsement of Murphy, who had been employed as the disbursing agent since September 1929. Like J. George Wright, Murphy began his career in the Indian service at the Rosebud Sioux agency in South Dakota.[66]

Julia Whitehorn's father, the distinguished orator, Charles Whitehorn, was a fullblood leader who had served as assistant principal chief from 1924 to 1928, and would go on to serve two more terms in that leadership role on the tribal council. (Charles Whitehorn is not to be confused with Charlie Whitehorn, a young Osage murder victim.) Charles married Lillie Hoag, a Caddo woman.[67] The great Oklahoman artist Charles Banks Wilson sketched him in 1960. Wilson and Mathews became friends by the early 1970s.

The Osage women's tea brought together many of the most prominent and interesting Osage women in the community. They and their families contributed to the rich history of the Wahzhazhe people and their Osage Nation. They were strong women who offered untold invaluable assistance to their husbands and family members who held public offices and powerful positions.

THE CARDINAL

Tuesday, January 20, 1931, #49

Many species of birds are wintering in the Osage. Along with the natives, there are many species that came to the blackjacks from the north. They are seedeaters, as seeds and grain are the only food to be had during the winter. They are found along the creek bottoms among the reeds, where their food abounds, and where they are protected from the winter winds. They are calm and inconspicuous, and drab in color, having lost their nuptial plumage. They are full brown, slate-colored, grey, dull yellow, and mottled—wonderfully in harmony with the drab branches, stems, and rusty leaves of winter. On sun-shiny days, their chirrups of contentment may be heard as they feed quietly. There are no displays of prancing and strutting; there is no song, though some species as the chickadee and the titmouse send out cheerful notes as they search for food.[68] This is the season of the metabolic low point of life. There is only one urge: to survive.

All members of the flycatcher family have departed, as well as other spe-cies that live on insect and grubs.[69] They have gone to the far south, where their food can be found. Those species that live on grain and seeds remain to contribute actively to the drab creek-bottoms.

But there is one remarkable bird of the Osage who carries his nuptial plumage all year round. His actions and voice are quiet as he searches the seedpods. His color is scarlet, and when he flashes across the line of vision, the solemn fields are colored by his passing; a streak of red like a ball of fire, brings life to the whole valley. There is life in his flight over the pastel world of winter; he is a symbol of the sleeping life of earth, awaiting to throb with the wild joy of living.

This bird of startling red is the cardinal (red bird). Books have been written about him. He has received many poetic tributes, but mostly tributes to the cheer and the flashing color he brings to the spring woods. Indians gave his name to their sons. An appreciative lady honored him in a book titled *The Song of the Cardinal*. He has appealed to the poetic fancy through the ages. A Greek philosopher said that when the gods wished to attract men's attention to some beautiful spot in Nature, that they caused a cardinal to flit across the scene.

Although his flute-like song thrills the woods of early spring and summer, and his fiery plumage symbolizes happiness in the spring world flooded with the ecstatic activity of life, to many, he is a symbol of Life in the obviously dead world of winter, dominated by sere, rasping leaves and dry branches.

GENE STRATTON-PORTER'S THE SONG OF THE CARDINAL

Published in 1903, *The Song of the Cardinal* was the first book by the popular Hoosier novelist and naturalist Gene Stratton-Porter, born Geneva Grace Stratton in 1863. This charming tale anthropomorphizes a special cardinal and narrates his relationship with an Indiana farm family, who can translate his songs into English. The hero of this sentimental novel is an übercardinal—bigger, redder, and more sonorous than any of his cardinal peers. His beautiful song has the power to revivify the marriage of an enchanted midwestern farmer and his wife.

A native of Wabash County in rural eastern Indiana, Gene Stratton-Porter found fame with her novel *Freckles* (1904) and its sequel, *Girl of the Limberlost* (1909)—which was adapted into three films and a teleplay. She became one of the most popular women novelists of her times. A romantic, Stratton-Porter believed that virtue was cultivated through intimate contact with Nature, differentiating her from her contemporaries of the Naturalist movement including Stephen Crane, Theodore Dreiser, and to a lesser extent, Edith Wharton.[70] Stratton-Porter contributed to the publication of the Izaak Walton League, *Outdoor America*.

The day before this column appeared, an "important meeting of the Pawhuska chapter of the Izaak Walton League" was held at the Chamber of Commerce rooms in the Duncan Hotel downtown. All current and former members were urged to attend, promised that the meeting would last no longer than thirty minutes and "no solicitations or requests for donations would be made."[71]

WILL ROGERS, THE PIONEER WOMAN, AND E. W. MARLAND

During the 1930s, thousands of Oklahomans and others suffered from the Dust Bowl and the Great Depression. The great entertainer and philosopher Will Rogers, who, like his fellow Cherokee, Lynn Riggs, hailed from the Claremore area, Indian Territory, was moved to do something to help. On February 2, 1931, the day after the preceding column appeared, in Oklahoma City Rogers kicked off his relief tour of the state, which he organized to "raise funds for the unemployed and drought-stricken farmers" through the American Red Cross.[72] Rogers was an outspoken advocate for the "little guy," the average American. Eight months later, Rogers gave a famous radio speech later called "Bacon, Beans, and Limousines," as a warmup for President Hoover, a Republican. Contending that "America is fundamentally liberal," Rogers boldly countered Hoover policy by declaring that the country needed to "arrange some way of getting more equal distribution of wealth in the country." As Amy M. Ware states in *The Cherokee Kid*, Rogers was a Cherokee with a great deal of political clout. He went on to become buddies with the next president, Franklin Delano Roosevelt.[73]

Will Rogers, born in 1879 on a ranch in the Cherokee Nation, Indian Territory, near Oologah, became celebrated as an expert trick roper, storyteller, radio personality, movie star, and witty columnist who rhetorically deployed what Amy Ware calls "Indian Territory slang." Perhaps the biggest celebrity of his times, Rogers "played an important cultural role" for most twentieth-century Americans by "mediating the bifurcated American scene marked by a dwindling rural and regional America on one hand and an emerging urban and metropolitan nation on the other," Ware writes.[74]

In February 1931, Will Rogers performed in seventeen Oklahoman cities in just six days that month, showing his prodigious generosity of spirit and love of his home territory. In many cases, he flew in a small airplane from city to city. Norman, Stillwater, Ada, Ponca City, Tulsa, and Miami were among the municipalities treated to Rogers's quips and charms, and though audiences did not know it, these shows were the last time that most Oklahomans would ever see Will Rogers alive. While performing fifty relief shows in afflicted areas of Oklahoma, Texas, and Arkansas in only eighteen days, he would joke: "Senators are drinking corn when two years ago they would have turned up their nose at anything less than Bourbon," "Wall Street Brokers have let their night Chouffers go [sic]," and "Rockefeller Sr. is only playing seven holes." His relief tour, widely covered by the national press, raised over $222,000 in relief funds and raised the spirits of countless folks hurt by the Dust Bowl and the Depression. Where there is a Will, there is a way.[75]

John Joseph Mathews seems to have met Will Rogers, and he knew Will's widow, Betty Blake Rogers.[76] Will definitely knew Mathews's work. On bookshelves at his California ranch, Will Rogers displayed copies of the works of John Joseph Mathews, along with those of his fellow Cherokee and one-time classmate, John M. Oskison.[77] Amy Ware writes that Rogers resembled his Indian Territory contemporaries Lynn Riggs, Oskison, and Mathews in that each "focused with equal ardor on their homeland while appealing to a national audience," creating counternarratives to White regionalist writers who represented the Indigenous but frequently got it wrong.[78]

It is possible Mathews encountered Will Rogers a year earlier on April 22, 1930, when the Cherokee flew from California to Ponca City, Oklahoma, for the grand unveiling of the tall *Pioneer Woman* statue by Bryant Baker, commissioned by oilman E. W. Marland, Jo's friend, and future governor of Oklahoma, after a popular vote chose Baker's design over other prototypes. Rogers thought "there must have been fifty thousand people" at the dedication, and "what made it look so colorful" was the large number of "Indians, of all tribes, Poncas, Otoes, Osages, and Cherokees. You see it was our tribe of Cherokee's that sold the original old Cherokee Strip that all this mess is living on." Cherokees didn't receive much money for it, though, because "we had it for hunting grounds, but never knew enough to hunt oil on it."[79] E. W. Marland had actually refused to invite Will Rogers, thinking his tone would be too irreverent for the occasion, but somehow Will was invited and spoke anyway, Mathews stated in his 1951 biography of Ernie Marland, *Life and Death of an Oilman*. Rogers delivered a brief, comical speech prior to the unveiling. One newspaper reported that Rogers began his speech by debunking the romanticizing of Sooners: "Now that the applesauce and 'boloney' is all over, we'll state a few facts about this affair. The pioneers here sneaked in ahead of the gun. You had to be a crook or you wouldn't be here. If you'd waited for the run you wouldn't have got any land."[80] Of his wife, Betty Rogers, Will joked that it "takes a pretty broadminded wife to allow her husband to come clear to Oklahoma to help take the clothes off another woman."[81] He spun a yarn about another "pioneer woman," this one "in the Cherokee country," who removed her corset at a country hoedown, and on the way home, spilled out over the width of a wagon seat. Such banter embarrassed Ernie Marland, but "the crowd loved this; they loved Will Rogers," Mathews wrote. "They forgot their sore feet and their fatigue when they looked at him. Just looking at him gave them a warm feeling inside and brought smiles and laughter of which they were unconscious. But for E. W., the dignity of the occasion had been marred."[82]

Although Will Rogers valued Mathews's books, as a Cherokee, he was heir to a degree of tribal antipathy toward Osages, with whom the Cherokees had a history of conflict and grudges including the Battle of Claremore Mound in 1817, which occurred near Will's birthplace.[83] Of course, most conflict arose from the federal government's haphazard relocation policies that positioned the Cherokees at odds with several other tribes. Taking a Tsalagi-centric worldview, Rogers employed intertribal humor, and often displayed what Amy Ware calls tribal elitism, privileging his tribe above all others, and disparaging others, particularly the Osages. In his newspaper columns, Rogers told jokes at the Osages' expense, but to Ware such jests seem "at times more antagonistic than they were funny." Acknowledging that "some of this may be friendly tribal banter," still "the jabs seem brutal." On May 4, 1930, Rogers pointed out that the Cherokees were thought to be the most civilized tribe while the Osages were supposedly uncivilized, yet an Osage receives more money from the government before breakfast each day than a Cherokee does in a lifetime. "So it really shows you it kinder pays not to know too much. I would trade my so-called superior knowledge right now for an Osage headright." Nevertheless he continued, probably thinking of Mathews among others: "But as a matter of fact, the Osages got some mighty smart men among them."[84]

In August 1935, beloved Will Rogers was silenced, killed in a tragic plane crash in Alaska while flying with his friend, Oklahoman aviator Wiley Post. Millions of his fans and admirers were heartbroken, even devastated. Who would get them through the remaining dark days of the Great Depression? A few months earlier, with the United States still in the clutch of the Depression, when countless Americans were receiving government assistance, Rogers had commented on air: "The Indian used to be the ward of the government, but now we all are. Everybody's an Indian."[85] Mainstream America had been humbled. Will Rogers made us laugh, and made us think too, and slipped in powerful Cherokee critiques of white American follies and injustice.

EARLY SPRING AND THE SWALLOWS OF GENEVA

Sunday, February 8, 1931, #52

The mild, spring-like weather of the last month will have the effect of throwing out of balance the usual program of Nature in the Osage. If it continues, which is not likely, the season will have been advanced, and the species in adapting themselves to the change will undoubtedly start breeding. Certainly the bud will swell, and the trees will be in leaf much earlier this year. Already many of the insects have been hatched, and the young are trying their wings. Many of the insects that have hibernated have emerged and are tuning up in the evenings. It is strange to hear the rasping chorus from the grassroots at this time of year.

It has been estimated that the least change in the atmosphere of the earth, or the least wobble of the globe on its axis would throw life into confusion, and many species would have to adapt themselves quickly in order to survive. The unseasonable weather locally then, will undoubtedly have a local effect. . . .

We know that there is a delicate, perfect balance in Nature, the balance being kept by the species themselves in the constant war for survival. Occasionally the scales tip. But immediately there is readjustment and the scales waver to perfect balance. The birds that migrate from the Osage for the winter are almost without exception the insectivorous species. They really follow their food south, when the insects of the Osage disappear in the autumn. These species return to the Osage in the spring when the young insects are hatched from the eggs that were laid last winter, and when the adult insects emerge from their hibernation. The insects have begun to appear, and if the weather remains balmy, will swarm over the Osage, long before the birds return from the south. This then will cause a slight tip of the scales in this region of the continent. Without their natural enemies, the insects will swarm in great numbers, and very likely do great damage to growing things before they are checked by the birds on their return, before the balance is adjusted. It is possible, however, that the birds may also return early to the Osage, but it is more likely that they will not. There seems to be great precision in the migratory flights of some species of birds. As an example, the swallows swarm all summer over the lake of Geneva in Switzerland, leaving on the exact date every autumn, and returning on an exact date in the spring. This would indicate a perfect schedule in the case of swallows at least, and it is possible that this is also the case of any of the species meeting in the Osage. This is simply a possibility that occurs to one as an effect of the unseasonable weather. Of course, there are many more that cannot be mentioned, since space is limited to this column as well as the knowledge of the writer.

GENEVA

In the preceding column, Mathews spoke of Geneva, Switzerland, from personal experience. In the summer of 1923, having recently graduated from Merton College, Oxford, Mathews wanted to learn more about the League of Nations and internationalism. So he enrolled in a short course at the University of Geneva in modern French and international relations, and earned a certificate. At the pension in Geneva where Mathews stayed, he met Virginia "Ginger" Winslow Hopper, an appealing young woman from an affluent family, who was nearly seven years his junior. A debutante from Newark, New Jersey, she lived in Geneva with her older sister Phyllis and her mother, Gertrude Louise Winslow Hopper. In 1923, Ginger and Phyllis were day students at Brilliantmont International School, a French boarding school in nearby Lausanne, where she studied music and dance. Jo and Ginger's whirlwind relationship was interrupted by one post-undergraduate term at Oxford, while she stayed in Geneva. They married in April 1924 in Ouchy, south of Lausanne, Switzerland.

WILD BEAUTY OF THE OSAGE

Sunday, May 10, 1931, #77

One of the chief characteristics of the Osage, one certainly contributing much to its uniqueness and beauty, is the lack of order and the fact that its surface is not geometrically divided into neat, smug fields and meadows. Two factors—that it is primarily a grazing country and its development has been retarded by the plan of allotment—have contributed much to this lack of standardization. It has this aspect of being natural and in the original; the hills and the prairie are as they were in the beginning, where they are included in the larger ranches. Even the ploughed fields do not lie in neat squares along the roadsides, but lie along the valleys and often along the sides of hills as though by mere chance.

Herein lies much of the wild beauty of the Osage. The wildflowers of blue, yellow, and white seem to have been dropped from the indolent, careless hand of a pagan goddess, and bloom by whim in the most unexpected places. A lone tree whipped by the prairie breezes looms on the limestone hills far from others of its kind, cutting the horizon, its leaves whispering continually. The winding streams marked by elms, sycamores, willows and blackberries, traced among the blackjacks, their basins unmarred by the scars of the plow and the neat squares of farmsteads. Clumps of blackjacks far from the wooded hills cling to a high point on the prairie, apparently without reason, but breaking the monotony of prairie and sky.

MRS. LAURA E. TUCKER

Juxtaposed with the preceding piece was a feature on one of Mathews's mentors, a retired teacher, Laura E. Tucker, who started a private subscription school in Pawhuska on the hill opposite to where the white Osage Agency building once stood. She taught Mathews as a boy for several years. The article praises her "lifelong interest in the education of children, attempting to make of them good citizens according to her high standards and ideals." Jo and his three younger sisters were enrolled at Mrs. Tucker's Preparatory School, which was established to educate the children of White traders, clerks, and Indian agents. Mrs. Tucker's school was close to the Mathews home, on a hill on Grandview Avenue. Laura Tucker was a crucial influence on Jo and many others. "Mrs. Tucker, with her brightness and her rugged certainties, laid a wonderful foundation upon which later I was to build my formal education and culture," Mathews recalled in *Twenty Thousand Mornings*. Though strict, she encouraged Jo's attraction to words and became an early mentor.

NOTES

1. Donna Colleen Jones, "The Osages—Chief Fred Lookout," *Nancy Bellzona's Picture Book*, Electric Scotland, www.electricscotland.com/history/america/donna/picturebook/5455.htm, accessed February 19, 2019.

2. United Press, "Osages, Poncas Mourn Loss of Colorful Tribe Members," *Pittsburgh Press* [Kansas], November 7, 1929, Newspapers.com.

3. Ruthanna M. Simms, "Friends and the Osages: History of Hominy Friends Church," 1970. Friends University, Edmund Stanley Library Special Collections, 32; "In Memory of Paul Pitts," *Indian Progress*, June 1, 1970, 7.

4. "Osage Scenes in Big New Talkie," *Journal-Capital*, June 3, 1930.

5. Phillip Fortune, personal interview, February 20, 2015, Pawhuska, Oklahoma.

6. Maria Tallchief with Larry Kaplan, *Maria Tallchief*, 12.

7. "Local Indians Now in Talkies," *Journal-Capital*, May 28, 1930.

8. Richard Green, *Te Ata*, 150, 166–67; Linda W. Reese, "Mobley, Tessie," *Encyclopedia of Oklahoma History and Culture*, www.okhistory.org/publications/enc/entry.php?entry=MO035.

9. Tara Browner, "Native Songs, Indianist Styles, and the Processes of Music Idealization," in *Opera Indigene: Re/Presenting First Nations and Indigenous Cultures*, edited by Pamela Karantonis and Dylan Robinson (London: Routledge, 2011), 180–81; Deloria, *Indians in Unexpected Places*, 183–87.

10. Philip Deloria, *Indians in Unexpected Places*, 205–15.

11. Reese, "Mobley, Tessie"; "Vinay, Lushanya, 1964," Member Archives, *Oklahoma Hall of Fame, Gaylord-Pickens Museum*, oklahomahof.com/member-archives/v/vinay-lushanya-1964, accessed August 28, 2019.

12. Michael Snyder, *John Joseph Mathews* (Norman: University of Oklahoma Press, 2017), 68.

13. "Fifty-one Millionaires Extras in *Cimarron*," *Evening News* (Harrisburg, PA), March 12, 1931.

14. "Cimarron," *Variety*, January 27, 1931, variety.com/1931/film/reviews/cimarron-1200410377/.

15. "Cimarron (1931)," *Rotten Tomatoes*, www.rottentomatoes.com/m/1004177_cimarron, accessed February 16, 2019.

16. Given Mathews's references to all human beings as "man" and his use of masculine pronouns to represent all humankind regardless of their gender, this paragraph especially exemplifies the masculinist language that was then commonplace.

17. On the ground, the Horned Lark is distinctive. It is mostly brown-grey above and pale below, with a striking black and yellow face pattern. Except for the central feathers, the tail is mainly black, contrasting with the lighter body. The summer male has black "horns," giving this species its name. Its song is high-pitched, lisping or tinkling, and weak: a few chirps are followed by a warbling, ascending trill.

18. Fleur Feighan Jones, telephone interview, January 13, 2015; "Penney's Here Since Back in '25," *Pawhuska Journal-Capital*, September 29, 1972.

19. Mathews to Marie Mathews, April 16, 1923, Box 1, folder 22, John Joseph Mathews Collection, Western History Collection, University of Oklahoma; "Feighan-Mathews Wedding Solemnized Here Saturday," *Daily Journal-Capital*, June 22, 1930.

20. Fleur Feighan Jones, telephone interview, January 13, 2015.

21. "Feighan-Mathews Wedding Solemnized Here Saturday," *Daily Journal-Capital*, June 22, 1930.

22. "Fullblood Osage Women to Be Guests at Tea in Wright Home Here Monday," *The Daily Journal-Capital*, January 18, 1931, 1.

23. "Julia Pryor Student File," Carlisle Indian School Digital Resource Center, Dickinson College, carlisleindian.dickinson.edu/student_files/julia-pryor-student-file.

24. "Fred Lookout Student File," Carlisle Indian School Digital Resource Center, Dickinson College, carlisleindian.dickinson.edu/student_files/fred-lookout-student-file.

25. Terry P. Wilson, *Underground Reservation*, 89.

26. "Chief Fred Lookout," *Oklahoma Hall of Fame*, Gaylord-Pickens Museum, oklahomahof.com/archives/l/lookout-chief-fred-1948, accessed February 17, 2017.

27. Snyder, *John Joseph Mathews*, 134, 163.

28. Thoburn, *Standard History of Oklahoma*, 5: 1947; Wilson, *Underground Reservation*, 54–55.

29. Wilson, *Underground Reservation*, 110; Thoburn, *Standard History of Oklahoma*, 5: 1770.

30. C. A. Henrie, "Osages Argue They Alone Should Settle Trust Question," Wichita *Daily Eagle*, January 23, 1921, 36.

31. Wilson, *Underground Reservation*, 110.

32. Wilson, *Underground Reservation*, 110–11.

33. Louis Burns, *A History of the Osage People* (Tuscaloosa: University of Alabama Press, 2003), 470–71.

34. "Prominent Oklahoma Woman's Rites Set," *Miami Daily News-Record* (Oklahoma), May 21, 1948; Joseph B. Thoburn and Muriel H. Wright, *Oklahoma, A History of the State and its People*, Volume IV (New York: Lewis Historical Publishing, 1929); Evett Dumas Nix, *Oklahombres: Particularly the Wild Ones* (University of Nebraska Press, 1993 [1929]), 156.

35. Wilson, *Underground Reservation*, 146.

36. Thoburn, *Standard History of Oklahoma*, 5: 1947.

37. Thoburn, *Standard History of Oklahoma*, 5: 1795.

38. Wilson, *Underground Reservation*, 88–89.

39. Wilson, *Underground Reservation*, 32.

40. Wilson, *Underground Reservation*, 33.

41. *Moodys Manual of Railroads and Corporation Securities* (Moodys, 1917), 439.

42. According to "Statehood Bill Floating Bait," *Guthrie Leader*, February 5, 1906, 1, William Leahy was serving as vice president of Pawhuska National Bank in 1906.

43. "Constitution of the Osage Nation" [November 26, 1890], *Treaties and Laws of the Osage Nation*, edited by W. S. Fitzpatrick (Cedar Vale, Kansas: Cedar Vale Commercial, 1895).

44. Maria Tallchief with Larry Kaplan, *Maria Tallchief*, 4.

45. Quoted in Fairfax Area Historical Society, *From a Field of Cane*, 57.

46. "Pawhuska Girl Will Wed Former City Man," *Oklahoman*, June 10, 1934, 40, Oklahoman Digital Archives, archive.newsok.com.

47. Mathews, *Twenty Thousand Mornings*, 145–46.

48. "Indians Plead to Save Peyote in Prohibition," *Evening News* [Harrisburg, Pennsylvania], February 10, 1919, 7; Thomas C. Maroukis, *The Peyote Road: Religious Freedom and the Native American Church* (Norman: University of Oklahoma Press), 2012, 105–06; "News of Former Students," *Indian Leader* [Lawrence, Kansas], October 28, 1921, 19.

49. Shannon Shaw Duty, "George Tallchief, Former Principal Chief, Dies at 96," *Osage News*, 9, no. 9, September 2013, 1, 5, s3.amazonaws.com/static.osagenews.org/cms_page_media/43/2013_09_September.pdf.

50. Russ Tall Chief, personal interview, Norman, Oklahoma, April 25, 2019.

51. "Osage Murder Case Speeded," *Oklahoman*, October 24, 1926, 12, Oklahoman Digital Archives, archive.newsok.com.

52. "Death Alarms Osage Family," *Daily Oklahoman*, October 25, 1926, 3, Oklahoman Digital Archives, archive.newsok.com. Confoundingly, "Tall Chief" is misspelled as "Fallthies" throughout the article.

53. Duty, "George Tallchief."

54. Warehime, *History*, 212.

55. Deloria, *Indians in Unexpected Places*, 206.

56. "Costume of Indians Adds Event Color," *Waxahachie Daily Light*, April 14, 1937, 3.

57. Homer Grunn was an American composer, teacher, and performer. Born in 1880 in Salem, Wisconsin, he studied piano and composition in Chicago and Berlin. After teaching at music schools in Chicago, from 1903 to 1907, and Phoenix, from 1907 to 1910, he settled in Los Angeles. During visits to New Mexico, Grunn encountered Native American music and appropriated the melodies he collected in ballets, songs, and piano pieces, harmonizing them per Romanticism. He also composed operettas, children's operas, and ballets, often produced locally. Grunn died in Los Angeles in 1944. Source: "Homer Grunn papers, 1880-1984," Collection Guide, UCLA Library Special Collections, Performing Arts, Online Archive of California, www.oac.cdlib.org/findaid/ark:/13030/tf9j49p2k9/, accessed February 12, 2017.

58. "Indian Baritone Sings and Presents Program before Women's Club," *Covina* (California) *Argus*, November 29, 1934, 11.

59. United Press, "Indian Singer on Warpath, Seeks Divorce," *Santa Ana Register*, July 29, 1936; Associated Press, "Languishing American?" *Pampa Daily News* (Texas), July 29, 1936.

60. Associated Press, "Indian Woman Says Mate's Love Stolen," *San Bernardino Sun*, December 19, 1936.

61. Maria Tallchief with Larry Kaplan, *Maria Tallchief*, 1–2.

62. "Helen Tallchief Robertson," *Find-a-grave*, www.findagrave.com/memorial/127789962, accessed January 12, 2018.

63. "South Dakota Girl is Bride Today in Brilliant Washington Wedding," *Argus-Leader* (Sioux Falls, South Dakota), January 3, 1925, 6.

64. "Commissioner of Indian Affairs to Retire Wright," Pawhuska *Daily Journal-Capital*, December 9, 1930; Wilson, *Underground Reservation*, 123.

65. Grant Foreman, "J. George Wright." *Chronicles of Oklahoma* 20, no. 2 (June 1942), 121–23.

66. "New Osage Agent Meets with Hearty Approval of Tribe," *Daily Journal-Capital*, December 23, 1930.

67. Charles Whitehorn interviewed by B. D. Timmons, January 25, 1969, T-46-1, Doris Duke Collection, University of Oklahoma Libraries, digital.libraries.ou.edu/utils/getfile/collection/dorisduke/id/11308/filename/11290.pdfpage.

68. The titmouse is a small but hardy, cheery-voiced, non-migratory woodland bird of the same family as the chickadee, the Paridae. This family of songbirds has short, stout, pointed bills, nostrils concealed by thick feathers, strong feet, and rounded wings ("Titmouse," "Chickadee," "Paridae," *Encyclopedia Britannica*, www.britannica.com, accessed February 5, 2017.)

69. The label Tyrant flycatcher, also called New World flycatcher, includes any of about four hundred species of aggressive insect-eating New World birds of the family Tyrannidae, sometimes called kingbirds. This genus earned its name because several of its species are highly aggressive on their breeding territories, where they will attack larger birds such as crows, hawks, and owls. Most tyrannids are plain, in shades of gray, brown, or olive above, and tan, white, or yellow below; a few are strikingly patterned in black and white. Many have a patch of red or yellow on the crown. In all but a few, the sexes are marked alike. In 1951, the scissor-tailed flycatcher became Oklahoma's official state bird. Its striking, black-and-white tail is usually eight-to-ten inches long, with a fork that splits it six inches deep. The scissortail's body is soft gray with a white underbelly; its only vivid colorings are splashes of red or pink beneath the wings. Its nesting range is within a narrow belt stretching from southern Nebraska to southern Texas. During the summer, Oklahoma's state bird can be observed across the state. "Tyrant flycatcher," *Encyclopedia Britannica*, www.britannica.com; Tobie Cunningham, "Scissor-tailed Flycatcher," *Encyclopedia of Oklahoma History and Culture*, www.okhistory.org, accessed February 05, 2017.

70. "Gene Stratton-Porter," *Encyclopedia Britannica*, www.britannica.com/biography/Gene-Stratton-Porter.

71. "Izaak Walton League to Meet Here Monday," *Journal-Capital*, January 18, 1931.

72. "Rogers Opens Oklahoma Relief Tour Tonight," *Journal-Capital*, February 2, 1931, 1.

73. Rogers, "President's Organization on Unemployment Relief," October 19, 1931, quoted in Amy Ware, *The Cherokee Kid: Will Rogers, Tribal Identity, and the Making of an American Icon*. (Lawrence: University Press of Kansas, 2015), 180–81.

74. Ware, *Cherokee Kid*, 2.

75. Dale Ingram, "Will Rogers: His Best Effort Tour Hits 75th Anniversary," *Oklahoman*, February 13, 2006, newsok.com/article/2931437; Will Rogers, *Autobiography of Will Rogers*, 218 [entry for February 12, 1931, "*Sample of What Will Said in His Relief Talks*"]; Will Rogers, *The Papers of Will Rogers: The Final Years, volume 5: August 1928-August 1935* (Norman: University of Oklahoma Press, 2006), 192.

76. Mathews diary, January 12, 1946, Box 1, Folder 48, John Joseph Mathews Collection, Western History Collection, University of Oklahoma.

77. Amy Ware, *Cherokee Kid*, 95.

78. Ware, *Cherokee Kid*, 173.

79. Rogers, "Prairie and Oil News," May 4, 1930, in *Will Rogers' Weekly* Articles, volume 4, edited by Steven K. Gragert (Stillwater: Oklahoma State University Press, 1981), 140–43.

80. Ware, *Cherokee Kid*, 101.

81. Will Rogers, *The Papers of Will Rogers*, 5: 163.

82. John Joseph Mathews, *Life and Death of an Oilman: The Career of E. W. Marland* (Norman: University of Oklahoma Press, 1951), 203–04.

83. Ware, *Cherokee Kid*, 157.

84. Will Rogers, "Prairie and Oil News," May 4, 1930, in *Will Rogers' Weekly Articles*, 4: 140–43.

85. Will Rogers, "Good Gulf Show," May 19, 1935, quoted in Ware, *Cherokee Kid*, 184–85.

Part IX

Conservation

NATURE IS OUR CLASSROOM AND LABORATORY

Monday, February 9, 1931, #53

No refining of one's taste in matters of art or literature, no sharpening of
one's powers of insight or psychology, can ever take the place of one's
sensitiveness to the life of the earth. This is the beginning and the end of
a person's true education. Art and literature have been shamefully abused,
have been perverted from their true purpose, if they do not conduce to it.

—John Cowper Powys

The above is an excerpt from a chapter in *The Meaning of Culture* by John
Cowper Powys.[1] Not that this seems any more true because he as an example
of highly educated, cultured man, has written it, but because one feels that
it is a beautifully expressed truism, and worthy of a highly-cultured man.
One has attempted to stress the importance of being in tune with his natural
environment in this column, the ultimate purpose being to incite an appreciation of that which surrounds us—of which we are a part, the foundation
and origin of all human enterprise. The column's purpose has been, first, to
reveal to people the broader fields, in which they may come in contact with
the elemental forces and come into a better understanding of their fellow
creatures and the forces that make us what we are; and second, to help us to
find ourselves in our true relationship with other actors on this stage, upon
which we strut for a brief time and pass on.[2]

Whatever is the chief concern of life, it is always a pleasure to know more
of ourselves, and being essentially sensual, we naturally seek happiness and
contentment, and there is no happiness like the feeling of oneness with nature.
Our laboratory and classroom surrounds us, where Nature shows her every
mood, and creeps up to our very doors.

OIL AND POLLUTION OF OUR STREAMS

Wednesday, February 11, 1931, #54

During the period of frantic oil activity in the Osage, it was almost impossible for the exploring companies to properly take care of the oil from gushers, and the saltwater brought up from the depths. All was exuberant, excited activity, and inasmuch as this germ of prosperity had stung almost every citizen in the Osage, there was not much time to think of the effect that this oil and saltwater flowing down the tributaries into the creeks would have upon the game, fish, and natural beauty of the hills.

At present, it is different. We are waking up to the ravages caused by this period of exhilaration, this fevered dream of an indefinite, gilded Utopia. We have taken steps to restock the streams that were polluted by the oil and saltwater, and replenish the cover with game; much of our native game having been killed out by the hardy hordes of employees and indifferent camp followers.

Now, there is no excuse for the releasing of saltwater into the ravines, whence it flows into the streams and kills the fish. Yet information comes to us that saltwater is being released intermittently into such ravines. Recently, this has been done and the result is hundreds of dead fish. It is useless to attempt restocking of streams if the fish are to be thus carelessly killed. There is a sort of philosophy in America, which may be summed up in the phrase, "all right, if you can get away with it." This philosophy has influenced much of the activity in the Osage, but the point which makes this philosophy a practical one is the fact the public are indifferent. This is not the characteristic of a civilized community. Indifference puts inefficient politicians or their favorites into office, and makes of public servants swaggering dictators. Indifference is a curse, and it is difficult to imagine how any community can progress if it remains lethargic under the influence of this poison.

When those citizens of the Osage, who are working toward the objective of bringing this county back to a semblance of its former state, as a paradise for the hunter, the fisherman, and the lover of beauty, they should feel more confidence in themselves if they knew that other citizens assumed interest in their activities—such activity, for instance, inspired by a determination to end wanton pollution of our streams.

SUNDOWN *III: THE OLD SWIMMING HOLE*

Mathews's environmentalist message remains sadly relevant today, as repeated incidents of oil spills and pipeline leaks taint our rivers, lakes, ponds,
and oceans. In Oklahoma, geological studies show that the byproducts of
hydraulic fracturing techniques cause earthquakes; they also threaten drinking water sources. In Osage County, river and creek pollution is a grave
concern. In January of 2017, bold "water protectors" continued to risk their
safety opposing the Dakota Access Pipeline at and near the Standing Rock
Sioux Reservation; in Osage County, nearly five months after the discovery
of "dead fish and turtles, a creek with 100-degree water twice as salty as
seawater, and a public water supply scare for the city of Pawhuska," investigators examined "nearby oilfield underground injection control wells as
a possible source," the *Tulsa World* reported.[3] The contaminated portion of
Bird Creek is just a few miles west of the Joseph H. Williams Tallgrass Prairie Preserve, the largest protected area of tallgrass prairie. In April 2017, a
spokesman for the U.S. Environmental Protection Agency (EPA) said the
agency had "identified three injection well operators in the area for further
investigation." Also in April, dozens of syringes were found right off Lynn
Avenue near Bird Creek in Pawhuska, at the "go-to summer hotspot for
kids" that locals call Hobo's Island.[4] In May, Kelly Bostian of *Tulsa World*
reported that Osage County Sheriff Eddie Virden, who is also a "Pawhuska-
area rancher who has had issues with oil production contamination on his
ranch" told visiting EPA Administrator Scott Pruitt, whose security retinue
he was part of, that the problem is not limited to this Bird Creek site. "This
is a common problem all over the county."[5] A Trump appointee, Pruitt is a
climate change denier and a fierce opponent of the Paris Agreement, same-
sex marriage, and abortion rights. He represented polluters fighting court
battles *against* the EPA. By all appearances, Trump's appointment of Pruitt
to administrator of the EPA was like appointing the fox to guard the chicken
coop. Pruitt was quickly embroiled in scandal and stepped down in July
2018. John Joseph Mathews would be horrified that his beloved Bird Creek
was still so wretchedly contaminated.

Late in Mathews's only novel, *Sundown*, Challenge Windzer, following
college and his stint as a military aviator and flight instructor stateside during the World War I years, returns to his hometown. Chal drifts aimlessly,
speeding around in his roadster and drinking bootleg liquor with his pals.
Longing for something pure from the past, he decides to take Marie Fobus,
a lively young woman who smokes, drinks, and wears the shortest skirts in
town, out to a swimming hole he remembered fondly from his boyhood. This
"certain spot" was a "round hole of water with elms arching above it; elms

in which the prairie breezes talked eternally. That was the place he wanted to find now." When Chal finally locates the swimming hole, however, the sight is grim: "several black wells stood about on the prairie above the trees and from each, a path of brown sterile earth led down to the creek, where oil and saltwater had killed every blade of grass and exposed the glaring limestone. Some of the elms had been cut down, and the surface of the water had an iridescent scum on it."[6] Little seems to have changed in one hundred years.

"Spring!" by John Joseph Mathews
Courtesy of the Osage Nation and the Mathews family

QUESTIONING THE PRAIRIE FIRE RITUAL

Monday, March 2, 1931, #58

The buds are swollen, and the elms and other trees along the creek have begun to relieve the monotony of bare, dark-grey branches with the light green and yellowish clusters of buds just bursting into leaf. In the valleys, under the protection of trees, are green carpets of new grass, and hidden at the roots of the sere winter grass of the prairie and hills, are green shoots. In the early morning, the robin sings with surprising confidence, and the cardinal gives his attitude toward all those promise with his clear, flute-like notes. He seems to say "cheer-cheer-cheer," but one believes that he is not completely "sold" on the idea.

Thousands of little midges and other insects are flitting about. One even sees millers and species of nocturnal moths. However, "one swallow does not make a spring," and one is not sure whether nimble-footed, provocative Primavera has come to the Osage, or whether it is just gnarled, bearded Old Man Winter doing a Spring Dance with flowing veils and cornucopia complete.[7]

Now comes the time of year when we shall be greeted with blackened hills and charred trees. A prairie fire is a beautiful thing against the night sky, but what a desolate picture is the result in the hard light of day. One wonders if the yearly burning of the winter grass is an economic aid, or just a habit or a tradition. The reason for burning the grass of the hay meadows is obvious, but there seem to be arguments on both sides of the question in the case of the pastureland. Both arguments definitely stated, neither is very convincing since they are not based on scientific facts. Such facts from scientific findings may exist, but the casual observer or partisan does not often come into contact with them, and his attitude is apt to be colored by his interests in the matter.

THE GREAT DRAMA OF NATURE

Friday, April 4, 1931, #69

In the great drama of Nature, it is difficult for man to determine causes. He sees the effect, but the causes are still a mystery to him. He is aware of the terrific struggle for existence, but the interdependence of the species is so intricate, so delicate, that it has become a most fascinating mystery to him, and one which has challenged his thirst for knowledge. Someday, he will discover in this drama of life romance as great as that found in the Crusades, and tragedy as great as that found in Shakespeare. It will be most intensely interesting romance and tragedy, because it will be man's own story as a part of the life of the earth. He will come to know himself much better, through knowing his brothers of the fields and woods.

ALDO LEOPOLD

In the omitted opening section of this column that concludes so eloquently, Mathews again contemplates the mystery of the missing quail and cites an article just published by the father of wildlife ecology, Aldo Leopold, and his co-author, John N. Ball: "The Quail Shortage of 1930." Their piece appeared in *Outdoor America*, the organ of the Izaak Walton League.[8] Investigating six states, Leopold and Ball considered the hard winter and the previous summer's drought as possible causes of the dearth of quail, but failed to arrive at definite conclusions. Leopold continued to address quail in later articles appearing in *Outdoor America* (see bibliography).

Aldo Leopold went on to find literary fame after he published *A Sand County Almanac* (1949), which like its predecessor, *Talking to the Moon* (1945), uses an organizational structure of months, or in Mathews's case, Osage Moons. Leopold describes the natural environment of his rural home in Wisconsin, the depletion of prairie chickens in the region, and the behavior of birds on and near his property. Leopold was an early theorist of the Land Ethic, which urges humans to forge an ethical relationship between themselves, the land, and other species that live on that land. "We abuse land because we regard it as a commodity belonging to us," Leopold writes in the foreword to *Sand County Almanac*. "When we see land as a community to which we belong, we may begin to use it with love and respect."[9] Resonances between the work of John Joseph Mathews and Aldo Leopold are worth further exploration.

THE BLACKJACKS AND THE WHISPERING PRAIRIE'S CALL

Tuesday, March 24, 1931, #66

I have seen the polished disc of a desert moon hanging in a palm tree,
Making ghosts of white-robed men, and flooding the sands with eerie silence.
I have watched the seething whitecaps dance madly o'er the howling sea,
And heard the demented winds moan and shriek in unleashed violence.
I have seen the dawn burst upon the wild, primordial world of pine,
And heard the bull-elk's challenge echo along the canyon's wall.
But there are things of wonder which by my birth are mine,
Above the desert silence, the sea: the blackjacks and the whispering prairie's call.

—John Joseph Mathews

Birdsong breaks from most unexpected places: from the pink peach trees, from the swaying top of the white-blossomed pear tree, from the green-budded elm. The whimsical winds swirl and eddy the pink and white petals, and deck the emerald grass with gay color. Hundreds of nameless flowers make the carpet of crazy pattern in the glades among the blackjacks, and the clouds race across the blustering sky. At night, the prairie fires flicker and reflect against the horizon, and cold breezes rattle the dead, rusty leaves, as the moon in harmony with the new life of the earth, hangs like silver horns, aloof and cold above the hills.

The wind whistles across the prairie, muffling the first diffident voices of Spring, screaming its importance to a world that is waiting for the throbbing of life, the cheerful song of the meadowlark and the sad whistle of the kill-deer, and for the long, rolling, booming call of the prairie chicken, as the sun peeps over the limestone escarpments.

HUNTING IN ALGERIA AND YELLOWSTONE

Mathews makes reference to his varied travel experiences in this poem, which appears only in this wonderful column. Although he occasionally wrote poems, this is the only Mathews poem known to have been published. The first stanza is informed by Mathews's experiences in early 1922 hunting in northern Africa. He pursued gazelles and shot a Barbary leopard. Mathews rang in the New Year with champagne in Algiers, and in early January, he was in Sidi Okba, which sits on an oasis in the Biskra province of Algeria. Sidi Okba boasts the oldest Mohammedan building in Africa. Here, near the religious capital of the Ziban people, he traveled on horseback with two American friends, led by a guide named Ahmed. They rode among the shifting sand dunes of the vast Sahara Desert.

The first two lines of the second stanza evoke Mathews's long hunting trip to Yellowstone in Wyoming in late 1920. This experience stirred something deep in his soul. In an unpublished poem, "I Thought," Mathews writes, "I thought a violin expressed life's yearning, / Then I heard a bull-elk's challenge burning."[10] After college graduation, he decided to embark on an elaborate, expensive big-game hunting trip in the Rockies, in the Wyoming Yellowstone area. He was joined on the first leg by Josephine's husband, Henry Benjamin Caudill, Sr. They picked up their "saddle horses and pack string at Holmes Lodge on the Shoshone River, on the trail to the east gate of the Park." In addition to the five saddle horses, "one for Bill the guide, one for Jim the cook, one for Wuff the wrangler and one each" for Henry and Jo, they had a "string of perhaps fourteen or fifteen pack horses," he wrote.[11] They hunted nonstop and camped out in the snow. "Glad to be alive," Mathews listened enraptured to the "challenge of the bull wapiti" and felt "proud of [his] manhood," he wrote in 1929. "In his bugle there seemed to be virility, passion, power, courage, a primitive freedom, the will to survive, and a plaintive insatiable yearning."[12]

Surprisingly, Mathews opted to extend his hunting trip instead of attending his first semester at Merton College, Oxford University. His mentor Walter Stanley Campbell alerted Merton College of Mathews's changed plans. Oxford sent him a letter scolding him but allowed him to attend Trinity term in the spring. Mathews thought Campbell would be disappointed, but when the two men met prior to Jo's trip to England, Campbell grinned delightedly and told him, "You're getting away with murder."[13]

ONE LAST CAPER OF OLD MAN WINTER

March 31, 1931, #68

We laughed too soon at the senile caperings of Old Man Winter; his seasonal mildness was misunderstood. The spirt was not yet extinct. Like an all-powerful potentate, he emerged from the death chamber and shouted defiance, saving the last ounce of his strength for a magnificent gesture, and putting everything into this last regal appearance, presenting himself in full panoply to a surprised world.

The shrieking of the cold winds was his sardonic laughter; school children were frozen and flower and fruit buds blasted by his imperial whim. By his twisted, imperial will, he is determined to die standing. . . .

White snow patches on the brown grasses of winter and against the background of the green sprouting grass of the burnt-off areas, make a striking, unfamiliar picture on the prairie: rather a dreary picture of resignation.

THE IZAAK WALTON CULTURE POND

Thursday, April 23, 1931, #71

The Izaak Walton Culture Pond is now complete. It was built by the local chapter of the League for the citizens of the Osage. Fingerlings will be brought here and kept in the ponds until they are large enough to take care of themselves in the streams and lakes of the country.[14] There will be a constant stocking of streams from the ponds so that the fishermen of the Osage need not go outside of their own county to enjoy this great sport, perhaps the most popular sport in the nation.

Now that the Culture Pond is complete, there is another possibility—a dream as yet, but a dream within the realm of reality. A lake can be built in the hills of the Osage which would draw fishermen from all over the district. This would be satisfying to the merchants of the county, and to all who take pride in having our hills appreciated by others, since the ego in each man desires the appreciation of others of the things that are his.

Somehow, people who do things silently and thoroughly, who expect no praise or reward, who spurn puerile, though often very acceptable publicity, have an appeal that is lasting and sincere. Many of the members of the local chapter of the League have done such work for the citizens of the Osage. Work which the other members of the local chapter of the League have no knowledge, but it would detract from the spirit in which the work was done if their names were mentioned, and such mention would likely be distasteful to them. However, one cannot refrain from mentioning Mr. W.A. Blasingame's work on the construction of the Culture Pond.[15] He not only directed the work, but also paid the dam-builders from his personal funds and gave not a few hours of his time each day but all his time to community improvement. It is true that the chapter has compensated him for his actual expenditures, but his time was a contribution, and the spirit in which he undertook the work is commendable and certainly worthy of mention in this column dedicated to the Osage hills and their wildlife.

THE IZAAK WALTON LEAGUE AND
CONSERVATION OF THE OSAGE

Monday, May 11, 1931, #78

At all times, the Izaak Walton League, through its divisions and as a national organization, moves toward its objectives: restocking cover and streams, reforesting the hills, conserving wildlife, creating recreation areas, and working to inspire the people of the United States to take a greater interest in their great outdoors.

This organization did not spring perfect from the ear of a god. It must go through the slow process from the carrying out of an idea to efficiency, and in this progress toward that which is accepted as a very laudable purpose, cooperation of the local divisions is necessary. We of the Osage, ready as we are to do what we can for the wildlife of our region, would naturally become phlegmatic[16] were it not for the constant inspiration of the national organization; were it not for the periodical contact we make with the other chapters and the men who inspire us with their enthusiasm.

Such inspiration is needed for the work of educating the average man in the conservation of the wildlife of his state and country. Habit is strong, and men have been in the habit of killing where and when they please without thought for the future. To make them see that they are destroying their own game is difficult and calls for utmost patience. Then, in America, and one makes this statement advisedly, people create laws for the express purpose of breaking them, as though the laws were the prohibitions of some eternal enemy. It would seem that game laws actually inspire the average man to disregard all things except a desire to defeat the law that protects his game and assures future sport. Seemingly, somewhere in the back of his mind is a half-formed idea that freedom and independence are synonymous with the word American, and he expresses this freedom and independence in wanton destruction of that which as a citizen of a democracy belongs to him.

This average man's attitude must be changed, and it can only be changed by his education in such matters. This education cannot be carried on by the few who deplore the situation, but by cooperation with the organization dedicated to that purpose. Dislike for some of the men identified with this organization is not contributing to the conservation of the wildlife; the idea is what really matters. The wildlife of the Osage cannot be saved by personal jealousy, prejudices, and disillusionment. It has besides its natural enemies, pariah dogs, half-wild housecats, and the hunter. The extra burden of human pettiness should not exist.

DISILLUSIONMENT

The tone of the last paragraph and the allusion to "personal jealousy, prejudices, and disillusionment" makes one wonder what events or communica-
tions were in the background of these statements, and if it was meant to be
a message to certain individuals in particular. Who was showing "dislike for
some of the men identified with this organization"? The degree to which
Mathews maintained his activities the Izaak Walton League after wrapping
up *Our Osage Hills* is not known. Although it seems he did not subsequently
refer to the Izaak Walton League in his writing, he remained a committed
conservationist and a sensitive and attuned nature writer.

PRAIRIE CHICKEN, QUAIL, AND
THE IZAAK WALTON LEAGUE

Monday, June 1, 1931, #82

Late in the afternoon, usually after a rain, one can hear the prairie chickens sending their sonorous, booming call over the prairie. This is always encouraging, since it reminds us that they are still with us, even though in small numbers. Whether privately or officially, one intends to bring the situation of the prairie chicken in the Osage to the attention of the Izaak Walton League convention at Lawton, meeting on June 7, 8, and 9.

It cannot be ascertained at this time whether or not the quail situation will be better this autumn, due to unmolested nesting and rearing, but so far there has been no reason why there should not be the usual number when the hunting season comes. The quail is a most prolific bird, and under favorable conditions soon overcomes depletion. The Osage is one of his natural habitats, and here he finds his food and protection and has struck a balance with his enemies—except, of course, in unusual cases of epidemic, extremely hard winters, wet springs and summers. It has never been proven, one believes, that a long drought is really such a disturbing factor in the propagation of quail.

About 12,000 bass eyes[17] were put into the Culture Ponds on Dial Hill[18] one day last week. These eyes, when they have attained the fingerling stage, will be distributed among the streams of the Osage. It is the hope of the local chapter of the Izaak Walton League that they will be able to supply the streams constantly from these Ponds.

REKINDLING THE PASSION FOR CONSERVATION

Wednesday, June 3, 1931, #83

In our endeavors to protect the game and fish in the Osage, and to restock streams and cover, we oftentimes grow rather listless. The spirit is still there, and certainly the determination to bring to success the plans that we have formulated is still evident. But even the most spirited protagonist of wildlife conservation will be dulled by the constant contact with conditions and things that he meets every day. The people with whom he works often detract from his spirited activity through their quiescence, and give to the whole matter the complexion of their attitude. It is an attitude acquired through monotony—the familiar, everyday rounds of the business of life, which slowly pales the vivid colors of enthusiasm, and covers a community with the fog of indifference, wherein arises petty vanities and ineffective but constant defense of their state of satisfied dissatisfaction.

Man is so constituted that his enthusiasms cannot live upon themselves; contacts with men of other communities who are working toward the same goals are necessary to him. His old enthusiasms spring into life again and new ideas come to him. He suddenly realizes that the object of his work retains all the meaning and importance that he attributed to it when he first took it up. He comes home inspired by what he has seen and heard, determined to never allow himself to fall into lethargy again.

This is one of the most important results of a state convention; it is almost the reason for being of all conventions, inasmuch as national and state organizations depend upon the small units for their success, and their success in turn depends upon the spirited activity of the members.

At Medicine Park, on June 7, 8, and 9, the Oklahoma Division of the Izaak Walton League will host its convention. The spot is most beautiful. The program is replete with pistol shooting, casting, and other competitions; there will be fish frys, and scenic drives through Oklahoma's National Park, a great game preserve wherein live the wildlife that once had Oklahoma as its habitat.[19] There will be fishing and boating, and many will bring their camp equipment, and make of the convention a short vacation along the mountain streams, and find pleasure in the beauty of the Wichita Mountains.

Members of the local chapter of the League are requested to attend this convention, for their personal pleasure in enjoying the vacation and the freshening of their spirits.

THE BIG CONVENTION!

Juxtaposed vertically with Mathews's preceding column is a news article headlined "State Ikes Will Convene Sunday." The piece added details unmentioned in Mathews's piece, including a "bathing beauty contest," underscoring the pre-feminist sexual politics of this almost entirely male organization, and a barbeque at Lost Lake. Notable speakers included Senator Elmer Thomas, who in a few years would become Mathews's nemesis during his tenure on the Osage Tribal Council; Walter M. "Skipper" Harrison, managing editor of two newspapers, the *Oklahoman* and the Oklahoma City *Times*; Congressman Jed Johnson; Congressman James V. "Sunny Jim" McClintic; and federal "government representatives of the Forest Service Bureau of Fisheries and Biological Survey." This gave Mathews an opportunity to deepen his contacts among influential politicians and pressmen, and he no doubt relished the experience. Those attending the "Ike convention" witnessed "the greatest game-proof fencing project ever attempted." At the national game preserve, they took in wildfowl and herds of buffalo, elk, and deer.

IN THE WICHITA MOUNTAINS

Tuesday, June 16, 1931, #84

A great thing has been done in the Wichita Mountains. There the wildlife of the state is being preserved to form a nucleus from which the state may be restocked. Really it is a very noble effort on the part of a few farsighted men, and certainly no part of the state is so well adapted to this type of preservation. The rugged granite hills and mesas with luxuriant grasses make an ideal home for the herds of elk and buffalo, and the lakes and streams are sanctuaries for the migratory waterfowl. It is a great grazing land accommodating both cattle and wild game.

It is pleasant driving through the hills of the Wichitas when the white clouds float lazily. The hills are green and untouched, yet the green fails to cover the distorted strata of upturned granite, as they twist like pinkish snakes over and around the peaks and across the valleys. Here is a disharmony to which one cannot accustom himself at first, especially if he has lived in the Osage, where the green prairie is a carpet that seems to undulate in to the far horizon.

Perhaps prejudice plays a part, but one has failed so far to find a region in the state that can compare with the Osage. The Wichitas are primitive and appealing, yet they are neither mountains nor hills. They possess none of the grandeur of the Rockies, nor yet the tranquil beauty of the Adirondacks; they are neither wild nor peaceful. They are rock-banded and disturbed, and there lingers about them an unrest that is not definite enough to be alluring, yet they may be called beautiful.

NOTES

1. The quotation is taken from *The Meaning of Culture*, chapter IX, "Culture and Nature," from Part II: Application of Culture. John Cowper Powys, *The Meaning of Culture* (New York: W. W. Norton, 1929), 148. In the 1920s and 1930s, Powys was an influential British novelist and critic, possessing a hearty, original style. He lectured in America from 1950 through the early 1960s, summering in England. This book seems to have influenced Mathews's sense of style.

2. Mathews of course refers to Macbeth's famous soliloquy in Shakespeare's *Macbeth*, Act V, scene five: "Life's but a walking shadow, a poor player / That struts and frets his hour upon the stage / And then is heard no more: it is a tale / Told by an idiot, full of sound and fury, Signifying nothing."

3. Kelly Bostian, "Extreme Contamination in Bird Creek Tributary an Ongoing Mystery," *Tulsa World*, January 11, 2017, www.tulsaworld.com/news/state/extreme -contamination-in-bird-creek-tributary-an-ongoing-mystery/article_18777940-7a2a -5650-82ab-16f6fb3c2c06.html.

4. Ziva Branstetter, "EPA Investigating Osage County Saltwater Leak," *The Frontier*, December 22, 2016, www.readfrontier.org/stories/epainvestigativesalterwa- terleak/; Kelly Bostian, "EPA Narrows Search for Cause of Bird Creek Contamination in Osage County," *Tulsa World*, April 21, 2017, www.tulsaworld.com/homepagelat est/epa-narrows-search-for-cause-of-bird-creek-contamination-in/article_d9ee9c32 -788d-5b84-ac6a-a03c41e460f3.html; Maureen Wurtz, "Dozens of Syringes Found Near Bird Creek in Pawhuska," April 10, 2017, KTUL Tulsa ABC, ktul.com/news/ local/dozens-of-syringes-found-near-bird-creek-in-pawhuska.

5. Kelly Bostian, "EPA's Pruitt: Agency is 'Doing What It's Supposed to Do' at Osage Pollution Site," *Tulsa World*, May 28, 2017, www.tulsaworld.com/news/state/ epa-s-pruitt-agency-is-doing-what-it-s-supposed/article_882efaf6-f06b-5f77-8663 -ba2791234b48.html.

6. Mathews, *Sundown*, 250.

7. "Primavera" means spring in many romance languages, and Mathews seems to allude to Sandro Botticelli's famous Italian Renaissance painting called *Primavera*, also known as *Allegory of Spring*.

8. Aldo Leopold and John N. Ball, "The Quail Shortage of 1930," *Outdoor America* 9, no. 9 (April 1931): 14–15, 67.

9. Aldo Leopold, *A Sand County Almanac and Sketches Here and There* (New York: Oxford University Press, 1949), viii.

10. Mathews, "I Thought," Box 4, Folder 30, John Joseph Mathews Collection, Western History Collection, University of Oklahoma.

11. Mathews, *Twenty Thousand Mornings*, 236.

12. Mathews, "Hunting in the Rockies," *Sooner Magazine* (May 1929): 279.

13. Mathews, *Twenty Thousand Mornings*, 252–53.

14. Fingerlings are small, young fish.

15. Wade A. Blasingame was an Osage County rancher and landowner who be- came interested in the real estate business. He came to the Osage in 1897 as a sur- veyor and decided to stay. Warehime, *History*, 131.

16. Apathetic or indifferent.

17. The rock bass (*Ambloplites rupestris*), also known as the northern rock bass, rock perch, goggle-eye, or red eye, is a carnivorous freshwater fish native to east-central North America. It is similar to the smallmouth bass, but is usually much smaller.

18. Dial Hill was named for the aforementioned businessman Wesley M. Dial, whose large property lay near there.

19. Since 1907, the area was designated Wichita National Forest, under the supervision of the U.S. Forest Service. In 1936, five years after this column appeared, it became Wichita Mountains Wildlife Refuge, having been placed under the control of the Bureau of Biological Survey, precursor of the U.S. Fish and Wildlife Service, which was formed in 1940.

Part X

Critique of Settler Colonialism

MISSING THE TRUE SAGA OF OUR NATION:
A CRITIQUE OF SETTLER COLONIALISM

Wednesday, March 4, 1931, #60

While the stage is set for the Osage, and we await the decision of Old Man Winter—whether he intends to continue his senile caperings, or make his welcome adieu, so that Spring, who must be standing impatiently in the wings, shivering in her cheesecloth, can lead on her toe-dancing ballet—we turn to another topic, ignoring Winter's presence. His act has been mild and without interest this year anyway.

It has always been one's pet idea that the pioneer Europeans who came in contact with the Indians of America were almost as ignorant and barbaric as they thought the Indians to be; vide history, and stories that have come down to us. If this idea cannot be confirmed by what has been actually written, then one can find confirmation by reading between the lines. The average European pioneer was a chauvinist, a rabid nationalist or religionist, and he could not see anything nor understand anything that did not conform with his own opinions and teachings, and people who did not measure up to his standards were pagans, savages quite beyond the pale and not worthy of his "civilized" interest. Not that that made any difference to the original American, but it does make a great difference to us who are left without the true saga of our country, because of this lack of broad sympathy and intelligent understanding on the part of the pioneers.[1]

In 1827, a Frenchman named Paul Vissiers visited the Osages and he wrote a very plausible book titled *Histoire des Indians Osages*.[2] He gushes and spills over occasionally, but despite his enthusiasm, he proved to be, if not a deeply understanding and exact observer, at least a keen and interested one, and his little book is filled with information. But alas, he was a nationalist, a child of the artificial atmosphere, and one imagined him tingling pleasantly with the warm consciousness of superiority, and ever busy flicking the dust of the Osage encampments from his riding trousers. One cannot blame him for his smug Europeanism, but he had no sense of humor, and that is unforgivable. A really civilized man ought to have a sense of humor. Following is a translation of the last two paragraphs under the chapter heading "Des Femmes" (The Woman):

> Chastity is one of their virtues; the girls attend with calm the time of their marriage, which takes place from the age of 15 to 20 years, and the boys from the age of 16 to 25. The girl who abandons herself to promiscuity is despised by her sisters and abandoned by her family, and is forced to follow her ravisher, who is always known at the time of her confinement; at that time, she makes known

the father of the infant. The father then shares in the blame and disrespect which has come to his accomplice, and, as in her case, he cannot hope to make a decent marriage, unless his war exploits are brilliant or his success in the chase outstanding, to efface the memory of his deed. From the whole Osage tribe he may then regain favor. But the girl is barred from this way of returning to consideration. She is never raised from the status of a Messalina,[3] and drags her days out under this stigma, having only fleeting and secret relationship with the men.

Adultery of the women, a capital crime, one for which the husband revenges himself on the woman and her accomplice, is extremely rare in this tribe, and one sees, after the preceding paragraph, that this tribe has a code of morals, especially as to chastity, nearly the same as our own.

Anyone who has read just a little French history knows of the code of morals existing at the time of the writing of this book and of the code before the Revolution, after the Revolution, and up to the Third Republic, will agree that this superior observer among a primitive people showed an amazing lack of a sense of humor, when he wrote that last line.

OLD MAN

Sunday, March 8, 1931, #61

A spring snowstorm always seems indefinite, without purpose—more of a whim of Nature than a well-planned, routine occurrence. No matter how the winds howl and bluster, they show a certain lack of conviction, like one attempting to portray himself as courageous or awe-inspiring as he wishes to be. It is the colossal bluff.

Green grass blades peep through the snow, and swelling buds hint of spring and growth. The robin, the blue jay and the cardinal have an attitude of impatience rather than one of hopelessness, and though the storm may still their early spring voices, their activity is not curbed. This gives the storm the fleeting significance only, and makes of it an annoyance rather than a prolonged, seasonable performance.

Last autumn, an old man asked permission to stay in the second-growth elms and walnuts across the creek from the farmhouse. He spent the summer there under a tarpaulin raised on four short poles. He had a team of mules, a wagon and bedclothes, and he depended on infrequent work for his mules and his hoe for his living. On rainy days or when he was not working, he would come to the house, borrow a pair of glasses, and lose himself in the unearthly romances of Zane Grey.[4] One was forced to believe that the borrowed glasses filled a psychological need rather than a physical one, but he seemed happy as his withered old spirit rode under the Arizona skies with the Artemis-like heroine and the handsome hero.[5]

One day he came into the house, and asked to borrow a shotgun. When asked what he wanted it for, he said with mild pride: "Well, I seen me a bunch of quail over there in the field—first I've seen on the crick fer a coon's age I reckon, and I thought I'd get me a mess."

"Yes, but they are out of season and besides that, the covey is probably a pair with the half-grown young."

"Hell boy, them's the kind—tender." He had an expression of pity for one's ignorance in such matters.

"Suppose you know that the law protects quail at this season of the year?"

"Who's goin' a know it?"

"No one is going to know it for the simple reason that you're not going to shoot them."

He looked surprised and hurt. He began to look down at his toe, and then with defiance and bitterness, said, "I reckon yu lay claim to all God-a-Mighty's creatures just 'cause they're on you; why, I've trapped quail by the thousand right on this crick long before you was born—used to sell 'em up in Kansas to a feller in the business, fer a dollar, and a dollar-and-a-quarter a doben [sic]."

CITY SLICKERS

Monday, March 16, 1931, #62

One always feels sorry for people in large cities in the springtime. They have so little evidence that spring has come, unless it be artificial. Of course, the shops create a spring atmosphere in their windows, and there appears a most lavish display of fishing rods and cabins, camp equipment, and apparel. These things make longing and desire a little more poignant, dreams perhaps a little sweeter, and gives to the son of the city keen anticipation of his allotted two weeks' vacation. But the bursting of the bud is missed, the bird song in the early morning hours and in the calm of the evenings when the hills become violet and the western sky is splashed with pink; the balmy air and the unobtrusive scents of earth and things growing, are not for him of the pavements.

Sometimes during the summer, this man of the city goes West, dressed in clothes sold to him by pale-faced clerks in the large sports stores, and jogs up and down on a stiff-legged cowpony for a few delightful days. Or else he walks. He takes long hikes, then returns to his world of steel and concrete, taking great pride in his sunburned arms, and becomes an authority on the particular type of vacation in which he has indulged. Again he takes up the monotonous life of catching trains and ferries and subways, between his office in the steel canyons of the business district, and his home an hour away.

This is the business of living perhaps, and no doubt he is happy in his daily routine, but one is more apt to believe that living has something to do with wide expanses of whispering prairie and blackjack-covered hills, which creep up to his door, where he may live daily in the heart of the things of the earth.

URBAN MATHEWS

Mathews had lived in Geneva, Switzerland; Montclair, New Jersey, a commuter suburb of New York City; and Pasadena, near Los Angeles. He had also spent time in London, Paris, Berlin, Munich, Rome, Algiers, and other cities, so he knew something about urbanites and city life. He never grew fond of cities, however. Visiting Cleveland, Ohio, in 1943, he wrote his partner, Elizabeth, "I don't know what to make of Cleveland. The people one meets downtown are rather barbaric; a lower order of civilization."[6]

THE OSAGE COUNTY HOME OWNERS ASSOCIATION: TROUBLING REVELATIONS

The Sioux-Osage author Fred Grove wrote that some "enemies of the tribe wore blue-serge suits, white shirts and ties, sang in church, and were regarded as pillars of their community." One of them, a banker and lawyer who defended murder plotter Bill Hale, was even a lay minister.[7] Widespread land lease schemes preyed on Osage landowners, and brazen though they were, they "seem mild compared to the audacity of the Osage County Home Owners Association," Terry P. Wilson writes.[8] Indeed, like Old Man Winter, the association tried to impose its "twisted, imperial will" upon coveted mineral rights held by Osages. The Osage County Home Owners Association (OCHOA), which was comprised of landowners, bankers, guardians, and other businessmen, sought to terminate the Osage headright system and thus, their communal oil profits, when the Osage trust period with the government expired in April 1931, the month we have now reached in Mathews's "Our Osage Hills" columns.

The OCHOA strongly opposed any congressional extension of the trust period. In fact, they formed in 1919 with the avowed purpose of fighting Oklahoma house bill 5009, introduced by Senator Wheeler, which proposed to extend the Osage trust period with the federal government to 1959. The group therefore openly worked to rob the inheritance of all Osages with headrights and their descendants. This proved challenging, however, because unlike most tribes, the Osages had purchased their land outright from the Cherokees when they traveled south from Kansas Territory, after having sold their land there to the federal government in multiple treaties during the nineteenth century. The Wahzhazhe had undeniable rights to their underground reservation, even if much surface land had been transferred to Whites. The association's efforts were blocked by fierce and effective opposition from the Osage Tribal Council.

Surprisingly, there are several Mathews-family connections to the original officers of the OCHOA, some of whom are associated with Bill Hale and his nefarious Fairfax contingent. This is disconcerting, though it should be recalled that Jo's Osage father, William S. Mathews, who had been a tribal councilman before and after allotment, had died back in 1915 with a strong reputation for honesty.

The first example is the association president in its early years, George G. LaMotte of Pawhuska, a mixed-blood Anishinaabe (Chippewa) who became a big-time Osage County rancher. Born in Minnesota in 1880, and raised there and in Wisconsin, Michigan, and Canada, George was graduated from Carlisle Indian School and Haskell Indian School, where he was a football and baseball star. In 1905, LaMotte moved from Kansas City to Pawhuska and was employed by the Osage agency until 1910. During those years, La-Motte played semi-pro ball on the Pawhuska baseball club, which reputedly had a "fast team in the field," especially from 1906 through 1908, when it was "feared by all rival teams in that section," stated a Haskell student reporter. As noted earlier, William S. Mathews, a sports fan like his son, had helped finance the Pawhuska team, and he and Jo's mother, Jennie, would be seen cheering them on.[9] An outfielder, LaMotte was considered "a dangerous and hard hitter," and this aggression was seen in subsequent areas of his life. La-Motte became a wealthy Osage County rancher who, by hook or by crook, came to lease more than four hundred thousand acres from Osages, becoming one of the largest cattle producers in the state. George LaMotte, whom John Joseph Mathews knew, as his father had before him, was not only the president of the OCHOA, but also a person who, with his second wife, had repeatedly run afoul of the federal government for profiting from Osages and their land illegally and unethically. During most of the early activity of the OCHOA, Mathews was finishing college at the University of Oklahoma after serving in the Army Air Corps, hunting in the Rockies, studying at Oxford, and traveling in Europe and Algeria, so he was likely unaware of George La Motte's fierce endorsement of terminating the communal headright system.

In 1921, La Motte publicly argued that since 1906, business of all kinds in Osage County had been "predicated upon the limitations of the 25-year period." Deeds and leases had specified the clause marking 1931 as the year in which the Osage "would become a citizen and the white man the owner of the property which he had purchased." LaMotte maligned the proposed extension by rhetorically linking it with German and Russian tyranny, claiming he found it hard to understand why "the government should now emulate the Bolsheveki or adopt the Hun theory that a written contract is but 'a scrap of paper.'" In an analysis of propaganda, Kristen Williams Backer writes,

> perhaps the most directly influential antecedents to the Bolshevik monster were derogatory personifications of Germany created by allied propagandists in World War I. Following the German invasion of Belgium, whose neutrality, previously guaranteed in the Treaty of London of 1831 and 1839, was dismissed as a "Scrap of Paper," Germany was increasingly portrayed as "the Hun."[10]

LaMotte declared: "The welfare of the Osage Indian, justice to the white man who has sought to make his home in the county, and a decent regard for the progress of agriculture and commerce, demand a removal of the hobbles that have been placed on the development of Osage county and its citizens."[11] Of course, the possibility of extension had always been an option, so any such deeds or leases with such a provision were premature and perhaps misleading.

It is not as though the LaMottes needed more money. George had accumulated so much, he embarked on a two-year tour of Europe, hanging out in metropolitan cafes while his daughter took music lessons. At Carlisle and in touring bands, LaMotte had played double bass in the Wheelock Indian band; his daughter, Georgette, who inherited his musical talent, was studying piano repertory in Paris with two teachers. Philip Deloria writes that Dennis Wheelock led both the Carlisle and the Haskell Institute bands, and converted the Haskell band into the U.S. Indian Band, a fifty-piece touring ensemble that became widely known.[12] In July 1922, while visiting Paris during a trip through Europe, Jo Mathews was enjoying the ambience of a sidewalk café when George LaMotte approached. At the café, George invited Jo to dinner at his apartment that same night. The two men went to Jo's hotel to wait for Jo's friend, the wealthy French-Osage Grace Soldani, who arrived for a social call with the Comtesse de Sonis and her daughter, Miss Morgan. After the ladies departed, Jo and George went to LaMotte's apartment, where Jo met George's beautiful fifteen-year-old daughter. Such was the beginning of a charming week during which Mathews mixed with Grace Soldani, Mr. and Miss LaMotte, the Count and Countess, and Miss Morgan, enjoying sophisticated conversation over coffees, aperitifs, and scrumptious meals. The countess and Mathews were the most outspoken, holding the floor on politics, war, and other non-musical subjects.[13]

It may seem surprising that George LaMotte, a Chippewa who had been so closely associated with Osages, would be hostile to the financial well-being of Osages with headrights, or so concerned over the suppositious contractual rights of "the White man." Yet LaMotte and his White, politically connected wife, Anna Marx LaMotte, had already accumulated a scandalous track record, rife with arrests and accusations of exploitation of Osages. After LaMotte's first wife died in 1908, two years later, he, a Democrat, married Anna Marx McGuire, who in 1909 divorced Oklahoma Republican Congressman Bird S. McGuire, also a lawyer and rancher who owned a large acreage outside of Bartlesville. Anna LaMotte became George's business partner in LaMotte & LaMotte, at a time when women magnates were rare, leasing Osage land for farming and grazing. They pooled their strengths and connections to expand their wealth and power, and Anna's charms drew business. Within five years, they were handling leases on more than three hundred thousand acres per year. To get there, however, the LaMottes employed sharp practices, and soon ran afoul of the federal government. In October 1913, an indictment "charging the endorsement of a false acknowledgement to a grazing lease was returned against Mrs. LaMotte." In November, George and his wife were arrested in Pawhuska by U.S. Marshal W. S. Cade, "under warrants based on indictments returned by the federal grand jury at Lawton" some weeks prior. These emerged from the Osage oil lease cases that had "caused the indictment and arrest of several prominent oil men several days ago," it was reported.[14] This was the previously discussed Uncle Sam Oil Company controversy, during which the Department of the Interior expelled the Osage Tribal Council. George LaMotte countered that his and Anna's indictments were merely retaliation for "open resentment" they had revealed after being refused a "square deal from the agency," and protesting too strongly against practices that created "the troubled conditions of this country." The men they had criticized struck back through the federal courts, he claimed.[15]

Their legal trouble was not an isolated incident, however, because in February 1914, Rosa Neal Hill, a fullblood Osage, sued the LaMottes and W. T. Leahy in the district court. Hill requested the cancellation of nine different deeds of conveyance, which purported "to convey title to an undivided interest in about 4,000 acres of Osage lands." The petition alleged that Rosa Hill had employed Mrs. LaMotte to look after and lease her lands, but the Osage woman had been duped into signing over the deeds based on Mrs. LaMotte's misrepresentation that the deeds were only powers of attorney she must sign so that Anna could lease and best care for Rosa Hill's interest in those lands. All of the transactions were with Anna LaMotte, but in some cases, Anna acted as agent for her husband, George.[16]

In April 1917, George and Anna LaMotte were yet again on trial, on a charge of conspiring to defraud the government through the purchase of Osage property. The charge centered around the deed to a house that had been owned by an Osage woman, Mollie Lamont, who had borrowed money several times from LaMotte & LaMotte. Lamont's house was mortgaged to Anna LaMotte, who then issued another loan. The federal government called it fraud, and in October 1917, they secured a temporary injunction restraining the LaMottes from "obtaining leases on lands of incompetent Osage Indians." John Fain, U.S. district attorney, charged that the LaMottes had "obtained through guardians valuable leases on Osage Indian lands without the approval of the secretary of the interior." The lands had been "released to cattlemen for valuable considerations, and the government and Indian owner have not derived their just share from the property." So George and Anna were ripping off both Osages and the federal government regularly; only federal action seemed to slow them. This injunction was modified in 1921, saying that only allotted and inherited lands were restricted from leasing.[17] Described as attractive and charming, avaricious Anna LaMotte was associated with political power and Oklahoma statehood; she was declared a "romantic figure" by the press even amid the LaMottes' 1917 scandal. The *Oklahoman* wistfully recalled that Anna, during her previous marriage to Oklahoma first district Republican congressman Bird McGuire, along with the state delegation, had been hosted by President Theodore Roosevelt in a special reception at the White House. Moreover, upon Oklahoma statehood, she was "presented by Joe Cannon, then speaker of the house, with the flag then waving from the capitol," along with the flag of the new state of Oklahoma, the latter she gifted to the Daughters of the American Revolution.[18] The LaMottes were crooked capitalists who took advantage of their situation, one a Native American who was fine with exploiting other Natives, the other a glamorous symbol of statehood with a track record of fleecing Osage women.

Paul Nightingale Humphrey, secretary of the association in 1921, was later John Joseph Mathews's personal attorney who handled his will. Responding to requests made by the Osage tribal council, Paul Humphrey said he did not own a single acre of land in the county and had no personal interest in the matter, and was only acting professionally as a lawyer in his representation of the OCHOA. In 1921, Humphrey argued against the proposed extension; if it were granted, the oil and gas interests would get "something for nothing." But unless the extension was passed, Osages would get nothing at all after 1931.

The OCHOA vice president was prominent Hominy trader and rancher, Frederick Gentner Drummond. Gentner had been a guardian of many Osages until recently and was a partner in the First National Bank of Hominy. A 1914 graduate of Oklahoma A&M who attended Harvard Business School, Drummond learned to speak Osage fluently and was reportedly given an Osage name. After his father's death, he helped run the family business, the Hominy Trading Company. John Joseph Mathews knew Gentner Drummond and his wife, Grace Ford Drummond, and their children. Mathews and his second wife, Elizabeth, became older friends of Gentner and Grace's son, the rancher Frederick Ford Drummond, and his wife, Janet Trahern Drummond, who were repeat guests at The Blackjacks during the 1960s and early 1970s. Fred Drummond later played an important role in the establishment of the Tallgrass Prairie Preserve, which now includes the land on which The Blackjacks sits.[19] Les Warehime writes that Gentner Drummond operated a ranch that once held twenty-five thousand acres devoted to Hereford cattle, but he "primarily confined himself to banking and operation of the trading company." His brothers, Cecil and Alfred A. (Jack), however, started buying up ranches prior to World War I and continued to actively "buy ranches in partnership throughout the 1920s including the Bill Hale Ranch near Fairfax." Jack and Cecil were able to buy and lease huge tracts of land. After Jack joined the Army during World War II, Cecil focused on setting up his three sons in ranching. Supported by their family's resources, the young Drummonds bought up "the land of ranchers who had been badly weakened, first by drought and then by the depression." It is not surprising that most non-Osage ranchers and cattlemen would favor turning over the subsurface

mineral rights owned communally by the Osage Nation, to surface landowners. Those buying up the land of Osages stood to gain vast sums of money.

The methods by which such massive ranching empires (including the Hale,
Mullendore, Drummond, and Chapman-Barnard ranches) secured leases and
purchases of land from Osages could be aggressive, dishonorable, or sometimes even criminal. Beginning with Osage allotment in 1908, cattlemen saw
themselves as being in a desperate situation. The *Wichita Eagle* put it in a
nutshell in January:

> tract by tract, the immense pastures of Oklahoma and Indian Territory have
> dwindled until only the Osage Nation, sixty miles square, remains, and to-
> day with the allotment of the Osage Indians and the coming of statehood, the
> cattlemen sees this last feeding ground slipping away and he is making a death
> struggle to hold that portion which constitutes the best pastures.[20]

This was forecasted by the character Curly in Lynn Riggs's play *Green Grow
the Lilacs*, set in 1900 in Indian Territory: "The ranches are breakin' up fast.
They're puttin' in barbed w'ar, and plowin' up the sod fer wheat and corn.
Pretty soon they won't be no grazin'—thousands of acres—no place for the
cowboy to lay his head."[21] Many cattlemen flouted laws and regulations
governing the Osages and their land use. Chicanery and defrauding of Osage
landholders ran rampant.[22] Banker, Indian loan shark, and future murder
plotter, H. G. Burt managed to buy up "considerable Indian lands," his partner John Bird testified.[23] During the early period of Osage allotment, when
individuals were selecting their tracts, Superintendent Hugh Pitzer testified
that when he took over the Osage agency, he "found locators, middlemen and
agents of cattlemen doing an extensive business," and they seemed to serve
the interests of cattlemen, not of the Osages. Pitzer found that the reservation
was occupied by White men "under informal, that is to say illegal, leases or
contracts." Conditions were in "a most chaotic state" and clearly "financially
detrimental to the Indians." Pitzer explained most Osage allottees would
readily offer their land for leasing, often being offered cash incentives, and
gradually, an aggressive rancher could control vast tracts. "If a rancher was
successful in securing most of the leases within a given pasture or control
of its water, he would command control of the entire pasture, as the remaining land owners had little choice but to lease to him." This tactic was how a
single cattleman or small partnership could establish dominance over a huge
acreage, Warehime reports.[24] Erd Mullendore and other prairie moguls were
known for aggressive and hostile practices; Erd built his ranching empire by
buying out cattlemen "who were forced out of business for one reason or
another," sometimes for suspicious reasons. In the 1920s, Erd did whatever
it took to get his son, Gene, established in ranching. One of the operators he

bought out was Bill Hale, the Osage murder plotter, who controlled many parcels of land; thus both Drummonds and Mullendores took over properties of Hale, the kingpin. In 1929, the year in which Hale was found guilty, Erd established the Mullendore Trust and eventually acquired as many as eighty thousand acres, mostly in the vicinity of Fairfax.[25]

In 1915, capitalists Horace G. Barnard and "reticent and shrewd" James A. Chapman formed a partnership and purchased a ranch property. Chapman was also a partner with Robert McFarlin—his uncle and later, father-in-law, and Barnard's brother-in-law—in the hugely successful McMan Oil Company and the Exchange National Bank of Tulsa, which is now Bank of Oklahoma, a major bank in the state. With a lust for land, Chapman and Barnard rapidly expanded their ranch holdings. "When they could," Warehime writes, "they bought land that had been held by lease and any available that bordered their ranch. At one time they owned more than 100,000 acres in Osage County."[26] Not infrequently, it seems, opportunity to buy land they had bordered or leased arose through the death of the Osage landowner. In 2001, Jim Roan Gray, great-grandson of murder victim Henry Roan, and soon to become principal chief of the Osages, and Osage writer Wilhelm Murg co-authored an article using material from their interview with anthropologist Dr. Garrick Bailey of University of Tulsa, who shared his research and insights. "While the death rate for Osages was twice as high as the non-Osages in the area, Osages who owned tracts of land that would later become a part of the Chapman-Barnard Ranch had a death rate that was four times as high." They claimed "at its peak, the ranch covered 1/5 of the land in Osage County."[27] These figures are startling, when recalling that Osage County is about the size of Delaware. The ranch started to decline with Chapman's death in 1966. In 1983, the Nature Conservancy purchased a thirty thousand-acre ranch that had been part of the Barnard-Chapman holdings.

Clyde F. Lake of Pawhuska, the secretary-treasurer of the OCHOA, was also linked with the Mathews family. It is a bit distressing to find the name of "the ebullient Clyde Lake," who had been the Mathews family's business advisor, among the officers of this group so hostile to Osage interests. C. F. Lake was the cashier at the Citizens National Bank in Pawhuska, formerly Citizens State Bank, which John Joseph Mathews's father had co-organized, and for which he had served as president and as a director, the latter until the day he died. Clyde Lake was also a guardian. In *Twenty Thousand Mornings*, Mathews explains that after William's death in March 1915, he worked with Lake and their family lawyer on his father's business affairs, reluctantly because at the time he disliked anything related to business. Lake was quick, self-assured, and efficient even while enjoying his "long light brown cigars, which he smoked with delicacy." Yet Mathews implies there was more to Lake than met the eye. "He exuded bright efficiency, which precluded any urge to be casual," Mathews wrote in the first volume of his unfinished autobiography. "Like many completely absorbed businessmen, he laughed often—at nothing. His laughing was like that of certain other businessmen, protective; you couldn't see his thoughts beyond it: a veritable smokescreen, or even a species of distraction display, as practiced by the brooding killdeer or the upland plover."[28] A Killdeer parent will lure predators away from the nest by calling loudly while feigning a limp and a broken wing; upland plovers—now called upland sandpipers—also make loud distraction displays.[29] Clyde Lake's laughter may have also been a nervous display called "duper's delight." Yet "he had been a favorite" of Jo's father, and "he kept faith," Mathews believed, feeling that his mother Jennie Mathews and he were fortunate in their advisors. Neither he nor his mother knew much about finances and did not fully understand the proceedings, though he concluded nothing went amiss. Mathews apparently had no idea that Lake worked to take away the communal headright system.

Along with Clyde Lake, Jo Mathews had worked with Elmer E. Grinstead, the Mathews family's primary attorney. Mathews considered Grinstead cautious, honest, and serious. Grinstead, however, would go on to defend Bill Hale, mastermind of the Osage murders, and his compliant nephew, Ernest Burkhart. E. E. Grinstead was not just a lawyer, he was also in banking, as the secretary and trust officer of the Citizens Trust Company in Pawhuska, who handled the estates of wealthy Osages. In retrospect, we know Grinstead was thus doubly in the "Indian business," as the widespread racketeering and exploitation was called. It turns out that Grinstead, like Lake, did not have the interests of the Osages in his heart or mind. In 1919 and 1920, Grinstead as an attorney worked for the Osage County Home Owners Association to prepare a legal brief presenting a case opposing the extension of the Osage mineral trust period. Grinstead argued at length against the extension before a U.S. House committee. Grinstead was not just a hired gun; in April 1931, he revealed himself a leading advocate of their position when he served notice to the Finance Oil Company that he "owned Osage land under lease by the company and claimed all minerals underlying the land or extracted from it after midnight, April 8." The mineral trust period had already been extended through 1958, yet many surface land owners, mostly White men, refused to accept this. Grinstead threatened legal action if his demands were not met. He was only one of many "white men who [had] purchased land allotments from individual tribesmen," who then claimed the subsurface rights that had been "reserved to the tribe since the land was parceled out by the government" during allotment. Others were also planning lawsuits. Despite his scheming, Grinstead was the lay preacher referred to at the beginning of this chapter.[30] Grinstead had already shocked and betrayed Osages in 1923 for being Hale's lawyer in suing the Capitol Insurance Company of Denver, attempting to make them "pay up on the fraudulent Henry Roan policy of $25,000," Osage author Dennis McAuliffe, Jr., reveals in *Bloodland: A Family Story of Oil, Greed and Murder on the Osage Reservation*.[31] Hale arranged to have Henry Roan murdered. This was not the last time Grinstead worked for the bad guys. When Hale and gunman John Ramsey had their arraignment set in January 1926, their defense attorneys plotted "to introduce a motion to quash all charges" against them, Underhill noted. Hale's defense team, Grinstead, Scott, Hamilton, and Cross, argued that Hale and Ramsey should be returned to Pawhuska, "where their defense could be planned." The Pawhuskan firm had also represented Ernest Burkhart.[32] Knowing this, E. E. Grinstead's photo staring out at the viewer from the *Osage County Profiles* book looks especially creepy.

Ed T. Kennedy, Robert Stuart, Eugene S. Shidler, A. N. Ruble, H. G. Burt, Dr. Roger L. Hall, and J. L. Hudson were all on the executive committee of the OCHOA, which met with an Indian Affairs Committee of Congress when it visited Oklahoma, with Congressman Phil Campbell of Kansas at its head.[33] Herbert G. Burt became a conspirator with Bill Hale and participated in the murder of W. W. Vaughan, the attorney of the Osage murder victim, George Bigheart. Banker and former rancher J. L. Hudson, at the time the cashier at the First National Bank of Fairfax, was a confederate of Hale and C. E. Ashbrook, the latter also of that bank, in which Hale held interest and which served as the financial epicenter of the Osage reign of terror. The vast majority of the executive committee were bankers or members of banking institutions.[34] The attempted land grab of the OCHOA, although ultimately a failure, exposed individuals who up to then had pretended to be friends of the Osages.

In the late teens and through 1920, the OCHOA publicly argued that it would be best for everyone—even the Osages themselves—if the trust period and the communal headright system was allowed to expire. Surface land owners would then be granted the subsurface oil mineral rights to the land they had purchased. The association even used as a point in their argument that the fullbloods were rapidly dying out. This, of course, was being hastened by crooked doctors and bootleggers, and was about to explode into a gruesome series of murders in a few months. The original officers' names appeared in a series of three articles published in the Wichita *Daily Eagle* about factions feuding over the future of Osage County oil and mineral rights post-1931. Wichita was more favorable to the agricultural development of the county, opposing oil development, which made land less useful for grazing and agriculture. They stressed the saltwater and oil overrunning into streams, poisoning fish and cattle. The surface right owners of the OCHOA complained that oil and gas wells could be drilled on their land, ruining their agricultural potential, and they had little or no recourse. They were legal nonentities, they claimed, greatly exaggerating.[35] But a statement signed by Principal Chief Charles Brown and five tribal council members made the Osage position clear: oil and gas development would take priority over agricultural land use. Soon, the activities of the OCHOA turned private, for the reason that their livelihoods were now being threatened by a righteous Osage boycott, whose financial future health was threatened by the actions of the OCHOA.

In early 1920, the Osage Tribal Council took powerful actions—called "bludgeon resolutions" by the Kansan press—against the OCHOA. They were prepared by George E. Tinker, secretary of the Osage Council, in Washington, DC, with "the assistance of a lady stenographer," and signed by Principal Chief Charles Brown and Assistant Principal Chief Paul Red Eagle. At that time, the resolution noted, the OCHOA executive committee was almost entirely comprised of bankers, and "several of the most active members of the Association were guardians for one or several" Osages. The law then allowed an individual to act as guardian to up to five "Indian wards," and considering the "large incomes to be handled, the position is one of considerable financial value." Regardless, the Wichita *Daily Eagle* stressed, "these men, so loosely allied with the interests of Osage County and the Indian [sic], were antagonistic to an extension of the trust period." This line of argument failed to consider that many of these landowners could stand to make a great deal *more* money if they owned the subsurface rights of their land, than if they remained guardians within the current system. The Osage Tribal Council mailed many letters to bankers and guardians of Osages announcing that they had passed a resolution. The Osage tribe felt, reasonably, that "banks and persons who are receiving benefits from the Osage tribe of Indians and from members thereof, ought not to, in any way, interfere with, bring any influence to bear against" the granting of an extension of the period, and "if they continue to do so, said banks ought not to be permitted to have deposits of money belonging to the Osage tribe, and such persons ought not to be permitted to longer act as guardians of estates of members of the tribe." The council requested to

> withdraw from any bank whose officers and directors use any influence to prevent the granting of the extension of the mineral period, all funds of the Osage tribe deposited therein, and that they use their influence and efforts to cause to be removed any guardian of the estate of an Osage Indian who is using his efforts or influence to prevent the granting of the extension of the mineral period.

This hardline imposed by the Osage council proved effective.

In their written responses, bankers and guardians equivocated and flip-flopped. Executive committee member Ed T. Kennedy, president of Bank of

Commerce of Pawhuska, claimed his bank was neutral, but he, the owner of considerable land in the area, naturally had his own opinions on the subject; rather than embarrassing his employer, however, he vowed to take a neutral stand. Clyde Lake, cashier of Citizens Bank of Pawhuska and secretary-treasurer of the OCHOA, co-signed a verbose letter with the president, A. W. Hurley, saying that the bank "had not as an institution exerted any effort for or against such legislation," nor did it expect to take part in the contro-versy out of good business sense. Lake and Hurley admitted Citizens Bank had been "a house divided against itself," because its officers, directors, and stockholders were split on their views, "each more or less active as their re-spective natures, personal opinion as to a public policy or self-interest might dictate." That said, Lake and Hurley assured the Osage Tribal Council that all officers and directors would thereafter hold their tongues on the subject of defeating potential legislation by Congress.[36] F. Gentner Drummond, vice president, advised the Osage council that he no longer had any "Indian wards, it having become necessary to resign from such position on account of a State law recently enacted which affected state, county, and city officials." This law limited the amount of money a guardian could collect from his ward. R. G. Drummond, still a guardian, claimed he had taken no active interest in the matter, "other than that of a payment of a small assessment made on all landowners in Osage County." E. S. Shidler of Stockgrowers' State Bank of Pawhuska, and founder of the oil boom town of Shidler in late 1921, vowed to "take no further active interest in this matter and to undertake no work in harmony with the department on matters in which the tribe's interests seem to be affected"; Shidler seems to be refusing to cooperate.

The OCHOA immediately felt the pressure from these letters from the tribal council. Almost all of the bankers and guardians pledged they would not fight the extension. A member of the executive committee, A. N. Ruble was the father of Jo Mathews's good friend, Jack Ruble, who had been a fra-ternity brother at the University of Oklahoma. A. N. Ruble, the cashier of the First National Bank of Pawhuska and the secretary-treasurer of the Pawhuska Oil Company,[37] sidestepped, specifying that "none of the officers or directors in this bank are at this time using their influence, nor do they propose to use such effort, to defeat such legislation by Congress." By 1925 A. N. Ruble was being called "one of Pawhuska's leading citizens and greatest philan-thropists," and "responsible for much of Pawhuska's growth."[38] The OCHOA reorganized, so that in early 1921, only one banker sat on their executive committee, "and the assistance of bankers and guardians to protect the white man home owner in Osage county can be better imagined than described," the *Eagle* stated intriguingly. They kept a low profile.

In 1931, the Osage trust period was ultimately renewed through 1958, but in the wake of this action, the OCHOA still filed three pesky lawsuits. Fortunately, in June 1932, the OCHOA was finally defeated in court. Judge Franklin E. Kennamer of the federal district court in Bartlesville granted the government a temporary injunction to prevent any more legal action by surface right holders of Osage land to obtain oil and mineral rights.[39] Thus, these well-heeled foes of the tribe were vanquished.

THE KILLING OF A PRESIDENT'S NEPHEW

Juxtaposed with Mathews's beautifully written column of June 16, 1931, "In the Wichita Mountains" is a news article with a striking headline: "Mexican Organization Demands Death for Ardmore Deputies." The organization was a labor union, and Ardmore is a small city in south-central Oklahoma.[40] With three pistol shots, William E. Guess, an Ardmore plainclothes sheriff, silenced forever two Mexican students who had stopped in the town on their way back to Mexico City. One of them, Emilio Cortez Rubio, was a nephew of Pascual Ortiz Rubio—the president of Mexico—and the son of a wealthy Mexican landowner and attorney. The other student, Manuel Gomez, was the son of another elite family. A third student, Salvador Cortes Rubio, also a nephew of President Rubio, was unharmed. The three students were headed home from their respective colleges: Salvador Rubio and Manuel Gomez studied at St. Benedict's College in Atchison, Kansas, and Emilio Rubio was a sophomore at the Rolla School of Mines in Missouri. Father F. D. McCreedy of St. Mary's Catholic Church in Ardmore knew the three students personally and vouched for their good character.[41]

Bill Guess and his partner, Cecil Crosby, racially profiled the Mexican students. The *Daily Ardmoreite* reported that the lawmen "first saw the youths at the root beer stand on Twelfth Avenue," then pulled into a gas station and waited for the students to pass in their car, for no apparent reason. Between Tenth and Eleventh avenues, the car stopped and Salvador Rubio got out to relieve himself. The officers tailing them claimed Salvador was making an "indecent exposure of himself," so they stopped to admonish him. Crosby stepped out of the plainclothes officers' unmarked car.

"What authority have you to question us?" Rubio demanded, according to Crosby.

The officers said they identified themselves and showed their badges. The *Ardmoreite* stated: "Guess got out of his car, and taking a flashlight, started towards the coupe in which the Mexicans were riding. As he did so, one of the Mexicans, his shoulders draped in a blanket, climbed from the seat. He turned, facing the officer." Guess claimed he saw "the muzzle of an automatic pistol peering from under the folds of the blanket," so he immediately shot the young man. The youth "spun sharply around and the officer, uncertain as to his aim, fired a second time." It would appear this was a rash decision. Another account states the student had a gun on his lap, which fell to the ground when Guess yanked him out of the car. The *Ardmoreite* reported that "Guess flashed his light into the car. The Mexican was fumbling after a gun, Guess said, and he fired point blank," killing him. The officers found three pistols and a shotgun in the car; additionally "the youths had nearly 300 rounds of ammunition for the new automatic pistols they possessed as well as other ammunition."

Fernando Ortiz Rubio and Guillermo Ortiz Rubio, sons of the president, and companions of the two students who were killed, telephoned authorities of St. Benedict's College in Kansas, explaining that their cousins and friend had mistaken the plainclothes officers for bandits. The president's sons attended St. Benedict's with Salvador and Manuel. Emilio Rubio was a former student who transferred to the Rolla School of Mines, where he had been studying for two years. A St. Benedict's College official said both the Rubios and Gomez were young men of excellent character and high standing there. College authorities said the youths were carrying a large sum of money, so they carried arms both for protection and to have the weapons for hunting at home.[42]

As one might expect, this tragic event caused a great deal of diplomatic tension between Mexico and the United States, including the Mexican labor union calling for the heads of Guess and Crosby. Incidents such as this one and the 1930 lynching in Chickasha evidence the high level of racism, racial tension, and violence that existed in the state of Oklahoma while Mathews was typing these columns. Such events were preceded in the previous decade by the monstrous 1921 Tulsa massacre, and the 1920s Osage reign of terror, the general climate of which seemed to continue in some ways through the 1930s and beyond. Much of this troubled history has been generally concealed from official histories until relatively recently.

NO PRECEDENT

Wednesday, July 8, 1931, #85

Oftentimes, when one is pursuing a subject in which he is intensely interested, and is following conversation on the subject very closely, he finds in
this conversation isolated statements or incidental ones which reveal much.
Of course, they just reveal; nothing is ever done about it—there is nothing
on which to base action. There is nothing except that the statement reveals
sometimes the whole attitude of a race; even a raison d'etre for certain historical facts, and they are valuable for this fact alone.

In June, the State Division of the Izaak Walton League held a convention
at Medicine Park. There were men from all over the State, men interested in
conversation and the outdoors. The conversation was about game, fish, and
forests and state parks. National representatives of the people, home from
Washington, were there, as well as officers of the State and National Park
system. One day, one talked with a man intensely interested in the enlarge-
ment of the Wichita National Park [Forest].

"Yes," he said, "I want to see it; someday I shall see it. All this forest that
included the Park was land owned by the Comanche and Kiowa; it was just
lying there. Then, moved by the public-spirited people of this section, the
government took it over from the Indians and made a park for the people. I
certainly want to see it extended."

"Why can't it be extended?"

"You can't do it; here are all these people who own their little farms here.
We'll have to condemn it, and that would hardly be fair."

"Won't they sell?"

"As soon as they found out that the government wanted it, they would hike
the price."

"The land the government would be interested in would not be valuable for
agriculture certainly. These hills are almost worthless for that, are they not?"

"Certainly, worthless. Many of these fellows would make a living making
whiskey, but you see, there is no precedent for taking this land away from
the owners."

The hills and forests that were the homes of the Kiowa and the Comanche
must have been converted into a "whoopee" ground for the people and tax-
payers with such subtlety, that not even precedent was established.

QUANAH PARKER HONORED

The preceding late column is a prime example of Mathews's pithy Osage critique and his great wit and attention to ironic detail. It also testifies to the development of his writing style over the course of the column. It amounted to a parting shot.

Connecting to the subject of Jo's column, an article that appeared two days before noted that many Kiowas, Comanches, Apaches, and other tribespeople gathered in Post Oak Mission—near Medicine Park and the Wichita National Forest—to pay tribute to Quanah Parker, who had died twenty years earlier in 1911. The great leader of Comanches, Parker was both a fierce warrior and strong advocate for Comanche interests, and a committed defender of the Native American Church's peyote ceremonies. Comanche critic Dustin Tahmahkera notes: "Quanah is our Crazy Horse and Geronimo, our Sitting Bull and Chief Joseph."[43] Parker became a Johnny Appleseed of peyote, bringing the sacrament from Texas to the Southern Plains tribes of Indian Territory, from where it continued to spread like a prairie fire. Ultimately, many prominent Osage families such as the Lookouts, Red Eagles, and Tall Chiefs became practitioners of the peyote religion, which became organized as the Native American Church. Parker's mother, the daughter of a Texas rancher, was taken from her family as a child and was raised as Comanche.[44] Parker became enthralled with the power of peyote after being induced by his Parker relative to travel to Texas to learn the ways of White ranchers. He fell ill and asked for a medicine man. His Parker grandmother found the next best thing, a *curandera*, a northern Mexican healer woman who used herbs, plants, prayer, and magic to cure. She administered peyote, and Quanah was healed by this medicine.[45]

After the U.S. military defeat of the Comanches at the Battle of Adobe Walls, Parker helped the tribe to settle into their new agrarian life on the Kiowa-Comanche-Apache reservation. A role model to many Natives who successfully negotiated White and Indian worlds, Quanah Parker ultimately became very wealthy as a rancher and stockholder, co-owning the Quanah, Acme, and Pacific Railway.[46] According to anthropologists Alice Marriott and Carol K. Rachlin,

> when the western Oklahoma Indian lands were allotted in individual holdings of one hundred sixty aces in early 1900, Quanah cannily took his own allotment, those of each of his eight wives, and those of his then-living children in one huge block in the neighborhood of the little town of Cache, near what is now the Wichita Wildlife Refuge, in southwestern Oklahoma.[47]

In May 1930, five thousand people attended the unveiling of a monument erected to honor the Comanche Man of Destiny. In 1957, Mathews read with appreciation *The Comanches: Lords of the South Plains* by Ernest Wallace and E. Adamson Hoebel.[48]

THE OSAGE AND THE WHITE MAN'S ROAD

In a sense, Mathews's last column was the one just cited, "No Precedent," published on July 8, 1931, since the final installment of *Our Osage Hills* was comprised of a lengthy excerpt from the impressions of an unnamed newspaper columnist who had "recently visited the Osage" for the June In-Lon-Schka dances, a subject Mathews had covered in an earlier piece.

His column writing now complete, on July 4, 1931, Mathews devoted himself to composing his first book, *Wah'Kon-Tah: The Osage and the White Man's Road*. Mathews had tracked down Oakley Miles, the son of Laban J. Miles, former agent to the Osages and family friend, who had passed away in April, and asked him if he had an old house somewhere he might use to write about Laban Miles and the Osages. Oakley's neighbor had an abandoned shack sitting eighteen miles northeast of Pawhuska on Rock Creek, and Oakley helped Mathews clean it out. The budding Osage author dived into an ascetic existence, his few possessions including a dog, a horse, and a typewriter. He used a bucket to shower and ate canned goods plus whatever he could hunt or fish. He listened to records of Native music for inspiration on a portable phonograph. In retrospect, this was a trial run for his future life at The Blackjacks, which he would build a year later. When news of Mathews's project spread over Osage communities, some elders sought him out to share stories of the early days of the Osage Nation, which enhanced his Osage perspective.

Mathews began writing his book on Independence Day, a symbolic gesture. He may have had Henry David Thoreau on his mind, who first occupied his cabin at Walden pond on July 4, 1845. Mathews asserted his autonomy, and through Nietzschean willpower and a little help from his friends—University of Oklahoma Press Director Joseph A. Brandt, and University of Oklahoma professor and author Walter S. Campbell—he soon became a book author. Mathews finished composition on Thanksgiving 1931, he built The Blackjacks sandstone cabin in summer 1932, and *Wah'Kon-Tah: The Osage and the White Man's Road* was published in the fall of 1932. This beautiful book was praised by critics, sold extremely well for a book from an academic press, and was chosen as an alternate selection of the Book of the Month club. By the end of the year, John Joseph Mathews was a nationally known American Indian author—at a time when such a thing was almost completely unknown.

NOTES

1. This is an idea that is given fuller expression in *Wah'Kon-Tah: The Osage and the White Man's Road* (1932) and *The Osages: Children of the Middle Waters* (1961).

2. The contemporary translator of this book into English writes, however, that there is "no indication" that Vickers's "knowledge of Osage life drew upon anything other than locally and recently printed sources, and we can't be sure he even so much as caught a glimpse of visiting Osages [to Paris], since all his comments about them during their first weeks in France seem to have been taken from other published accounts." *An Osage Journey to Europe, 1827-1830: Three French Accounts*, edited and translated by William Least Heat-Moon and James K. Wallace (Norman: University of Oklahoma Press, 2013), 67.

3. Valeria Messalina married the Roman Emperor Claudius. She was related to the emperors Nero, Caligula, and Augustus. A powerful and influential woman reputed to have been promiscuous, Messalina allegedly conspired against her husband and was executed when the plot was discovered.

4. Ohio native Zane Grey (1872–1939) was a baseball player, dentist, and a famous author of copious Westerns, many of which were adapted into movies, such as his most popular novel, *Riders of the Purple Sage* (1912), which was adapted five times. The novel was illustrated by Mathews's friend, W. Herbert "Buck" Dunton.

5. Artemis is the Hellenic goddess of the hunt, wild animals, childbirth, and virginity; Diana is her Roman analog.

6. Mathews Diary, April 9, 1943, Box 1, Folder 46, John Joseph Mathews Collection (JJM), Western History Collection (WHC), University of Oklahoma (OU).

7. Fred Grove, *The Years of Fear* (Waterville, Maine: Five Star, 2002), 52–53; "E.E. Grinstead," *Osage County Profiles* (Pawhuska: Osage County Historical Society, 1978).

8. Wilson, *Underground Reservation*, 137.

9. William Hampton, "Athletic Activities," *Indian Leader* [Haskell College, Lawrence, Kans.], April 1, 1921, 1; Osage County Historical Society, *Osage County Profiles*, 1978, 27.

10. Kristen Williams Backer, "*Kultur-Terror*: The Composite Monster in Nazi Visual Propaganda," *Monsters and the Monstrous: Myths and Metaphors of Enduring Evil*," edited by Niall Scott (New York: Rodopi, 2007), 83.

11. George LaMotte quoted in C. A. Henrie, "Osage County—A Land of Three Title Deeds," Wichita *Daily Eagle*, January 16, 1921, 38.

12. Deloria, *Indians in Unexpected Places*, 207.

13. Mathews diary, July 25, 26, 28–31, 1922; August 5, 7–9, 1922, Box 1, Folder 45, JJM, WHC, OU; "Georgette La Motte Views Passion Play," *Musical Courier*, August 24, 1922, 39; Joseph Thoburn, *A Standard History of Oklahoma*, 5: 2136–37; "The Founding Meeting of NCAI," National Congress of American Indians, www.ncai.org/about-ncai/mission-history/the-founding-meeting-of-ncai, accessed January 25, 2019.

14. "LaMottes are Arrested," Fort Gibson [Oklahoma] *New Era*, November 20, 1913, 3.

15. "Another Scandal," Arkansas City [Kansas] *Daily News*, November 13, 1913, 2.

16. "Osage Sues for Deed Cancellation," Muskogee [Oklahoma] *Times-Democrat*, February 3, 1914, 3.

17. "LaMottes Find Paper in Court," *Daily Oklahoman*, April 29, 1917, 9, Oklahoman Digital Archives; "Grazing Land Appeal Affirmed by Court," *Galveston Daily News* [Texas], January 25, 1921, 4.

18. "Anna M. LaMotte Romantic Figure," *Daily Oklahoman* [Oklahoma City], April 29, 1917, 9.

19. Les Warehime, "Drummond Ranch," *Encyclopedia of Oklahoma History and Culture*, www.okhistory.org/publications/enc/entry.php?entry=DR007; John Roy Drummond, "Frederick (Fred) Drummond," *Osage County Profiles* (Pawhuska, OK: OCHS, 1978); Snyder, *John Joseph Mathews*, 111, 171–72, 195, 197.

20. *Wichita Eagle*, January 12, 1908, quoted in Warehime, *History*, 106.

21. Lynn Riggs, *Green Grow the Lilacs*, in *Cherokee Night and Other Plays*, by Lynn Riggs (Norman: University of Oklahoma Press, 2003), 70–71.

22. Jonathan Kwitny, *Mullendore Murder Case* (New York: Warner, 1976 [1974]), 34–37; Terry P. Wilson, *Underground Reservation*, 137.

23. Joint Commission to Investigate Indian Affairs, "Osage Reservation," 1539.

24. Warehime, *History of Ranching the Osage*, 107.

25. Warehime, *History of Ranching the Osage*, 117.

26. Randy Krehbiehl, "Fields of Gold," *Tulsa World*, January 12, 1998, www.tulsaworld.com/archive/fields-of-gold/article_eaf1689e-fe09-55fd-8d2e-a0b780edae53.html; Warehime, *History of Ranching the Osage*, 116; Carl N. Tyson, "McMan Oil Company," *Encyclopedia of Oklahoma History and Culture*, www.okhistory.org/publications/enc/entry.php?entry=MC036.

27. Jim Gray and Wilhelm Murg, "Osage Oil Boom and Reign of Terror collide in new book by Osage historian," *Native American Times* [Tulsa, Oklahoma], November 15, 2001, 4B, ProQuest.

28. Mathews, *Twenty Thousand Mornings*, 144–45.

29. "Killdeer—Master of Distraction," *BirdNote*, 2018, www.birdnote.org/show/killdeer-master-distraction; "Upland Sandpiper," *South Dakota Birds, Birding, and Nature*, www.sdakotabirds.com/species/upland_sandpiper_info.htm, accessed February 5, 2019.

30. "Richest Indians in Legal Fight," *Boston Globe* [Associated Press], April 10, 1931, 35; "E.E. Grinstead," *Osage County Profiles* (Pawhuska: OCHS, 1978).

31. Dennis McAuliffe, Jr., *Bloodland* (Tulsa: Council Oak Books, 1999), 296–97.

32. Underhill, *Osage Indian Reign of Terror*, 86, 128.

33. "Opening of Osage County to Agriculture Is Biggest Question in Indian Affairs," *Oklahoman*, August 10, 1919, 43–44, *Oklahoman* Digital Archives.

34. "Home Owners Coming Here," Wichita *Daily Eagle*, January 23, 1921, 22.

35. C. A. Henrie, "Osage County—A Land of Three Title Deeds," Wichita *Daily Eagle*, January 16, 1921, 38.

36. *Indians of the United States: Investigation of the Field Service* (Washington, DC: U.S. Government Printing Office, 1920).

37. *Moodys Manual of Railroads and Corporation Securities*, 1917, 439.

38. "Banker Charged with Alienation," *O'Collegian* [Stillwater, Oklahoma], January 23, 1925, 1, Digital Collections, Oklahoma State University.

39. "Injunction Granted in Osage Land Suit," Miami [Oklahoma] *Daily News-Record*, June 16, 1931, 2.

40. "Mexican Organization Demands Death for Ardmore Deputies," *Daily Journal-Capital*, June 16, 1930.

41. "Officer Kills Two Mexican Youths," *Daily Ardmoreite* [Ardmore, Oklahoma], Monday, June 8, 1931, www.oklahomahistory.net/rubio.html.

42. "Youths on Way to Mexico City Stopped Here," *Daily Ardmoreite*, June 8, 1931.

43. Dustin Tahmahkera, "Hakarʉ Marʉʉmatʉ Kwitaka? Seeking Representational Jurisdiction in Comanchería Cinema." *NAIS* 5:1 (2018): 106.

44. Alice Marriott and Carol K. Rachlin, *Peyote* (New York: New American Library, 1972), 23–24, 26–27.

45. Marriott and Rachlin, *Peyote*, 28–29.

46. Dustin Tahmahkera, "Hakarʉ Marʉʉmatʉ Kwitaka? Seeking Representational Jurisdiction in Comanchería Cinema," 106.

47. Marriott and Rachlin, *Peyote*, 48–49.

48. "Indians Honor Quanah Parker," *Journal-Capital*, May 6, 1930; John Joseph Mathews diary, April 1, 1957, Box 2, Folder 9, JJM, WHC, OU.

Part XI

Murder

THE FRENZY BEGINS:
THE MURDER OF SAUCY CALF

"In 1932 the frenzy ended," John Joseph Mathews writes in *The Osages*. The Great Frenzy was what Mathews called the hyperactive period of Osage oil development, wealth, exploitation, and, eventually, murder that peaked in 1923. Before analyzing the causes of the end of the frenzy, it behooves us to jump back two decades to the beginning to understand how the dark side of the frenzy began much earlier than most understand.

The unsolved murder of Saucy Calf, elder and leader, in February 1912, is the earliest recorded case in the series of killings that are now widely known as the Osage murders. Despite this, Saucy Calf's murder is not mentioned by the published authors who have probed these crimes; that is, except for John Joseph Mathews. Saucy Calf is in fact the only murder victim Mathews names in his massive history of his people, *The Osages: Children of the Middle Waters*. Mathews spoke with special authority because he remembered the terrible incident from his youth. On the other hand, Mathews had much less immediate knowledge of the flurry of murders of the early 1920s and the resulting trials of the late 1920s. They occurred while he was abroad, studying at Oxford, traveling in Europe and North Africa, and living with his first wife, Virginia, in New Jersey and in Pasadena, California; he did not return to Pawhuska until the fall of 1929.

Mathews cited Saucy Calf not just because he remembered the elder's demise, but because Saucy Calf had been a distinguished leader as a younger man and a friend of his family. Considered the greatest deer hunter among the Osages, Saucy Calf gave the name Little Deer to Josephine Mathews, the oldest Mathews sibling.[1] Further, Mathews, writing in the late 1950s, doubtless made a point to mention the unsolved case because journalists and other writers had failed to connect Saucy Calf's killing to the later spate of Osage murders, an oversight that persisted in the literature until now. Mathews explained that during the frenzy, "the amounts of royalty payments were headlined in the state newspapers, and this drew some prostitutes and petty thieves and murderers to the agency, and things happened. One night the house of Saucy Calf (called Sassy Calf) in the village was robbed and set afire, and he was burned with the evidence."[2] Some evidence did remain, fortunately. Although the fire was at first called an accident, the Osages demanded an investigation into what they strongly suspected was murder. Because of their valiant efforts, an inquest and exhumation were performed, which found the elder had indeed been murdered.

Saucy Calf's slaying occurred not only well before the early 1920s Osage reign of terror, but also predated what has been cited as the earliest case, the gruesome murder of Mary C. DeNoya Bellieu Lewis in August 1918. Lawrence

Hogan briefly describes the case of Mary Lewis (which was solved), in *The Osage Indian Murders*; later, David Grann provides more detail and forwards this case as evidence of the broadened scope of the Osage murders beyond the established period of the 1920s. Yet Hogan, Grann, and Lonnie Underhill all overlook the murder of Saucy Calf that occurred over six years earlier—which many Osages blamed on the elder's much younger White girlfriend.

As has been established, Osage tribal wealth, regarded by many Whites as unearned, attracted parasitism, guardianship abuse, and rampant exploitation. Readily available and tempting to many Osages were hard liquor, addictive opiates, and other drugs. Eventually the frenzy culminated in the nefarious reign of terror on the Osages that peaked in 1923. In the early 1920s, while residents of New York City and other diversifying metropolises were enjoying the Jazz Age as flappers liberated themselves, dancing the Charleston, and toasting one another with bootleg gin, and F. Scott Fitzgerald wrote *The Great Gatsby*, Oklahoma became a hell on earth for many people of color, who were dehumanized by the virulent white supremacism that surrounded them. As previously noted, the most glaring examples are the Tulsa massacre, in which an entire African American neighborhood was burned, and the Osage reign of terror. The Ku Klux Klan, revitalized by the popularity of D. W. Griffith's 1915 film *The Birth of a Nation*, became very popular in Oklahoma in the early 1920s, with a University of Oklahoma dean among their leadership; a student chapter of the Ku Klux Klan were even allowed a page in the 1920 yearbook.[3] Envious Whites at various levels of society constructed Osages in modernity as useless anomalies, examples of what Hannah Arendt called "the superfluous man," an idea she derived from nineteenth-century Russian literature. The Holocaust historian Raul Hilberg later showed Arendt how "the bureaucratic state could eradicate such people in the twentieth century," Timothy Snyder explains in concluding *Bloodlands: Europe between Hitler and Stalin*. The Osage murders can be seen as a part of the larger history of interaction between Euro-Americans and American Indians, telling of the former's unabashed attempts to subjugate and displace the indigenes, liquidate their natural resources, and eradicate their culture and identity, all in the name of progress and Christian decency. If the federal government no longer exterminated American Indians directly, the bulk of their project of displacement and expropriation having been completed, still state and local agencies gladly turned the other way as private wealth and power further enriched itself and confederates through the predation and death of Osages, while keeping the wheels greased; federal authorities could not protect the Osages and were slow to step in as the number of Osage victims grew. Like the regimes Arendt analyzes in *The Origins of Totalitarianism*, the U.S. national narrative and Oklahoman statehood narrative surrounding the Osages were "capable of placing death within a story of progress and joy," in Snyder's phrase, for example expressed in parades and pageants celebrating land theft and settler colonialism.[4]

During the Osage reign of terror murders, which mostly occurred while Mathews was overseas, a group of White men, respected citizens such as bankers and lawyers among them, conspired against and murdered at least two dozen Osages, possibly up to hundreds, plus a few non-Osages, in a sinister plot to inherit headright payments. The murderers and their confederates covered up the killings by clumsily disguising them as accidents or suicides. Many potential witnesses who might have testified were murdered. Former Federal Bureau of Investigation (FBI) employee Lawrence J. Hogan notes in *The Osage Indian Murders* that many Osage County law enforcement officers "were unscrupulous and a number of them were directly affiliated" with Bill Hale and "his gang of outlaws."[5] After local and state authorities proved ineffective or corrupt, the Osage Tribal Council requested federal assistance, and J. Edgar Hoover's new FBI finally stepped in, but at first were ineffectual and made mistakes. Bill Hale and his nephews, Ernest and Byron Burkhart, also known as Bryan, were indicted, along with conspirator John Ramsey, but many more were involved in or aware of the plot. Shockingly, Hale and John Ramsey were paroled and pardoned in 1947, which of course angered the Osages; this was a major insult that seemed to hold their lives cheaply. Byron Burkhart, who testified for the federal government, never served time; Ernest was conditionally released from prison in 1946, formally released in 1959, and pardoned in 1966. Justice was not truly found for the victims. Some investigators knew or strongly suspected that banker Herbert G. Burt (previously discussed) and others were also major players and intimate confederates of Hale's; however, Burt was never arrested. Several murders were never directly linked to Hale, and many more were never investigated. But J. Edgar Hoover, anxious to cover the FBI's mistakes and conclude the long, embarrassing matter, declared they had their man and the case was all wrapped up.[6]

One crucial fact has eluded writers covering the Osage murders: the victims were almost entirely of Mathews's own band, the Big Hill band, whose members mainly lived in the vicinity of Gray Horse Indian Village near Fairfax, the hometown of Maria and Marjorie Tall Chief. Osage County is a large land mass comparable in size to Delaware, something often not realized, and Osage social and cultural groupings are complex; that is why this lack of acuity has been a major oversight in the literature. Another fact overlooked by Grann and others is the Fairfax First National Bank was central to the murder plot and the wholesale plunder of Osage wealth.

Mathews discussed the Osage murders briefly toward the end of *The Osages*, and he dramatized their effects on Osages in the last section of his

1934 novel, *Sundown*. This began a tradition of Osage and other Indigenous authors delving into this dark history. In 1958, Fred Grove, an Osage author of Western novels, published *Flame of the Osage*, set in Osage County during the murders, as were two of his 1970s novels, *Warrior Road* and *Drums Without Warriors*. In 1968, Mathews's stepson John Clinton Hunt's Faulknerian second novel, *The Grey Horse Legacy*, was partly set during the Osage murders. Twenty-two years after that, Chickasaw novelist Linda Hogan used this setting for *Mean Spirit* (1990). Twelve years later, Osage author Charles H. Red Corn published his sole book, the historical novel *A Pipe for February* (2002), which addressed and dramatized the context of the Osage reign of terror of the 1920s from an Osage perspective.

Chief Saucy Calf, as he was sometimes called, with "saucy" pronounced as "sassy," had served on the Osage council several times. At his death he was deemed a prominent and well-regarded member of the tribe who "served his people on numerous occasions."[7] Saucy Calf even served as one of the models for Osage figures depicted in the famous stained-glass "Indian window" at Immaculate Conception Church in Pawhuska, along with the leaders Chief Bacon Rind and Arthur Bonnicastle. The famous Bacon Rind has been discussed, but the life and death of the latter, Bonnicastle, merits a brief detour.

The life of Arthur Bonnicastle, who was named after the titular hero of *Arthur Bonnicastle, an American Novel* (1874) by a then-popular author, Josiah Gilbert Holland, might form the material for a novel superior to his namesake book.[8] The son of a Wahzhazhe woman named Me-tse-he, Arthur Bonnicastle as a youth became a devoted follower of the peyote religion and later became a peyote roadman in the Native American Church. Because W. J. Pollack, agent to the Osages, opposed young Arthur's faith but Arthur ignored his disapproval, in 1900 Pollack sent him away to Carlisle Indian Industrial School in Pennsylvania, though the Osage was, "at age twenty-two, several years older than the average male students at that time," Omer Call Stewart notes in *Peyote Religion: A History*. Arthur had previously studied at the Osage Boarding School and Haskell Institute in Lawrence, Kansas. Arthur fled Carlisle School that same year, enlisted in the Army (Company E of the Ninth Infantry), and was sent to the Philippines during the Philippine–American War, where he was wounded, stabbed by Filipino revolutionary fighters he called "bolomen." The United States was trying to take over imperial control of the Philippines from Spain per the Treaty of Paris of 1898, but this treaty was not recognized by Filipino leaders, whose troops dominated most of the country besides Manilla. Thus the United States was receiving much resistance from Filipinos, who naturally wanted to control their own destiny, as they had struggled to do under imperial Spain. Then in 1901, Sergeant Bonnicastle fought in China, becoming a war hero during the defeat of the anti-imperialist, anti-Christian Boxer Rebellion or Uprising. Arthur's company was reportedly the first to plant the American flag on the walls of Peking in August 1901. John Joseph Mathews wrote in his memoir that he recalled the Boxer War in China "because of an Osage Indian who was the first man of the foreign allied army over the wall, and had missed fame because the fourth man reached down for the flag, and planted it on the wall. This incident of the turn of the century was still being talked about and commented on in my town and county in 1914." Later, after Mathews's curiosity was stoked by his college education, he asked Arthur Bonnicastle about the flag planting. Bonnicastle's reply epitomized "the difference between the Quixotism of civilized European influence and the protective-coloration consciousness of the Neolithic man" to Mathews: "Them fellas shootin' at us could see me better with that flag."[9] Ironically, around the same time that Bonnicastle was fighting for the religious freedom of Christians in China (an issue that remains at time of writing), Agent Oscar A. Mitscher, whose son Tom was a friend of Jo Mathews, "forbade an Osage chief to invite a Caddo peyote leader to visit the Osage reservation," Stewart writes. Because no law justified Mitscher's order, the Osages simply disregarded him. Of course, there is irony in an Osage fleeing a severely assimilationist and colonizing school to fight for imperialism and colonialism, albeit heroically. Bonnicastle was honorably discharged and readmitted to Carlisle in 1903 but he ran away later that year and returned to his people, becoming active in Osage Nation politics. In 1918 and 1922, he testified in Washington, DC, in defense of his peyote religion. In a 1922 issue of *Congressional Digest*, Arthur Bonnicastle, along with Omaha ethnologist Francis La Flesche, represented the "Con" perspective on proposed legislation that would suppress peyote, stressing that Osages only used peyote in religious ceremonies and as medicine in cases of sickness. "It trains the mind to higher ideas in worshipping God." He had never seen "any bad effects from its use." From 1920 to 1922, Bonnicastle served as principal chief of the Osages.[10]

On the morning of May 30, 1923, the war hero and Osage leader Arthur Bonnicastle died suspiciously at only forty-six years of age, in a Kansas City hospital, after being treated for less than two days. His great wealth had been widely broadcast in newspapers the year before.[11] Mr. Bonnicastle's cause of death was registered as chronic interstitial nephritis, a kidney disorder, with uremia the contributory cause, resulting from the breakdown of his kidney. No operation was performed before his death, nor was there an autopsy; unspecified "clinical symptoms" were the sole confirmation of the diagnosis.[12] Though not discussed in the literature on the Osage murders, this suspicious death may well have been a covered-up murder, especially considering the context of slayings and swindles occurring in early 1923, some involving Kansas City, one of which still to be discussed. The Osage Nation published an online piece on Bonnicastle, which, while mistaking his cause of death, noted the forty-six-year-old leader's demise was never investigated and "many still find the circumstances surrounding his death to be quite mysterious."[13] Both Bonnicastle's life and death bear further scrutiny. Arthur Bonnicastle was not forgotten by the Osages: he makes a cameo in *A Pipe for February* by Charles H. Redcorn, which is set in Pawhuska during the early 1920s reign of terror.[14]

Nor should Saucy Calf's life and his mysterious death be forgotten. The Osage name of Saucy Calf is Tse-zhi'n-ga-wa-da-i'n-ga.[15] A saucy or sassy calf is a playful bison calf; John Joseph Mathews writes in *The Osages* that a fearless young warrior counting coup on a Pawnee foe, for example, might be called "Saucy-Calf" by his companions. "Saucy or playful buffalo calves did not always escape from their merry adventures unsullied; they sometimes butted a skunk or a porcupine," Mathews explains.[16] Saucy Calf's mother, Wanna Wood, had died the previous year; until her death she had been the oldest living Wahzhazhe woman, well over one hundred years old, it was reported. Wood had been "intimately acquainted with many high government officials who frequented the Indian Territory in territorial days," readers were told.[17] Saucy Calf was eighty years old when he was murdered, living alone in his cabin without known family support. His only reported vice was occasional excess drinking, which he did on the day before he died, the *Oklahoman* reported.[18]

A fullblood, Saucy Calf had been a traditional "little chief" or sub-chief among the Wahzhazhe, along with serving as tribal councilman. Despite his status and service to the tribe, some Kansan newspapermen broadcast chauvinism and cruelty. "He was an uncivilized blanket Indian," sneered the Douglass *Tribune* after Saucy Calf's death.[19] Back in 1893, Saucy Calf had lost his son to an accidental shooting. The Independence *Daily Reporter* at the time stated: "Sassy Calf is the name of an Osage Indian who died last week. He is probably roast veal by this time."[20] The editor had appended this obnoxious sentence to an item that appeared in other Kansan newspapers. Many of these journalists, of course, were pressing for the Osage Reservation to be opened up for white ranchers and settlers. Such dehumanization helped clear a path for land-grabbers, exploiters, and murderers to justify their heinous actions.

As his son's death and his own demise suggest, Saucy Calf's life was marred by violence. In 1895, the supreme court of the Osage Nation "acquitted Sub-Chief Saucy Calf of the charge of murder," because he shot Mr. Bigheart, a relative of the wealthy Osage chief James Bigheart, in self-defense. Most newspapers named the victim as James or Jim Bigheart, calling him a son of James Bigheart (but a son of the chief named James had died two decades earlier); the Arkansas City paper, which interviewed a stenographer, at first called the deceased Walter Bigheart, a son-in-law of James Bigheart. Saucy Calf was defended by the influential Osage Sylvester J. Soldani, a state politician and co-publisher of the *Wah Sha She News* along with founder George E. Tinker, in the first murder trial the Osage Nation had found necessary to hold in about fourteen years.[21] This did not mean the reservation was immune to murder. On the contrary, Mathews explains that during the 1880s, "when there was horse stealing from across the border or murder, or there were white men taking refuge from the law in their camps, they refused to inform the agent," Captain Carell H. Potter, who served between the two terms of the favored agent, Major Laban J. Miles, a Quaker.[22] A stenographer named H. Mark Journey was hired by a commission aiming to negotiate an allotment treaty with the Osages; Journey told a Kansan journalist of Saucy Calf's self-defense killing. Mr. Bigheart was "a full blood and very quarrelsome, an embryo desperado" (sic) who in general scared most of the fullbloods. On December 20, 1894, "the old Indian" Saucy Calf was a guest at Bigheart's home. He and his host argued, but before things became overheated, the older and wiser Saucy Calf left the house and walked toward his home in the village. Belligerent Bigheart, wielding a Winchester rifle and shouting, chased after Saucy Calf, quickly overtaking him. Leaping from his horse, Bigheart ran toward his foe, and "within a few feet of him, placed the muzzle of the Winchester against his stomach and pulled the trigger," but Saucy Calf twisted and the bullet passed between his arm and body. The older man grappled with Bigheart, seized his gun, tossed it away, and then threw Bigheart to the ground. While down, Bigheart drew his clasp knife, but Saucy Calf managed to take that from him and threw it away, readers were told. "He then let Bigheart up, who started for the knife." While Bigheart reached for the blade, Saucy Calf retrieved the Winchester, and "shot Bigheart in the heart, killing him instantly." Saucy Calf gave himself over to officers and was placed in prison but was acquitted of all charges.[23]

Dr. Garrick Bailey explains that to Omaha ethnologist Francis La Flesche, Saucy Calf was his "closest friend and main source of information about the Osages" after the death of tribal leader, Black Dog (Shon-ton-ca-be). Saucy Calf and Francis La Flesche had met in Washington, DC, soon before the Omaha began his research on the Wahzhazhe. "A very warm, father-son relationship" between them rapidly developed. Saucy Calf, a priest of the Buffalo Bull clan, had become a follower of the peyote religion, yet his commitment was "lukewarm" and he did not emerge as a leader. A witness to the dissolution of the traditional religion, Saucy Calf wished to leave a written record of some of his knowledge to benefit future Osages, Bailey writes.[24] Yet he often "expressed fear that some harm might come to him for parting with these religious secrets," as one journalist reported. "The murder of Saucy Calf, a man of high standing in his tribe, and the burning of his house" happened, according to general Osage sentiment, because "he gave away certain rituals and songs of the sacred ceremonies." The rites in question were "held in such deep awe that, in the opinion of the Osage, persons officiating who have made mistakes in the form of recitation of the rituals or in the singing of the songs have become insane, or blind, or met with violent death."[25] I have heard of similar curses that befell naïfs who revived an element of the old traditional religion that had been collectively "put away" by the tribe. In Saucy Calf's case, it seemed, retribution was swift. The Wahzhazhe elder was only able to provide the Omaha ethnologist with material on a single esoteric ritual—the Buffalo Bull clan version of the Songs of the Waxo'be—before he was murdered and his house burned.

After Saucy Calf's death in February 1912, rumors spread among the community that his White girlfriend arranged to have him murdered and the house burned to make it appear an accident, according to Garrick Bailey.[26] Although Saucy Calf was an elder, he was reputedly a "widower with an eye for women." The *Oklahoman* printed a special report presenting a theory: "it was known that the old man had at least $100 on his person or concealed in his house," the equivalent of about twenty-six hundred dollars in 2019. This money had been "paid to him by one Mary Prior, a friend of the deceased, who claimed at the inquest that she had given it to him on the promise that he would marry her" earlier Saturday before his murder that night.[27] Little is known of Mary Prior; she may have been the alleged White girlfriend.

An alternate account appeared in mid-February in adjacent Washington County, claiming Saucy Calf had collected $180 from a businessman while in Pawhuska. The Osage had been drinking early that afternoon and displayed the money freely, it was reported, as though to blame the victim for targeting himself by flashing cash.[28] (In 2018, $180 would be worth about $4,650.) The Osages declared "Saucy Calf was murdered," and they demanded an inquest. They believed he was "murdered for his money and that the assassin used fire to hide the crime."[29] Because Saucy Calf was considered to be very wealthy, it is possible that whoever was behind the murder stood to gain more than that amount.

The funeral of this respected Osage elder and leader was attended by two thousand people.[30] After the funeral service and burial, growing rumors of foul play finally began to concern the county attorney and other authorities.

They decided to exhume the body and perform an autopsy, the inquest presided over by Justice of the Peace Hargis. It was found Saucy Calf had been stabbed in the side and in the heart with his own "handsome sword" that had been given to him by President William McKinley during one of the councilman's many trips to Washington representing the Osage Nation.[31] The sword, found near his body in the charred ruins, was known to be difficult to pull from its scabbard, so a great effort had been required to remove it. At first, strong suspicion pointed to "well-known characters of Indian extraction who live in this vicinity," readers were told, and authorities thought they had enough evidence to make arrests. In February, the aforementioned H. H. Brenner, president of First National Bank, and John L. Bird, vice president of the Citizens National Bank, both of Pawhuska, had offered a "reward of $500 for the arrest and conviction of the perpetrators of the crime."[32] It will be recalled that John Lyman Bird was a friend of John Joseph Mathews's father, William, who had co-established the Citizens National Bank, served as its president, and remained a bank director until his death in 1915. Unfortunately, although Bird was loved and trusted by most fullbloods, Bird and Brenner had their own side partnership—they were loan sharks who charged Osages illegal interest rates and who enjoyed insider access to Osage agency records, thanks to their friendship with the corrupt Superintendent Carroll. Before long, H. G. Burt took over half of Brenner's "Indian business" in the firm. Knowing all this and the fact that Bill Hale would later offer reward money for Osage murders, even the reward offer itself might be deemed suspicious; there is no risk in offering reward money if you have insider knowledge that the perpetrator will not be caught.

Some believed Saucy Calf was murdered for money he had won that night gambling. In April, a fullblood Osage man, Laban Miles, was arrested and jailed, charged with the murder. Ironically, he was named after the Quaker, a favored agent to the Osages and family friend of the Mathewses. Miles was later exonerated.[33] Newspapers said little about the Osage's alleged connections to the crime. In October 1913, Jim Pappan, a Kaw-Pottawatomie man, and two brothers and former Kansans, Bill and Frank Galloway, were taken into custody following investigation into the murder.[34] The case was built by County Attorney Cope, "after all expectation of finding the murderers had vanished from the public mind," the *Oklahoman* reported. Born on the Kaw Reservation, Jim Pappan back in 1891 was shot at a party by Bob Warren, a ranch manager, during a fight over Pappan's wife, the former Fannie Cross, formerly Warren's longtime sweetheart. Kaw witnesses told the attending doctor the shooting was unjustified. Jim Pappan had been alerted by Louis Pappan, called "Big Louie," that things were amiss at a dance party he was hosting at his home, attended by several mixed-bloods. Despite Fannie's marriage to Jim three months earlier, Mrs. Pappan had "continued to be quite friendly" with Bob Warren; the two had even exchanged rings at the dance, it was reported. Jim Pappan invited Warren to step outside to fight; Warren refused, then Pappan approached him emptyhanded, the Kaws said, contrary to what Warren and his friends claimed, that he wielded a knife. Warren drew his .44 revolver and fired, the bullet passing through Pappan's side, hitting his lung, running through his thigh, and into the leg of bystander Mrs. Joe Pappan, who was sitting nearby in a chair. Jim Pappan was seriously injured, suffering "several hard hemorrhages" and Joe's wife suffered great pain.[35] The shooting caused uproar among the Indians and ranchmen, most of whom said it was totally uncalled for. Jim Pappan moved to Pawhuska in 1909, where he ran a taxi service—though he knew not how to drive and hired a longtime chauffeur—rented out a house, and owned racehorses.[36] Returning to the Saucy Calf case, in November 1913, Pappan and the Galloway brothers were released and the evidence was judged circumstantial. "That a man should go broke at an Osage poker game and appear the next morning with a fat roll of bills is not good evidence on which to hold him over for the grand jury on a charge of first degree murder and robbery, was held by Justice of the Peace Hargis" of Pawhuska in discharging the trio on a preliminary hearing.[37]

No further arrests were ever made, and no more newspaper stories appeared calling for a continued investigation into the murder. Saucy Calf's murder remains a mystery, like scores of other suspicious deaths of Osages that followed.

Twenty-seven years before discussing Saucy Calf in *The Osages: Children of the Middle Waters*, John Joseph Mathews had alluded to this early murder and cover-up in his novel *Sundown*, in which Chief Saucy Calf is called Saucy Chief. Proceeding from a scene in the novel described earlier, out on the Osage prairie, Challenge Windzer, during his Oklahoman university's summer break, runs into his beloved Professor Granville, the Englishman who is currently doing contract work for an oil company. Wanting to spend more time with his beloved mentor, Chal invites Granville back to the ranch house to share the noon meal with him, despite the fact that sophisticated Granville would therefore be subjected to a rustic rancher and his wife. After entering the house, Chal introduces the professor to the ranch worker, Cal Carroll, and his reticent wife, who live there. Mr. Carrol's incessant, provincial stream of questions and his rough prairie dialect embarrass Chal, but Granville is gracious and patient. The Englishman shows interest in Carroll's world and gets the rancher talking, which Chal finds clever, because Granville would then not have to continue to be obliged to answer his barrage of unsophisticated questions.

Cal explained to Granville that Indians are honest and always keep their word. He told a story about how a prominent, wealthy rancher with the very

American name of Daniel Webster Harris made a deal with Saucy Chief with no written contract, to partner on a cattle deal. Harris flagrantly cheated Saucy Chief by having Carroll and the other ranch hands "lose" two hundred steer; then Harris paid the Osage his share of the market value for eight hundred steer instead of the thousand that were shipped. Saucy Chief came out to the ranch with an employee of the Osage agency to investigate, but Harris merely made a show of yelling at his ranch hands about the "missing" two hundred cattle while Sassy Chief just watched this performance silently. Carroll said that particular theft empowered Webster to start his business; he eventually became a millionaire rancher and oilman, and was running for office. After narrating the crime in which he participated shamelessly, Carroll called Harris one of the smartest men in the country and wished to see him become governor of Oklahoma. In the White world that Chal knows, he can apprehend and even dimly accept such theft contextually as "smart" and "just business." Regardless, Chal is flustered, dying to tell Granville and the Carrolls that Sassy Chief was well aware of the rancher's machinations. When the cattle counted short, the Osage followed the trail and found them, though the cowboys did not spy him. But even with this knowledge, to protest beyond what he did was beneath his dignity as a great man and a chief; further, his peyote religion forbade revenge. The following spring, Harris came to the village and begged Sassy Chief to continue the partnership, but the Osage just listened, looked at the hills, and said, "no." He refused to explain.

Cal Carroll, whose last name is surely a jab at the corrupt former superintendent to the Osages, went on to tell Professor Granville about how Saucy Chief "was later burned to death in his house in the village, because some white settlers had heard that he had much money there," and as Cal talked, "he looked at his wife significantly." Cal Carroll even says he believes that he knew and used to work with one of the men who "had a hand in it," but would not name him. At this, Granville promptly rose and thanked the Carrolls for "the pleasant afternoon." Although Granville is distressed in his undemonstrative English way, Cal misjudges, believing that Granville is impressed by his squalid story, and thus Cal perversely

> felt distinctly that there was something romantic about his obscure life after all; he felt distinctly that there had been somewhat of glory in it. Many white men who came into contact with the Plains Indian had felt that glory in the very contact; reflected glory which had set them to strutting. Cal was not the least important of these as he went to the barn to hook up the mules.

Though subtle, Mathews's satire is scathing. The lack of humanity shown by Carroll and Harris toward the Osages is astonishing; such people of Osage

County think little of defrauding an Indian, and for the more low-bred, even a hideous murder plot throws off reflected "glory." Mathews exposes the sick and disgraceful attitudes prevalent among settlers in his homelands through his characters' reflections.

Chal still wants to tell Granville the truth about Saucy Chief. In fact, out of all the people in the world, Chal wants Granville most to know, "but he couldn't bring himself to tell him." Chal thought "he ought to let him know that Cal hadn't known the whole story, and that white men never had been able to see both sides."[38]

RAYMOND REDCORN

The May 1, 1931, issue of the *Journal-Capital* was filled with stories marked by worry over the possibility of urban May Day communist demonstrations spurred by joblessness and despair in depressed Oklahoma. Amid the tumult of International Workers' Day, the newspaper quietly reported in a small front page item that an Osage gentleman, Raymond Wesley Redcorn, Sr., or Tsa-moie, had passed away the previous night in his home on Bigheart Street following an unspecified "extended illness," not providing much detail of his life or death.

Raymond W. Redcorn, Sr., was born in the Osage Nation in March 1885 to his father, Wy-e-gla-in-kah, and mother, Me-tsa-he. In 1908, Mr. Redcorn married a local white girl, Bertha Kathryn Hudson, known as Kate. A native of Chillicothe, Missouri, Bertha Hudson had four sons with Raymond between 1909 and 1919: Raymond W. Redcorn, Jr., Douglas Gilbert Redcorn, and Harold Ambrose Redcorn; the oldest son died in infancy. Raymond Redcorn's World War I draft card checked the boxes of "short" and "stout" to describe his physique.[39] Redcorn became an active Southern Baptist.

In May 1917, Raymond inadvertently caused alarm when he went missing in New Orleans when he was a delegate to a Southern Baptist Convention held there, as reported in the *Times-Picayune*. Raymond left the Grunewald Hotel baggage in tow, but did not arrive at the Mino House, where he was expected to meet the Reverend B. N. Crane and an unnamed "married Indian couple." The missing Osage was "said to be one of the wealthiest Indians in the state and his friends fear[ed] foul play." The story even specified that "Redcorn had considerable money in his possession," a detail that might have put the missing Osage at more risk. Redcorn owned large tracts of land in the Pawhuska area and was "in the automobile business," readers were told. His desciption—five foot, four inches, 220 pounds, with short black hair parted in the middle, and wearing a soft, light hat with a wide brim, a brown suit, and tan shoes—was relayed to all police stations.[40] It is unknown what Raymond Redcorn, flush with cash, did in the meantime while missing during his first visit to the Big Easy, but he survived and, it is assumed, eventually rejoined his party. Redcorn became active in tribal affairs and cultivated numerous friends throughout Osage County.

Curiously, but unnoted in his brief obituary, Redcorn was only forty-six years old when he died. He was survived by a brother, Wakon Iron Redcorn.[41] Raymond Redcorn's granddaughter, Kathryn Redcorn, former longtime curator of the Osage Tribal Museum, believes her grandfather was murdered by his second wife through slow poisoning. He had been in good health prior to his death, she said.[42] For unknown reasons, in 1922, Raymond divorced Kate Hudson Redcorn, who lived on until 1971. In July 1923, amid the Osage reign of terror, Raymond married another White woman, Grace Bernice Horner, born in Iowa in 1889, who went by her middle name, and apparently also used the nickname Camila.[43] This period reaching its nadir in 1923 was thick with murder and conspiracy among crooked doctors, bankers, lawyers, sheriffs, even undertakers, many of whom were legal guardians of so-called incompetent Osages. Many White residents of Fairfax and Pawhuska were on the take, scheming and bilking Osages of their headright payments; in fact, both cities were premised on the "Indian business." Even if most did not resort to murder, many were aware of the plots and looked the other way out of fear, cowardice, or craven self-interest. In May 1929, with the aid of two attorneys, Bernice Redcorn traveled to Love County, Oklahoma, lying about 250 miles south, near the Texas state line. There, at the county courthouse, she attempted to file for divorce from Redcorn. Because neither she nor Raymond was known to have resided in Love County during their marriage, this was a ploy to squeeze more money out of the Osage. A few days later, Bernice returned to Osage County and resumed living with Raymond Redcorn as his wife. The District Court presiding over Love County then tried to force Raymond to pay alimony to Grace plus court fees, and charged him with contempt of court. Raymond shrewdly petitioned the Oklahoma Supreme Court, which ruled in February 1930 that the divorce filing was null and Redcorn need not pay any alimony.[44] Later that year, Bernice and Raymond Redcorn lived in California, in a home in Monrovia, Los Angeles County; the 1930 census reported that neither had an occupation. Yet Redcorn's obituary of May 1931 stated "he had spent his entire life" in the Osage.[45]

In early 1931, Raymond began to suspect he was being poisoned, Kathryn Redcorn said. He told relatives who were visiting not to eat or drink anything in the house, and then died shortly thereafter, on the last day of April. His son, Raymond Redcorn, Jr., later told his own son, Raymond W. Redcorn III, that Redcorn, Sr., had uttered that warning. No medical or legal record indicating poisoning as cause of death has been located; however, this is also the case with many of the murders that were covered up and never officially investigated. In a 1995 essay on Osage oil, Rennard Strickland, the Cherokee-Osage attorney and scholar, wrote: "Rethinking the so-called Osage murders suggests that as many as two hundred tribesmen may have been killed in the 1920s in order to transfer their headrights to intermarried whites."[46] Many Osages therefore lost hope for any justice. According to Kathryn Redcorn, Bernice fled the area after Redcorn's death, walking away with a headright—

"our birthright"—but her attorney ultimately gained control of the headright. Bernice later remarried a Mr. Buffum, moved to St. Louis, and died there in late 1961. Kathryn Redcorn said she had wished to have a tête-à-tête with Bernice, but could not make it happen in time.

Raymond Redcorn, Sr., was linked to the banker and reign of terror conspirator, Herbert G. Burt, so he had actually been at risk for several years prior to his death in 1931. Although David Grann brought H. G. Burt to popular attention, he fails to connect Burt and Redcorn in his book, and never actually names Raymond Redcorn, Sr., although he introduces Kathryn Redcorn's suspicions about her grandfather's death quite late in his true crime bestseller. Raymond Redcorn's name appears prominently in a 1929 trial, *Vaughan v. Burt*—a case deeply intertwined with the Osage reign of terror murders.[47] This case, its record easily found online, closely links Redcorn to the murder victim, George Bigheart; these Osage men shared an attorney, William W. Vaughan, who was murdered and thrown from a train the day after George died suspiciously in Oklahoma City in June 1923, amid the apex of the Osage murders. All three were closely tied to H. G. Burt, who conspired with the master plotter, Bill Hale, against Redcorn's counterpart, George Bigheart. George was married to Grace Bigheart, a half-sister of the daughters of the late Lizzie Q. Kyle, two of whom, Anna Brown and Rita Smith, had been murdered; Mollie Burkhart survived but was at great peril. Lizzie Q.'s first marriage had been to Jim Bigheart, and Grace Bigheart was their only child. Therefore, Grace stood to inherit portions of her half-sisters' estates, and that of her husband.[48] In the summer of 1922 Grace Bigheart's son, Joe Bigheart, and daughter-in-law, Bertha Bigheart, adopted Anna Burkhart, the youngest child of Mollie Burkhart and murder conspirator, Ernest Burkhart. Bertha Bigheart shared with FBI investigators the speculation she had heard: Bill Hale and Ernest and Byron Burkhart had also planned to murder her and her parents so that Bertha's entire estate could be inherited by Anna Burkhart (who died at age four).[49] Police and FBI reports prove that H. G. Burt, though he was never arrested, was a major player in the Osage murders, a close partner and friend of Bill Hale, and an intimate friend of the murder victim, attorney W. W. Vaughan. Much evidence shows that Burt betrayed and murdered his friend Vaughan with the help of at least one accomplice. Despite this body of evidence that led at least one FBI investigator to call Burt a "murderer," as noted, J. Edgar Hoover publicly declared that the FBI had found their man, Hale, and concluded their investigation. Their foreclosed narrative was immortalized in Don Whitehead's *The FBI Story: A Report to the People* (1956, with a foreword by Hoover) and its fictionalized movie adaptation in 1959 starring lovable Jimmy Stewart.[50]

Considering both the sickening context of widespread collusion, and H. G. Burt's seeming control of Raymond Redcorn's affairs, it is quite possible that Bernice Redcorn secretly plotted with H. G. Burt against her Osage husband. Retrospectively it seems that in 1923, Raymond was fortunate to have escaped the fates of George Bigheart, Vaughan, and many more victims of the scheming and treachery of Hale, Burt, and other rich and prominent White men, their gunmen, and lackeys who colluded and covered up. Yet, ironically, Raymond escaped poisoning then, only to be poisoned by his second wife eight years later, it would seem.

On June 29, 1923, Raymond Redcorn's attorney, William Watkins Vaughan, was thrown from a speeding train thirty miles north of Oklahoma City. Born in Kentucky, Vaughan was a fifty-four year-old father of ten who had moved his family from Anadarko, Oklahoma, to Pawhuska seven years earlier. During his years in Pawhuska, Vaughan had made several friends and built an impressive law practice, first with Preston Shinn, who had been attorney for the Osages and testified on their behalf against exploitation, and later with Charles B. Wilson, his partner at the time of his death.[51]

Vaughan was working closely with private investigators attempting to crack the Osage murders, it was reported, but the exact nature of his work has never been made clear. It is established that Vaughan discussed with federal agents the murders of Anna Brown and her cousin Charlie Whitehorn, who was shot in his car on Dial Hill within days of Anna's body being found.[52] In June 1923, Vaughan received a call from a friend of George Bigheart. George had apparently been poisoned and had been hospitalized in Oklahoma City. Alarmingly, H. G. Burt and Bill Hale were there with Bigheart shortly before his death, according to a local policeman, so they may have poisoned him then.[53] George Bigheart held information on the Osage murders that he would reveal only to Vaughan, his trusted lawyer, who was urged to hurry to Oklahoma City. Before Vaughan departed, he allegedly told his wife of a safe in a secret location where he had stashed cash and evidence he had collected on the murders. William told her if anything should happen to him, she must retrieve the evidence right away and give it to authorities, and use the money for the children and herself. In David Grann's account, after Vaughan reached Bigheart at the hospital, the Osage waved others from the room, and "apparently shared his information, including incriminating documents."[54] For several hours, Vaughan remained by Bigheart's side until he died, Grann claimed.

That makes for a dramatic story, but Grann seems to have ignored FBI reports and some of the reportage of the Pawhuska *Journal-Capital*, possibly in favor of family lore, which promoted the image of Vaughan as an absolute good guy. Author of *The Osage Indian Murders*, Lawrence J. Hogan, who had full access to FBI files, and Lonnie E. Underhill, author of *The Osage Indian Reign of Terror*, who combed through the Pawhuska *Journal-Capital* archive, differ somewhat from Grann's synthesis. Bigheart, who had "previously signed over management of his headright to William K. Hale, went on a prolonged drinking binge." An Osage named John Kenny told FBI agents that Grace Bigheart had conversed with his wife, Necia Kenny. Grace had said that Bill Hale had induced her husband to sign a deed transferring a great deal of the family's land over to Hale, Underhill reports.[55] The kingpin and his conspiring nephew, Ernest Burkhart, transported George from Gray Horse to Hominy, where they boarded a train together to Oklahoma City. They checked him in to Wesley Hospital, supposedly for treatment of his alcoholism. When George began recovering, he called his attorney, Vaughan, and asked him to travel quickly to Oklahoma City to protect him. Over the phone, but not in person, Bigheart "apparently gave his lawyer important information about the mysterious murders." On June 29, 1923, "before Vaughan could reach Oklahoma City, Bigheart died," Hogan writes. Although an autopsy did not show anything unusual, the attending physician said he had some important testimony to deliver "if he were summoned before a Court of Inquiry," Hogan stated. George Bigheart was allegedly given poisoned whiskey. An argument erupted at Bigheart's deathbed over a deed that the Osage had allegedly made out to Hale a few days before, which Vaughan claimed was fraudulent. Vaughan phoned the new Osage County sheriff to report that he had all the evidence on the Osage murders he needed and was hurrying back on the first available train. According to Hogan, Vaughan told several people that he then had enough evidence "to put a certain party in the electric chair" as he had identified the ringleader, who, he could show, had paid a certain attorney five thousand dollars to halt investigation of the Osage murders.[56] When the sheriff asked Vaughan if he knew who had poisoned Bigheart, Vaughan replied he knew that and much more. Together, Vaughan and Burt boarded an overnight train in Oklahoma City, Burt claimed, along with Albert Jackson, proprietor of the Jackson Theater, and L. M. Colville, another attorney.[57] Burt was the last known person to see Vaughan alive, and he reported Vaughan's disappearance, yet he was not investigated. In 1926 the *Oklahoma City Times* reported that evidence pointed to the conclusion that Vaughan had been murdered in Oklahoma City, and his cadaver was carried onto the departing train and into the sleeping car, from which it was later thrown; this story was picked up by the Associated Press.[58] Tom White's biographer casually stated that apparently Vaughn "was shot and his body pushed off the train." Indeed, one witness reported seeing an unconscious man being dragged and lifted onto the train by two men, each supporting an arm, who claimed the limp man was drunk; this was likely Vaughan, drugged or already murdered.[59] The attorney's body was found stripped nearly naked, and his widow found the hiding place empty.

Germane to the murders of Bigheart and Vaughan, Herbert G. Burt had been the guardian of George Bigheart's son, Charles, who died at age twelve in 1918, and was guardian of his daughter, Pearl Bigheart, who would inherit her late father's headright, plus that of four other Osages.[60] In an interview, the Fairfax town marshal who investigated the Osage murders concluded that not only had Burt been involved in Vaughan's murder, but also a "mayor of one of the boomtowns—a local tough—had helped Burt throw Vaughan off the train."[61] An FBI report made by T. F. Weiss shares the results of interviews held in March 1924 with a confidential informant in Wichita, Kansas, who stated the outlaw and conspirator Kelsey Morrison had recently signed over to Burt the same oil interests that Morrison had once signed over to Bill Hale.[62] This transpired in Arkansas City, Kansas, a place where Burt frequently conducted business outside of Pawhuska and the state of Oklahoma.[63] Former Boy Scout Harold Burt, the son of H. G. Burt, and Sam Turner, mayor of Shidler, surely the same boomtown mayor who was Burt's accomplice, met Kelsey Morrison in Arkansas City and paid him $250 to sign these papers to H. G. Burt. Because "H. G. Burt and Hale are very intimate," Weiss noted, "this was done for Hale."[64] In 1925, Burt was reportedly so scared that he would be arrested, he suddenly fled to Kansas. An FBI informant "who had been close to Hale" and had "provided critical evidence against him in the other murder cases" was asked about Vaughan's death: "I think Herb Burt pulled that," he replied.[65] In early 1926, the *Oklahoma City Times* ran a story picked up by the Associated Press claiming that new testimony was going to be heard by the federal grand jury that had already returned murder charges against Bill Hale and John Ramsey for the killing of Henry Roan: "A prominent Pawhuska businessman, heretofore unmentioned, is to be drawn into the net." This did not transpire, but this likely refers to H. G. Burt. One wonders if a great deal of money changed hands to prevent that testimony from being heard. Burt was seemingly very close to being arrested.[66]

Just like George Bigheart, Raymond Redcorn, Sr., was a wealthy Osage who had been under guardianship and condescendingly designated as "incompetent." As their attorney, William W. Vaughan was successful in legally restoring the status of Bigheart and Redcorn to competency. He charged each man the hefty fee of ten thousand dollars, but ultimately, H. G. Burt seems to have embezzled most of this money. In 1929, Vaughan's widow Rosa Vaughan was forced to sue Burt, who had owed William Vaughan money from the ten thousand dollars Burt collected from Redcorn. Oddly, the court did not rule in her favor in the Redcorn case, only in the case of the deceased,

George Bigheart. It was claimed Redcorn had understood that "Burt had full authority in the premises" and thus his transaction was conducted solely with Burt. The commissioner's opinion, however, casts doubt on the ruling in Redcorn's case and perhaps the whole legal system in its utter failure to protect Osages from predation and murder.

> We shall not disturb the judgment of the trial court in that part of the case which relates to the Raymond Redcorn matter, the $10,000 note in connection herewith, and a small payment thereon, and the one-third distribution thereof to plaintiff and the surviving law partner of the deceased. We may not altogether agree with the findings of fact of the trial court on this particular phase of the case, but, for good and sufficient reasons, as to that transaction, we prefer to leave the parties where we found them.[67]

Raymond Redcorn, Sr., was dead a little over two years following this decision.

David Grann portrays W. W. Vaughan as a White savior who was sacrificed for his devotion to hapless Osage victims and their community. Vaughan is not alone in this role because Grann's most prominent White messiah is FBI investigator Tom White, who dominates a lengthy section of the book. But a more careful examination of the historical facts reveals a more complex picture. In the 1920s and 1930s, Pawhuska was lousy with lawyers, about seventy-five to eighty of them—approaching 10 percent of the population—and nearly all of them took advantage of their monied Osage clients. Vaughan was no exception. Charging Redcorn and Bigheart ten thousand dollars each to restore them to "competency" was outrageous; that sum of money had the buying power of about $140,000 in 2018. Furthermore, the Osages might have paid nothing; according to Terry Wilson, lawyers "profited by representing Osages applying for competency even though the agency handled all such cases free." Attorneys were found to have "regularly billed their Indian clients according to a sliding scale running from $50 to 10 percent of their surplus funds."[68] This practice was grossly exploitative, regardless of whether most Osages were willing to pay the fee, evincing an "Olympian indifference" toward money, to quote Mathews.[69] Another disturbing revelation is that Vaughan and Burt were very close friends: "relations of a business and professional nature" between them "were of an extremely confidential and intimate nature." According to testimony, "for a considerable time before Vaughan's death," he and Burt were "constantly together," and Burt "directed or referred prospective clients to Vaughan." This portrayal is not one of a friend of the Osages in particular; if Burt and Vaughan were constantly together in 1923, it seems likely that Vaughan would have known something of Burt's dealings with Bill Hale. Even if Vaughan was somehow totally deceived, it is clear Burt and Vaughan were helping each other to help themselves to fat stacks of Osage cash. Among those that Burt "directed to Vaughan or promoted in conjunction with him were two wealthy Osage Indians, one George Bigheart and one Raymond Redcorn, who were under guardianships as incompetents."[70] Grann's construction of Vaughan as a pure White savior, and by implication, his portrayal of the Osages as helplessly waiting for him and the main hero, fittingly named White, is flawed and detrimental to a fuller understanding of the Osage murders. Grann's emphasis upon such figures seems condescending to Osages, who are depicted as passive victims, and perhaps has as its aim the consoling of its White readers, as the puffing up of such saviors works some measure of redemption against the widespread predation and evil displayed by the large cast of White plotters and enablers in Osage County.

Raymond Wesley Redcorn, Jr., was born to Kate and Raymond in August 1911. He was an early Boy Scout and later became an Eagle Scout. In fact, the first Boy Scout troop in the United States was established in Pawhuska in 1909, even before there was a Boy Scouts of America. When Reverend John Forbes Mitchell was sent from England to the St. Thomas Episcopal Church in Pawhuska, he exported the English scouting tradition. Mitchell had been associated with scouting because of his friendship with Scouts founder Robert Baden-Powell. In June 1929 Raymond, Jr., was asked by the scoutmaster at Bacone College in Muskogee, a school for American Indians (that in the 1930s became famous for its art school), to help him raise funds for five of his scouts to travel to England for the Great Jamboree. Redcorn helped to raise three thousand dollars in three days, and the Osage Agency allowed Redcorn to draw from his surplus funds to pay his own expenses and travel. Thus Raymond Redcorn became a Bacone Scout delegate, which put him on a path to meeting royalty. The party traveled to Philadelphia to Washington, DC, where they were guests at the home of Secretary of State Patrick J. Hurley. The Natives traveled to New York to pick up their Eagle Scout badges; then they sailed across the Atlantic to Liverpool, and then to Birkenhead, England, where sixty thousand scouts were gathered for the Jamboree.

Redcorn recalled that in the middle of August, he and the other five Bacone Scouts were at their camp at the Jamboree, dressed in Indian regalia and making fry bread, when Robert Baden-Powell, the founder of the Scouts, sauntered up and introduced himself and two young men to the Indians. They were Edward, the Prince of Wales, and his brother Albert (Bertie), both future kings. Edward asked what they were cooking, and asked if they might partake. Raymond made the royals some Indian frybread, which they enjoyed. Albert soon remarked that he wanted to return home with the Osages. The Prince of Wales took Baden-Powell aside, and then the latter returned and asked Raymond if he and his group could come spend the next weekend at Buckingham Palace! That Friday evening, a limousine came to pick up the Indian scouts, their duffle bags, and tepees. That evening, the group dined with King George V, Queen Mary, Edward, and Albert, Redcorn said. They were invited to drum and sing in a big celebration at the palace the next night. The king, queen, and about four hundred spectators enjoyed their performance. The Native scouts from Oklahoma were royally entertained for three days and two nights; they viewed the crown jewels in the basement and spent a night in Windsor Castle.

As a coda to this story, less than seven years later, in January 1936, the Prince of Wales became King Edward VIII, only to abdicate the throne in December to marry an American socialite, Wallis Simpson, "the woman he loved." Thereupon, Albert became King George VI. Redcorn left scouting after his return from the Jamboree because the Depression hit Pawhuska and he had to get a job.[71]

In July 1931, a few months after his father's death, Raymond Redcorn, Jr., commenced studies at Chillicothe Business College in Missouri.[72] His mother Kate Hudson may have returned there, because Chillicothe was her hometown. Raymond was described as a fullblood Osage and a "track and football man" who had been "sent to the college by the Osage Indian Agency."[73] After oil payments slumped in the early 1930s, many Osages made efforts to receive a practical education to promote self-determination of tribal resources. A decade later, Raymond was again enrolled in the school, along with Verne Tall, a Sioux from Pine Ridge, South Dakota.[74] In 1932, Raymond married Waltena Comel Myers, born in Ralston in 1915, after a three-week courtship. In May 1934, a son, Wakon Iron RedCorn, was born, and soon afterward the couple moved to New Orleans, where Raymond attended the Baptist Bible Institute there to train for the ministry, now a family tradition. According to his son, Raymond Redcorn III, he was part of a group of Osage men forming the core of the Osage Union Baptist Church. In the 1940s, Raymond painted portraits in oils, including one of Mary Hope Cannon. He was also gifted musically, playing the piano and singing in a vocal quartet with Harold A. Redcorn and Wakon Iron Red-Corn. During the World War II period, he worked as a pipefitter, traveling from state to state on assignment.[75] In 1950, he became the first Osage to be ordained in the Baptist ministry and his first preaching job was at Foraker, in Osage County not far from his paternal allotment. For decades he served as a Baptist minister; in the 1970s he led Sunday School classes of the

Pawhuska Indian Camp Church.[76] His son said he preached at one thousand funerals, many for indigent families.

In April 1958, a group of Osage men including Buddy Gray and painter and sculptor, Romaine Shackelford, all members of the Osage Association, very much wanted John Joseph Mathews to stand as a candidate for the Osage Tribal Council. Mathews kept his word to meet with nineteen Osages at Raymond Redcorn's campsite "in the Indian camp" at Pawhuska. They pleaded with Mathews to run, but he repeatedly refused, because he was busy with the rapid composition of his tribal history, *The Osages: Children of the Middle Waters*.

Waltena Redcorn, under the tutelage of Mary McFall, a fullblood Osage woman and others, became skilled at fry bread cooking. In 1973, the Red Corn family started a fry bread mix company and a restaurant on Main Street in Pawhuska that served Native American food.[77] Raymond Redcorn, Jr., retired from the ministry in an official capacity in 1977.

Raymond Redcorn, Jr., passed away in 2003 and Waltena, his lifelong partner, followed four years later. In 2018, his grandson, graphic designer, filmmaker, and comedian Ryan RedCorn, published an article in *Oklahoma Today*: "So how does my grandpa . . . not only live through this time period but adapt, survive and thrive to the age of ninety-four? How does he lay the foundation for a family when he's surrounded by so much murder and corruption?" Ryan RedCorn concluded his piece affirmatively: "These stories would not exist if our people had not survived this time. And we would not have survived this time without each other. Much has been written about Osage murders. I want people to know about Osage survival. I would not be here if it were not for my grandfather's ability to navigate and survive this time period."[78]

In 2016, Ryan's father, Raymond Redcorn III, was elected the Assistant Principal Chief of the Osages, serving with Principal Chief Geoffrey Standing Bear, the great-grandson of Principal Chief Fred Lookout. Redcorn III is intensely interested in Osage history and donated a massive collection of around a thousand photographs, books, and ephemera to the Osage Nation Museum in 2017. Redcorn dedicated this collection to the memory of his parents. "My father had a collection of Ho-ta-moie photographs and rare 1895 stereoviews of Pawhuska, which he gave me, forming the core of this collection." Ho-ta-moie (Rolling Thunder) was better known as John Stink, a folkloric Osage who lived alone with his pack of dogs in the Pawhuska area, hunting in the hills and mostly refusing to acculturate to settler ways. Stories circulated of Ho-ta-moie dying and resurrecting repeatedly, and these plus his unwanted wealth gave him fame and made him the subject of magazine and newspaper articles. "I hope people enjoy seeing these photographs as much as I enjoyed collecting them," Redcorn said. His son Ryan Redcorn runs Buffalo Nickel Creative in Pawhuska; another son, Sean Alexander RedCorn (Alex), earned a Ph.D. in education from Kansas State University, and his dissertation, "Set the Prairie on Fire," was inspired and influenced by Osage writers and intellectuals such as John Joseph Mathews, Robert Allen Warrior, and Jean Dennison.

THE END OF THE FRENZY:
C. E. ASHBROOK, HOMER HUFFAKER, MARY ELKINS,
AND THE FIRST NATIONAL BANK OF FAIRFAX

If "in 1932 the frenzy ended," as Mathews wrote nearly three decades later, the general cause was the drastic reduction in Osage headright payments resulting from the Great Depression and the drop in demand for oil. Having to step down from an aristocratic position dealt a blow to the vanity of some tribespeople, Mathews explained in *The Osages*.[79] But it also made them less attractive to predators, some of whom during the 1920s had been imprisoned or killed in the midst of criminal acts. That was the general cause, but two major, related events making headlines in the spring of 1932, preceded by the death of a local banker, mark that year in particular as the end of the Great Frenzy, supporting Mathews's claim.

The first event, in January 1932, was unheralded in the press: the death of Osage County merchant, loan shark, and banker, Herbert G. Burt. We now know he was a suspect in the Osage murders but never arrested. Burt's death meant that the Osages were free of another leech and predator, who, by all indications, participated in the reign of terror and helped throw W. W. Vaughan from a train. The second event occurred in March: the arrest and imprisonment of Charles Earl Ashbrook, for embezzling vast sums. C. E. Ashbrook was not only the head cashier of the First National Bank of Fairfax, but also the Fairfax city treasurer. The money he pilfered repeatedly belonged not only to the city, but, more grievously, to Osage wards residing in the area whose funds were held in trust at the bank.[80] The third event was the suspicious death in June of an exceedingly wealthy Osage heiress, Mary Elkins, reportedly a vivacious flapper and the subject of juicy and condescending newspaper stories.

Mary Elkins's guardian was C. E. Ashbrook's boss—Homer Huffaker, president of the First National Bank of Fairfax. This bank was co-organized in 1913 by Huffaker's brother-in-law Lew A. Wismeyer, who served as its first president for several years, after founding and naming the townsite of Fairfax. In the early 1920s, the First National Bank of Fairfax became the main financial hub of the Osage murders, a fact heretofore unnoted. First of all, William K. Hale owned interest in the bank and did most of his banking there; Underhill even states that Bill Hale "controlled" a Fairfax bank. Agent Tom White's biographer said Hale owned "large banking interests," an elaborate ranch house near Gray Horse, and townhouses in Pawhuska and Fairfax, along with vast acreages of leased and owned ranchland. Don Whitehead's chapter on the murders in *The FBI Story* begins with a reference to "banker William K. Hale."[81] Lew Wismeyer had come to the Osage Reservation in 1878 as chief clerk at the Osage agency office at Pawhuska; in 1884, he obtained a trader's license and opened a store in Pawhuska, later moving it to Grey Horse, and finally Fairfax.[82] Wismeyer was retired by the time the murders were hatched and was said to be a kindly and generous man; thus, he was not involved in murder plots, just the raking in of huge profits from Osage largesse. Both Charley Ashbrook and Homer Huffaker, however, were intimate friends with treacherous Bill Hale. In fact, Ashbrook, Huffaker, Hale, and Scott S. Mathis, president of the Big Hill Trading Company, were all very closely connected and in league, according to a 1925 FBI report from undercover investigator John K. Wren, a Native American who treasured his Ute ancestry.[83]

Back in 1892, Homer Huffaker moved from Council Grove, Kansas, to the Osage Nation with Wismeyer and assisted him in the trading post at Gray Horse; in 1903, Homer joined his brother-in-law in the transplanting of businesses from Gray Horse to the new railroad depot town, Fairfax. Huffaker, who allegedly quickly became fluent in the Osage language, was assistant cashier for two years in the Osage Bank of Fairfax, built in 1904. John Joseph Mathews's Osage father, William S. Mathews, another trader and merchant turned banker, was an organizer of the Osage bank of Greyhorse, which became the Osage Bank of Fairfax. Therefore, W. S. Mathews most likely knew Huffaker before Mathews sold his interest in the bank, and his interest in two other banks he had helped organize, to focus on the Citizens National Bank of Pawhuska.[84] Huffaker next became the secretary and treasurer of the Wismeyer Mercantile Company, where he worked for a decade, and around 1912 he was elected County Commissioner.

In 1913, Homer Huffaker organized the Big Hill Trading Company with John L. Bird, Dyke C. Maher, and Will Baldruff, and became its first president. The retail company occupied the entire lower floor of the large Kizer building, offering a great variety of dry goods, furniture, shoes, vehicles, harnesses, and "Indian supplies." John Bird, it will be recalled, was a Mathews family friend and a powerful business associate of William S. Mathews. In 1913, Bird was both the vice president of the Fairfax National Bank and the vice president of the Citizens National Bank of Pawhuska—where W. S. Mathews was a director, past president, and co-organizer—plus, Bird was an Indian loan shark in Pawhuska partnered with H. H. Brenner and joined by future Osage murder suspect, H. G. Burt. John Bird was not only deeply trusted by the fullbloods, he and a few of his associates were given privileged access to Indian agency records.[85]

The Big Hill Trading Company and its undertaking company, and its later president, Scott Samuel Mathis, did not just rip off countless Osages with grossly inflated prices, as the Osage Tribal Council protested in 1921.[86] In the 1920s, like the First National Bank of Fairfax, the Big Hill Trading Company and its president became a hub of the hideous murder plots and their cover-ups.[87] In 1922, Scotty Mathis consolidated his Eagle Trading Company with the Big Hill Trading Company and became a member, with Huffaker, Burt, and Baldruff as the principal stockholders. A large modern brick building was constructed to house the furniture store, undertakers, ready-to-wear, grocery, meat market, and variety store under one roof.[88] After murder victim Anna Brown's body was found in May 1921, Mathis and Hale ordered her body examined by the Big Hill Trading Company, which then offered funeral services, and they helped cover up the crime. Mathis boldly offered a five thousand dollar reward for the arrest and conviction of her murderer; private detectives were hired to work the case. Hale's nephew Byron Burkhart was "almost immediately arrested as a suspect." But just when it seemed a case was about to be made against Byron, Mathis "suddenly withdrew the reward, Burkhart was released from jail, and years passed before anything more was done to prosecute the case," Underhill reveals in *Osage Indian Reign of Terror*.[89] This was, of course, incredibly suspicious.

In October 1925, FBI Agent John Wren called Scott Mathis, who was also a guardian, "a crook and evidently in the power of Hale," who "handles him." Mathis, Huffaker, C. E. Ashbrook, and Hale knew "so much on each other" that none of them would ever spill the beans "regarding any of the others." The four men had "all been in various deals together cheating the Indians out of money," Wren reported. These businessmen shared a long history, and their circle included suspect Herbert G. Burt, who had an entire career in Fairfax prior to living in Pawhuska. In May 1912, a group of Fairfax businessmen established a permanent Merchants' Association; the elected officers included H. G. Burt as the commercial finance officer, Ashbrook and C. E. Riley as advertising officers, and Huffaker, Mathis, and W. E. Copeland, future banking associate of Huffaker and Ashbrook, in charge of entertainment.[90] Corruption and rot was widespread; other guardians, Wren wrote, had conspired "with Hale in cheating the Indians, in the sale of horses, cattle, automobiles, etc." The main "detective or spy" for the Hale contingent and the trading company was Bob Shrofe, a "crook" who gathered "all the dope on the Indians" and did "all the framing for them in their crooked deals in skinning the Indians," Wren noted in vintage hardboiled prose. Not only did Shrofe keep Hale apprised of all activities affecting him and his allies, he was also a "very close friend" of Hale's subservient nephews, Ernest and Bryan Burkhart (Byron). Wren derided Shrofe as "yellow" and was sure he would crack "if put under the 'hammer' when the time comes," suggesting the FBI men could be tough interrogators, which aligned with their reputation.[91]

This Fairfax coterie was deeply loyal to the plotter of many Osage murders, Bill Hale, and they received benefits from their collusion. Bank president Homer Huffaker and Fairfax mayor and councilman Pitts Beaty were included on an FBI list of men who remained steadfast in their defense of Hale.[92] Huffaker's sycophancy toward Hale is especially nauseating. In January 1926, when the Tulsa *Tribune* sent a reporter to Fairfax in advance of Hale's trial, Huffaker proclaimed that good ole Bill Hale had given five hundred dollars to the Baptist Church when they asked for help: "he's always been for law and order a mighty good man who loves his family and home."[93] Moreover, Huffaker backed up an alibi for Hale's nephews, Bryan Burkhart and Ernest Burkhart, suspects in the May 1921 murder of Anna Brown. Bryan had allegedly held Anna Brown in a lover's embrace before Kelsey Morrison struck Anna, then shot her in the head.[94] While Bill Hale was prepared for his trip to Leavenworth penitentiary in November 1926, the *Oklahoman* reported: "Tears came in the eyes of Homer Huffaker, president of the First National Bank at Fairfax, and S. S. Mathis, manager of the Big Hill Trading Company, as they told their lifelong friend goodbye. They said they will visit him as often as the Leavenworth rules will allow."[95] The plotters needed to keep their stories straight, for one thing; had there been a thorough investigation, these men would have been skating on thin ice.

Scott S. Mathis was somehow appointed administrator of the estate of Hale's archenemy, William E. Smith, whose new Fairfax home had been exploded with nitroglycerin in March 1923. Bill Smith's Osage wife, Rita Kyle Smith, and their young White servant, Nettie Brookshire, were killed instantly.[96] The crime scene was ghastly; one neighbor found one of Brookshire's legs in their tree. Rita was a sister of Minnie Smith, Bill Smith's first wife, who had died, perhaps suspiciously, of a rare wasting disease in 1918; of Anna Brown, murdered in 1921; and of Mollie Burkhart, who yet survived, but who was married to Ernest Burkhart—an accomplice in the murder of the Smiths and Brookshire. Bill Smith, terribly maimed and emasculated, died a few days later. Scott Mathis was the guardian of several Osages, some of whom were murdered, such as Anna Brown, or who died under suspicious circumstances, such as Lizzie Q. Kyle—the mother of Minnie, Rita, Anna, and Mollie—whom some believe was slowly poisoned.[97] Born circa 1849, Lizzie Q. (Elizabeth, born Frances) first married Jim Bigheart, and they had one child, Grace Bigheart. Grace later married George Bigheart, who as noted was murdered in June 1923. In 1929, the very year in which Hale was imprisoned, Scott Mathis suddenly became interested in the cattle business and assembled a ranch of several thousand acres northwest of Fairfax.[98]

Bank cashier Charles E. Ashbrook was a moneyman of the murder operation, overseeing the hauls from crooked deals and outrageous frauds deposited in and withdrawn from his bank—and pocketing money along the way. Ashbrook was thus a major player in the exploitation and predation of Osages, along with Hale and Burt, and helped empower Hale's sinister plot, yet has never been named as such in the literature on the murders. Ashbrook was a "close friend of Bill Hale" and would not "say anything against the Hale faction, for the reason that Hale has too much on him," FBI Agent Wren reported. Ashbrook's boss Homer Huffaker oversaw the financial epicenter of the Osage reign of terror, which, as noted, mainly preyed on Osages of the Big Hill band who lived in the vicinity of the Osage village of Greyhorse and Fairfax. Regardless, the names of Ashbrook and Huffaker have not been featured, even though Ashbrook stole Osage money time and again, and both were friends and confederates of Hale. A reporter for the *Oklahoman* put it aptly in November 1926, after Hale was imprisoned: "Other strands of a rope that appeared to bind together a number of Osage Indian killings, which might have converged" were still "dangling in the air." Many cases were investigated but were never solved or attracted much press attention; many more possible murders were never reported or investigated. Verdon R. Adams, biographer of FBI Agent Tom White, wrote:

> Any FBI Agent who took part in the investigation that Tom supervised follow-ing his conference with Mr. [J. Edgar] Hoover can testify that for every case of this nature that was prosecuted, there were dozens where the guilty parties were never brought to trial. In some cases, key witnesses were dead or could not be located. In others, the evidence, while thoroughly convincing to the investigator on the scene, was of too tenuous a nature to provide a reasonable likelihood of conviction. Even in the courtroom, the very fountainhead of justice, what was handed out to the Indian was frequently a caricature of equity.[99]

Therefore, many Osage relatives of those who died suspiciously, possible murder victims, came to feel that seeking justice was hopeless. In a climate of corruption, distrust, and fear, even asking for an investigation or autopsy might put an Osage at risk.

Back in 1909, C. E. Ashbrook had moved to Fairfax from Charleston, Illinois, no doubt lured by the promise of Osage wealth. Over the next decade, he and his wife, the former Lila Lee Spillman, quickly insinuated themselves in the power structure of this twisted town on the take, and before long, lived "surrounded by comfort and conveniences."[100] In April 1912, Ashbrook was elected city treasurer and Huffaker was a councilman. Not only did Ashbrook repeatedly steal vast sums of money from Osages and from the city of Fairfax, but also, further solidifying his complicity in the murders, Ashbrook's wife was the official administrator of the estate of Henry Roan, who was murdered in February 1923 so that Bill Hale could collect on a fraudulent life insurance policy.[101] It was actually Charley Ashbrook, of course, who handled the Roan estate and collaborated with Hale to defraud and cheat Osages, both living and recently dead. The *Oklahoman* even stated "Ashbrook was administrator of the estate of Henry Roan, wealthy Osage Indian, for whose death W. K. Hale is serving a life sentence in federal prison. Roan was slain allegedly for collection of a $25,000 insurance policy. Ashbrook testified for Hale at the trial." Yet Ashbrook was never indicted in the Osage murders.[102]

In October 1926, Ashbrook testified that he had seen Hale and Roan together several times and considered them good friends.[103] Hale had hired local lowlife John Ramsey to lure and murder Henry Roan. The unfortunate Osage was allegedly depressed and alcoholic because of his wife's infidelity, and he had made a previous failed suicide attempt, as Hale learned. If Roan had completed suicide, the life insurance policy Hale had taken out would become void, so Hale wanted Roan killed before he might kill himself. Hale testified that the last place he saw Roan was the First National Bank of Fairfax. "Roan appeared sober. He asked for twenty-five dollars to get some liquor. I let him have it."[104] When Hale was a defendant in a 1929 federal trial for the killing of Henry Roan, C. E. Ashbrook again served as witness for the magnate. In 1932, newspapermen inferred the collaboration between Hale and Ashbrook, but the connection didn't take hold in court and was lost to time. J. Edgar Hoover must take much of the blame because he lost interest in making further arrests after they nabbed Hale. Ashbrook's name ought to be held in infamy for his crimes against the Wahzhazhe people.

By any means the bankers enriched themselves, and it seemed like too much was never enough. By the early 1920s, the First National Bank of Fairfax building had been greatly expanded, doubling its square footage.[105] By October 1924, Ashbrook had somehow accumulated enough capital to open a new apartment house enterprise in Fairfax he had built. Ashbrook had personally invested twenty-five thousand dollars (worth about $375,000 in 2019) in the seven-apartment house, the first of its kind in Fairfax. Immediately moving in were J. J. Quarles, cashier, and later president of the Osage Bank of Fairfax, also a guardian, and his wife. Years earlier, J. J. Quarles had purchased a store from his cousin, S. S. Mathis, placed his son Frank in charge, and called it The Quarles Store.[106]

In the midst of the 1926 murder trial of Hale and Ramsey, C. E. Ashbrook ran afoul of the federal government for embezzling a great deal of money from his Osage ward, Charles Fletcher—and Bill Hale himself was named as another defendant in the lawsuit. Some backdrop to the case is helpful. In February 1923, at the peak of the murders, C. B. Peters, an oilman and president of the Chamber of Commerce of Tulsa, secured control of the First

National Bank of Fairfax. In 1920, the Tulsa Chamber had passed resolutions supporting the Osage County Home Owners Association (OCHOA) in their opposition to an extension of the Osage mineral trust period. In other words, as noted earlier, the OCHOA and the Chamber proclaimed that after 1931, the owners of surface land rights, Whites and others, should own the subsurface oil and gas rights, too, and Osages with headrights should lose their communal underground reservation. Later, however, under pressure from certain oil interests, and "to avoid friction, a special directors' meeting annulled the resolution and the report"; nonetheless, representatives of the Chamber still placed it before a Congressional Committee investigating Osage Indian affairs and the resolution was printed in the report of that committee.[107] Thus the Tulsa Chamber, the OCHOA, and certain oilmen placed on record their hostility to Osage sovereignty and interests. When the First National Bank of Fairfax came into C. B. Peters's control, Huffaker remained the president and Ashbrook remained the cashier. The other two major stockholders were bankers, former officers of the First National Bank associated with Bill Hale: J. C. Stribling, a "former cowman" and former president of the bank, and J. L. Hudson, former cashier of the bank.[108]

The 1926 federal trial of Ashbrook, which named Bill Hale, did not receive much publicity, overshadowed as it was by the simultaneous murder trial of Hale and John Ramsey. From Ashbrook, the government sought to recover a missing $49,514, which had been paid to him. Bill Hale and J. L. Hudson, bank stockholders, reportedly gave surety on Ashbrook's bond, each pledging fifteen thousand dollars. The government sued Hale and Hudson for fifteen thousand dollars each. Under a then-recent court ruling, an act of Congress governing distribution of Osage incomes stated that guardians were allowed to collect only one thousand dollars quarterly and were denied from any part of their wards' proceeds from land. The government was trying to recover all excess funds paid to Osage guardians following the passage of that act, and thereby discovered Ashbrook's embezzlement. In vain I searched for a follow-up story to learn the result of this suit filed by the government; as Terry Wilson explains, of the twenty-five suits filed in 1924 by the Interior Department against dishonest guardians to recover Osage money, not a single one went to trial. Instead, all the defendants made settlements out of court to avoid criminal prosecution. Most such cases had been resolved without formal litigation, as in 1923, J. M. Humphrey, field solicitor for the Osage superintendency, "offered one hundred guardians with flagrantly fraudulent accounts" the opportunity to make amends voluntarily, Wilson writes.[109]

In 1929 the *Oklahoman* thought it well to run a large photograph of a smiling Bill Hale, his wife, and attractive daughter, Willie Hale Oller, which had been taken on the Pawhuska courthouse steps, captioned "Hale Family

Shows No Worry Signs at Trial."[110] The press therefore was not necessarily concluding Hale was guilty. In September 1926, Willie Hale had married Willard Oller of Fairfax, the son of her father's ranching partner, Lou Oller, and macabrely, "they lived within a few hundred yards of the spot where Anna Brown had been murdered," according to Lawrence Hogan. Willie was nineteen, and Willard was twenty-one. On the day in 1921 that the home of Bill and Rita Smith was blown up, Lou Oller sent Hale a telegram saying the "Deal Stands Good. I Will Go in the Morning."[111] This let Hale know the plan was in motion and further gave him a documented alibi when he signed for the telegram in Fort Worth, where he had gone to a livestock show. After Hale's incarceration, his wife moved in with their daughter and son-in-law. Hogan stated Mr. Oller was Osage; however, though he was born in Osage County and had lived in Big Hill Township in the western part of the county, his race was registered as "white" on census records. Hogan also claimed Willie Hale married an Osage named Frank Simkins; though Simpkins was an Osage engaged in cattle ranching, raising race-horses, and driving a truck, no record of a marriage with Hale has been located.[112] Ms. Hale later married Sam Cohen, an ex-convict whom her father had befriended while in prison, and they dwelt in Phoenix, sometimes with dear ole dad. Perhaps it was a case of like father, like daughter. The doings of this Hale scion bear further investigation.[113]

In March 1932, C. E. Ashcroft's huge embezzlement scandal closed the bank and sent him to prison the following year. One of the worst pilferers of Osage money, and one of the many players in the Osage murders at large, was finally halted. The First National Bank of Fairfax had closed after a routine federal audit showed that Ashbrook's personal account was grossly overdrawn. Ashbrook resigned and then went missing on March 16, after being "pressed by city officials to be bonded for $100,000" for the treasurer position. His previous bond of fifty thousand dollars had elapsed, liquidated when a bonding firm folded.[114] After further auditing, it was discovered that of the funds Ashbrook embezzled, a great deal of it "was money on deposit for Osage Indian wards of the government" that had been pilfered over a period of several years.

Even though Ashbrook had already been in trouble in 1926 for stealing from his Osage ward, the 1932 newspaper stories feigned shock, painting him as a "leader in Fairfax society, for 25 years a faithful associate in the bank, ten years city treasurer, elected almost invariably without opposition." Good ole Charley Ashbrook had just been elected president of the Chamber of Commerce; he was also former school district treasurer and treasurer of the Masonic Lodge and the Fairfax Country Club. Ashbrook was "the man who was trusted with more of the private affairs of our citizens than any other," his supporters said. This "respected citizen" was "one of the most popular members of the community; active in civic affairs as well as the financial affairs of southern Osage County."[115] Townspeople acted surprised, but this was not Ashbrook's first scandal, and a large percentage of Fairfax townspeople were in on the take themselves. Stealing from Osages was the status quo; what was maybe shocking was that Ashbrook had taken from fellow Whites on the take.

C. E. Ashbrook was missing for two and a half weeks, leaving behind a confused wife and twenty-year-old daughter, who had returned home from studies at the University of Oklahoma. Homer Huffaker's brother, Carl I. Huffaker, vice president of the bank, did his best to cover for Ashbrook and put the best face on a desperate situation, dubiously claiming that after Ashbrook resigned, he secured "his overdraft with acceptable securities," and the bank would not lose any money. Carl Huffaker had previously been an electrician, telegrapher, and beginning in 1911, postmaster of Fairfax; using suggestive language, a waggish journalist reported that as postmaster, Carl was fastidious, "exactly precise in the most minute detail, but he is an outlaw of the holy writ and the laws of nature, and although he is a tempting morsel in the eyes of many a fair damsel, he has steadfastly refused to take a rib."[116] This seems to imply that Carl Huffaker was a gay man. Pitts Beaty, member of the city council, said that five audits had been performed since 1923. Beaty had been the mayor of Fairfax in 1925; Wren said Beaty was a "very close personal friend" of Bill Hale; "further it was ascertained that this man is an arch crook and is the guardian of Molly Burkhart, the wife of Ernest Burkhart." Beaty the crook claimed that the auditor, trying to figure the balance on hand in the bank, would visit, and "each time, Ashbrook had a certificate of deposit ready, signed by an assistant cashier." Neither the auditor nor the assistant cashier questioned the CD or checked it with the ledger sheet. The assistant cashier, W. E. Copeland, was "friendly with the Hale faction, and is N.G. [no good]," Wren reported. In August 1926, Copeland confirmed this when he testified for Hale, saying that Henry Roan frequented the First National Bank, and Roan and Hale were close friends. He portrayed Hale positively, noting Bill had lent Henry money on occasion and sold him livestock on credit. The assistant cashier had served on the coroner's jury and saw blood on Roan's clothing. Henry Roan was a man of some education, Copeland said, and considered him "intelligent and shrewd."[117] From 1910 through 1923, no audits of city of Fairfax books were performed. This means that during the worst years of the reign of terror, whose victims were mostly Big Hill band Osages in the Gray Horse/Fairfax area, no one was checking the finances of the city, whose treasurer was also cashier at the First National Bank, where vast sums of Osage money were held. One article reporting the bank closing noted: "The other bank here, the

Fairfax National, was robbed recently." Robbery and theft operating under various guises were ubiquitous.[118]

On the night of May 1, 1932, Ashbrook gave himself up to Jim Pyle, special officer of the Osage Indian Agency in Pawhuska. He surrendered at the Indian Agency because he had stolen monies held in trust for Osages, along with city money. While hiding out in Santa Fe, New Mexico, Ashbrook faced federal charges of violating national banking laws, along with state charges of stealing city funds. On May 3, Ashbrook sat in the county jail at Sapulpa, awaiting trial on charges of taking $105,200. He pleaded not guilty when arraigned in the federal court at Tulsa, before a U.S. commissioner. "When a fellow gets into a jam, then there doesn't seem to be anything that he can do," Ashbrook rued to a reporter. He protested he did not "take a dirty dime of anyone's money" and claimed it could not be proved that he, "as a banker, took any funds from the bank," adding he needed a "fighting attorney."[119] In late September, the city of Fairfax sued the First National Bank, its receiver F. M. Overstreet, and Ashbrook, for $37,389. The petition alleged that the sum was taken illegally while funds were on deposit at the bank.[120]

When Ashbrook's federal trial arrived, although receivers asserted Ashbrook's accounts were short $105,000, he admitted to taking only fifty thousand dollars and was handed a four-year sentence by Judge Franklin Kennamer.[121] In January 1933, Ashbrook was sent to Leavenworth federal penitentiary, where Bill Hale and John Ramsey were confined, and where former FBI Agent Tom White, who had directed the Osage murder investigation, was now in charge. In prison, Ashbrook contracted a throat ailment, and in June 1933, five months into his sentence, he died of throat cancer. His body was sent to his former home of Charleston, in southern Illinois. His obituary in his local paper omitted the embezzlement and stated falsely that he had died in Fairfax.[122]

Mary Jacqueline Elkins (E-he-ke-op-pe), the supremely wealthy Osage heiress and symbol of the Great Frenzy, died in June 1932. The death of Mary Elkins, like her life over the course of a decade, was the material for sensational newspaper stories. Like John Joseph Mathews, Elkins was a member of the Big Hill band. Her guardian since her twelfth birthday was Homer Huffaker. Mary was a graduate of Haskell Indian School in Lawrence, Kansas, and a fancy finishing school in Los Angeles. E-he-ke-op-pe was born in Gray Horse village in January 1905, one of five children of her mother, Mo-se-che-he, and father, Me-ti-an-kah, who had lived humbly, but became wealthy when headright payments boomed. Sadly, the family suffered a debilitating tuberculosis outbreak, cutting lives short. Mary Elkins spent much of her childhood and teenage years in sanitaria in California and Colorado. By the end of 1916, when Mary was only eleven years old, all of her family members had died except for her brother, Ernest Elkins (Wah-ne-en-kah). E-ne-op-pe died in 1906, Bernadette Elkins in 1909, and Edward Elkins (Ne-wal-la) in 1911. Their mother passed away in 1912, and her father in 1916.[123] Imagine the sadness and isolation that she faced as a girl.

Mary Elkins spent most of her adult life in the Colorado Springs area, where many affluent Osages enjoyed visiting, often staying at luxurious Broadmoor Hotel. In March 1926, Will Rogers joked that Colorado Springs was "the Osage Indians' Summer Resort. There being the richest people in the world, are naturally able to pick out the best resort there is [sic]. When the Osages come, Marland, of Ponca City, and Spencer Penrose [Colorado gold and copper magnate] and the smaller fry have to move out and give way to wealth." Rogers added that "a teepee in every room" made "the Osages feel at home."[124] According to Terry Wilson, Mary Elkins purchased a home in a suburb called Ivy Wild and allegedly abandoned herself to a "career of drinking, drugs, and high living" with "other like-minded Osages congregated there" who were enjoying wealth and leisure during the Roaring Twenties.[125] Elkins was frequently reckless in her drinking, driving (despite hiring chauffeurs), and horseback riding, scattering pedestrians from crosswalks and sidewalks, it was reported. She was said to become belligerent when drinking, picking fights with Ute men and women gathered at the Garden of the Gods who offered their handicrafts to tourists, belittling their ancestry. Later, she would become remorseful, returning to offer money and apologies to assuage her fellow Natives. Mary Elkins, still quite young, reportedly started drinking heavily after the death of her first husband, Jack Daugherty, a "steady young businessman." Mr. Daugherty died soon after their daughter, Marie Jacqueline, was born in April 1922. Mary had been happy with Jack, newspaper readers were told. But Mary also lost her brother Ernest, her last living family member, during that same month.[126]

In early 1923, amid the apex of the murders, Mary Elkins, already tubercular, was at great risk of joining her family in the afterlife. In late June of that year, she filed suit for divorce against Wilbur L. Corbett (Bobby), a welterweight boxer from Fairfax, Oklahoma.[127] Mary Elkins made the shocking claim that she had been drugged and forced into marrying Corbett in Kansas City on May 3, after knowing him for only a few days. During a visit to Oklahoma, she met Corbett, and, apparently taken by the prizefighter, agreed to accompany him to Kansas City. Her complaint alleged Corbett invited her to dinner, during which he "plied her with liquor and drugs until she became unconscious and thereafter removed her to his room and had a marriage ceremony performed." Ms. Elkins charged him with cruelty and trying to browbeat her into signing over to him her land and headrights.[128] This was a conspiracy originating in her childhood hometown of Fairfax, "where certain parties conspired to obtain the Elkins fortune, hiring Corbett's services for that purpose," Wilson explains.[129] Possessing large land holdings in Osage County and eight and a half headrights, Mary was almost unimaginably wealthy.

Mary Ekins's activities in Colorado Springs and her marriage to Bobby Corbett were made known to her guardian, Homer Huffaker, via newspaper coverage of a drinking and driving incident labeling her a "firebrand flapper." On the way to and from the Garden of the Gods, the stunningly beautiful natural rock formations Mary loved, she was inclined to stop for a drink at "numerous shady resorts," readers were told. After returning to Colorado Springs, she caused an accident that wrecked her car and damaged two others, sending a driver to the hospital with a serious injury. The next day, she pleaded guilty to all charges, paid a steep fine, paid for the damages to the other cars, pledged to pay medical expenses of the hospitalized man, bought another edition of her fancy roadster, and went about her business.[130] Seeing a newspaper article, Huffaker sprang into action; wishing to regain control over his ward from the second-rate pugilist, he initiated "legal actions to have her marriage annulled" upon her request. Homer also conferred with Superintendent J. George Wright, and they commenced a full investigation into rumors surrounding the marriage. An attorney hired by the tribe, along with Huffaker's personal lawyer, traveled to Kansas City, then on to Colorado Springs, learning that the courtship of Elkins and Corbett had indeed been a whirlwind: between their meeting and the moment of their marriage, they did little but drink and joyride. After the marriage, Corbett burned through a great deal of Mary's money, whipped and beat her, and supplied her with a constant pipeline of liquor and drugs including opiates in an attempt to accelerate her death, so he could inherit her headrights. When an attorney confronted Corbett, saying he knew all about the plot, the scoundrel "quickly reduced his demand for $10,000 in exchange for not contesting the annulment, to $1,000 for his cooperation." The attorneys unfortunately could not gather enough evidence to enable them to file a "charge of conspiracy to obtain the property of a ward of the United States, much to the chagrin of Superintendent Wright," who had urged a robust prosecution. Mary Elkins was nearly another victim of the Osage reign of terror as it peaked in 1923.[131]

Sadly, Ms. Elkins's life, though it clearly had its bright moments, continued to be fraught with excess and violence. She later married Harry Bowles, a Colorado Springs taxi driver. Although Bowles had married an extremely wealthy woman, he sought a divorce, because, he claimed, his Osage bride "beat him so severely and so often that he was ill" throughout the previous year; it was granted in May 1929. Mary later married a smalltime tradesman, David Derryberry, but divorced him in January 1932, charging that he, like Corbett, had beaten her and blacked her eyes.[132] Even Mary's final days involved man trouble and legal trouble. When Elkins' body was found, "Sheriff's officers had been seeking her for a week to serve papers on her in connection with an alienation of affections suit" brought by LaVerne Hayden, an African American woman—her chauffeur's wife.

Six months after her final divorce, Mary Elkins was dead. Newspapers trumpeted Mary's insatiable lust for jewelry, and before she died, she had spent twenty to twenty-five million dollars of the "wealth the Oklahoma oil wells were continuously pouring into her lap," a sum equating to at least 293 million dollars in 2018. The 1930 census even reports a jeweler named Grant A. Alford was actually living in her house as a lodger! Despite Ms. Elkins's alleged free spending, upon her death, it was reported, she still had six hundred thousand dollars cash in the bank (worth nearly eleven million dollars in 2018), fifty thousand acres of valuable land, "three luxurious homes, a whole fleet of expensive motor cars," closetsful of haute couture, and, of course . . . jewels![133]

When Mary Elkins passed away on June 8, 1932, at only twenty-seven years of age, the coroner pronounced the cause was "excessive use of liquor," which "removed earlier suspicion that she might have been the victim of violence. He said it was learned she had been intoxicated for several days."[134] Learned how, and by whom? What was the nature of the suspicions of violent death? The details are vague. Ms. Elkins was a woman long accustomed to drinking. It seems questionable that even multiple days of drinking would have killed her. Given Ms. Elkins's lifestyle and tolerance to alcohol, her death remains mysterious and should be viewed in light of the previous attempt made on her life and the wider context of concurrent plots against Osages. E-he-ke-op-pe was buried in Gray Horse cemetery with her family members. After Mary's death in 1932, her daughter Marie Jacqueline was placed in a California convent, the sole heir of the family estate and headrights.

In 1935, a few years after the end of the frenzy, Mary Elkins's guardian, Homer Huffaker, was profiled in an Associated Press story, not described as a former bank president, but rather as a rustic old-time trader, a White who had "for half a century lived among the Osages and studied their habits and traditions." Huffaker said the "fullbloods are passing away; the younger generations have not been assimilated by the white race; that means the Indian race is deprived of many of its former characteristics and has not attained those of the whites." He described living at the Greyhorse agency as a youth in the days when most of the Osages were fullbloods, whom he recalled as "honest and upright men, possessing a native shrewdness and wisdom which many a white man envied." But in 1935, he said, most of the Osages were partly white. In what sounds both confessional and regretful, Huffaker said that sadly, most Osages had "learned many of the white man's bad ways. They've learned dishonesty—I say it frankly and I believe other early residents will back me up—from us. They're discovering the fact that truth and sincerity don't always pay when dealing with a paleface."[135]

NOTES

1. "Indian Heiresses Invade Capital," *Washington Herald*, September 7, 1914, 5.

2. John Joseph Mathews, *The Osages* (Norman: University of Oklahoma Press, 1961), 778.

3. Larry O'Dell, "Ku Klux Klan," *The Encyclopedia of Oklahoma History and Culture*, https://www.okhistory.org/publications/enc/entry.php?entry=KU001; Snyder, *John Joseph Mathews*, 38.

4. Timothy Snyder, *Bloodlands*, 380–81.

5. Lawrence J. Hogan, *Osage Indian Murders*, 141.

6. Lonnie Underhill, *Osage Indian Reign of Terror*, 257–60; Hogan, *Osage Indian Murders*, 266–76.

7. "Saucy Calf Was Murder Victim," *Oklahoman*, February 18, 1912, 12, Oklahoman Digital Archives, archive.newsok.com; "Indian Turned the Joke," *Chronicle-Telegram* [Elyria, Ohio], March 29, 1912, 12; "'Sassy Calf' was Victim of Robbers Who Stole Money," Arkansas City [Kansas] *Daily Traveler*, February 17, 1912, 1.

8. Oscar Faye Adams in *Handbook of American Authors* (Boston: Houghton Mifflin, 1885) notes that Josiah Gilbert Holland's "work has met with severe criticism from a literary point of view, but remains widely popular. As editor of *Scribner's Monthly* he exercised a wide and excellent influence" (82).

9. Mathews, *Twenty Thousand Mornings*, 134.

10. "Pleads to Save Oklahoma Oil Resources for Native Red Men," *Boston Post*, December 19, 1920, 103; "Arthur Bonnicastle's Own Story," *Red Man and Helper* [Carlisle Indian Industrial School, Pennsylvania], March 4, 1902, 2, carlisleindian. dickinson.edu/sites/all/files/docs-publications/RedMan-Helper_v02n30_0.pdf; Hazel W. Hertzberg, *The Search for an American Indian Identity: Modern Pan-Indian Movements* (Syracuse: Syracuse University Press, 1971), 268; Omer Call Stewart, *Peyote Religion: A History* (Norman: University of Oklahoma, 1987), 132; Griffin Paul Jackson, "US Report Bashes China's Religious Freedom Violations," *Christianity Today*, May 2, 2019, www.christianitytoday.com/news/2019/may/uscirf-religious -freedom-violators-report-china.html; "The Lobby Discusses Legislation to Suppress the Use of Peyote," *Congressional Digest*, February 1922, 15.

11. "Pleads to Save Oklahoma Oil Resources for Native Red Men," *Boston Post*, December 19, 1920, 103.

12. "Former Chief of Osage Dies," *Osage Chief*, June 8, 1923; Missouri State Board of Health Certificate of Death, online records.

13. "Did You Know?" n.d., *Osage Nation*, www.osagenation-nsn.gov/news -events/news/did-you-know-7, accessed October 17, 2019.

14. In Red Corn's *A Pipe for February*, the veteran Arthur Bonnicastle and a group of his friends from out of town descend the stairs to the Bon Bon café in Pawhuska where the narrator, John Greyeagle, Barbara, and Molly are sitting. "Arthur Bonnicastle has quite a history and Roper once read that the *New York Times* referred to him as a soldier of fortune. I found myself relaxing and fantasizing just a little about who the people with Arthur Bonnicastle might be. Maybe other soldiers of fortune

or mercenaries who followed him over the Great Wall of China during the Boxer Rebellion" (126).

15. His name is also spelled Tsa-shin-kah-wah-ti-an-kah. Sassy Calf is not to be confused with Sassy Chief of the Heart-Stays People.

16. Mathews, *Osages*, 428.

17. Ada *Evening News* [Oklahoma], February 16, 1911, 2.

18. "Saucy Calf Was Murder Victim," *Oklahoman*, February 18, 1912, 12, Oklahoman Digital Archives.

19. Douglass *Tribune* [Kansas], March 1, 1912, 8.

20. Cedar Vale *Star* [Kansas], April 7, 1893, 3; Independence *Daily Reporter* [Kansas], April 12, 1893, 2.

21. "The Osage Proposition," *Weekly Republican-Traveler*, January 3, 1895, 7; "Chief Saucy Calf Acquitted," Lawrence *Daily Journal*, February 16, 1895, 2; "Territory News," Muskogee *Phoenix*, March 13, 1895.

22. Mathews, *Osages*, 725.

23. "Treating with the Osage," Arkansas City *Weekly Republican-Traveler*, December 20, 1894, 7.

24. Garrick Bailey, introduction to *The Osage and the Invisible World: From the Works of Francis La Flesche* (Norman: University of Oklahoma Press, 1999), 19.

25. Thomas F. Logan, "Behind the Scenes at Nation's Capital," Philadelphia *Inquirer*, December 7, 1914, 8.

26. Garrick Bailey, introduction to *The Osage and the Invisible World*, 21.

27. "Saucy Calf Was Murder Victim," *Oklahoman*, February 18, 1912, 12, Oklahoman Digital Archives.

28. "Saucy Calf Was Murdered," Washington County [Oklahoma] *Sentinel*, February 16, 1912, 1, Gateway to Oklahoma History.

29. "Chief Saucy Calf Slain," *Coffeyville Daily Journal* [Kansas], February 16, 1912, 1.

30. "Chief Saucy Calf Slain," *Coffeyville Daily Journal* [Kansas], February 16, 1912, 1.

31. William McKinley was president from March 1897 to September 1901, when he was assassinated six months into his second term.

32. "Saucy Calf Was Murder Victim," *Oklahoman*, February 18, 1912, 12.

33. "Did Laban Miles Kill Saucy Calf?" Guthrie [Oklahoma] *Daily Leader*, April 4, 1912, 1.

34. "For Killing Saucy Calf," Fort Gibson *New Era* [Oklahoma], October 23, 1913, 2.

35. "Further Particulars," Arkansas City [Kansas] *Weekly Republican-Traveler*, April 30, 1891, 6; "Shooting at Kaw," *Industrial Free* Press [Winfield, Kansas], May 7, 1891, 4.

36. Arkansas City [Kansas] *Daily Traveler*, January 12, 1892, 5; "Three Arrested on Murder Charge," *Daily Oklahoman*, October 12, 1913, 9; "Shooting at Kaw," *Canal City Dispatch* [Arkansas City, Kansas], May 1, 1891, 5; "Jim Pappan Story," *Osage County Profiles* (Pawhuska: OCHS, 1978).

37. "Indians Freed of Murder Charge," *Daily Ardmoreite* [Ardmore, Oklahoma], November 3, 1913.

38. Mathews, *Sundown*, 182–86.

39. World War I draft card via Ancestry.com.

40. "Baptist Delegate Reported Missing: Friends Fear for Safety of Raymond Redcorn, Indian, of Oklahoma," New Orleans *Times-Picayune*, May 18, 1917, 9, America's Historical Newspapers.

41. "Raymond Redcorn Taken by Death," *Journal-Capital*, May 1, 1931, 1.

42. Kathryn Redcorn, personal interview, her home in Pawhuska village, July 6, 2018.

43. *Oklahoma, County Marriages, 1890-1995* [database] (Lehi, Utah: Ancestry .com), 2016.

44. "Redcorn v. District Court of Eight Judicial District," *Justia, US Law*, February 11, 1930, Supreme Court of Oklahoma, law.justia.com/cases/oklahoma/supreme-court/1930/44316.html, accessed January 12, 2018.

45. 1930 U.S. Federal Census, Ancestry.com.

46. Rennard Strickland, "Osage Oil: Mineral Law, Murder, Mayhem, and Manipulation," *Natural Resources & Environment* 10, no. 1 (summer 1995): 39.

47. *Vaughan v. Burt*, case number 19197, Supreme Court of Oklahoma, January 22, 1929, *Justia*, law.justia.com/cases/oklahoma/supreme-court/1929/44873.html, accessed January 12, 2018.

48. Underhill, *Osage Indian Reign of Terror*, 18, 23, 26, 92, 239, 255.

49. Underhill, *Osage Indian Reign of Terror*, 222.

50. Don Whitehead, *The FBI Story: A Report to the People* (New York: Random House, 1956), 113–18.

51. Underhill, *Osage Indian Reign of Terror*, 27.

52. Charlie Whitehorn (Charles), the son of John and Dona Whitehorn of Hominy [source: 1920 federal census, Osage County, Hominy, Ancestry.com] is not to be confused with the assistant principal chief, Charles Whitehorn, who lived until 1972.

53. David Grann, *Killers of the Flower Moon*, 263.

54. Grann, *Killers of the Flower Moon*, 93–94.

55. Underhill, *Osage Indian Murders*, 23–24.

56. Hogan, *Osage Indian Murders*, 71.

57. Underhill, *Osage Indian Reign of Terror*, 24, citing Pawhuska *Journal-Capital*, June 30, 1923.

58. Reported in Associated Press, "Newspaper Claims Indictments Will Combat Meddlers," *Ada Evening News* [Oklahoma], January 28, 1926, 1.

59. Arthur H. Lamb, *Tragedies of the Osage Hills*, Pawhuska, n.d., c. 1929, 152.

60. *United States v. William K. Hale*, No. 485, 39 F.2d 188 (1930), March 24, 1930.

61. Grann, *Killers of the Flower Moon*, 264.

62. T. F. Weiss, FBI report, March 21 to April 9, 1924, vault.fbi.gov/Osage%20 Indian%20Murders/Osage%20Indian%20Murders%20Part%2010%20of%2065, accessed January 12, 2018.

63. *Arkansas City Traveler*, June 10, 1913, 4; December 23, 1916, 2; May 6, 1922, 4.

64. T. F. Weiss, FBI report, March 21 to April 9, 1924, vault.fbi.gov/Osage%20 Indian%20Murders/Osage%20Indian%20Murders%20Part%2010%20of%2065.

65. Grann, *Killers of the Flower Moon*, 264.

66. Associated Press, "Newspaper Claims Indictments Will Combat Meddlers," *Ada Evening News* [Oklahoma], January 28, 1926, 1.

67. *Vaughan v. Burt*, case number 19197, Supreme Court of Oklahoma, decided January 22, 1929, *Justia*, law.justia.com/cases/oklahoma/supreme-court/1929/44873 .html, accessed January 12, 2018.

68. Wilson, *Underground Reservation*, 140.

69. Mathews, *Sundown*, 91.

70. *Vaughan v. Burt*, case number 19197, Supreme Court of Oklahoma, decided January 22, 1929, *Justia*, law.justia.com/cases/oklahoma/supreme-court/1929/44873.html.

71. Raymond Redcorn III, personal interview, July 6, 2018; Ralph W. Marler, "City Celebrates Scouts," *Tulsa World*, October 10, 1999, www.tulsaworld.com/ archives/city-celebrates-scouts/article_2ea6caae-1aff-5807-be0f-7b5c7ef0cd6e.html; Raymond Redcorn, Jr. [narrative], "The Great Scout Jamboree 1929" [exhibit], Osage County Historical Society Museum, Pawhuska, Oklahoma, viewed November 2018.

72. *Chillicothe* (Missouri) *Constitution-Tribute*, July 29, 1931, 8; *Stanberry* (Missouri) *Headlight*, January 25, 1940, 4.

73. "Osage Indian Enrolls," *Chillicothe* (Missouri) *Constitution-Tribute*, August 1, 1931, 1.

74. *Herald* [Sisketon, Missouri], January 25, 1940.

75. Raymond W. Redcorn III, personal interview, July 6, 2018, Pawhuska.

76. "Pleasant Ridge News," *Arkansas City Traveler* [Kansas], October 15, 1953, 30; "Blue, Gold Banquet Set by Neosho Cubs," *Joplin Globe* [Missouri], February 26, 1960, 12; "Granola News of Interest," *Arkansas City Traveler* [Kansas], December 30, 1970, 12; Waltena RedCorn and Sandra RedCorn, "Raymond, Jr. and Waltena Redcorn," *Osage County Profiles* (Pawhuska: OCHS, 1978).

77. "About ha-pah-shu-tse," Red Corn Native Foods, 2018, redcorn.com/?page_ id=2.

78. Ryan RedCorn, "The Collections," *Oklahoma Today*, July/August 2018, 69–73.

79. Mathews, *Osages*, 779.

80. "Ex-Charleston Man Held as Embezzler," *Journal Gazette* [Mattoon, Illinois] May 14, 1932, 2.

81. Lawrence J. Hogan, *Osage Indian Murders*, 114; John Wren, FBI report, October 6, 1925, Osage Indian Murders part 22 of 56, Federal Bureau of Investigation, Vault .fbi.gov; Underhill, *Osage Indian Reign of Terror*, 256; Vernon R. Adams, *Tom White: Life of a Lawman* (El Paso: Texas Western Press, 1972), 59; Whitehead, *FBI Story*, 113.

82. Fairfax Area Historical Society, *From a Field of Cane*, 68.

83. John Wren, FBI report, October 6, 1925, Vault.fbi.gov, accessed December 26, 2018.

84. Snyder, *John Joseph Mathews*, 14.

85. Fairfax Area Historical Society, *From a Field of Cane*, 72, 78; Thoburn, *Standard History of Oklahoma*, 5: 2133–34.

86. Fred Grove, *Years of Fear*, 229.

87. Grann, *Killers of the Flower Moon*, 164, 280–81, 290.

88. "Scott and Harriet Mathis," *Osage County Profiles* (Pawhuska: OCHS, 1978).

89. Underhill, *Osage Indian Reign of Terror*, 212.

90. Fairfax Area Historical Society, *From a Field of Cane*, 45.

91. John Wren FBI report, October 6, 1925, Osage Indian Murders, part 22 of 65, vault.fbi.gov.

92. Underhill, *Osage Indian Reign of Terror*, 44.

93. Quoted in Grove, *Years of Fear*, 63–64, 156.

94. Grove, *Years of Fear*, 156.

95. "Iron Nerve of 'Osage King' is Yet Unbroken," *Oklahoman*, November 17, 1926, 5.

96. Her first name is spelled "Reta" on her tombstone, but seems to be spelled Rita elsewhere.

97. David Grann, *Killers of the Flower Moon*, 280–81.

98. "Scott Mathis," *Osage County Profiles* (Pawhuska: OCHS, 1978).

99. Adams, *Tom White*, 47.

100. Quoted in Fairfax Area Historical Society, *From a Field of Cane*, 76.

101. "Former Fairfax Banker Succumbs," *Tulsa World*, June 7, 1933, 1, microfilm, Oklahoma History Research Center.

102. "Fairfax Civic Leader Missing in $105,000 Shortage in City Funds," *Daily Oklahoman*, March 26, 1932, 1.

103. Underhill, *Osage Indian Murders*, 200.

104. Quoted in Grove, *Years of Fear*, 195–96.

105. Underhill, *Osage Indian Reign of Terror*, 182, illus.

106. "Fairfax Apartment House is Completed," *Daily Oklahoman*, October 19, 1924, 47; Fairfax Area Historical Society, *From a Field of Cane*, 68.

107. "Osage County—A Land of Three Title Deeds," Wichita *Eagle*, January 16, 1921, 38.

108. "Fairfax Bank is Purchased by Tulsa Man," *Daily Oklahoman*, February 17, 1923, 3; Joseph B. Thoburn, *Standard History of Oklahoma*, 5: 2122.

109. Wilson, *Underground Reservation*, 138.

110. "Hale Defense Blames [Roy] Bunch in Roan Death," *Daily Oklahoman*, January 22, 1929, 5.

111. Underhill, *Osage Indian Reign of Terror*, 126.

112. Warehime, *History of Ranching the Osage*, 204.

113. Underhill, *Osage Indian Reign of* Terror, 91; Lawrence J. Hogan, *Osage Indian Murders*, 269.

114. "C.E. Ashbrook in Sapulpa Jail," *Daily Ardmoreite*, May 3, 1932, 1.

115. "Cashier Surrenders on $100,000 Charge," St Louis *Post-Dispatch*, May 3, 1932, 22; "Fairfax Civic Leader Missing in $105,000 Shortage in City Funds," *Daily Oklahoman*, March 26, 1932, 1, Oklahoman Digital Archives.

116. Quoted in *From a Field of Cane*, Fairfax Area Historical Society, 66.

117. Underhill, *Osage Indian Reign of Terror*, 174.

118. "Bank at Fairfax Is Closed Voluntarily," *Oklahoman*, March 22, 1932, 18, Oklahoman Digital Archives.

119. "Banker Denies Taking Money," *Oklahoman*, May 4, 1932, 18, Oklahoman Digital Archives; "C.E. Ashbrook in Sapulpa Jail," *Daily Ardmoreite*, May 3, 1932, 1; "Ex-Charleston Man Held as Embezzler," *Journal Gazette* [Mattoon, Illinois] May 14, 1932, 2.

120. "Fairfax Sues to Recover Deposit In Closed Bank," September 30, 1932, 5, Oklahoman Digital Archives.

121. "Fairfax Banker to Prison for Thefts," Miami [Oklahoma] *News-Record*, January 5, 1933, 8.

122. "Former Fairfax Banker Succumbs," *Tulsa World*, June 7, 1933, 1, microfilm, Oklahoma History Research Center.

123. Wilson, *Underground Reservation*, 144; *Journal of American Indian Family Research* 10, no. 1, 10.

124. Will Rogers, "More and Better Relatives Is Rogers' Claim Made on His Last Oklahoma Trip," March 28, 1926, in *Will Rogers' Weekly Articles, vol. 2 The Coolidge Years: 1925-1927* (Stillwater: Oklahoma State University Press, 1980), 170.

125. Terry P. Wilson, "Women of the Osage: A Century of Change, 1874-1982," in *Women in Oklahoma: A Century of Change*, edited by Melvena K. Thurman (Oklahoma Historical Society, 1979), 83.

126. American Weekly, "America's Richest Indian Heiress Dies of Too Much Money," *San Francisco Examiner*, August 7, 1932, 81.

127. Corbett listed his residence as Fairfax, Oklahoma, on their Missouri marriage license.

128. American Weekly, "America's Richest Indian Heiress Dies of Too Much Money," 81; "Rich Indian Bride is Suing for Divorce," Sioux City *Journal*, June 24, 1923, 28.

129. Wilson, "Women of the Osage," 84.

130. American Weekly, "America's Richest Indian Heiress Dies," 81.

131. Wilson, "Women of the Osage," 84.

132. "Rich Girl Divorced," *Pittsburgh Press* [Pennsylvania], May 6, 1929; American Weekly, "America's Richest Indian Heiress Dies."

133. American Weekly, "America's Richest Indian Heiress Dies."

134. "Osage Oil Heiress Found Dead in Home after Long Rum Orgy; Marital Tangles Won Notoriety," Philadelphia *Inquirer*, June 9, 1932, 2.

135. "Indians Now Face Critical Period," Ada [Oklahoma] *Evening News*, December 26, 1935, 6.

Acknowledgments

Very special thanks go to the Mathews family, including John Joseph Mathews's three wonderful grandchildren, Sara Dydak, Laura Edwards, and Chris Mathews, for their continued support and enthusiasm for the project, and for giving permission to publish excerpts from their grandfather's letters and diaries archived at the Western History Collection at the University of Oklahoma in Norman. I thank the past and present employees of the Western History Collection who have assisted me with my research over the years including curator Todd Fuller more recently, and very special thanks go to librarian Jacquelyn Reese. My family members have provided invaluable help including my brother, Timothy Snyder, whom I cite in this book, and my parents, Christine Snyder and Dr. Gene Snyder, for reading drafts of chapters, or in Tim's case, the entire manuscript, and offering much helpful advice and guidance. My father's comments on the Indian baseball chapter were most helpful, and Tim's suggestions for revision of the introduction were gems. Thanks go to Marci Shore, Mary Snyder, Lori Snyder, Ivy Snyder, and Cora Snyder for their moral and familial support. *Our Osage Hills* columns and many other news items were photocopied from the microfilm archives at the Research Center of the Oklahoma History Center in Oklahoma City; I want to thank Oklahoma Historical Society Executive Director Dr. Bob Blackburn, and all of the employees there, especially those in the microforms area, for their continued assistance over many years. I also want to thank past and present employees of the Keith Leftwich Memorial Library at Oklahoma City Community College, including Rachel Butler and Monica Carlisle, who provided me with rarities through interlibrary loan and other supports during my early research for the book. I also want to thank Professor Pamela S. Stout of Oklahoma City Community College for her consistent support and research and editorial assistance. Likewise, I also thank the librarians at Bizzell Library at the University of Oklahoma in

Norman, where I did my PhD and where I currently teach, for their enduring and deeply appreciated help, especially in the interlibrary loans area. I also want to give deep thanks to my friend, photographer, and retired attorney Harvey Payne of the Joseph H. Williams Tallgrass Prairie Preserve, owned by the Nature Conservancy, on which sits John Joseph Mathews's renovated Blackjacks cabin, for his continued support and conversation efforts; I am also grateful for his foreword and his deep love and appreciation of Mathews. I am grateful for the continued hospitality, assistance, and shared knowledge of my friend Russ Tall Chief of Oklahoma City University and his sweet and talented family. I am grateful to Russ for sitting for a formal interview and writing another foreword about his beloved Mathews. Deep gratitude goes to the Osage Traditional Cultural Advisors for allowing me to access digitized Mathews audio and photographic materials archived at the Wahzhazhe Cultural Center in the Osage Nation, Pawhuska, and for later granting permission to publish Mathews's photographs in this book. Deep thanks go to the Cultural Center and especially to John Horsechief, audio-video technician and growing aficionado of John Joseph Mathews, for his assistance and interest in the project. Thanks also to Kathryn Redcorn and Hallie Winter, former curators of the Osage Nation Museum, for their continued support. Kathryn Redcorn and Assistant Principal Chief Raymond Redcorn III sat for interviews especially for this project, for which I am very grateful. Thanks are also due to Garret Hartness of the Osage County Historical Society Museum for his assistance and support. Thanks also go to the Pawhuska *Journal-Capital* newspaper and its publisher, Matt Tranquill. Hearty thanks go to the most capable, admirable, and eloquent Dr. Kate Crassons, director of Lehigh University Press, for taking an interest in this manuscript and for her thoughtful and insightful advice and support; along with my brother Tim, Kate helped me to make the introduction much stronger. Thanks also go to Tricia J. Moore, managing editor, for her counsel. I thank those who supported me in innumerable or unquantifiable ways whom I may be overlooking or forgetting. And finally, thanks to all of the readers and fans of the incomparable John Joseph Mathews, especially those of the Wahzhazhe, who made the existence of this book possible.

Bibliography

WORKS BY JOHN JOSEPH MATHEWS

Books

Wah'Kon-Tah: The Osage and the White Man's Road. Norman: University of Oklahoma Press, 1932.

Sundown. New York: Longmans, Green, 1934.

Talking to the Moon. Chicago: University of Chicago Press, 1945.

"Within Your Dream." Unpublished novel manuscript written in 1949 and revised through 1955. Now lost.

Life and Death of an Oilman: The Career of E. W. Marland. Norman: University of Oklahoma Press, 1951.

The Osages: Children of the Middle Waters. Norman: University of Oklahoma Press, 1961.

Talking to the Moon. Second edition. Foreword by Elizabeth Mathews. Norman: University of Oklahoma Press, 1981.

Sundown. Introduction by Virginia H. Mathews. Norman: University of Oklahoma Press, 1988.

Twenty Thousand Mornings: An Autobiography. Edited and introduced by Susan Kalter. Norman: University of Oklahoma Press, 2012.

Old Three Toes and Other Stories of Survival and Extinction. Edited and with afterword by Susan Kalter. Norman: University of Oklahoma Press, 2015.

Selected Articles and Short Stories

"Admirable Outlaw." *Sooner Magazine* vol. 2, no. 7 (April 1930): 241, 264.

"Boy, Horse and Dog." (Full-length volume 1 of three planned autobiographical volumes). John Joseph Mathews Collection, Western History Collection, University of Oklahoma, Box 4, Folder 33.

"Chief Fred Lookout Saw Great Changes Come to His Tribesmen of the Osage." *Oklahoman*, April 23, 1939.

"Dance at Dawn." *Oklahoma Today* 19, no. 2 (1969): 28–36.

"From the Osage Hills." *Sooner Magazine* 3, no. 8 (1931): 280, 308–10.

"Gallery." *Space* vol. 1, no. 1 (1934).

"Hunger on the Prairie." *Sooner Magazine* 2, no. 9 (1930): 328–29.

"Hunting in the Rockies: The Wary Bull Wapiti Worthy Foe of Hunter's Skill." *Sooner Magazine* 1, no. 8 (1929): 263, 278–80.

"Hunting the Red Deer of Scotland: The Thrill of Conquering the Monarch of the Highlands." *Sooner Magazine* 1, no. 7 (1929): 213–14, 246.

"John L. Bird Early Osage Trader Dies," Pawhuska *Daily Journal-Capital*, January 28, 1935, 1.

"Our Osage Hills." *Pawhuska Journal-Capital*, March 16, 1930–July 10, 1931.

"Passing of Red Eagle: An Osage Goes to His Happy Hunting Ground." *Sooner Magazine* 2, no. 5 (1930): 160, 176.

"Red Man's Gold." *Service* (Cities Service Magazine), October 1946, 12–13.

"Romance of the Osages." Transcript of radio show recorded in Tulsa, broadcast April 30, 1937, NBC Blue network. Lilly Library, Indiana University, Bloomington.

"The Royal of Glen Orchy." 1963. John Joseph Mathews Collection, Western History Collection, University of Oklahoma, Box 4, Folder 21.

"Singers to the Moon." *Oklahoma Today*, August–September 1996, The OKT Reader section, II–VII.

Lecture

"Hawks of Oklahoma." Oklahoma City Academy of Science, Sixth Annual Meeting, December 1916.

ARCHIVES AND SPECIAL COLLECTIONS

Gateway to Oklahoma History (online database). Oklahoma Historical Society. gateway.okhistory.org.

John Joseph Mathews audio, video, and photographic archives. Wahzhazhe Cultural Center, Pawhuska, Osage Nation.

John Joseph Mathews Papers, 1921–1979 (JJM). Western History Collection (WHC), University of Oklahoma (OU), Norman, Oklahoma.

NewspaperArchive. www.newspaperarchive.com.

Newspaper microfilm archives. Oklahoma Historical Society Research Center, Oklahoma History Center, Oklahoma City.

Newspapers.com Publishers Extra. Newspapers by Ancestry. www.newspapers.com.

Oklahoman Digital Archive. archive.newsok.com. University of Oklahoma Bizzell Library database.

Walter Stanley Campbell Papers (WSC). Western History Collection (WHC), University of Oklahoma (OU).

INTERVIEWS WITH THE AUTHOR

Phillip Fortune, personal interview, February 20, 2015, Pawhuska, Oklahoma.

Fleur Feighan Jones, telephone interview, January 13, 2015.

John Hopper Mathews and Mary Abigail "Gail" Painter Mathews. Personal interview, August 2, 2013, Allenville, Pennsylvania.

Kathryn Redcorn, personal interview, July 6, 2018, Pawhuska.

Raymond Redcorn III, personal interviews, January 7, 2013, and July 6, 2018, Pawhuska.

Russ Tall Chief, personal interview, April 25, 2019, Norman, Oklahoma.

SELECTED OTHER BOOKS AND ARTICLES

Adams, Oscar Faye. *Handbook of American Authors*. Boston: Houghton Mifflin, 1885.

Adams, Verdon R. *Tom White: The Life of a Lawman*. El Paso: Texas Western Press [University of Texas at El Paso], 1972.

American Weekly. "America's Richest Indian Heiress Dies." *San Francisco Examiner*, August 7, 1932, 81.

Armer, Laura Adams. *Waterless Mountain*. New York: Alfred A. Knopf, 1993 [1931].

"Arthur Bonnicastle's Own Story." *Red Man and Helper* [Carlisle, Pennsylvania]. March 4, 1902, 2.

Askew, Rilla. *Most American: Notes from a Wounded Place*. Norman: University of Oklahoma Press, 2017.

Bach, Steven. *Marlene Dietrich: Life and Legend*. University of Minnesota Press, 2013.

Backer, Kristen Williams. "*Kultur-Terror*: The Composite Monster in Nazi Visual Propaganda." In *Monsters and the Monstrous: Myths and Metaphors of Enduring Evil*, edited by Niall Scott, 81–102. New York: Rodopi, 2007.

Barthel, Thomas. *Pepper Martin: A Baseball Biography*. Jefferson, NC: McFarland, 2003.

Benjamin, Roger. *Orientalist Aesthetics: Art, Colonialism, and French North Africa, 1880-1930*. Berkeley: University of California Press, 2003.

Bleiler, Lyn, and Society of the Muse of the Southwest. *Taos*. Mt. Pleasant, SC: Arcadia, 2011.

Braunlich, Phyllis Cole. *Haunted by Home: The Life and Letters of Lynn Riggs*. Norman: University of Oklahoma Press, 1988.

Brosman, Catherine Savage. *Southwestern Women Writers and the Vision of Goodness: Mary Austin, Willa Cather, Laura Adams Armer, Peggy Pond Church and Alice Marriott*. Jefferson, NC: McFarland, 2016.

Brown, Dee. "Land Fever: The Strange Jekyll-Hyde Life of Arthur Manby." Review of *To Possess the Land: A Biography of Arthur Rochelle Manby* by Frank Waters, *Chicago Tribune*, March 3, 1974.

Browner, Tara. "Native Songs, Indianist Styles, and the Processes of Music Idealization." In *Opera Indigene: Re/Presenting First Nations and Indigenous Cultures*, edited by Pamela Karantonis and Dylan Robinson, 173–85. London: Routledge, 2011.

Burke, Flannery. *From Greenwich Village to Taos: Primitivism and Place in Mabel Dodge Luhan's*. Lawrence: University Press of Kansas, 2008.

Burns, Louis F. *A History of the Osage People*. Tuscaloosa: University of Alabama Press, 2003.

Cunningham, Elizabeth. *Remarkable Women of Taos*. Taos: Nighthawk, 2013.

Lord Curzon. *Travels with a Superior Person*, edited by Peter King. London: Sidgwick & Jackson, 1985.

Deloria, Philip J. *Indians in Unexpected Places*. Lawrence: University Press of Kansas, 2004.

Donald, David Herbert. *Look Homeward: A Life of Thomas Wolfe*. Cambridge, MA: Harvard University Press, 2002.

Duty, Shannon Shaw. "George Tallchief, Former Principal Chief, Dies at 96," *Osage News* 9, no. 9 (September 2013): 1+.

Ellison, Ralph. *Flying Home and Other Stories*. New York: Vintage, 1996.

Engle, Paul. "Thoreau and Simple Life, Modernized." Review of *Talking to the Moon*. Chicago *Daily Tribune*, June 17, 1945.

Fairfax Area Historical Society. *From a Field of Cane: The Early Years of Fairfax, Oklahoma, 1903–1913*. Fairfax, OK: Fairfax Area Historical Society, 1999.

Ferber, Edna. *Cimarron*. Garden City, NY: Doubleday, Doran, 1929.

———. *A Peculiar Treasure*. Garden City, NY: Doubleday, Doran, 1939.

Fisher, Ada Lois Sipuel. *A Matter of Black and White: The Autobiography of Ada Lois Sipuel Fisher*. Norman: University of Oklahoma Press, 1996.

Fixico, Donald L. *The Invasion of Indian Territory in the Twentieth Century*. Boulder: University of Colorado Press, 2011.

Foreman, Grant. "J. George Wright." *Chronicles of Oklahoma* 20, no. 2 (June 1942): 121–23.

Franks, Kenny. *The Osage Oil Boom*. Oklahoma City: Oklahoma Heritage Association, 1989.

"Fred Lookout." *Encyclopedia of North American Indians*, edited by Frederick E. Hoxie, 346–47. Boston: Houghton Mifflin, 1996.

Frost, Laura. "The Romance of Cliché: E. M. Hull, D. H. Lawrence, and Interwar Erotic Fiction." In *Bad Modernisms*, edited by Douglas Mao and Rebeca L. Walkowitz, 94–118. Durham, NC: Duke University Press, 2010.

Fuller, Todd. *60 Feet, Six Inches and Other Distances from Home: The (Baseball) Life of Mose YellowHorse*. Duluth: Holy Cow!, 2002.

Grann, David. *Killers of the Flower Moon: The Osage Murders and the Birth of the FBI*. New York: Doubleday, 2017.

Gray, Jim, and Wilhelm Murg. "Osage Oil Boom and Reign of Terror collide in new book by Osage historian." *Native American Times* [Tulsa, Oklahoma], November 15, 2001, 4B.

Grove, Fred. *Drums without Warriors*. New York: Dorchester, 2002 [1976].

———. *Flame of the Osage*. Trowbridge, UK: Gunsmoke, 1998 [1958].

———. *Warrior Road*, Chippenham, UK: Gunsmoke, 2007 [1974].

———. *The Years of Fear*. Waterville, Maine: Five Star, 2002.

Hassrick, Peter H., and Elizabeth J. Cunningham. *In Contemporary Rhythm: The Art of Ernest L. Blumenshein*. Norman: University of Oklahoma Press, 2008.

Hearings Before the Senate Committee on Indian Affairs on Matters Relating to the Osage Tribe of Indians. Washington, DC: Government Printing Office, 1909.

Henrie, C.A. "Osages Argue They Alone Should Settle Trust Question." Wichita *Daily Eagle*, January 23, 1921.

———. "Osage County—A Land of Three Title Deeds." Wichita *Daily Eagle*, January 16, 1921.

Hertzberg, Hazel W. *The Search for an American Indian Identity: Modern Pan-Indian Movements*. Syracuse: Syracuse University Press, 1971.

Hogan, Lawrence J. *The Osage Indian Murders*. Second edition. Frederick, MD: Amlex, 1998.

Hogue, Alexandre. "W. Herbert Dunton: An Appreciation." *Southwest Review* 13, no. 1 (October 1927): 48–59.

Howe, LeAnne. *Choctalking on Other Realities*. San Francisco: Aunt Lute, 2013.

———. *Miko Kings: An Indian Baseball Story*. San Francisco: Aunt Lute, 2007.

Hunt, John. *The Grey Horse Legacy*. New York: Knopf, 1968.

Hurston, Zora Neale. "Spunk." In *The New Negro*, edited by Alain Locke, 105–11. New York: Simon & Schuster, 1997 [1925].

Joint Commission to Investigate Indian Affairs. "Osage Reservation." *Hearings Before the Joint Commission of the Congress of the United States, Sixty-third Congress*. March 9, 1914. Washington, DC: U.S. Government Printing Office, 1914.

Kafka, Franz. *Amerika*. Translated by Edwin Muir. New York: New Directions, 1946.

Kalter, Susan. Introduction to *Twenty Thousand Mornings* by John Joseph Mathews, edited by Susan Kalter, XVII–LII. Norman: University of Oklahoma Press, 2012.

Kwitny, Jonathan. *The Mullendore Murder Case*. New York: Warner, 1976 [1974].

La Flesche, Francis, and Garrick Bailey. *The Osage and the Invisible World: From the Works of Francis La Flesche*, edited and with an introduction by Garrick Bailey. Norman: University of Oklahoma Press, 1995.

Lamb, Arthur H. *Tragedies of the Osage Hills*. Pawhuska, Oklahoma, n.d., c. 1929.

Leopold, Aldo. *A Sand County Almanac and Sketches Here and There*, illustrated by Charles W. Schwarz. New York: Oxford University Press, 1949.

———. "Rebuilding the Quail Crop." *Outdoor America* 10, no. 4 (November 1931): 38.

———. "Report of the Iowa Game Survey, Chapter One: The Fall of the Iowa Game Range." *Outdoor America* 11, no. 1 (August-September 1932): 7–9.

———. "Report of the Iowa Game Survey, Chapter Two: Iowa Quail." *Outdoor America* 11, no. 3 (December-January 1933): 11–13, 30–31.

——— and John N. Ball, "The Quail Shortage of 1930." *Outdoor America* 9, no. 9 (April 1931): 14–15, 67.

Logsdon, Guy. "John Joseph Mathews—A Conversation." *Nimrod* 16 (April 1972): 70–75.

Lunde, Darrin. *The Naturalist: Theodore Roosevelt, a Lifetime of Exploration, and the Triumph of American Natural History*. New York: Broadway, 2016.

Maroukis, Thomas C. *The Peyote Road: Religious Freedom and the Native American Church*. Norman: University of Oklahoma Press, 2012.

Marriott, Alice, and Carol K. Rachlin. *Peyote*. New York: New American Library, 1972.

May, Jon D. "Bacon Rind." *The Encyclopedia of Oklahoma History and Culture*. Oklahoma Historical Society. www.okhistory.org/publications/enc/entry.php?entry=BA003.

McAuliffe, Jr., Dennis. *Bloodland: A Family Story of Oil, Greed and Murder on the Osage Reservation*. Tulsa: Council Oak Books, 1999.

Momaday, N. Scott. *House Made of Dawn*. New York: Harper & Row, 1968.

More, Hannah. *The Works of Hannah More: with a Sketch of Her Life, Volume 1*. Boston: Goodrich, 1827.

Nix, Evett Dumas. *Oklahombres: Particularly the Wild Ones*. Lincoln: University of Nebraska Press, 1993 [1929].

Oklahoma Historical Society. *The Encyclopedia of Oklahoma History and Culture*. www.okhistory.org.

Osage County Historical Society. *Osage County Profiles*. Pawhuska, OK: Osage County Historical Society, 1978.

An Osage Journey to Europe, 1827-1830: Three French Accounts, edited by William Least Heat-Moon and James K. Wallace. Norman: University of Oklahoma Press, 2013.

Osage Tribal Museum. *The Osage Timeline*, researched and developed by Lou Brock. Pawhuska, OK: Osage Tribal Museum, 2013.

Owens, Louis. *Other Destinies: Understanding the American Indian Novel*. Norman: University of Oklahoma Press, 1994.

Oxendine, Joseph B. Foreword to *The American Indian Integration of Baseball* by Jeffrey Powers-Beck, IX–XIII. Lincoln: University of Nebraska Press, 2004.

Powers-Beck, Jeffrey. *The American Indian Integration of Baseball*. Lincoln: University of Nebraska Press, 2004.

Powys, John Cowper. *The Meaning of Culture*. New York: W. W. Norton, 1929.

Raper, Arthur F. *The Tragedy of Lynching*. Chapel Hill: University of North Carolina Press, 1933.

Redcorn, Charles H. *A Pipe for February*. Norman: University of Oklahoma Press, 2002.

RedCorn, Ryan. "The Collections." *Oklahoma Today* (July/August 2018): 69–73.

Red Eagle, Ed [Sr.]. Interview with Robert Miller [cassette and transcript]. Doris Duke Collection, Western History Collection, University of Oklahoma, T-108, vol. 48.

Reese, Linda W. "Tessie Mobley." *The Encyclopedia of Oklahoma History and Culture*. Oklahoma Historical Society. www.okhistory.org/publications/enc/entry.php?entry=MO035.

Riggs, Lynn. *Green Grow the Lilacs*. In *The Cherokee Night and Other Plays*, 6–105. Norman: University of Oklahoma Press, 2003.

Rogers, Will. *The Autobiography of Will Rogers*, edited by Donald Day, foreword by Bill and Jim Rogers. New York: Lancer, 1963 [1949].

———. *The Papers of Will Rogers: The Final Years, volume 5: August 1928-August 1935*. Norman: University of Oklahoma Press, 2006.

———. *Will Rogers' Weekly Articles, volume 2 The Coolidge Years: 1925-1927*. Stillwater: Oklahoma State University Press, 1980.

———. *Will Rogers' Weekly Articles, volume 4 The Hoover Years: 1929-1931*. Stillwater: Oklahoma State University Press, 1980.

Rowland, Ann Wierda. "Sentimental Fiction." In *The Cambridge Companion to Fiction in the Romantic Period*, edited by Richard Maxwell and Katie Trumpener, 191–206. Cambridge: Cambridge University Press, 2008.

Rudnick, Lois Palken. *Mabel Dodge Luhan: New Woman, New Worlds*. Albuquerque: University of New Mexico Press, 1987.

Runstedtler, Theresa. *Jack Johnson, Rebel Sojourner: Boxing in the Shadow of the Global Color Line*. Los Angeles: University of California Press, 2012.

Schimmel, Julie. *The Art and Life of W. Herbert Dunton, 1878-1936*. Austin: University of Texas Press for the Stark Museum of Art, 1984.

Simms, Ruthanna M. "Friends and the Osages: History of Hominy Friends Church." Circa 1970. Edmund Stanley Library Special Collections, Friends University, Wichita, Kansas.

Smith, Robert Barr. *Outlaws: Tales of Bad Guys Who Shaped the Wild West*. New York: Rowman and Littlefield, 2013.

Snyder, Michael. "Friends of the Osages: John Joseph Mathews's *Wah'Kon-Tah* and Osage-Quaker Cross-Cultural Collaboration." *Chronicles of Oklahoma* 88, no. 4 (2010–11): 438–61.

———. *John Joseph Mathews: Life of an Osage Writer*. Norman: University of Oklahoma Press, 2017.

Snyder, Timothy. *Bloodlands: Europe between Hitler and Stalin*. New York: Basic, 2010.

Stewart, Omer Call. *Peyote Religion: A History*. Norman: University of Oklahoma, 1987.

Strickland, Rennard. "Osage Oil: Mineral Law, Murder, Mayhem, and Manipulation," *Natural Resources & Environment* 10, no. 1 (summer 1995): 39–43.

Tahmahkera, Dustin. "Hakaru Maruumatu Kwitaka? Seeking Representational Jurisdiction in Comanchería Cinema." *NAIS* 5, no. 1 (2018): 106.

Tallchief, Maria with Larry Kaplan. *Maria Tallchief: American's Prima Ballerina*. New York: Henry Holt, 1997.

Thoburn, Joseph Bradfield. *A Standard History of Oklahoma, volume 5*. Chicago: American Historical Society, 1916.

——— and Muriel H. Wright. *Oklahoma: A History of the State and its People, volume 4*. New York: Lewis Historical, 1929.

Treaties and Laws of the Osage Nation, edited by W. S. Fitzpatrick. Cedar Vale, KS: Cedar Vale Commercial, 1895.

Turnbull, Andrew. *Thomas Wolfe*. New York: Scribner's Sons, 1967.

Underhill, Lonnie. *Osage Indian Reign of Terror*. Gilbert, Arizona: Roan Horse, 2010.

U.S. Congress House Committee on Indian Affairs. *Leases for Oil and Gas Purposes, Osage National Council*. Washington, DC: U.S. Government Printing Office, 1913.

Urban, Mark. *Generals: Ten British Commanders Who Shaped the Modern World.* London: Faber and Faber, 2005.

Vaught, Michael. "Osage Scribe." *Oklahoma Today* 46, no. 5 (August-September 1996): 34–37.

Voight, William, Jr. *Born with Fists Doubled: Defending Outdoor America.* Spirit Lake, IA: Izaak Walton League of America Endowment, 1992.

Ward, Geoffrey C. *Unforgivable Blackness: The Rise and Fall of Jack Johnson.* New York: Knopf, 2004.

Ware, Amy M. *The Cherokee Kid: Will Rogers, Tribal Identity, and the Making of an American Icon.* Lawrence: University Press of Kansas, 2015.

Warehime, Les. *History of Ranching the Osage.* Tulsa: W. W. Publications, 2000.

Warrior, Robert Allen. *Tribal Secrets: Recovering American Indian Intellectual Traditions.* Minneapolis: University of Minnesota Press, 1995.

Waters, Frank. *To Possess the Land: A Biography of Arthur Rochford Manby.* Chicago: Swallow Press, 1973.

Weaver, Jace. Foreword to *The Cherokee Night and Other Plays.* Norman: University of Oklahoma Press, 2003, ix–xv.

Webb-Storey, Anna. "Culture Clash: A Case Study of Three Osage Native American Families." Ph.D. dissertation, Oklahoma State University, 1998.

White, E. E. *Experiences of a Special Indian Agent.* Norman: University of Oklahoma Press, 1965 [1893].

Whitehead, Don. *The FBI Story: A Report to the People.* Foreword by J. Edgar Hoover. New York: Random House, 1956.

Wilson, Terry P. *Indians of North America: The Osage.* New York: Chelsea House, 1988.

———. "John Joseph Mathews." In *Native American Writers of the United States,* edited by Kenneth M. Roemer, 154–62. Dictionary of Literary Biography 175. Detroit: Gale Research, 1997.

———. "Osage Oxonian: The Heritage of John Joseph Mathews." *Chronicles of Oklahoma* 59 (Fall 1981): 264–93.

———. *The Underground Reservation: Osage Oil.* Lincoln: University of Nebraska Press, 1985.

———. "Women of the Osage: A Century of Change, 1874-1982." In *Women in Oklahoma: A Century of Change,* edited by Melvena K. Thurman, 57–102. Oklahoma City: Oklahoma Historical Society, 1979.

Wolfe, Thomas. *Of Time and the River: A Legend of Man's Hunger in His Youth.* New York: Simon & Shuster, 1999 [1935].

Index

About the Contributors

Russ Tall Chief is an Osage writer, educator, and actor, as well as a Tail-dancer and former Drumkeeper for the Greyhorse District of the Osage In'lonshka ceremonial dances. From 2000 to 2015, Tall Chief served as the Art Galleries Editor for *Native Peoples Magazine* and currently serves as the Director of Student Diversity and Inclusion at Oklahoma City University. Tall Chief earned his master's degree in English from Bemidji State University in Minnesota and a bachelor's degree in Communication from the University of Central Oklahoma.

Harvey Payne practiced law in Pawhuska, Oklahoma, for forty years and represented several members of the family of John Joseph Mathews beginning in 1980.

About the Authors

Michael Snyder is the author of *John Joseph Mathews: Life of an Osage Writer* (University of Oklahoma Press, 2017). Praised by the *TLS* of London, closer to home the biography was a finalist for the Oklahoma Book Award and an Oklahoma bestseller, according to *The Oklahoman* newspaper. He has published many peer-reviewed articles and book reviews on American and American Indian literatures, along with scattered poems. An Assistant Teaching Professor in the College of Arts and Sciences at the University of Oklahoma, Dr. Snyder is writing the biography of the gay author James Purdy and a novel and continues his research and writing on Native American literature and culture, especially that of the Osages.

One of the first American Indian novelists, **John Joseph Mathews** (1894–1979) was the preeminent Osage author, naturalist, and historian of the twentieth century. Born in Pawhuska, capital of the Osage Nation, Indian Territory, well before Oklahoma statehood, Mathews grew up riding his horse and camping all over his Osage homeland, observing birds and animals, with only his dog as companion. During World War I, he interrupted his undergraduate study of geology and zoology at the University of Oklahoma to enlist in the Army and became an aviator and teacher of aviation. He earned a second degree in natural sciences from Merton College, Oxford University. A few years after returning to Pawhuska in 1929, Mathews had a sandstone cabin home built upon a prairie ridge, on his family allotment acreage outside of Pawhuska. He served on the Osage Tribal Council for two four-year terms in the 1930s and early 1940s, and began publishing works in a variety of genres including the novel *Sundown* (1934), the philosophical nature study *Talking to the Moon* (1945), and his magnum opus, *The Osages: Children of the Middle Waters* (1961). Mathews married twice and had two children and two stepchildren.